Introduction to
Messianic
JUDAISM

At last, we have a book written by top scholars, thinkers, and leaders in the Messianic Jewish and larger Christian communities that addresses all the major questions of faith, praxis, and biblical interpretation among Jewish believers in Jesus. It is an extremely rich and important book, certain to stimulate fruitful discussion for years to come and covering a topic that the church can no longer ignore.

— MICHAEL L. BROWN, President, FIRE School of Ministry

This book is a landmark contribution on the nature and significance of Messianic Judaism. It shows clearly that Messianic Judaism is not an ephemeral epiphenomenon that can any longer be ignored or marginalized; on the contrary, it poses an acute set of theological and ecclesiological questions that will take years to resolve. Written with pleasing economy and depth, this volume is indispensable reading for anyone who has forgotten the Jewish origins of Christianity or who has become complacent about the contested nature of their current ecclesial identity. I recommend it with enthusiasm.

— WILLIAM J. ABRAHAM, Outler Professor of Theology and Wesley Studies and Altshuler Distinguished Teaching Professor, Perkins School of Theology, Southern Methodist University

This volume provides an unmatched resource for anyone wanting to understand Messianic Judaism today. In the first section, the accessible yet deeply informative essays written by scholars from within its own ranks cover the history and dynamics of Messianic Judaism. In the second, many topics relevant to the theological concerns of this movement are discussed by New Testament specialists.

— MARK D. NANOS, Soebbing Distinguished Scholar-in-Residence, Rockhurst University

Introduction to
Messianic
JUDAISM

Its Ecclesial Context and Biblical Foundations

DAVID RUDOLPH &
JOEL WILLITTS
GENERAL EDITORS

ZONDERVAN®

ZONDERVAN.com/
AUTHORTRACKER
follow your favorite authors

ZONDERVAN

Introduction to Messianic Judaism
Copyright © 2013 by David Rudolph and Joel Willitts

This title is also available as a Zondervan ebook. Visit www.zondervan.com/ebooks.

Requests for information should be addressed to:

Zondervan, *Grand Rapids, Michigan 49530*

Library of Congress Cataloging-in-Publication Data

Introduction to messianic Judaism : its ecclesial context and Biblical foundations / Daniel Rudolph
    and Joel Willitts, general editors.
        p. cm.
    Includes index.
    ISBN 978-0-310-33063-9 (pbk.)
    1. Messianic Judaism. I. Rudolph, Daniel, 1967– II. Willitts, Joel.
BR158.159 2013
289.9—dc23   2012029606

Cover design: www.wdesigncompany.com
Cover image: © 2012 Artists Rights Society (ARS), New York / ADAGP, Paris
                CNAC/MNAM/Dist. Réunion des Musées Nationaux / Art Resource, NY
Interior design: Beth Shagene

Printed in the United States of America

HB 08.16.2023

Contents

PART 1

The Messianic Jewish Community

PART 2

The Church and Messianic Judaism

Contributors

Richard Bauckham (PhD, Cambridge University) is senior scholar at Ridley Hall, Cambridge.

Darrell Bock (PhD, University of Aberdeen) is research professor of New Testament studies at Dallas Theological Seminary.

Markus Bockmuehl (PhD, Cambridge University) is professor of biblical and early Christian studies at Oxford University.

William S. Campbell (PhD, University of Edinburgh) is reader in biblical studies at the University of Wales, Lampeter.

Akiva Cohen (PhD, Tel Aviv University) is a New Testament scholar and researcher who resides in Israel.

Stuart Dauermann (PhD, Fuller Theological Seminary) is senior scholar at the Messianic Jewish Theological Institute.

John Dickson (PhD, Macquarie University) is senior research fellow at the Department of Ancient History, Macquarie University, and director of the Centre for Public Christianity.

Mitch Glaser (PhD, Fuller Theological Seminary) is executive director of Chosen People Ministries in New York City.

Scott J. Hafemann (ThD, Eberhard-Karls-Universität Tübingen) is reader in New Testament studies at the University of St. Andrews.

Justin K. Hardin (PhD, Cambridge University) is tutor in New Testament at Oxford University.

Douglas Harink (PhD, St. Michael's College) is professor of theology at The King's University, Alberta, Canada.

Daniel J. Harrington (SJ, PhD, Harvard University) is professor of New Testament at Boston College School of Theology and Ministry.

Daniel C. Juster (MDiv, McCormick Theological Seminary) is executive director of Tikkun International, an international network of Messianic Jewish synagogues and emissaries.

Craig Keener (PhD, Duke University) is professor of New Testament at Asbury Theological Seminary.

Carl Kinbar (D.Litt. et Phil., University of South Africa) is director of the New School for Jewish Studies.

Mark S. Kinzer (PhD, University Michigan) is the rabbi of Congregation Zera Avraham in Ann Arbor, Michigan, and senior scholar at the MJTI Center for Jewish-Christian Relations.

Elliot Klayman (JD, University of Cincinnati) is director of the School of Jewish Studies at the Messianic Jewish Theological Institute in Los Angeles, California.

Seth N. Klayman (PhD, Duke University) is the rabbi of Congregation Sha'arei Shalom in Cary, North Carolina.

Russ Resnik is executive director of the Union of Messianic Jewish Congregations (UMJC).

Jennifer M. Rosner (PhD, Fuller Theological Seminary) teaches at Azusa Pacific University in Azusa, California.

David Rudolph (PhD, Cambridge University) is the rabbi of Tikvat Israel Messianic Synagogue in Richmond, Virginia, and lecturer in New Testament at the MJTI School of Jewish Studies.

Anders Runesson (PhD, Lund University) is associate professor of early Christianity and early Judaism at McMaster University.

R. Kendall Soulen (PhD, Yale University) is professor of systematic theology at Wesley Theological Seminary.

Joel Willitts (PhD, Cambridge University) is associate professor of biblical and theological studies at North Park University.

Todd A. Wilson (PhD, Cambridge University) is senior pastor at Calvary Memorial Church in Oak Park, Illinois.

Rachel Wolf is an instructor in Jewish history and thought at the International Alliance of Messianic Congregations and Synagogues (IAMCS) Yeshiva.

Introduction

David Rudolph

One of the earliest publications of the modern Messianic Jewish community, *The Messianic Jew*, rolled off the printing press more than a hundred years ago in December 1910. Reading this journal, one is struck by the grand vision for Messianic Judaism that its authors articulated soon after the turn of the century. A straight line can be drawn between the dreams of these Jewish pioneers and the emergence of the twenty-first-century Messianic Jewish community.

Introduction to Messianic Judaism is a portal into this movement. It provides a description of what the Messianic Jewish community looks like today at its center and on its margins. The first section of the book traces the ecclesial contours of the community, providing a sociohistorical and theological snapshot of where the community is presently and where it is heading. Alongside these chapters, part 2 includes a number of essays on biblical and theological issues central to the identity and legitimacy of Messianic Judaism.

There are now over five hundred Messianic synagogues around the world.[1] In North America, the majority of Messianic synagogues are affiliated with the Union of Messianic Jewish Congregations (UMJC) and the International Alliance of Messianic Congregations and Synagogues (IAMCS). The UMJC defines Messianic Judaism as "a movement of Jewish congregations and congregation-like groupings committed to Yeshua [Jesus] the Messiah that embrace the covenantal responsibility of Jewish life and identity rooted in Torah, expressed in tradition, renewed and applied in the context of the New Covenant."[2]

I grew up in one of these UMJC synagogues from the age of eight. How I became a Messianic Jew is in many ways paradigmatic of how God is moving in the lives of thousands of Jews today. The realization that Yeshua is the Messiah of Israel, the one foretold by the prophets of Israel, is often followed by a second life-transforming realization: that the God of Israel calls Jews who follow the Jewish Messiah to remain Jews and become better Jews in keeping with his eternal purposes.

This is my story. In 1975, our house was robbed. My father called 911 and the officer who received the dispatch raced to our house. While on the way, the policeman

---

1. David H. Stern, *Messianic Judaism: A Modern Movement with an Ancient Past* (Clarksville, Md.: Lederer, 2007), 271–72.

2. Union of Messianic Jewish Congregations, "Defining Messianic Judaism," 2005. Cited 27 February 2012. Online: http://www.umjc.org/home-mainmenu-1/global-vision-mainmenu-42/13-vision/225-defining -messianic-judaism.

heard Jesus say to him, "Tell the person you meet about me." When the policeman arrived at our home, he said, "Mr. Rudolph, I think you should sit down. I have something to tell you." The policeman proceeded to tell my father about Jesus — who he was and why God sent him into this world.

My father, who was a criminal lawyer at the time, felt sorry for the policeman, thinking that he had lost his mind. But as the policeman shared the message of the gospel, my father experienced being surrounded by the presence of God. It was tactile and like a force field. While this was happening, the policeman left without taking a report, having done what Jesus told him to do. After about an hour, the presence of God departed, my father fell to the floor, and he prayed, "God, I am so sorry that I have not believed in you all these years. Now I know that you are real. But why did you send a Christian? Is Jesus who the Christians say he is?" My father did not know the answer to this question, but he knew he was going to find out.

Over the next couple of months, my father read large portions of the Hebrew Bible and New Testament, and came to believe that Jesus was the Messiah of Israel foretold by the prophets. He began attending a local church. When the pastor of the church learned that my father was Jewish, he encouraged our family to visit a nearby Messianic synagogue, where we would be able to live out faith in Jesus in a Jewish communal context.

My father took the pastor's advice and visited the Messianic synagogue, but he did not like it because most of the service was in Hebrew. So my father returned to the church. When the pastor saw my father again, he asked what happened and my father shared his experience. Amazingly, rather than the pastor welcoming my father into his church, the pastor said, "Mr. Rudolph, I think you should give the Messianic synagogue another chance since it will be difficult to maintain your Jewish identity at our church. We do not celebrate Jewish festivals, have bar mitzvahs, teach Hebrew, etc. This is a very important decision." So my father went back to the Messianic synagogue, and this time he felt it was where God wanted our family to be. Today my father is the rabbi of a UMJC Messianic synagogue.

Because this pastor encouraged my father in the direction of Messianic Judaism, I was raised as a Messianic Jew. I now have three daughters, all of whom have been raised in Messianic synagogues and identify as Messianic Jews. My oldest daughter is a student at Johns Hopkins University, and she tells me that she will raise her future children as Messianic Jews. The Messianic synagogue option enabled my parents (both of whom are halakhically Jewish) to pass on Jewish identity to their children and grandchildren. But things could have turned out differently had the pastor not intervened. If the pastor had welcomed my father into his church, without welcoming his Jewish calling, the likelihood is that I (like the vast majority of Jesus-believing Jews in churches) would have assimilated and left behind my Jewish identity.

The Messianic Jewish community is made up of thousands of Jews like my father who, since the late 1960s, have described the Messiah of Israel entering their lives and calling them to become better Jews. Along with these Jews who became followers of Yeshua as adults, there is also a second (even a third and fourth) generation of Messianic Jews like myself who have grown up in the Messianic Jewish community. We

stand on the shoulders of those who pioneered the modern Messianic Jewish movement, and we have a unique contribution to make as those who have always thought
and lived as Messianic Jews.

This book is written primarily for rabbis and pastors, informed laity, undergradu-
ate students, and seminarians in the Messianic Jewish, mainstream Jewish, and Gentile Christian world. It is understandable why Jews would be interested in Messianic
Judaism. But why would Gentile Christians want to learn about the Messianic Jewish community? Joel Willitts answers this question in the concluding chapter of this
volume. For now, I would like to offer several reasons why Messianic Judaism is relevant to Gentile Christians. The first reason is *epistemological* — Messianic Judaism
helps Gentile Christians to understand their own faith better. In his book *The Jewish-
Christian Schism Revisited*, John Howard Yoder describes early Christianity as a form
of "Messianic Judaism" and the early church as a body composed of "Messianic Jews"
and "Messianic Gentiles."[3]

Many today view Judaism and Christianity as separate and distinct religions by
God's design. However, Yoder argues that this was not God's intention. A more objec-
tive understanding of the Jewish-Christian schism requires setting aside the "had to"
and allowing for the possibility that "it did not have to be." Historical development
does not always reflect the will of God. A critical reading of history will allow for the
"defectibility of the church of the past" and bear in mind that "divine providence"
readings of church history are sustained in part because they validate Christian
self-definition:[4]

> There was never a single event by that name [the Jewish-Christian schism]. After
> it had conclusively taken place, it seemed to everyone to be utterly natural that it
> should have come to pass. Yet there was a space of at least fifty years — twice that
> in most respects — during which it had not happened, was not inevitable or clearly
> probable, and was not chosen by everyone, not even by everyone who finally was
> going to have to accept it. We do violence to the depth and density of the story
> if, knowing with the wisdom of later centuries that it came out as it did, we box
> the actors of the first century into our wisdom about their children's fate in the
> second. We thereby refuse to honour the dignity and drama of their struggle, and
> the open-endedness of their questioning and the variety of paths available to them
> until one answer, not necessarily the best one, not necessarily one anyone wanted,
> was imposed on them.... If God's purpose might have been to offer a different
> future from the one which actually came to be, then we do not do total justice to
> God's intent in the story by reading it as if the outcome he did not want but which
> did happen, had to happen.[5]

As historians have increasingly recognized, the parting of the ways between Judaism and Christianity occurred between the second and fourth centuries, and this
parting did not necessarily reflect apostolic example or teaching:

---

3. John Howard Yoder, *The Jewish-Christian Schism Revisited* (ed. Michael G. Cartwright and Peter Ochs; Grand
Rapids: Eerdmans, 2003), 32 – 33.

4. Yoder, *Jewish-Christian Schism Revisited*, 137.

5. Yoder, *Jewish-Christian Schism Revisited*, 43 – 44, 47.

We have learned that instead of thinking of "Christianity" and "Judaism" as systems, existing primordially in a "normative" form, and instead of thinking of "Christians" and "Jews" in the early centuries as separate bodies existing over against each other, we must think of two initially largely overlapping circles. The circle "Church" and the circle "Jewry" overlapped for generations, in the persons whom we may call either messianic Jews or Jewish Christians, who for over a century at least stood in fellowship with both wider circles. They were not split apart from one another by Jesus' being honoured as Messiah, not by anyone's keeping nor not keeping the law. The split which was ultimately to push the circles apart began, we saw, not in the first century but in the second. It began not as a cleft between the two larger circles but as a schism within each of the communities. People like the "apologetic father" Justin began splitting the Church over the issue of respect for Jewish culture, and some rabbis began pushing out the *nozrim* who wanted to stay in their synagogues. "Justin's wedge" is dated about 150; the "rabbis' wedge" returned the insult at least a generation later.[6]

Messianic Judaism is the bridge between the Jewish people and the church, and as such it helps the church to understand better its origin and identity.

A second reason why the Gentile Christian world should concern itself with Messianic Judaism is *ecclesiological* — God designed the church to be a Jew-Gentile body. Markus Barth wrote in 1969, "The church is the bride of Christ only when it is the church of Jews and Gentiles.... [T]he existence, building, and growth of the church are identified with the common existence, structure, and growth of Jews and Gentiles."[7] Why is this? *It is because the church is a prolepsis of Israel and the nations in the eschaton.* Interdependence and mutual blessing between Jew and Gentile reflect the *raison d'être* of the church and anticipate the consummation when Israel and the nations, in unity and diversity, will worship Adonai alone. As George Howard asserted in 1979, a Jew-Gentile church testifies to the oneness of God and the ultimate plan of God:

> The gospel as Paul preached it demanded a continued ethnic distinctiveness between Jews and Gentiles in order that ... [Adonai], the God of the Hebrews, could be conceptualized by both Jews and Gentiles as the God of all nations....
> This is certainly his point of view in Rom. 3:29 – 30 where he says: "Or is God the God of the Jews only? Is he not the God of the Gentiles also? Yes, of the Gentiles also, since God is one." His thought is: if God is one he must be the God of both Jews and Gentiles.... We may even go further and say that any attempt on either side to erase the ethnic and cultural nature of the other would be to destroy Paul's particular concept of unity between Jews and Gentiles.[8]

Countering Paul van Buren's argument that "Only one Jew is essential to the Church and that is the Jew Jesus,"[9] Isaac Rottenberg points out that "Jewish-Gentile

---

6. Yoder, *Jewish-Christian Schism Revisited*, 69.

7. Markus Barth, *Israel and the Church: Contributions for a Dialogue Vital for Peace* (Richmond, Va.: John Knox, 1969), 90 – 91.

8. George Howard, *Paul: Crisis in Galatia: A Study in Early Christian Theology* (Cambridge: Cambridge University Press, 1979), 66, 79 – 81.

9. Paul M. Van Buren, *Discerning the Way* (New York: Seabury, 1980), 155.

unity belongs to the *esse* [being], not just the *bene esse* [well-being] of the Church."[10] R. Kendall Soulen has made a formidable case for Jew-Gentile ecclesiological variega-tion in his book *The God of Israel and Christian Theology*:

> Traditionally, the church has understood itself as a spiritual fellowship in which the carnal distinction between Jew and Gentile no longer applies. The church has declared itself a third and final "race" that transcends and replaces the difference between Israel and the nations.... The proper therapy for this misunderstanding is a recovery of the church's basic character as a table fellowship of those who are — and remain — different. The distinction between Jew and Gentile, being intrin-sic to God's work as the Consummator of creation, is not erased but realized in a new way in the sphere of the church. The church concerns the Jew as a Jew and the Gentile as a Gentile, not only initially or for the period of a few generations but essentially and at all times.[11]

Peter Hocken describes this fellowship between Jesus-believing Jews and Gentiles in the church as inherently "dialogical":

> The vision of the church as "the two made one" profoundly challenges all our inherited views of the church, whether Catholic, Orthodox or Protestant. First, it challenges what we may call all "monopolar" models of the church. The New Testament model is "bipolar," a union of contrasts or of opposites: of the Jews (oriented by their original calling toward the nations) and of the Gentiles (oriented by the gospel calling toward Israel and their Messiah). The bipolar model excludes a self-serving church, a church that sees its role as subordinating all else to itself — even in the name of Christ. There is something dialogical built into the consti-tution of the church as there is in the eternal "constitution" of the Trinity. There is the dialogue of the Bridegroom with the Bride (Eph. 5:22 – 23) and there is the dialogue of the "two made one," of Jew and Gentile, already on earth.[12]

One of the main purposes of this book is to give Gentile Christians vision for the dialogical relationship they share with Messianic Jews so that they will *come alongside* the Messianic Jewish community and assist it. Coming alongside can take many forms, including (a) praying for the Messianic Jewish community, (b) sharing the good news of Yeshua in a way that affirms the calling of Jews who follow Yeshua to remain Jews and to become better Jews, (c) encouraging Jews in churches to be involved in the Messianic Jewish community, (d) supporting Messianic Jewish education, (e) contrib-uting to the welfare of Messianic Jews in Israel, (f) helping local Messianic synagogues, (g) collaborating with Messianic Jewish ecclesial leaders and scholars, (h) preaching and teaching the Scriptures in a way that affirms God's covenant faithfulness to the Jewish people and the bilateral (Jew-Gentile) nature of the church, and (i) including Messianic Jews in Jewish-Christian dialogue.

---

10. Isaac C. Rottenberg, *Jewish Christians in an Age of Christian-Jewish Dialogue* (1995), 99. A collection of essays published "by the family and friends of the author in honor of his 70th birthday for distribution among circles engaged in Christian-Jewish dialogue."

11. R. Kendall Soulen, *The God of Israel and Christian Theology* (Minneapolis: Fortress, 1996), 169 – 70.

12. Peter Hocken, "The Messianic Jewish Movement: New Current and Old Reality," in *The Challenges of the Pentecostal, Charismatic and Messianic Jewish Movements: The Tensions of the Spirit* (Burlington, Vt.: Ashgate, 2009), 106.

A third reason why the Gentile Christian world should take an interest in Messianic Judaism is *Christological* — Jesus is a Jew. Therefore, he has a particular relationship to the Messianic Jewish community.[13] In the last six verses of the New Testament, the resurrected Messiah says, "I am [present tense] the Root and the Offspring of David" (Rev 22:16). He remains today a Jew, the resurrected Jew, the son of David (i.e., the Jewish Messiah = Christ), the king of Israel. As Bruce Marshall notes, the resurrected Jew upholds the continuing validity of a Jew/Gentile distinction: "in the person of the Logos God makes his own the flesh of the particular, Jesus of Nazareth. God's ownership of this Jewish flesh is permanent.... So in willing his own incarnation, it seems that God wills the permanence, indeed the eschatological permanence, of the distinction between Jews and Gentiles."[14]

To love Jesus is to love him in the fullness of his divinity and humanity, and being a Jew is fundamental to his humanity. As Paul said, "Remember Yeshua the Messiah, raised from the dead, descended from David. This is my gospel" (2 Tim 2:8 NIV NCPE).

There is a tendency in today's church for Gentile Christians to think of the Son of God as having left behind his humanity. Typically, Gentile Christians do not have difficulty worshiping Jesus, but many experience difficulty thinking of Jesus as fully human, having a national/ethnic identity and returning in bodily form to establish his kingdom on earth. The Jesus worshiped today is often a Christ of the Spirit who has transcended earthly existence. N. T. Wright notes:

> The idea of the human Jesus now being in heaven, in his thoroughly embodied risen state, comes as a shock to many people, including many Christians. Sometimes this is because many people think that Jesus, having been divine, stopped being divine and became human, and then, having been human for a while, stopped being human and went back to being divine (at least that's what many people think Christians are supposed to believe).[15]

---

13. For Messianic Jews, Yeshua is "the incarnation of the Divine Word through Whom the world was made, and of the Divine Glory through Whom God revealed Himself to Israel and acted in their midst. He is the living Torah, expressing perfectly in His example and teaching the Divine purpose for human life. Yeshua is completely human and completely divine. As the risen Messiah and the heavenly *Kohen Gadol* (High Priest), Yeshua continues to mediate God's relationship to His people Israel, to those of the nations who have joined the greater commonwealth of Israel in Him, and to all creation. God's plan of salvation and blessing for Israel, the nations, and the entire cosmos is fulfilled only in and through Yeshua, by virtue of His atoning death and bodily resurrection, and God's gift of life to both Jews and Gentiles, in this world and in the world to come, is bestowed and appropriated only in and through Him" (Union of Messianic Jewish Congregations, "Statement on the Identity of Yeshua," November 12, 2003; online: http://www.umjc.org/home-mainmenu-1/faqs-mainmenu-58/14-umjc-faq/17-who-is-yeshua). This was followed by the UMJC's 2004 "Statement on the Work of Yeshua" — "Yeshua is the Messiah promised to Israel in the Torah and prophets. Through His death, burial, and resurrection, He provided the atoning sacrifice that gives assurance of eternal life to those who genuinely trust in Him. Jewish people, along with all people, need the spiritual redemption that is available only in Messiah Yeshua, and need to put their trust in Him and His sacrificial work. Our role as a union of congregations is to embody the message of life and redemption through Messiah in the context of the larger Jewish community" (http://www.umjc.org/home-mainmenu-1/faqs-mainmenu-58/14-umjc-faq/19-what-are-the-standards-of-the-umjc).

14. Bruce D. Marshall, "Christ and the Cultures: The Jewish People and Christian Theology," in *The Cambridge Companion to Christian Doctrine* (ed. Colin E. Gunton; Cambridge: Cambridge University Press, 1997), 178.

15. N. T. Wright, *Surprised by Hope: Rethinking Heaven, the Resurrection, and the Mission of the Church* (New York: HarperCollins, 2008), 111.

When Gentile Christians see Jesus as the resurrected son of David, the king of Israel, post-human conceptions of him fade away. This is because Jesus' past, present, and future as "the son of David, the son of Abraham" (Matt 1:1), the particularity of his humanity, becomes vividly clear. This in turn leads many Jesus-believing Gentiles to become interested in the Messianic Jewish community.

The beginnings of this book go back to England. Joel Willitts and I met as PhD students in New Testament at Cambridge University, where we studied under the same supervisor, Professor Markus Bockmuehl. We had readers' desks at Tyndale House, a biblical studies research center, and regularly discussed issues related to post-supersessionist interpretation of the New Testament and Messianic Judaism.

Joel and I became good friends and found that much mutual blessing took place whenever we had conversations about the Bible and theology. I valued Joel's perspective as a Gentile Christian and Joel valued my perspective as a Messianic Jew. There was a synergy in our exchange that often led to fresh insights and unforeseen avenues of theological inquiry. My experience at Tyndale House with Joel and other Gentile Christian friends taught me that there is indeed a God-designed interdependence between the Messianic Jewish and Gentile Christian ecclesial perspectives, and that one without the other is woefully inadequate.

Those were magical days in Cambridge. Joel and I talked about what we wanted to accomplish after we completed our doctoral programs and agreed to write a book together. We felt that the time was ripe for a Messianic Jew and a Gentile Christian to collaborate on a writing project, and we hoped to set a precedent for this in the field of biblical and theological studies. It is exciting to see our dream realized with the publication of *Introduction to Messianic Judaism*, authored by twenty-six Messianic Jews and Gentile Christians.

Of the twelve authors in part 1, all are recognized leaders in the Messianic Jewish community. They work with various organizations, including the Union of Messianic Jewish Congregations (UMJC), the Messianic Jewish Alliance of America (MJAA), the International Alliance of Messianic Congregations and Synagogues (IAMCS), the Messianic Jewish Rabbinical Council (MJRC), Tikkun International, Chosen People Ministries (CPM), Messianic Jewish Theological Institute (MJTI), Israel College of the Bible (ICB), and the New School for Jewish Studies. A third of the Messianic Jewish contributors are leaders in their thirties and forties, and two of the essays ("Messianic Jewish Synagogues" and "Messianic Jewish Worship and Prayer") are authored by Elliot Klayman and Seth Klayman — father and son — to underscore the cross-generational impact of Messianic Judaism.

Fourteen scholars from a wide spectrum of Christian backgrounds have written essays for the second part of the book. Their participation signals a growing academic and ecclesial interest in Messianic Judaism. Since the 1970s, a sea change has taken place in New Testament studies that has far-reaching implications for how the church evaluates Messianic Judaism. A broad reassessment of the New Testament writers' view of Judaism has occurred since the publication of E. P. Sanders's seminal work *Paul and Palestinian Judaism* (1977), and this reevaluation continues unabated. The contributors to the second part of *Introduction to Messianic Judaism* draw from this recent scholarship and demonstrate how post-supersessionist interpretation of the New Testament results in readings of the biblical text that are consistent with Messianic Judaism. The final section of the book is written by Joel Willitts, who provides a summary and synthesis of the essays, explaining how they shed light on the ecclesial context and biblical foundations of Messianic Judaism.

It is our hope that this book will become a standard reference for introductory information on Messianic Judaism. May it help Messianic Jews and mainstream Jews to understand better the history and contours of the Messianic Jewish community, and may it inspire Gentile Christians to enter into closer relationship with Messianic Jews. May the collaboration that Joel and I experienced in working on this book lead to a wider collaboration between Jew and Gentile in the body of Messiah.

הנה מה־טוב ומה־נעים שבת אחים גם־יחד
How good and pleasant it is when God's people live together in unity!
— PSALM 133:1

PART 1

The Messianic Jewish Community

CHAPTER 1

Messianic Judaism in Antiquity and in the Modern Era

David Rudolph

When we speak of Messianic Judaism in antiquity and in the modern era, we are referring to a religious tradition in which Jews have claimed to follow Yeshua (Jesus) as the Messiah of Israel while continuing to live within the orbit of Judaism. Communities of such Jews existed in the first four centuries of the Common Era and then reappeared in the eighteenth century. The aim of this essay is to survey this history up until the present day.

Messianic Judaism in the New Testament Period

During the New Testament period, Messianic Judaism existed in the Land of Israel, Syria, and beyond. Here I will focus on two communities that practiced Messianic Judaism: Matthew's community and the Jerusalem community.

In his published dissertation *Community, Law and Mission in Matthew's Gospel*, Paul Foster describes an emerging "new consensus" in New Testament studies concerning the social identity of Matthew's community.[1] An increasing number of scholars are now identifying Matthew's community as a "deviant movement operating within the orbit of Judaism."[2] The case for this view is made by Anthony Saldarini, J. Andrew Overman, Phillip Sigal, Daniel Harrington, Joel Willitts, and Anders Runesson, among others.[3] Roland Deines, who disagrees with this perspective, nonetheless acknowledges the existence of a new consensus emerging over three points:

1. The Matthean community in the last third of the first century CE is composed of mainly Jewish believers in Christ.

---

1. Paul Foster, *Community, Law and Mission in Matthew's Gospel* (Tübingen: Mohr Siebeck, 2004), 78, 253. Foster challenges the consensus view.

2. Foster, *Community, Law and Mission in Matthew's Gospel*, 77.

3. Anthony J. Saldarini, *Matthew's Christian-Jewish Community* (Chicago: University of Chicago Press, 1994); J. Andrew Overman, *Matthew's Gospel and Formative Judaism: The Social World of the Matthean Community* (Minneapolis: Fortress, 1990); Phillip Sigal, *The Halakhah of Jesus of Nazareth according to the Gospel of Matthew* (Atlanta: Society of Biblical Literature, 2007); Daniel Harrington, *The Gospel of Matthew* (Collegeville, Minn.: Liturgical Press, 1991); Joel Willitts, *Matthew's Messianic Shepherd-King: In Search of "The Lost Sheep of the House of Israel"* (Berlin: Walter de Gruyter, 2007); Anders Runesson, "Rethinking Early Jewish-Christian Relations: Matthean Community History as Pharisaic Intragroup Conflict," *Journal of Biblical Literature* 127, no. 1 (2008): 95–132; Anders Runesson, "From Where? To What? Common Judaism, Pharisees, and the Changing Socioreligious Location of the Matthean Community," in *Common Judaism: Explorations in Second-Temple Judaism* (ed. Wayne O. McCready and Adele Reinhartz; Minneapolis: Fortress, 2008), 97–113.

2. These Christian Jews see no reason to break with their mother religion just because they believe that Jesus is the Messiah, although they are experiencing some pressure in this direction from mainstream Judaism.

3. These Christian Jews live according to the Law of Moses and its valid halakhic interpretations of their time, with some alterations, softenings, or modifications based on the teachings of Jesus. Jesus is seen as a Law-observant Jew, who offered his own individual points of view on some matters and gave his specific interpretations of disputed halakhic rules, but they remained — as Markus Bockmuehl points out — "conversant with contemporary Jewish legal debate and readily accommodated on the spectrum of 'mainstream' first-century Jewish opinion." The Law-critical aspects in the Jesus tradition have to be interpreted within this frame.[4]

It is now commonly recognized that Matthew viewed his community as a reformist Messianic movement *within* first-century Judaism.

Similarly, New Testament scholars have long held that the Jerusalem community headed by Ya'akov/James was (1) primarily composed of Yeshua-believing Jews who (2) remained within the bounds of Second Temple Judaism and (3) lived strictly according to the Torah (Acts 15:4 – 5; 21:20 – 21).[5] Michael Fuller, Richard Bauckham, Craig Hill, Darrell Bock, Robert Tannehill, and Jacob Jervell are among the many Luke-Acts scholars who maintain that the Jerusalem congregation viewed itself as the nucleus of a restored Israel, led by twelve apostles representing the twelve tribes of Israel (Acts 1:6 – 7, 26; 3:19 – 21).[6] Their mission, these scholars contend, was to spark a Jewish renewal movement for Yeshua the Son of David *within* the house of Israel (Gal 2:7 – 10; Acts 21:17 – 26).

The Jerusalem congregation functioned as a center of halakhic/ecclesiastical

4. Roland Deines, "Not the Law but the Messiah: Law and Righteousness in the Gospel of Matthew — An Ongoing Debate," in *Built Upon the Rock: Studies in the Gospel of Matthew* (ed. Daniel M. Gurtner and John Nolland; Grand Rapids: Eerdmans, 2008), 54 – 55.

5. Joshua Schwartz, "How Jewish to be Jewish? Self-Identity and Jewish Christians in First Century Palestine," in *Judaea-Palaestina, Babylon and Rome: Jews in Antiquity* (ed. Benjamin Isaac and Yuval Shahar, Tübingen: Mohr Siebeck, 2012), 55 – 73. Scholars as far back as Jerome have tendentiously labeled this historical footprint of Messianic Judaism in first-century Jerusalem as sub- or pre-Christian: "In the first instance, the Jerusalem church is regarded as having been too Christian to be Jewish; in the second, it is thought too Jewish to be Christian. The assumption in either case is that one could have been truly Christian only to the extent that one was not authentically Jewish. On a popular level, it is the first approach that dominates. Christians such as James and Peter, both leaders of the Jerusalem church, are thought to have thrown off the shackles of their Jewish past. It is not difficult to see this view as an uncritical retrojection of modern Gentile Christianity onto the primitive church. Issues more characteristic of Judaism, such as the restoration of Israel (a concern repeatedly mentioned in the description of the Jerusalem church in Acts 1 – 3), are therefore ignored. The opposite approach, more common in scholarly circles, is to regard figures such as Peter and, especially, James as *too* Jewish, and therefore sub- or pre-Christian. Christianity instead is the product of the Hellenistic church (ironically, those who did not have the benefit — or, apparently, the distraction — of having known Jesus), especially the apostle Paul. Hence, 'Jewish Christianity' becomes secondary, problematic, and largely dismissible — except, that is, as a foil, the source of whatever one finds distasteful in early Christianity" (Craig C. Hill, "The Jerusalem Church," in *Jewish Christianity Reconsidered: Rethinking Ancient Groups and Texts* [Minneapolis: Fortress, 2007], 41 – 42).

6. On the restoration of Israel in Luke-Acts, see Michael E. Fuller, *The Restoration of Israel: Israel's Re-gathering and the Fate of the Nations in Early Jewish Literature and Luke-Acts* (Berlin: Walter de Gruyter, 2006); Richard Bauckham, "The Restoration of Israel in Luke-Acts," in *Restoration: Old Testament, Jewish, and Christian Perspectives* (ed. James M. Scott; Leiden, Netherlands: Brill, 2001), 435 – 87; Craig C. Hill, "Restoring the Kingdom to Israel: Luke-Acts and Christian Supersessionism," in *Shadow of Glory: Reading the New Testament after the Holocaust* (ed. Tod Linafelt; New York: Routledge, 2002), 185 – 200; Hill, "The Jerusalem Church," 39 – 56. Cf. Darrell

authority, and its leaders, headed by James, resolved disputes for the international community of Yeshua believers by issuing council decisions of the kind we see in Acts 15. Here Luke writes that the Jerusalem Council exempted Yeshua-believing Gentiles from proselyte circumcision and full Torah observance. While the significance of the Jerusalem Council decision for Yeshua-believing Gentiles has long been recognized in New Testament studies, the implications for Yeshua-believing Jews has only recently come to the forefront of Acts scholarship. As F. Scott Spencer points out, "The representatives at the Jerusalem conference — including Paul — agreed only to release *Gentile* believers from the obligation of circumcision; the possibility of nullifying this covenantal duty for Jewish disciples was never considered."[7] If the Jerusalem leadership had viewed circumcision as optional for Yeshua-believing Jews, there would have been no point in debating the question of exemption for Yeshua-believing Gentiles or delivering a letter specifically addressed to these Gentiles. Michael Wyschogrod rightly notes that "both sides agreed that Jewish believers in Jesus remained obligated to circumcision and the Mosaic Law. The verdict of the first Jerusalem Council then is that the Church is to consist of two segments, united by their faith in Jesus."[8]

A growing number of New Testament scholars now concur with Wyschogrod that an important implication of the Jerusalem Council decision is that Yeshua-believing Jews were to remain practicing Jews.[9] To put it another way, the Jerusalem Council validated Messianic Judaism as the normative way of life for Jewish followers of Yeshua. In Acts 21:17 – 26 — the mirror text of Acts 15 — this validation is made explicit by Paul's example.[10] At the request of James, Paul sets the record straight before thousands of Torah-observant Messianic Jews in Jerusalem that he remained within the bounds of Judaism. He testifies in the holy Temple that (1) the rumours about him are false — he teaches Diaspora Jews not to assimilate but to remain faithful Jews — and (2) he observes the Torah (present active tense) like the "zealous for the

L. Bock, *Acts* (Grand Rapids: Baker Academic, 2007); Robert C. Tannehill, *The Narrative Unity of Luke-Acts: A Literary Interpretation* (vol. 2; Minneapolis: Fortress, 1990); Robert C. Tannehill, *The Shape of Luke's Story: Essays on Luke-Acts* (Eugene, Oreg.: Cascade, 2005); Jacob Jervell, *The Theology of the Acts of the Apostles* (Cambridge: Cambridge University Press, 1996); Jacob Jervell, *Luke and the People of God: A New Look at Luke-Acts* (Minneapolis: Augsburg, 1972); Hilary Le Cornu with Joseph Shulam, *A Commentary on the Jewish Roots of Acts* (2 vols.; Jerusalem: Academon, 2003).

7. F. Scott Spencer, *Acts* (Sheffield: Sheffield Academic Press, 1997), 159.

8. Michael Wyschogrod, *Abraham's Promise: Judaism and Jewish-Christian Relations* (ed. R. Kendall Soulen; Grand Rapids: Eerdmans, 2004), 194. Cf. Amy-Jill Levine, *The Misunderstood Jew: The Church and the Scandal of the Jewish Jesus* (New York: HarperSanFrancisco, 2006), 26, and chapter 16 below, Richard Bauckham, "James and the Jerusalem Council Decision."

9. Markus Bockmuehl, *Jewish Law in Gentile Churches: Halakhah and the Beginning of Christian Public Ethics* (Edinburgh: T&T Clark, 2000), 168 – 72; R. Kendall Soulen, *The God of Israel and Christian Theology* (Minneapolis: Fortress, 1996), 170 – 71; Richard Bauckham, "James and the Jerusalem Community," in *Jewish Believers in Jesus: The Early Centuries* (ed. Oskar Skarsaune and Reidar Hvalvik; Peabody, Mass.: Hendrickson, 2007), 75; Mark S. Kinzer, *Postmissionary Messianic Judaism: Redefining Christian Engagement with the Jewish People* (Grand Rapids: Brazos, 2005), 66 – 67, 158 – 60; Mark D. Nanos, "The Apostolic Decree and the 'Obedience of Faith,'" in *The Mystery of Romans* (Minneapolis: Fortress, 1996), 166 – 238; Jervell, *Luke and the People of God*, 190; Scot McKnight, "A Parting within the Way: Jesus and James on Israel and Purity," in *James the Just and Christian Origins* (ed. Bruce Chilton and Craig A. Evans; Leiden, Netherlands: Brill, 1999), 110; Daniel Marguerat, "Paul and the Torah in the Acts of the Apostles," in *The Torah in the New Testament: Papers Delivered at the Manchester-Lausanne Seminar of June 2008* (ed. Michael Tait and Peter Oakes; London: T&T Clark, 2009), 111 – 17.

10. David J. Rudolph, *A Jew to the Jews: Jewish Contours of Pauline Flexibility in 1 Corinthians 9:19 – 23* (Tübingen: Mohr Siebeck, 2011), 53 – 73.

Torah"[11] members of the Jerusalem Messianic Jewish community. Paul's testimony is fully consistent with his "rule in all the congregations" that Jews are to remain practicing Jews (1 Cor 7:17 – 24), a probable Pauline restatement of the Jerusalem Council decision.[12]

Messianic Judaism and the Parting of the Ways between Judaism and Christianity

For centuries, scholars have taught that a decisive parting of the ways took place between Judaism and Christianity during the New Testament period. Today this narrative is widely disputed. In their book *The Ways That Never Parted*, Adam Becker and Annette Yoshiko Reed document the history of this reassessment and demonstrate that the evidence supports a "variety of different 'Partings' at different times in different places."[13] Becker and Reed concur with Daniel Boyarin, Paula Fredriksen, Philip Alexander, John Gager, Judith Lieu, John Howard Yoder, Edwin Broadhead, and a growing number of scholars who have concluded, based on textual and archaeological evidence, that "the fourth century CE is a far more plausible candidate for a decisive turning point than any date in the earlier period."[14] This reassessment is strengthened by the recognition that communities of Yeshua-believing Jews who practiced Judaism existed as late as 375 CE. Epiphanius, the fourth-century church father, describes the Messianic Judaism of his day:

> [They] did not call themselves Christians, but Nazarenes.... [T]hey remained wholly Jewish and nothing else. For they use not only the New Testament but also the Old like the Jews.... [They] live according to the preaching of the Law as among the Jews.... They have a good mastery of the Hebrew language. For the entire Law and the Prophets and what is called the Scriptures, I mention the poetical books, Kings, Chronicles and Esther and all the others are read in Hebrew by them as that is the case with the Jews of course. Only in this respect they differ

---

11. The *kai* in Acts 21:24 is emphatic, as in the ESV ("you yourself *also* live in observance of the law").

12. David J. Rudolph, "Paul's 'Rule in All the Churches' (1 Cor 7:17 – 24) and Torah-Defined Ecclesiological Variegation," *Studies in Christian-Jewish Relations* 5 (2010): 1 – 23. Online: http://www.mjstudies.com; J. Brian Tucker, *Remain in Your Calling: Paul and the Continuation of Social Identities in 1 Corinthians* (Eugene, Oreg.: Pickwick, 2011), 62 – 114; and chapter 20 below, Anders Runesson, "Paul's Rule in All the *Ekklēsiai*."

13. Adam H. Becker and Annette Yoshiko Reed, eds., *The Ways That Never Parted: Jews and Christians in Late Antiquity and the Early Middle Ages* (Tübingen: Mohr Siebeck, 2003), 22.

14. Becker and Reed, *The Ways That Never Parted*, 23. See Daniel Boyarin, "Semantic Differences; or, 'Judaism'/'Christianity,'" in *The Ways That Never Parted*, 65 – 85; Daniel Boyarin, *The Jewish Gospels: The Story of the Jewish Christ* (New York: New Press, 2012); Daniel Boyarin, *Border Lines: The Partition of Judaeo-Christianity* (Philadelphia: University of Pennsylvania Press, 2004); Daniel Boyarin, *Dying for God: Martyrdom and the Making of Christianity and Judaism* (Stanford: Stanford University Press, 1999); Paula Fredriksen, "What 'Parting of the Ways'? Jews, Gentiles, and the Ancient Mediterranean City," in *The Ways That Never Parted*, 35 – 63; Philip S. Alexander, "'The Parting of the Ways' from the Perspective of Rabbinic Judaism," in *Jews and Christians: The Parting of the Ways A.D. 70 to 135* (ed. James D. G. Dunn; Grand Rapids: Eerdmans, 1999); John G. Gager, "Did Jewish Christians See the Rise of Islam?" in *The Ways That Never Parted*, 361 – 72; Judith Lieu, "'The Parting of the Ways': Theological Construct or Historical Reality?" in *Neither Jew nor Greek: Constructing Early Christianity* (London: T&T Clark, 2002), 11 – 29; John Howard Yoder, *The Jewish-Christian Schism Revisited* (ed. Michael G. Cartwright and Peter Ochs; Grand Rapids: Eerdmans, 2003); Edwin K. Broadhead, *Jewish Ways of Following Jesus: Redrawing the Religious Map of Antiquity* (Tübingen: Mohr Siebeck, 2010), 354 – 75; Anders Runesson, "Inventing Christian Identity: Paul, Ignatius, and Theodosius I," in *Exploring Early Christian Identity* (ed. Bengt Holmberg; Tübingen: Mohr Siebeck, 2008), 59 – 91.

from the Jews and Christians: with the Jews they do not agree because of their belief in Christ, with the Christians because they are trained in the Law, in circumcision, the Sabbath and the other things.[15]

In his essay "Jewish Believers in Early Rabbinic Literature (2d to 5th Centuries)," Philip Alexander notes that Messianic Jews who lived in Galilee during the Tannaitic period remained within the orbit of Judaism:

> They lived like other Jews. Their houses were indistinguishable from the houses of other Jews. They probably observed as much of the Torah as did other Jews (though they would doubtless have rejected, as many others did, the distinctively rabbinic interpretations of the *misvot*). They studied Torah and developed their own interpretations of it, and, following the practice of the Apostles, they continued to perform a ministry of healing in the name of Jesus.... [T]hey seem to have continued to attend their local synagogues on Sabbath. They may have attempted to influence the service of the synagogue, even to the extent of trying to introduce into it the Paternoster [the Lord's Prayer], or readings from Christian Gospels, or they may have preached sermons which offered Christian readings of the Torah. The rabbis countered with a program which thoroughly "rabbinized" the service of the synagogue and ensured that it reflected the core rabbinic values.[16]

Direct evidence of Jews who practiced Messianic Judaism after the First Council of Nicaea is scanty. This is because the view that Jews could not become Christians and remain Jews was backed by canon law and Constantine's sword. The Second Council of Nicaea in 787 was the first ecumenical council to ban Messianic Jews from the church. Messianic Jews were required to renounce all ties to Judaism through professions of faith like the one from the Church of Constantinople ("I renounce absolutely everything Jewish, every law, rite and custom").[17] From the fourth century until the modern period, millions of Jews converted to Christianity and left behind their Jewish identity.

Messianic Judaism and the Moravian *Judenkehille* in the Eighteenth Century

The earliest known post-Nicene attempt to restore Messianic Judaism was undertaken by the Moravian Brethren in Herrnhut, Germany (1735).[18] Count Nikolaus Ludwig

---

15. Epiphanius, Panarion 29, quoted in A. F. J. Klijn and G. J. Reinink, trans., *Patristic Evidence for Jewish-Christian Sects* (Leiden, Netherlands: Brill, 1973), 173. "The core traits of the Nazarenes — Jewish followers of Jesus with a Hebraic textual tradition, a commitment to the Law, and a location in the vicinity of Antioch — are supported by converging lines of evidence. In light of this analysis, the most plausible conclusion is that the core of the patristic representation of the Nazarenes is undergirded by a historical group who seek to continue God's covenant with Israel by both following Jesus and maintaining Jewishness" (Broadhead, *Jewish Ways of Following Jesus*, 187). Cf. Wolfram Kinzig, "The Nazoraeans," in *Jewish Believers in Jesus* (ed. Skarsaune and Hvalvik), 463 – 87.

16. Philip S. Alexander, "Jewish Believers in Early Rabbinic Literature (2d to 5th Centuries)," in *Jewish Believers in Jesus* (ed. Skarsaune and Hvalvik), 686 – 87.

17. Assemani, *Cod. Lit.* 1:105. See James Parkes, "Appendix 3: Professions of Faith Extracted from Jews on Baptism," in *The Conflict of the Church and the Synagogue: A Study in the Origins of Antisemitism* (New York: Atheneum, 1985), 397.

18. In 1730 – 31, Johann Georg Widmann and Johann Andreas Manitus, from Halle, entered into ongoing

von Zinzendorf established in the *Brüdergemeine* (the Brethren community) a congregation in which Yeshua-believing Jews were encouraged to live out Jewish life and identity. He called this congregation a *Judenkehille* (Jewish community):

> Soon the program of "gathering firstlings" emerged. The program aimed at integrating individual Jews into the *Brüdergemeine* without encouraging them to abandon their identity. To this end, several liturgical innovations were implemented. These included the celebration of the Day of Atonement and, later on, the Sabbath Rest and the intercession for Israel within the services on Sundays. A christianized Jewish marriage ceremony for the "firstlings" was created. The new converts were intended to be gathered in a Jewish-Christian congregation within the *Brüdergemeine*, the *Judenkehille* ("Jews' Qehillah," the latter part of the word being derived from the Hebrew word for "community").[19]

As the years passed, Zinzendorf reassessed his approach and concluded that it would be better for *Judenkehille* congregations to exist autonomously within the Jewish community rather than within Gentile Christian churches. He thus redirected German Pietist efforts toward this end:

> In the early 1750s, Zinzendorf reacted by modifying the project of the *Judenkehille* to the effect that he now aimed at establishing it *within* the Jewish communities. The converted Jews should, as an autonomous community, remain in their Jewish environment and form a sort of nucleus of the converted Israel. By this time Zinzendorf had moved to London to apply himself to the organization of the local branch of the *Brüdergemeine*. At that point, the new *Judenkehille* was also intended to be based in London and to be supervised by Lieberkühn and the convert Benjamin David Kirchhof (1716 – 1784).[20]

As late as the 1770s, the Moravian Brethren were facilitating the establishment of fully autonomous *Judenkehille* congregations in Germany, England, and Switzerland.

Messianic Judaism and Jewish Missionary Societies in the Nineteenth and Early Twentieth Century

With nineteenth-century Protestant missionary societies promoting cross-cultural evangelism, it became increasingly acceptable for Christians of Jewish descent to identify as "Hebrew Christians" and to form missionary societies to bring the gospel to their own people. These early Jewish mission agencies included the London Society for Promoting Christianity Amongst the Jews (1809), the Episcopal Jews' Chapel Abrahamic Society (1835), the Hebrew Christian Alliance (1867), the Hebrew Chris-

---

dialogue with members of the Plotzgo Jewish community in Poland about creating a Jewish-Christian synagogue where Jesus-believing Jews would continue to observe the Torah and Jewish customs. Acts 15; 21; and Rom 9:4 – 5; 11:11 – 21 were presented as the biblical basis for such a community. See Lutz Greisiger, "Israel in the Church and the Church in Israel: The Formation of Jewish Christian Communities as a Proselytising Strategy Within and Outside the German Pietist Mission to the Jews of the Eighteenth Century," in *Pietism and Community in Europe and North America 1650 – 1850* (ed. Jonathan Strom; Leiden, Netherlands: Brill, 2010), 133 – 34.

19. Greisiger, "Israel in the Church and the Church in Israel," 137 – 38.
20. Greisiger, "Israel in the Church and the Church in Israel," 139 – 40.

tian Prayer Union (1882), the British Hebrew Christian Alliance (1888), the Hebrew Christian Alliance of America (1915), and the International Hebrew Christian Alliance (1925).

It is important to recognize that Jewish mission agencies did not promote Messianic Judaism. They facilitated Jewish evangelism and encouraged "converted Jews" to join Protestant churches, which assimilated these Jews into Gentile Christianity. Hebrew Christians who were employed by Jewish missionary societies did not typically live within the orbit of Judaism or identify as Torah-faithful Jews. Most were fully at home in the symbolic universe of Gentile Christianity.

Despite (or perhaps because of) this Gentile Christian context, some Jewish believers in Yeshua who came to faith through Jewish mission agencies refused to assimilate into Gentile churches. They wanted to continue to live as Jews. These individuals called themselves "Messianic Jews" to distinguish themselves from the majority of Hebrew Christians who saw little to no value in Judaism, and who thought it was backsliding or heresy for Hebrew Christians to practice Judaism as a matter of covenant, calling, or national duty before God.

Prominent Messianic Jews in the late nineteenth and early twentieth centuries included Joseph Rabinowitz in Russia, Rabbi Isaac Lichtenstein in Hungary, Mark John Levy in the United States, Philip Cohen in South Africa, and Hayyim Yedidyah Pollak (Lucky) in Galicia. Other leaders included Moshe Imanuel Ben-Meir and Hyman Jacobs in Jerusalem, Paul Levertoff (who held the chair of Hebrew and Rabbinics at the Institutum Judaicum in Leipzig), Paulus Grun in Hamburg, Alex Waldmann, Israel Pick, Jechiel Tsvi Lichtenstein-Herschensohn, and John Zacker (who founded the Hebrew Christian Synagogue of Philadelphia in 1922).

Messianic Jews referred to their religious tradition as "Messianic Judaism,"[21] a term that implicitly called into question the traditional narrative of a first-century parting of the ways between Judaism and "Christianity." *It is important to recognize that Messianic Judaism challenged fundamental theological assumptions about the nature of the ecclesia and argued on the basis of New Testament texts — primarily Acts 15; 21:17 – 26; and 1 Corinthians 7:17 – 24 — that Yeshua-believing Jews had a continuing responsibility before God to live as Jews.*[22] Messianic Judaism took exception to eighteen hundred years of Gentile Christian theology and exegesis that precluded reading the New Testament in this way. Most Jewish mission agencies did not want to be identified with this new perspective and distanced themselves from Messianic Jews and Messianic Judaism.

In December 1910, the first volume of *The Messianic Jew* was published by Philip Cohen's organization, the Jewish Messianic Movement. The journal promoted the importance of Yeshua-believing Jews living within the orbit of Judaism and embracing a Torah-observant life.

---

21. Philip Cohen, "Ways and Means," *The Messianic Jew* 1, no. 1 (1910): 13. The March 1895 issue of *Our Hope* was subtitled *A Monthly Devoted to the Study of Prophecy and to Messianic Judaism.*

22. Ernst F. Stroeter, "An Urgent Call to Hebrew Christians," *The Messianic Jew* 1, no. 1 (1910): 7 – 8; J. N. Martins, "A Plea for Hebrew Christianity or Christian Judaism," *The Messianic Jew* 1, no. 1 (1910): 20 – 21; Ernst F. Stroeter, "Does the Jew, in Christ, Cease to Be a Jew?" *Our Hope* 2, no. 6 (December 1895): 129 – 34.

In response to this publication, David Baron, a Jewish missions leader who headed the Hebrew Christian Testimony to Israel, wrote an article titled "'Messianic Judaism'; or Judaising Christianity" in the October 1911 edition of *The Scattered Nation*. Here Baron called Messianic Judaism "dangerous" and described it as the agenda of spiritually immature Jews in Christ:

From different directions questions have been addressed to us as to our views and attitude in relation to the "Jewish Messianic Movement," which rather grand-sounding designation does not describe any movement of Jews in the direction of recognising our Lord Jesus Christ as the Messiah, but an agitation on the part of some Hebrew Christian brethren, who have evidently yet much to learn as to the true character of their high calling of God in Christ Jesus.... [The observance of Torah by the Hebrew Christian] is not only doubly incongruous, but, as experience has shown, a hindrance to his own full spiritual development; a means of confusion to his fellow-believers from among the Gentiles; and a stumbling-block to the Jews.

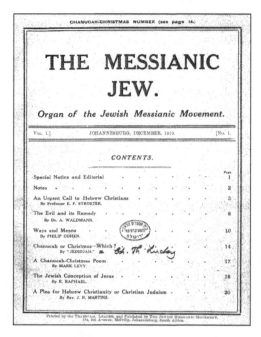

What these brethren preach and agitate for is, that it is incumbent on Hebrew Christians, in order to keep up their "national continuity," not only to identify themselves with their unbelieving Jewish brethren, in their national aspirations — as expressed, for instance, in Zionism and other movements which aim at creating and fostering "the national idea" and regaining possession of Palestine — but to observe the "national" rites and customs of the Jews, such as the keeping of the Sabbath, circumcision, and other observances, some of which have not even their origin in the law of Moses, but are part of that unbearable yoke which was laid on the neck of our people by the Rabbis.

To deal fully with this subject, and to point out all the dangers and fallacies of this "movement," one would require to write a very long treatise; but let us very briefly look at those observances which are included in the "Minimum programme" of these Judaising brethren. At the head of all stands circumcision. Now, from the physiological and hygienic point of view, there is a great deal to be said for the practice; but to say that it is incumbent upon the Jewish Christian to circumcise his children in order to keep up "his national continuity," is both erroneous and absurd.

This law-observing Judaism will not be contented were we to observe its national religious customs and yet believe in Jesus: if we would have its recognition we must deny Christ. This is the price required by the synagogue for our approach to it. Alas! some have paid this price who began by seemingly harmless "observances."[23]

The 1917 issue of *The Hebrew Christian Alliance Quarterly*, the official journal of the Hebrew Christian Alliance of America (HCAA), labeled Messianic Judaism a heresy that was banished from the alliance ranks. The *Alliance Quarterly* leaves no ambiguity about the HCAA stance on Messianic Judaism: "We felt it our duty to make it clear that we have nothing to do with this so-called 'Messianic Judaism,' in any shape or form, nor have we any faith in it." The journal goes on to state that the HCAA stands opposed to the "misguided tendency" of Messianic Judaism and that "we will have none of it!" They conclude with the statement, "We are filled with deep gratitude to God, for the guidance of the Holy Spirit, in enabling the Conference to so effectively banish it [Messianic Judaism] from our midst, and now the Hebrew Christian Alliance has put herself on record to be absolutely free from it, now and forever."[24]

Messianic Judaism and the Birth of the Congregational Movement in the Late Twentieth Century

Despite the social and theological marginalization of Messianic Judaism by Jewish mission agencies, the Messianic Jewish movement became a fixture in the worldwide community of Jewish believers in Yeshua. A shining source of inspiration was Joseph Rabinowitz's establishment of a Messianic synagogue in Kishinev, Russia, in 1884 called Beney Israel, Beney Brit Chadashah (Israelites of the New Covenant). Neither Rabinowitz nor his synagogue was connected to a Christian denomination; the government of Bessarabia legally designated the Messianic Jewish community a distinct Jewish sect.[25] Rabinowitz's synagogue considered circumcision, the Sabbath, and festivals incumbent upon Jews, as section 6 of the community's Twenty-Four Articles of Faith makes clear: "[As] we are the seed of Abraham according to the flesh, who was the father of all those who were circumcised and believed, we are bound to circumcise every male child on the eighth day, as God commanded him. And as we are the descendants of those whom the Lord brought out of the land of Egypt, with a stretched out arm, we are bound to keep the Sabbath, the feast of unleavened bread, and the feast of weeks, according as it is written in the law of Moses."[26]

Rabinowitz's congregation referred to their building (which seated 150–200 people) as a "synagogue," and they read from a Torah scroll.[27] Traditional synagogue

23. David Baron, "'Messianic Judaism'; or Judaising Christianity," *The Scattered Nation* (October 1911): 3, 11, 16.

24. "Messianic Judaism," *Hebrew Christian Alliance Quarterly* 1 (July/October 1917): 86. Cf. S. B. Rohold, "Messianic Judaism," *Prayer and Work for Israel* (January 1918): 8–11, 32–43.

25. Kai Kjaer-Hansen, *Joseph Rabinowitz and the Messianic Movement: The Herzl of Jewish Christianity* (Grand Rapids: Eerdmans, 1994), 64.

26. Kjaer-Hansen, *Joseph Rabinowitz and the Messianic Movement*, 104.

27. Kjaer-Hansen, *Joseph Rabinowitz and the Messianic Movement*, 146.

prayers were used with Messianic additions, and the Messiah was referred to by his original Hebrew name, Yeshua.

In the decades that followed, a number of missionary societies in North America and Europe attempted to start congregations in light of Rabinowitz's success. These included the First Hebrew-Christian Church of America in New York City (1885), the First Hebrew Christian Church of Chicago (1934; Presbyterian), the First Hebrew Christian Church of Philadelphia (1954; Presbyterian), and Emmanuel Presbyterian Hebrew Christian Congregation (1963). However, because these churches did not view Jewish life as a matter of covenant and calling before God, they struggled to transmit Jewish identity to the next generation. These Hebrew Christian churches were more often than not Presbyterian churches that put on a veneer of Jewishness to draw Jewish people to the gospel.[28] This was their *raison d'être*. It was not until the last quarter of the twentieth century that Messianic synagogues, reflecting the Rabinowitz model in theology and Jewish ethos, began to dot the landscape of major cities around the world.[29]

In the late 1960s and early 1970s, a large number of Jews in their twenties became believers in Yeshua and refused to assimilate into Gentile churches. They wanted to maintain their Jewish identity and live as Jews. Many had extraordinary experiences that pointed them in this direction. Marty Chernoff, a pioneer of the late twentieth-century movement, saw a vision of a banner stretched across the sky with the words "Messianic Judaism" on it.[30] His wife Yohanna writes about how they and their community of young Jewish believers in Yeshua came to reject the Hebrew Christian model and embrace Messianic Judaism:

> Almost every attempt by Hebrew Christians in the past to form congregations of Jewish believers had failed. Among the few notable exceptions was a congregation founded in Illinois in 1934, the First Hebrew-Presbyterian Church of Chicago, pastored by David Bronstein, Sr., under the auspices of the Presbyterian Church, USA. But David had to work to justify the use of the word "Hebrew" in the name, stressing that the liturgy was not patterned after that of the synagogue, but merely sprinkled with a few colorful Hebrew phrases and the reciting of the *Sh'ma*. While there were a few other isolated incidents of congregations of Jewish believers, most were more along the lines of a Jewish church rather than a synagogue and were an

---

28. Dan Cohn-Sherbok, *Messianic Judaism* (London: Cassell, 2000), 54.

29. An exception was the independent Messianic Jewish congregation established by Hyman Jacobs and Moshe Imanuel Ben-Meir in Jerusalem (1925–29). Also Kehilat haMashiach Betoch Israel (Congregation of the Messiah within Israel), a Messianic synagogue in Los Angeles in the 1950s planted by Dr. Lawrence Duff-Forbes. Rabbi Duff-Forbes led *Erev Shabbat* (Friday night) services that followed the *siddur* (traditional Jewish prayers). He also taught classes on modern and classical Hebrew, Yiddish, and Jewish history at his Yishivat Yahudat Meshichit (Academy of the Jewish Messiah). See Cohn-Sherbok, *Messianic Judaism*, 55–56. In 1960, Ed Brotsky of Toronto became the assistant rabbi of Kehilat haMashiach Betoch Israel. According to Brotsky, Rabbi Duff-Forbes "advocated that Jewish believers should follow what he called Messianic Judaism. For the next nine months until we returned to Canada, I learned a great deal about Messianic Judaism" (Robert I. Winer, *The Calling: The History of the Messianic Jewish Alliance of America, 1915–1990* [Wynnewood, Pa.: MJAA, 1990], 41–42). See also Joseph Shulam, "Rabbi Daniel Zion: Chief Rabbi of Bulgarian Jews during World War II," *Mishkan: A Theological Forum on Jewish Evangelism* 15 (1991): 53–57.

30. Yohanna Chernoff with Jim Miller, *Born a Jew ... Die a Jew: The Story of Martin Chernoff, a Pioneer in Messianic Judaism* (Hagerstown, Md.: Ebed, 1996), 124.

extension of the Christian church at large. Consequently, most Jewish members ultimately assimilated into the church, along with most other Jewish believers at this time, and were soon lost to their people.... Our congregation felt that it was time to rise up as one body to make a statement. In effect, we agreed that: "We are Jewish believers in *Yeshua* as our Messiah. We have our own destiny in the Lord. We will no longer be assimilated into the church and pretend to be non-Jews. If *Yeshua* Himself, His followers and the early Jewish believers tenaciously maintained their Jewish lifestyles, why was it right then, but wrong now?"[31]

Like the Chernoff family, many Yeshua-believing Jews in the 1970s wanted to live within the orbit of Judaism and to lift up the name of Yeshua within their local Jewish community. They established Messianic Jewish congregations to make this possible. Within a decade, the Messianic Jewish movement went from being a blip on the North American religious scene to being a grassroots congregational movement fueled by a new generation of Messianic Jews.

The Union of Messianic Jewish Congregations (UMJC) was formed in 1979 with nineteen member congregations, and the International Alliance of Messianic Congregations and Synagogues (IAMCS) followed in 1986 with fifteen member congregations. In 2012, these two umbrella organizations represented more than two hundred Messianic synagogues. There are an additional three-hundred-plus congregations around the world that are independent or linked to smaller Messianic Jewish networks.

Messianic Judaism and the Diversity of the Twenty-First-Century "Messianic Jewish" Movement

In 1975, the Hebrew Christian Alliance of America (HCAA) changed its name to the Messianic Jewish Alliance of America (MJAA) under pressure from young Messianic Jews who swelled its ranks. The name change reflected an about-face from the HCAA's stance in 1917 ("We felt it our duty to make it clear that we have nothing to do with this so-called 'Messianic Judaism,' in any shape or form ... and now the Hebrew Christian Alliance has put herself on record to be absolutely free from it, now and forever"). While the name change reflected an institutional commitment to move in the direction of Messianic Judaism, the MJAA did not immediately define "Messianic Jewish" or require its members to embrace new theological commitments. Thus, overnight, hundreds of Hebrew Christians with no prior commitment to "Messianic Judaism" as a historical theological concept became part of a Messianic Jewish national organization and in time began describing themselves as "Messianic Jews."

Compounding the confusion, a number of Jewish mission agencies (with no theological commitment to historic Messianic Judaism) began using the terms "Messianic Jewish" and "Messianic Jew," having found that potential Jewish "converts" resonated with the terms. The new terminology was also a way to connect with the growing number of Jewish believers in Yeshua who identified as Messianic Jews.

31. Chernoff, *Born a Jew ... Die a Jew*, 123–25.

Internally, however, these mission agencies were not unlike early twentieth-century Hebrew Christian missionary societies that opposed Messianic Judaism on theological grounds because of Christian theology's traditionally negative view of Judaism. One mission agency that quickly adopted the terms "Messianic Jewish" and "Messianic Jew" without embracing their original meaning is Jews for Jesus, a San Francisco – based organization that is known for its high-profile media campaigns and confrontational street evangelism.[32] Many Jews and Christians assume incorrectly that all or most Messianic Jews are part of this organization.[33]

A third factor that contributed to the muddling of the term "Messianic" was that evangelical Christian churches and ministries in Israel in the 1940s and 1950s began using the Hebrew term *Meshichyim* ("Messianic") instead of *Nozrim* ("Christians") because of its more positive connotation to Jews:

> Baptist Robert Lindsay noted that for Israeli Jews the term "Christians" (*nozrim* in Hebrew) meant, almost automatically, an alien, hostile religion. Because such a term made it nearly impossible to convince Jews that Christianity was "their" religion, the missionaries sought a more neutral term that did not arouse their strong negative feelings. They chose the term *Meshichyim* ("Messianic") to overcome the suspicion and antagonism that the term *nozrim* was provoking. The term *Meshichyim* also emphasized messianism as a major component of the Christian evangelical belief that the missions propagated. It held an aura of a new, innovative religion rather than an old, unfavorable one. The term was used to refer to those Jews who accepted Jesus as their personal Savior and did not apply, for example, to Jews accepting Roman Catholicism, who in Israel called themselves Hebrew Catholics.[34]

In sum, as a result of (1) the HCAA/MJAA name change, (2) the adoption of Messianic terminology by Jewish mission agencies for evangelism and networking,

---

32. Yaakov Ariel, *Evangelizing the Chosen People: Missions to the Jews in America, 1880 – 2000* (Chapel Hill: University of North Carolina Press, 2000), 200 – 219; David A. Rausch, *Messianic Judaism: Its History, Theology and Polity* (New York: Edwin Mellen, 1982), 88 – 91.

33. Many Messianic Jews view the Jews for Jesus organization as problematic for two reasons: (1) Confrontational street evangelism often offends the Jewish community and creates an unnecessary stumbling block to the *besorah* (gospel). See Walter Lieber, "Jews for Jesus and the Gospel Blimp: Why the Jewish Community Is Right to Reject Jews for Jesus," n.p. [cited 23 November 2011]. Online: http://www.messianicjudaism.me/media/2011/04/18/jews-for-jesus-and-the-gospel-blimp. (2) Contra historic Messianic Judaism, the Jews for Jesus organization maintains the classic Hebrew Christian view that Jewish life is not a matter of covenant responsibility or calling for Jewish believers in Yeshua but something that is optional: "There is nothing wrong with celebrating the biblical feasts or following certain rabbinic traditions, but we can do so only to the extent that we do not contradict the clear teaching of the Scriptures, both Old and New Testaments. And part of that New Testament teaching is that, in Messiah, we are fully free to practice these things or not as a matter of choice and conscience" (David Brickner, "A Final Word from David Brickner, Executive Director of Jews for Jesus," in *The Messianic Movement: A Field Guide for Evangelical Christians* [ed. Rich Robinson; San Francisco: Jews for Jesus, 2005], 187). Despite these theological differences, Jews for Jesus affirms the Messianic Jewish community: "In a statement released today [July 31, 2012], the Jews for Jesus Council (its global leadership body) issued the following statement of clarification on its position on the Messianic Jewish Movement: Moved by a desire for unity, and in the interest of mutual affirmation, we want to correct a long-standing misimpression to the contrary: we affirm both the Messianic Jewish Movement as a whole, as well as its Congregational component, as being legitimate and credible expressions of God's work today. We have been, and will continue to be, supportive of both" (http://www.jewsforjesus.org/about/news/jews-for-jesus-messianic-statement).

34. Ariel, *Evangelizing the Chosen People*, 222 – 23. The Hebrew term for "Messianic Judaism" is *Yahadut Meshichit*.

and (3) the Israeli Hebrew use of *Meshichyim* ("Messianic") as a substitute for *Noz-rim* ("Christians"), the term "Messianic Jew" took on a broader meaning in the late twentieth century. Consequently, today many people use the term "Messianic Jew" to refer to any "Jewish believer in Yeshua," whereas the historic term connotes a Jew who believes in Yeshua and continues to live as a Jew as a matter of covenant, calling, or national duty before God. Similarly, many people now use the terms "Messianic Jewish," "Messianic movement," and "Messianic" loosely to refer to the work of Jewish mission agencies and Christian ministries in Israel, whereas the historic terms refer to the way of life, thought, and communal experience of Yeshua-believing Jews who live within the orbit of Judaism. The only related term that has not been adopted by Jewish mission agencies and, for the most part, continues to maintain its historic, social, and theological connotation is "Messianic Judaism."

What is "Messianic Judaism" in the twenty-first century? The Union of Messianic Jewish Congregations offers the most comprehensive definition of the term,[35] and it is a definition in continuity with how the term has been used for over a hundred years:

Basic Statement

The Union of Messianic Jewish Congregations (UMJC) envisions Messianic Judaism as a movement of Jewish congregations and groups committed to Yeshua the Messiah that embrace the covenantal responsibility of Jewish life and identity rooted in Torah, expressed in tradition, and renewed and applied in the context of the New Covenant.

Messianic Jewish groups may also include those from non-Jewish backgrounds who have a confirmed call to participate fully in the life and destiny of the Jewish people. We are committed to embodying this definition in our constituent congregations and in our shared institutions.

Expanded Statement

Jewish life is life in a concrete, historical community. Thus, Messianic Jewish groups must be fully part of the Jewish people, sharing its history and its covenantal responsibility as a people chosen by God. At the same time, faith in Yeshua also has a crucial communal dimension. This faith unites the Messianic Jewish community and the Christian Church, which is the assembly of the faithful from the nations who are joined to Israel through the Messiah. Together the Messianic Jewish community and the Christian Church constitute the ekklesia, the one Body of Messiah, a community of Jews and Gentiles who in their ongoing distinction and mutual blessing anticipate the shalom of the world to come.

For a Messianic Jewish group (1) to fulfill the covenantal responsibility incumbent upon all Jews, (2) to bear witness to Yeshua within the people of Israel, and (3) to serve as an authentic and effective representative of the Jewish people within the body of Messiah, it must place a priority on integration with the wider Jewish world, while sustaining a vital corporate relationship with the Christian Church.

In the Messianic Jewish way of life, we seek to fulfill Israel's covenantal

---

35. Cf. Richard Harvey, *Mapping Messianic Jewish Theology: A Constructive Approach* (Milton Keynes, UK: Paternoster, 2009), 8–12.

responsibility embodied in the Torah within a New Covenant context. Messianic Jewish halakhah is rooted in Scripture (Tanakh and the New Covenant writings), which is of unique sanctity and authority. It also draws upon Jewish tradition, especially those practices and concepts that have won near-universal acceptance by devout Jews through the centuries. Furthermore, as is common within Judaism, Messianic Judaism recognizes that halakhah is and must be dynamic, involving the application of the Torah to a wide variety of changing situations and circumstances.

Messianic Judaism embraces the fullness of New Covenant realities available through Yeshua, and seeks to express them in forms drawn from Jewish experience and accessible to Jewish people.[36]

National Messianic Jewish organizations like the UMJC, the MJAA, and the IAMCS represent the mainstream of the Messianic Jewish movement in North America. Their statements on Messianic Jewish definition, vision, and theology ultimately delineate the center and the periphery of the movement.

The diversity of the twenty-first-century Messianic Jewish movement is reflected not only in its spectrum of religious observance and theological self-definition but also in its demographic makeup. Recent studies indicate that the Messianic Jewish community, like the wider Jewish community, is becoming increasingly multiethnic. A growing number of intermarrieds (i.e., Jews married to Gentiles) are embracing Messianic Judaism as an option for their families. Given that one out of every two American Jews intermarries,[37] the Messianic Jewish community in North America is poised to grow exponentially in the years ahead as more and more blended families find in Messianic Judaism a solution to the intermarriage dilemma.[38] In addition, thousands of Yeshua-believing Gentiles with a love for Jewish people are finding a

---

36. Union of Messianic Jewish Congregations, "Defining Messianic Judaism," 2005. Cited 27 February 2012. Online: http://www.umjc.org/home-mainmenu-1/global-vision-mainmenu-42/13-vision/225-defining-messianic-judaism. "What does the name 'Messianic Judaism' imply about the movement to which it refers? The decision to use the term 'Judaism' speaks volumes.... The term expresses our fresh consciousness that the earliest followers of Yeshua were all Jews and continued to live as Jews ... when we call our movement a type of Judaism, we are affirming that our relationship to the Jewish people as a whole, as well as our connection to the religious faith and way of life which that people have lived throughout its historical journey.... Though perhaps unrecognized at the time, the decision to employ the term 'Messianic Judaism' and not just the term 'Messianic Jew' was of great moment. It implied identification with the Jewish religious tradition as well as with the Jewish people. Finally, the name 'Messianic Judaism' implies that our movement is fundamentally among Jews and for Jews. It may include non-Jews, but it is oriented toward the Jewish people, and those non-Jews within it have a supportive role.... Messianic Judaism is Judaism, in all facets of its teaching, worship, and way of life, understood and practiced in the light of Messiah Yeshua" (Mark S. Kinzer, *The Nature of Messianic Judaism: Judaism as Genus, Messianic as Species* [West Hartford: Hashivenu Archives, 2000], 4 – 5, 11).

37. Arthur Blecher, *The New American Judaism: The Way Forward on Challenging Issues from Intermarriage to Jewish Identity* (New York: Palgrave, 2007), 163 – 91.

38. "Messianic Judaism is a natural option for intermarried couples because it is common ground for both partners. Also, children seek to *integrate* their identities, not separate them or eliminate them altogether (a drawback of the Jewish Only, Christian Only, Interfaith, and No Religion options). In addition, the Messianic Jewish option is rooted in the Scriptures and history, providing children with a strong sense of affirmation. First century Jewish followers of Jesus serve as an 'identity anchor' for twenty-first century Messianic Jews. For those intermarried couples who are looking for a way to bridge both backgrounds and raise their children with a clear and complete sense of identity, Messianic Judaism is a very good option" (David J. Rudolph, *Growing Your Olive Tree Marriage: A Guide for Couples from Two Traditions* [Clarksville, Md.: Lederer, 2003], 59).

home in the Messianic Jewish community and helping Messianic Jews to build congregations for Yeshua within the house of Israel.

Messianic Judaism is by definition a movement "fundamentally among Jews and for Jews."[39] Jews within the Messianic Jewish community represent the rich tapestry of the Jewish world and come from all branches of Judaism — including Orthodox, Conservative, Reform, Reconstructionist, Renewal — and the various Jewish subcultures of the world, such as Ashkenazi, Sephardic, Ethiopian, and Asian. Messianic Judaism is growing in Israel, and the center of the movement is slowly shifting to the Land. Among the hundreds of thousands of Jews in churches, more and more are connecting to the Messianic Jewish movement and finding in it a way to convey Jewish heritage to their children. Finally, there are now third- and fourth-generation Messianic Jews being raised in the Messianic Jewish community. These young Messianic Jews stand on the shoulders of their parents and grandparents and view the Messianic Jewish movement from a different perspective than Jews who have entered it from the wider Jewish or Christian world.

Like the miracle of the State of Israel rejoining the community of nations after millennia, the Messianic Jewish community has been restored to the Jewish-Christian world after a hiatus of more than sixteen hundred years. For centuries, the church and synagogue have marginalized Messianic Judaism, treating it as an excluded middle. Today there are signs of change. The Messianic Jewish movement is growing in support among churches as New Testament scholars and theologians increasingly demonstrate that Messianic Judaism is consistent with the teachings of the Jewish apostles and the experience of the earliest communities of Yeshua-believing Jews in the Land of Israel, Syria, and beyond. The movement is also winning sympathizers in the Jewish world as Messianic Jews demonstrate through their actions that Yeshua is good for the Jewish people.[40] The progress in the latter area is slow — often two steps forward and one step back — but incrementally there is movement toward the day Yeshua spoke about when Jewish leaders will say, *Baruch HaBa B'Shem Adonai* ("Blessed is he who comes in the name of the Lord").[41]

---

39. Kinzer, *Nature of Messianic Judaism*, 5.

40. E.g., Cohn-Sherbok, *Messianic Judaism*, ix – xiv, 203 – 13; Dan Cohn-Sherbok, *Voices of Messianic Judaism: Confronting Critical Issues Facing a Maturing Movement* (Baltimore: Lederer, 2001), ix – xiii; Pamela Eisenbaum, "They Don't Make Jews Like Jesus Anymore" (review of Daniel Boyarin, *The Jewish Gospels: The Story of the Jewish Christ*), *Moment Magazine Book Reviews*, March/April 2012. Cited 4 April 2012. Online: http://www.momentmag.com/moment/issues/2012/04/Books_Eisenbaum.html. "The notion of the humiliated and suffering Messiah was not at all alien within Judaism before Jesus' advent, and it remained current among Jews well into the future following that — indeed, well into the early modern period. The fascinating (and to some, no doubt, uncomfortable) fact is that this tradition was well documented by modern Messianic Jews, who are concerned to demonstrate that their belief in Jesus does not make them un-Jewish. Whether or not one accepts their theology, it remains the case that they have a very strong textual base for the view that the suffering Messiah is based in deeply rooted Jewish texts early and late. Jews, it seems, had no difficulty whatever with understanding a Messiah who would vicariously suffer to redeem the world" (Daniel Boyarin, *The Jewish Gospels: The Story of the Jewish Christ* [New York: New Press, 2012], 132 – 33).

41. Matt 23:39; cf. 21:9.

For Further Reading

Ariel, Yaakov. *Evangelizing the Chosen People: Missions to the Jews in America, 1880 – 2000.* Chapel Hill: University of North Carolina Press, 2000.

———. "Judaism and Christianity Unite! The Unique Culture of Messianic Judaism." Pages 191 – 222 in *Introduction to New and Alternative Religions in America.* Edited by Eugene V. Gallagher and W. Michael Ashcraft. Volume 2: Jewish and Christian Traditions. London: Greenwood, 2006.

Boyarin, Daniel. *Border Lines: The Partition of Judaeo-Christianity.* Philadelphia: University of Pennsylvania Press, 2004.

Broadhead, Edwin K. *Jewish Ways of Following Jesus: Redrawing the Religious Map of Antiquity.* Tübingen: Mohr Siebeck, 2010.

Carleton Paget, James. *Jews, Christians and Jewish Christians in Antiquity.* Tübingen: Mohr Siebeck, 2010.

Cohn-Sherbok, Dan. *Messianic Judaism.* London: Cassell, 2000.

Harvey, Richard. *Mapping Messianic Jewish Theology: A Constructive Approach.* Milton Keynes, UK: Paternoster, 2009.

Kinzer, Mark S. *Israel's Messiah and the People of God: A Vision for Messianic Jewish Covenantal Fidelity.* Edited by Jennifer M. Rosner. Eugene, Oreg.: Cascade, 2011.

———. *The Nature of Messianic Judaism: Judaism as Genus, Messianic as Species.* West Hartford: Hashivenu Archives, 2000.

———. *Postmissionary Messianic Judaism: Redefining Christian Engagement with the Jewish People.* Grand Rapids: Brazos, 2005.

Kjaer-Hansen, Kai. *Joseph Rabinowitz and the Messianic Movement: The Herzl of Jewish Christianity.* Grand Rapids: Eerdmans, 1994.

Pritz, Ray A. *Nazarene Jewish Christianity: From the End of the New Testament Period until Its Disappearance in the Fourth Century.* Leiden, Netherlands: Brill, 1988.

Rausch, David A. *Messianic Judaism: Its History, Theology and Polity.* New York: Edwin Mellen, 1982.

Rudolph, David, Joel Willitts, Justin K. Hardin, and J. Brian Tucker, eds. *New Testament after Supersessionism.* 18 vols. Eugene, Oreg.: Cascade, forthcoming.

Rudolph, David J. "History of Judeo-Christian Communities in the Jewish Diaspora." Pages 136 – 39 in *Encyclopedia of the Jewish Diaspora: Origins, Experiences, and Culture I.* Edited by M. Avrum Ehrlich. Santa Barbara: ABC-CLIO, 2008.

———. *A Jew to the Jews: Jewish Contours of Pauline Flexibility in 1 Corinthians 9:19 – 23.* Tübingen: Mohr Siebeck, 2011.

———. "Messianic Jews and Christian Theology: Restoring an Historical Voice to the Contemporary Discussion." *Pro Ecclesia* 14, no. 1 (2005): 58 – 84. Online: http://www.mjstudies.com.

———. "Paul's 'Rule in All the Churches' (1 Cor 7:17 – 24) and Torah-Defined Ecclesiological Variegation." *Studies in Christian-Jewish Relations* 5 (2010): 1 – 23. Online: http://www.mjstudies.com.

Skarsaune, Oskar, and Reidar Hvalvik, eds. *Jewish Believers in Jesus: The Early Centuries.* Peabody, Mass.: Hendrickson, 2007.

Tomson, Peter J., and Doris Lambers-Petry, eds. *The Image of the Judaeo-Christians in Ancient Jewish and Christian Literature.* Tübingen: Mohr Siebeck, 2003.

Willitts, Joel, David Rudolph, and Justin K. Hardin. *The Jewish New Testament: An Introduction to Its Jewish Social and Conceptual Context.* Grand Rapids: Eerdmans, forthcoming.

Winer, Robert I. *The Calling: The History of the Messianic Jewish Alliance of America, 1915 – 1990.* Wynnewood, Pa.: MJAA, 1990.

CHAPTER 2

Messianic Jewish Synagogues

David Rudolph and Elliot Klayman

When Agudas Shalom Synagogue burned down, along with its Torah scrolls, prayer books, and library, the president of the synagogue, Sheldon, was so depressed that he couldn't get out of bed. The insurance adjuster asked, "What's wrong? The synagogue is totally insured." Sheldon didn't respond. Sheldon's friend from the synagogue came by and said, "We will rebuild the synagogue!" Still no stir. Finally, Rabbi Gervitz visited Sheldon and reminded him, "We are the same synagogue community today that we were before the fire." The president of the synagogue opened his eyes, nodded in agreement with the rabbi, and stepped out of bed.

A synagogue is above all a sacred community of Jewish people who gather for worship, prayer, study, benevolence, social justice, lifecycle events, outreach, and other Jewish community activities.[1] What distinguishes Messianic synagogues[2] from mainstream synagogues is the centrality of Yeshua, the prominent place of the New Testament, and the presence of Gentile followers of Yeshua who come alongside Messianic Jews to build a congregation for Yeshua within the house of Israel.

Community Life

On a typical Shabbat (Sabbath) morning, prior to the main service, Messianic synagogues often have an adult education class that meets to study the *parsha* (the Torah reading for the week) and a related New Testament text. As the hour for the morning service approaches, musicians are heard finishing their practice, and prayer among the leaders typically takes place in the rabbi's office.

The Messianic Shabbat service is more upbeat than the traditional synagogue service. Modeled after worship described in the Psalms of David, Messianic Jewish services commonly incorporate song, dance, and instrumental music, along with Hebrew liturgy from the *siddur* (prayer book).[3] Although the average Messianic synagogue service includes instrumental music and dancing, some Messianic Jewish

---

1. Ron Wolfson, *The Spirituality of Welcoming: How to Transform Your Congregation into a Sacred Community* (Woodstock: Jewish Lights, 2007), 144–45; Sidney Schwartz, *Finding a Spiritual Home: How a New Generation of Jews Can Transform the American Synagogue* (Woodstock: Jewish Lights, 2003), 11–49, 226–68.

2. The earliest extant reference to a Messianic "synagogue" is Jas 2:2, "Suppose a man comes into your synagogue [*sunagoge*] wearing a gold ring and fancy clothes, and also a poor man comes in dressed in rags" (CJB) See chapter 1 of this volume for details about the Jerusalem Messianic Jewish community led by Ya'akov (James), the brother of Yeshua.

3. Shoshanah Feher, *Passing Over Easter: Constructing the Boundaries of Messianic Judaism* (Walnut Creek, Calif.: AltaMira, 1998), 139.

congregations follow a more classic synagogue model. High Holy Day services in Messianic synagogues tend to be more traditional and replete with Hebrew liturgy.[4]

The average length of a Messianic Shabbat service is two hours, and most congregations enjoy an *Oneg Shabbat* (a lunch and fellowship time) afterward,[5] followed by activities. Some synagogues have a *havdalah* service on Saturday evenings to mark the departure of Shabbat.

Larger Messianic Jewish congregations usually have weekly meetings for teens, college students, twentysomethings, young marrieds, and other social circles within the community. The Shabbat/Hebrew school program prepares children for *bar/ bat mitzvah*. *Chavurah* (fellowship) groups are venues to socialize, pray, and study together. Many synagogues have adult education institutes that offer courses on books of the Bible, Jewish history, Hebrew, and other areas relevant to Messianic Jewish life and thought.

Yeshua, the Messiah of Israel, is central to Messianic Jewish congregational life.[6] He is the sustaining focus in every aspect of the synagogue. This is because, from a Messianic Jewish perspective, Yeshua is divine and participates in the unique identity of the God of Israel:

> The Union of Messianic Jewish Congregations holds that the One GOD, the GOD of creation, the GOD of Israel, the GOD of our ancestors, of Whom our tradition speaks, reveals Himself uniquely, definitively, and decisively in the life, death, resurrection, and return of Yeshua the Messiah.
>
> Yeshua is the incarnation of the Divine WORD through Whom the world was made, and of the Divine GLORY through Whom GOD revealed Himself to Israel and acted in their midst. He is the living Torah, expressing perfectly in His example and teaching the Divine purpose for human life. Yeshua is completely human and completely divine.
>
> As the risen Messiah and the heavenly Kohen Gadol (High Priest), Yeshua continues to mediate GOD's relationship to His people Israel, to those of the nations who have joined the greater commonwealth of Israel in Him, and to all creation. GOD's plan of salvation and blessing for Israel, the nations, and the entire cosmos

---

4. David J. Rudolph, "Contemporary Judeo-Christian Communities in the Jewish Diaspora," in *Encyclopedia of the Jewish Diaspora: Origins, Experiences, and Culture I* (ed. M. Avrum Ehrlich; Santa Barbara: ABC-CLIO, 2008), 146.

5. For *Oneg Shabbat*, members and regular visitors bring dishes without pork or shellfish (Lev 11). Some Messianic synagogues also avoid mixing milk and meat. For a Messianic Jewish perspective on Israel's dietary laws, see Aaron Eby, *Biblically Kosher: A Messianic Jewish Perspective on Kashrut* (Marshfield, Mo.: First Fruits of Zion, 2012); Barney Kasdan, *God's Appointed Customs: A Messianic Jewish Guide to the Biblical Lifecycle and Lifestyle* (Clarksville, Md.: Lederer, 1996), 97–110; David J. Rudolph, "Yeshua and the Dietary Laws: A Reassessment of Mark 7:19b," *Kesher: A Journal of Messianic Judaism* 16 (2003): 97–119; David J. Rudolph, "Jesus and the Food Laws: A Reassessment of Mark 7:19b," *Evangelical Quarterly* 74, no. 4 (2002): 291–311. Online: http://www.mjstudies.com.

6. Union of Messianic Jewish Congregations, "Introducing Messianic Judaism and the UMJC" (Albuquerque: UMJC, 2010), 1–26. Online: http://www.mjstudies.com. Cf. Daniel C. Juster, *Growing to Maturity: A Messianic Jewish Discipleship Guide* (Clarksville, Md.: Messianic Jewish Resources International, 2011), 155–56; Sam Nadler, *Establishing Healthy Messianic Congregations: Planters, Planting, and Planning* (Charlotte: Word of Messiah Ministries, 2011), 12; Russell L. Resnik, *The Root and the Branches: Jewish Identity in Messiah* (Albuquerque: Adat Yeshua, 1997), 142.

is fulfilled only in and through Yeshua, by virtue of His atoning death and bodily resurrection, and GOD's gift of life to both Jews and Gentiles, in this world and in the world to come, is bestowed and appropriated only in and through Him.[7]

The Messianic Jewish lifestyle and lifecycle points back to Yeshua's story: his life, his mission, and his displays of love, grace, and healing. This reflects the mindset that "Messianic Judaism is Judaism, in all facets of its teaching, worship, and way of life, understood and practiced in the light of Messiah Yeshua."[8] Messianic Jews express their initial public identification with Yeshua through *tevilah* (immersion in water) in keeping with Yeshua's commandment (Matt 28:18 – 20). In Messianic synagogues, *tevilah* services often coincide with the fall and spring festivals.[9]

Messianic synagogues observe all of the major Jewish festivals and distinguish themselves from other Jewish congregations by interpreting festival tradition in light of Yeshua the Messiah. Rather than creating a new festival tradition, Messianic Jewish congregations enter into conversation with the present tradition and adapt it as needed to reflect their distinct beliefs.[10]

The typical Messianic synagogue mirrors the traditional synagogue when it comes to Jewish lifecycle events. Messianic Jewish boys are circumcised on the eighth day as a sign of the everlasting covenant between God and the Jewish people (Gen 17:9 – 13). It is a joyous community affair. Family members and friends from the synagogue are invited to the parents' home, where the ceremony takes place. Because there are only a few Messianic Jewish *mohelim* (covenant surgeons), parents typically employ a *mohel* from the wider Jewish community who is not Messianic. As part of the ceremony, the Messianic rabbi will read biblical texts about the covenant of circumcision (*brit milah*), usually including mention of Yeshua's circumcision in Luke 2:21, and offer up blessings and prayers over the child. The ceremony is followed by a *seudah* (party).[11]

In some congregations, *brit milah* is combined with a baby-naming ceremony, where a Hebrew name is conferred on the male infant. The baby is brought to the front of the synagogue, where dedicatory prayers are offered up, with the *zakenim* (elders) of the congregation present alongside the parents and the baby. In the case of

7. Union of Messianic Jewish Congregations, "Statement on the Identity of Yeshua," November 12, 2003. Cited 1 March 2012. Online: http://www.umjc.org/home-mainmenu-1/faqs-mainmenu-58/14-umjc-faq/17-who-is-yeshua. See Richard Harvey, "Yeshua the Messiah: The Shaping of Messianic Jewish Christology," in *Mapping Messianic Jewish Theology: A Constructive Approach* (Milton Keynes, UK: Paternoster, 2009), 96 – 139; Mark S. Kinzer, "Finding Our Way through Nicaea: The Deity of Yeshua, Bilateral Ecclesiology, and Redemptive Encounter with the Living God," *Kesher: A Journal of Messianic Judaism* 24 (2010): 29 – 52. Cited 1 March 2012. Online: http://www.kesherjournal.com/Issue-24/Finding-our-Way-Through-nicaea-The-Deity-of-Yeshua-bilateral-Ecclesiology-and-Redemptive-Encounter-with-the-Living-God; Akiva Cohen, "The Christology of Matthew's Gospel and the Trinitarian Baptismal Formula," *Mishkan: A Forum on the Gospel and the Jewish People* 39 (2003): 59 – 64; Michael Schiffman, "Messianic Jews and the Tri-Unity of God," in *Return of the Remnant: The Rebirth of Messianic Judaism* (Baltimore: Lederer, 1996), 93 – 104. Cf. Richard Bauckham, *Jesus and the God of Israel: God Crucified and Other Studies on the New Testament's Christology of Divine Identity* (Grand Rapids: Eerdmans, 2008).
8. Mark S. Kinzer, *The Nature of Messianic Judaism: Judaism as Genus, Messianic as Species* (West Hartford: Hashivenu Archives, 2000), 11.
9. Dan Cohn-Sherbok, *Messianic Judaism* (London: Continuum, 2000), 159 – 61; Kasdan, *God's Appointed Customs*, 111 – 22.
10. For a discussion of how Jewish festivals and liturgy are incorporated into the Messianic Jewish synagogue, see chapters 3 – 5 of this volume.
11. Cohn-Sherbok, *Messianic Judaism*, 142 – 45; Kasdan, *God's Appointed Customs*, 9 – 26.

a girl, there may be a *simchat bat* (joy of the daughter) ceremony. Naming of a baby ordinarily occurs when the mother first returns to the synagogue with her child.[12]

Messianic synagogues celebrate *bar mitzvah* (son of the commandment) ceremonies for boys when they turn thirteen and *bat mitzvah* (daughter of the commandment) ceremonies for girls when they turn twelve or thirteen. The young adult will lead portions of the Shabbat service, read from the *parsha* for that week, and give a *derash* (message) before the congregation. A Messianic Jewish *bar/bat mitzvah* also includes a reading from the New Testament, and usually the young man or woman will share about his or her faith as a Jewish follower of Yeshua. It is a joyful occasion attended by family and friends and often followed by a lavish party.[13]

Consistent with traditional Judaism, Messianic Jews marry under a *huppah* (wedding canopy), sign a *ketubah* (marriage contract), and break a glass at the conclusion of the wedding ceremony to shouts of "Mazel Tov!" (Congratulations).[14] It is common for the Messianic rabbi to share with the bride and groom passages from the New Testament that speak about love in marriage and the importance of abiding in Yeshua.[15] The ceremony is usually followed by a reception with food, music, and dancing.

Finally, Messianic Jewish families follow traditional Jewish practices related to burial and mourning:

> A Messianic Jewish funeral is based on the traditional model with most Messianic rabbis drawing from the *madrikh* (handbook for rabbis). The body is buried within twenty-four hours if possible. *Kaddish* (a prayer of praise to God during mourning) is recited along with other traditional Hebrew prayers. *Keriah* (tearing of the garments) is performed. One addition to the traditional service is the reading of verses from the New Testament as well as the Hebrew Bible.... It is typical for a Messianic Jewish family to sit *shiva* (mourn for seven days), light *yahrzeit* (memorial) candles and consult their rabbi about the traditional mourning process.[16]

Because Jewish cemeteries are often unwilling to provide their services for Jewish followers of Yeshua, a few Messianic Jewish congregations have established their own cemeteries or have acquired the rights to dedicated plots within cemeteries.

Symbols, Ritual Objects, and Language

Messianic synagogue buildings are diverse architecturally but similar in content. Jewish symbols like the *magen David* (star of David) or *menorah* (seven-branched candelabrum) are often seen on the outside and inside of the meeting place. Many

12. Cohn-Sherbok, *Messianic Judaism*, 140–42; Kasdan, *God's Appointed Customs*, 25–26.

13. Cohn-Sherbok, *Messianic Judaism*, 148–50; Kasdan, *God's Appointed Customs*, 37–46. See also Elliot Klayman, "The Bar/Bat Mitzvah: A Liturgy," *Kesher: A Journal of Messianic Judaism* 1 (1994): 122–35.

14. Stuart Dauermann, Michael Rudolph, and Paul L. Saal, "The Wedding Ceremony: Viable Models for Diverse Unions: Three Messianic Jewish Wedding Ceremonies," *Kesher: A Journal of Messianic Judaism* 9 (1999): 89–115.

15. Cohn-Sherbok, *Messianic Judaism*, 150–53; Kasdan, *God's Appointed Customs*, 47–70.

16. David J. Rudolph, *Growing Your Olive Tree Marriage: A Guide for Couples from Two Traditions* (Clarksville, Md.: Lederer, 2003), 127. See Cohn-Sherbok, *Messianic Judaism*, 153–55; Kasdan, *God's Appointed Customs*, 71–85.

congregations hang banners of the tribes of Israel and display Jewish artwork with Hebrew lettering.

The Messianic Jewish sanctuary resembles its traditional counterpart, with an ark containing the *sefer Torah* (Torah scroll), the *ner tamid* (eternal light) hanging above the ark, and a *bimah* (raised platform from which the Torah is read and services are led), centrally located and arranged so that the congregation faces Jerusalem. Messianic Jews attach great significance to Jerusalem:

1. Jerusalem is the eternal capital of the Jewish nation, which God is returning to the Land of Israel and to faith in her Messiah, Yeshua.
2. Jerusalem symbolizes Judaism, Jewish history, and the Jewish people; it also symbolizes Christianity, Christian history, and the Church. Messianic Jews have roots in both histories and affirm both aspects of Jerusalem's symbolic significance.
3. Jerusalem is the city to which Yeshua the Messiah will return. From there he will rule Israel and all the nations.
4. God's *Torah*, understood as including New Testament truth as well as that of the *Tanakh* [the Hebrew Scriptures], has gone forth, is going forth, and will go forth from Jerusalem.
5. The first Messianic Jews lived in and ministered from Jerusalem. Today's Messianic Jews, as the believing remnant of the Jewish people, have established a community there and intend to be part of the process of ministering *Torah* from Jerusalem.
6. Regardless of their political views, Messianic Jews generally agree that living for God is a more important value than holding onto territory. Nevertheless, God's promises to the Jews concerning territory — the Land of Israel and the city of Jerusalem — are not canceled and are not to be neglected.[17]

Many synagogues use mainstream or Messianic Jewish *siddurim* (prayer books) that follow the order and content of traditional Jewish prayer.[18] Men wearing *kippot* (head coverings) and *tallitot* (prayer shawls) dot the assembly on Shabbat morning.[19]

In addition to Jewish symbols and ritual objects, Messianic synagogues encourage the use of Hebrew to foster a Jewish ethos:

Messianic congregations are committed to Jewish continuity because they believe God is committed to Jewish continuity. Contemporary Messianic rabbis, like their mainstream counterparts, recognize the dangers of assimilation and labor to convey Jewish identity to the next generation of Messianic Jewish families. Messianic Jewish use of Hebrew expressions (even for New Testament terms) is in

---

17. David H. Stern, "The Significance of Jerusalem for Messianic Jews," in *The Enduring Paradox: Exploratory Essays in Messianic Judaism* (ed. John Fischer; Baltimore: Lederer, 2000), 102 – 3. See David H. Stern, "The People of God, the Promises of God, and the Land of Israel," in *The Enduring Paradox*, 79 – 94; Daniel C. Juster, "A Messianic Jew Looks at the Land Promises," in *The Land Cries Out: Theology of the Land in the Israeli-Palestinian Conflict* (ed. Salim J. Munayer and Lisa Loden; Eugene, Oreg.: Cascade, 2012), 63 – 81; David Miller, "Messianic Judaism and the Theology of the Land," *Mishkan* 26 (1997): 31 – 38.

18. For Messianic Jewish *siddurim*, see Barry Budoff, *Siddur Prayers for Messianic Jews* (Skokie, Ill.: Devar Emet Messianic Jewish Publications, 2006); John Fischer, *Siddur for Messianic Jews* (Palm Harbor, Fla.: Menorah Ministries, 2002); Jeremiah Greenberg, *Messianic Shabbat Siddur: A Messianic Prayer Book for Use in Sabbath Services and at Home* (Gaithersburg, Md.: Messianic Liturgical Resources, 2004).

19. Cohn-Sherbok, *Messianic Judaism*, 161 – 66; Kasdan, *God's Appointed Customs*, 123 – 39.

Baruch HaShem
Messianic Synagogue Building,
Dallas, Texas

Baruch HaShem
Messianic Synagogue Ark,
Dallas, Texas

Baruch HaShem Messianic Synagogue Torah Scrolls, Dallas, Texas

*Tikvat Israel Messianic
Synagogue Sanctuary (above)
and Ark and Bimah (right),
Richmond, Virginia*

*Beit Hashofar Messianic
Synagogue Ark and Bimah,
Seattle, Washington*

*Devar Emet Messianic Synagogue Torah Service,
Skokie, Illinois*

keeping with this spirit of resisting assimilation pressures in order to preserve Jewish identity. Jesus and the shlichim (apostles) were first-century Jews who taught in Hebrew/Aramaic. New Testament teaching was originally Hebraic. Messianic synagogues, therefore, see the use of Hebraic New Covenant terminology, such as the name "Yeshua" instead of "Jesus," as the restoration of something that is historically accurate. It links Messianic Jewish families to their first-century roots.[20]

Synagogue Leadership

A Messianic rabbi functions as a scholar, teacher, pastoral leader, guide, and representative of the Messianic Jewish community.[21] The Messianic Jewish Rabbinical Council (MJRC) defines a Messianic rabbi as

> a Jewish follower of Yeshua qualified by a supervised course of study, authorized by his or her ordaining authority, and empowered by the Spirit through the rite of ordination to expound and apply Torah as fulfilled in and mediated through the person, teaching, and work of Yeshua.... In the context of congregational life, the senior rabbi appointed by that community serves among them as their Mara d'Atra, i.e., mentor, guide, and authority in matters of religious practice and teaching, encouraging growth and unity that express the life of the Spirit of God.[22]

Messianic Jewish Theological Institute (MJTI)[23] and the Netzer David International Yeshiva[24] offer the core courses necessary to qualify for rabbinical ordination through the Union of Messianic Jewish Congregations (UMJC). Messianic rabbis are also ordained through the International Alliance of Messianic Congregations and Synagogues (IAMCS).[25] The UMJC offers a program for lay leaders that leads to licensure as a Madrikh (Hebrew for "guide"), a certification that is recognized in UMJC synagogues as valuable for teachers, synagogue officers, cantors, counselors, and other positions of leadership.[26]

---

20. Rudolph, "Contemporary Judeo-Christian Communities," 147–48.

21. A Messianic rabbi serves "as a custodian of Israel's revelation and traditions,... [a]dvises the community on matters of ritual life,... [a]cts as a judge in disputes,... [s]erves as a spokesperson for the congregation, the Jewish people, and Judaism to the outside world" (Stuart Dauermann, *The Rabbi as a Surrogate Priest* [Eugene, Oreg.: Pickwick, 2009], 259–60, 276–77). See David J. Rudolph, "The Rabbi as Pastor-Theologian: Torah Scholars Qua Ecclesial Leaders in the Post-Biblical Jewish Context" (paper presented at the Society for the Advancement of Ecclesial Theology [SAET] Symposium, Chicago, October 12, 2009). Online: http://tikvatisrael.com/pdf/Rabbi_as_Pastor-Theologian_Rudolph.pdf.

22. Messianic Jewish Rabbinical Council, "The Messianic Jewish Rabbi." Cited 26 February 2012. Online: http://ourrabbis.org/main/halakhah-mainmenu-26/introduction-mainmenu-27/the-messianic-jewish-rabbi. The UMJC and IAMCS have ordained several congregational leaders who are not Jewish. Whereas the UMJC leaves the question of title up to the local synagogue, the IAMCS uses "rabbi" for ordained Messianic Jews and "congregational leader" for ordained Messianic Gentiles.

23. Messianic Jewish Theological Institute, "The MJTI School of Jewish Studies." Cited 26 February 2012. Online: http://sjs.mjti.org.

24. St. Petersburg Theological Seminary, "The Netzer David International Yeshiva." Cited 26 February 2012. Online: http://www.sptseminary.edu/academics/the-netzer-david-international-yeshiva.

25. International Alliance of Messianic Congregations and Synagogues, "Welcome to the IAMCS Yeshiva!" Cited 8 March 2012. Online: http://yeshiva.iamcs.org.

26. Union of Messianic Jewish Congregations, "Madrikh: UMJC Licensure." Cited 26 February 2012. Online: http://www.umjc.org/education-mainmenu-49/madrikh-program-mainmenu-87.

The aging of Messianic synagogue leaders is a challenge that the Messianic Jewish community is facing. A recent demographic study found that two-thirds of all UMJC senior congregational leaders were between the ages of fifty-five and seventy.[27] In response, the UMJC has developed an initiative to attract younger leaders with the goal of seeing the average age of UMJC rabbis drop below fifty by 2020. The Kehilah (K20) program is a ten-year initiative that offers matching funds for congregations that mentor a young rabbinical intern, and it provides scholarships for those who enter UMJC-approved rabbinical training programs.[28]

The Purpose of Messianic Synagogues

Messianic Judaism is "a movement of Jewish congregations and groups committed to Yeshua the Messiah that embrace the covenantal responsibility of Jewish life and identity rooted in Torah, expressed in tradition, and renewed and applied in the context of the New Covenant."[29] The primary purpose of Messianic synagogues is to make it possible for Jews[30] who follow the Jewish Messiah to remain Jews[31] and become better Jews in keeping with the eternal purposes of the God of Israel.[32] This results in Messianic

---

27. David J. Rudolph, "A Wake-Up Call: Aging Trends of UMJC Congregational Leaders," May 3, 2010. Online: http://www.mjstudies.com.

28. Union of Messianic Jewish Congregations, "K20 Initiative Focuses on Future Leadership." Cited 26 February 2012. Online: http://www.umjc.org/donate-mainmenu-39/k20-program.

29. Union of Messianic Jewish Congregations, "Defining Messianic Judaism," 2005. Cited 27 February 2012. Online: http://www.umjc.org/home-mainmenu-1/global-vision-mainmenu-42/13-vision/225-defining-messianic-judaism.

30. While there is no center of halakhic (legal) authority in the Messianic Jewish community to rule on the issue of "who is a Jew," the movement as a whole is generally supportive of both the patrilineal and matrilineal definitions of Jewish identity. This is the official position of the International Messianic Jewish Alliance (IMJA) and the International Alliance of Messianic Congregations and Synagogues (IAMCS). The UMJC's "working definition of Jewish identity (July 27, 2010)" states: "Jewish identity is best understood as neither a strictly religious category nor a strictly ethnic category, but as membership in a people. Such a definition seems to underlie Paul's language in Philippians 3:4–5: 'If anyone else thinks he may have confidence in the flesh, I more so: circumcised the eighth day, of the stock of Israel, of the tribe of Benjamin, a Hebrew of the Hebrews ...' The primary criterion for defining Jewish identity is Jewish birth. Traditional Judaism recognizes one born of a Jewish mother as Jewish. Based on biblical precedent and reflecting the practice of some elements of the wider Jewish community, we also would consider one born of a Jewish father and a Gentile mother to be Jewish, if he or she identifies as a Jew. Since Jewish identity is not strictly ethnic, however, the discovery of Jewish ancestry beyond one's grandparents does not in itself render one Jewish" (online: http://www.mjstudies.com). In addition, there is the implicit recognition of converted Jews, i.e., Jews by choice, who had a formal conversion ceremony under a recognized authority. See David J. Rudolph, "Appendix A: Who Is a Jew?" in *Growing Your Olive Tree Marriage*, 131–38.

31. Outside of a Messianic synagogue context, it is very difficult for Jewish believers in Yeshua to remain practicing Jews and to pass on Jewish identity to their children. E.g., more than four hundred thousand Jews became members of churches between the early nineteenth century and World War II, but less than one percent of their descendants are self-identified Jews today. See Mitch L. Glaser, "A Survey of Missions to the Jews in Continental Europe 1900–1950" (PhD diss., Fuller Theological Seminary, 1998), 159–61; Yaakov Ariel, *Evangelizing the Chosen People: Missions to the Jews in America, 1880–2000* (Chapel Hill: University of North Carolina Press, 2000), 49–51; Rachel L. E. Kohn, "Ethnic Judaism and the Messianic Movement," *Jewish Journal of Sociology* 29, no. 2 (1987): 89; Philip Cohen, *The Hebrew Christian and His National Continuity* (London: Marshall Brothers, 1909), 37.

32. "One purpose is central to every goal we or any group of believers might have, and it is to live in the presence of God.... Without abiding in God, we can be a political movement, a therapy group, or a social club, but not the body of Messiah. To forward the expression of our faith in a Messianic Jewish way, I propose six goals, all subsidiary to this one purpose ... : seeking emotional healing, defining and pursuing community, developing a proper expression of Jewishness, engaging in evangelism, preparing for the land of Israel to become the center of Messianic Judaism, refining our theology so as to help end the schism between the body of Messiah and the

Jews being "a visible testimony of Yeshua from within the Jewish people."[33] Rabbi David Chernoff describes the unique mission of Messianic synagogues in this way:

> We have an eternal covenant with God that goes back to Abraham. Our history is unique in that we were not just chosen out of many nations, but were formed by God through Abraham, Isaac and Jacob to be a special blessing to this world. God has a purpose and calling for the nation of Israel and this covenant relationship is eternal (Gen. 17:1–8). If God has made an eternal covenant with us as Jewish people, then it is incumbent upon us to keep our covenant relationship with Him. It is God's desire for Jewish people not to assimilate but to continue to be Jewish. That desire and our eternal relationship with God are evidenced by preservation of the Jewish people for the past 2000 years, and the fact that God has supernaturally restored the State of Israel today. The primary way a Jewish believer can continue to live a life as a Jew and not assimilate away from his Jewish people is to be a member of a Messianic synagogue. In a Messianic synagogue, a Jewish believer can continue to worship the Lord in a Jewish way, celebrate the Jewish festivals, raise his children as Jews and be a testimony to his family and people.[34]

There are presently over five hundred Messianic synagogues in the world today.[35] These congregations are committed to Jewish continuity and work hard to pass on Jewish identity to the next generation of Jewish followers of Yeshua. They provide a weekly Messianic Jewish community experience that focuses on the Lord, follows the rhythm of Jewish life, and fosters a connection with the wider Jewish world. North American Messianic synagogues have established summer camps for teens and young adults (e.g., Or L'Dor on the East Coast and Dor Segulah on the West Coast), as well as intercongregational youth retreats, music festivals, and Israel aliyah programs that inspire young Messianic Jews to deepen their walks with the Lord and with one another.[36]

Intermarrieds

Messianic Jewish congregations are visited by thousands of Jewish-Gentile intermarried couples each year because Messianic synagogues offer a way to bring together core elements of the Jewish and Christian religious traditions:

Jewish people.... As Messianic Jews, let us connect intimately with our God, be true disciples who can transmit his love through Yeshua to others, and rise to the challenge of doing the works God has prepared for us to do (Ephesians 2:10) in these momentous days" (David H. Stern, "Summary Essay: The Future of Messianic Judaism," in *How Jewish Is Christianity? 2 Views on the Messianic Movement* [ed. Louis Goldberg; Grand Rapids: Zondervan, 2003], 178–79, 192).

33. Paul L. Saal, "Messianic Jewish Communities by Design: Open Doors and Reserved Seating" (paper presented at the annual Hashivenu Forum, Beverly Hills, Calif., 2012), 29. Online: http://www.mjstudies.com.

34. David Chernoff, *Messianic Judaism: Questions & Answers* (Havertown, Pa.: MMI, 1990), 22–23; David Chernoff, *An Introduction to Messianic Judaism* (Havertown, Pa.: MMI, 1990), 11. Cf. David J. Rudolph, *Understanding Messianic Judaism: Answers to Frequently Asked Questions* (Denver: Union of Messianic Jewish Congregations, 1993), 6–8.

35. David H. Stern, *Messianic Judaism: A Modern Movement with an Ancient Past* (Clarksville, Md.: Lederer, 2007), 271–72.

36. See Seth Klayman, "The Messianic Jewish Youth Experience: Our Past, Present and Future," *Kesher: A Journal of Messianic Judaism* 11 (2000): 117–41.

Many intermarried couples are drawn to Messianic synagogues because the Jewish-Christian gap is bridged (Cohn-Sherbok 2000, xii). Intermarriage tends to blur the traditional boundaries between Judaism and Christianity within the average family so that a quasi – Messianic Jewish religious expression naturally arises. Intermarried couples find common ground in Messianic synagogues. Children of intermarriage find a home where they can integrate their identities (Rudolph 2003, 56 – 59, 111 – 114). Messianic synagogues challenge the "law of excluded middle" by asserting that children of Jewish-Christian intermarriage can be simultaneously Jewish and believers in Jesus. For these reasons, Messianic (Judeo-Christian) communities are a very attractive option for intermarried couples and their children.[37]

The exponential growth of Messianic synagogues since the 1970s is in part due to the growing number of intermarrieds who are looking for a place they can call home. Many intermarried couples view the Messianic synagogue as a good option because it "honors the faith traditions of both spouses, conveys Jewish identity to the next generation and makes it possible for intermarrieds and their children to worship together comfortably as a family."[38]

One of the strengths of the Messianic Jewish option is that it offers an identity rooted in history.[39] Messianic Judaism challenges the notion that Judaism and Christianity are mutually exclusive religions and contends that Christianity was originally a form of Judaism. The Messianic synagogue fits together pieces from both religious traditions in an attempt to restore an ancient communal identity. Yeshua the Jew, and the first-century Jews who followed him as the Messiah (the twelve *shlichim* [apostles], Miryam [Mary], Ya'akov [James], Sha'ul [Saul]/Paul, Timothy, Eunice, Lois, and others), serve as identity anchors for twenty-first-century Messianic Jews. Consequently, Messianic synagogues are able to provide a clear and historically based identity for intermarrieds and their children.[40]

Messianic Gentiles

An important demographic that distinguishes most Messianic synagogues from mainstream synagogues is the presence of Gentile followers of Yeshua (for the most part not married to Jews) who come alongside Messianic Jews to build a congregation for Yeshua within the house of Israel. "Messianic Gentiles" are non-Jews who are called by God to participate in the life and destiny of the Jewish people.[41] They have a special

37. Rudolph, "Contemporary Judeo-Christian Communities in the Jewish Diaspora," 148.
38. Rudolph, *Growing Your Olive Tree Marriage*, xi. Intermarrieds also make an important contribution to the Messianic synagogue. See David J. Rudolph, "Intermarriage Can Have a Positive Effect on Messianic Judaism," in *Voices of Messianic Judaism: Confronting Critical Issues Facing a Maturing Movement* (ed. Dan Cohn-Sherbok, Baltimore: Lederer, 2001), 101 – 9.
39. See Gershon Nerel, "Primitive Jewish Christians in the Modern Thought of Messianic Jews," in *Le Judéo-Christianisme Dans Tous Ses États* (ed. Simon C. Mimouni and F. Stanley Jones; Paris: Les Éditions du Cerf, 2001), 399 – 425.
40. Rudolph, *Growing Your Olive Tree Marriage*, xi – xii.
41. In some Conservative synagogues, a Gentile who participates in the life and destiny of the Jewish people is referred to as a *K'rov Yisrael* (a relative or friend of Israel, close to the Jews). See Mark Bloom et al., *A Place in the Tent: Intermarriage and Conservative Judaism* (Oakland, Calif.: EKS, 2005), 13 – 18.

love for Jewish people, involve themselves in the Jewish world, learn Hebrew, honor Jewish customs, and serve as members of Messianic synagogues for decades. "*Ahavat Yisrael* [love of Israel], more than any other model, describes the calling of Gentiles within Messianic Judaism.... Gentiles in Messianic Judaism are not here for themselves, but for Messiah's own people."[42] Like Paul, who renounced his apostolic rights and freedom in order to serve the Corinthians whom he loved (1 Cor 9), Messianic Gentiles forego their rights and freedom in relation to Jewish life (Acts 15; 21:25)[43] in order to bless Messianic Jews and Messianic synagogues.

The demographic reality of Messianic Gentiles, including a second and third generation, raises a number of questions that the Messianic Jewish community is currently engaging.[44] Many of these questions relate to time-honored traditions in the Jewish world concerning the participation of non-Jews in Jewish life.[45] In mainstream synagogues, for example, Gentiles are generally not permitted to have a bar/bat mitzvah, wear a tallit, or read from the Torah[46] because these are all activities in which a Jew affirms his/her covenant responsibilities as a member of the people of Israel, something a non-Jew cannot do.[47] Some Messianic synagogues believe that these normative standards should be maintained for reasons of conscience and to

42. Russell L. Resnik, "Defining Messianic Judaism," *Kesher: A Journal of Messianic Judaism* 16 (2003): 67, 70. Cited 4 March 2012. Online: http://www.kesherjournal.com/Issue-16/Defining-Messianic-Judaism. See Schiffman, "The Role of Gentiles in Messianic Congregations," in *Return of the Remnant*, 113 – 20; H. Bruce Stokes, "Gentiles in the Messianic Movement." Cited 26 March 2012. Online: http://imja.org/gentiles-in-the-messianic-movement/.

43. Richard Bauckham, "James and the Jerusalem Council Decision," chapter 16 of this volume. Cf. Toby Janicki, *God-Fearers: Gentiles and the God of Israel* (Marshfield, Mo.: First Fruits of Zion, 2012), 49 – 72; Toby Janicki, "The Gentile Believer's Obligation to the Torah of Moses," *Messiah Journal* 109 (2012): 45 – 62.

44. E.g., can a Messianic Gentile who wants to become a convert to the Jewish people (i.e., a Jew by choice) do so? The debate over this question is still in session in the Messianic Jewish community. See *Kesher: A Journal of Messianic Judaism* 19 (2005): 7 – 85. Cited 1 March 2012. Online: http://www.kesherjournal.com/Issue-19/View-issue; Michael Wolf, "Conversion of Gentiles — 'No Way!'" in *Voices of Messianic Judaism*, 133 – 39; John Fischer, "The Legitimacy of Conversion," in *Voices of Messianic Judaism*, 141 – 49. Paul's "rule in all the congregations" (1 Cor 7:17 – 24, my trans.) is a general prohibition against conversion and consistent with the thrust of apostolic teaching that Yeshua-believing Jews and Gentiles should remain in their respective callings because the ekklesia is a prolepsis of Israel and the nations in the eschaton (Acts 15; Rom 3:29 – 30; 11:11 – 36; 15:7 – 12; Gal 2; Eph 2; etc.). See David J. Rudolph, "Paul's 'Rule in All the Churches' (1 Cor 7:17 – 24) and Torah-Defined Ecclesiological Variegation," *Studies in Christian-Jewish Relations* 5 (2010): 1 – 23. Online: http://www.mjstudies.com. This notwithstanding, many biblical prohibitions, including New Covenant ones (e.g., Yeshua's stance on divorce in Mark 10:10 – 12), have exceptions and the same may be the case with Paul's rule. Some Messianic rabbis contend that a compelling case can be made for an exception in the case of Messianic Gentiles who marry Jews and want to embrace the Jewish people as their own, as Ruth did (Ruth 1:16).

45. See Jon C. Olson, "Gentile Yeshua-Believers Praying in the Synagogue: Why and How," *Kesher: A Journal of Messianic Judaism* 23 (2009): 47 – 69. Cited 29 February 2012. Online: http://www.kesherjournal.com/Issue-23/Gentile-Yeshua-Believers-Praying-in-the-Synagogue-Why-and-How; Daniel C. Juster, "Jewish and Gentile Distinction in Messianic Jewish Congregations" (paper presented at the Tikkun Leadership Conference, 2008); Saal, "Messianic Jewish Communities by Design," 21 – 23.

46. Mainstream synagogues explain that a Gentile cannot say the traditional blessing before the Torah reading, "Blessed are You, O LORD our God, King of the universe, *Who chose us from all peoples and gave us His Torah.* Blessed are You, O LORD, Giver of the Torah."

47. Commission on Reform Jewish Outreach of the Union of American Hebrew Congregations and the Central Conference of American Rabbis, *Defining the Role of the Non-Jew in the Synagogue: A Resource for Congregations* (Cincinnati: Union of American Hebrew Congregations, 1990); Commission on Reform Jewish Outreach of the Union of American Hebrew Congregations and the Central Conference of American Rabbis, *A Supplemental Process Guide for Congregations: Defining the Role of the Non-Jew in the Synagogue* (ed. Dru Greenwood; Cincinnati: Union of American Hebrew Congregations, 1993); Jewish Reconstructionist Federation Task Force, *Boundaries and Opportunities: Report on the Role of the Non-Jew in Reconstructionist Synagogues* (ed. Shery Shulewitz; Wyn-

avoid blurring the distinction between Jew and Gentile in the body of Messiah, a differentiation that the New Testament upholds (1 Cor 7:17 – 24; Acts 15; 21:24 – 25). Other Messianic synagogues contend that these customs should be modified so that Messianic Gentiles may participate more fully in Jewish community life.

Gentile Christian Visitors

Many Gentile Christians visit Messianic synagogues to learn more about the Jewish roots of their New Covenant faith. Messianic rabbis welcome their Gentile brothers and sisters and seek to be a resource to them. Gentile Christian visitors should adapt to synagogue decorum in the same way that a guest would respond to the hospitality of his host by honoring the customs of the household he enters.[48] This is important because a Messianic synagogue is first and foremost a congregational home for Jewish believers in Yeshua and Jews who want to learn more about Yeshua of Nazareth, the Messiah of Israel.

Conclusion

Synagogues are above all sacred communities of Jewish people who gather for worship and prayer, fellowship, study, *simchas* (celebrations), outreach, and other Jewish community activities. Messianic synagogues have a special calling to be a place where Jews who follow the Jewish Messiah can remain Jews and become better Jews in keeping with the eternal purposes of the God of Israel. This includes conveying Jewish identity to their children and being a visible testimony of Yeshua from within the Jewish community. Messianic Jews, Jewish visitors who are not Messianic, intermarried couples, Messianic Gentiles, Gentile Christian visitors, and family and friends of all the above, together form the unique amalgam of people found in a healthy and vibrant Messianic Jewish congregation. This diversity enriches, but it can also divert the Messianic synagogue from staying focused on its calling. Because of the different backgrounds that converge in a Messianic synagogue, and the variety of expectations related to community life that naturally arise from this heterogeneity, synagogue leaders have

---

cote: Jewish Reconstructionist Federation, 1998); Charles Simon, *The Role of the Supportive Non-Jewish Spouse in the Conservative/Masorti Movement* (New York: Federation of Jewish Men's Clubs, 2005).

48. Many Gentile Christians who visit Messianic synagogues wrongly view the Gentile wing of the Church as apostate and think that Messianic synagogues alone represent authentic biblical faith. For a helpful corrective, see Boaz Michael, *Tent of David: Healing the Vision of the Messianic Gentile* (Marshfield: First Fruits of Zion, 2012). Other Gentile Christians erroneously claim that they are Jews due to a possibility of Jewish ancestry, often centuries ago, or based on what "the Lord told them" in a dream or vision. For a response to this challenge, see Boaz Michael, *Twelve Gates: Where Do the Nations Enter?* (Marshfield: First Fruits of Zion, 2012). Similarly, a large number of Gentile Christian visitors hold a "One Law" perspective and maintain that Gentile Christians should observe the Torah in the same way as Jewish people, contrary to Paul's letter to the Galatians and Acts 15; 21:25. For a mainstream response, see Daniel C. Juster and Russ Resnik, "One Law Movements: A Challenge to the Messianic Jewish Community," Union of Messianic Jewish Congregations, January 28, 2005. Cited 1 January 2012. Online: http://www.mjstudies.com. Cf. Boaz Michael and D. Thomas Lancaster, " 'One Law' and the Messianic Gentile," *Messiah Journal* 101 (2009): 46 – 70; First Fruits of Zion, "Divine Invitation: An Apostolic Call to Torah," 2010. Cited 26 February 2012. Online: http://ffoz.org/downloads/white_papers/. Messianic Jewish leaders have to walk a thin line between welcoming Gentile Christian visitors and guarding the vision, doctrinal standards, and traditions of their community. See Saal, "Messianic Jewish Communities by Design," 21 – 34.

to walk a fine line between being inclusive and upholding the Messianic Jewish vision and traditions of their congregation.

For Further Reading

Campbell, Alan L. C. "The *Non-Conversions* of Jews and Gentiles to Messianic Judaism: A Sense-Making Analysis of Interpersonal and Mass Communicative Influence on Spiritual Transformations." PhD diss., Regent University, May 2010.

Cohn-Sherbok, Dan. *Messianic Judaism*. London: Continuum, 2000.

———, ed. *Voices of Messianic Judaism: Confronting Critical Issues Facing a Maturing Movement*. Baltimore: Lederer, 2001.

Feher, Shoshanah. *Passing Over Easter: Constructing the Boundaries of Messianic Judaism*. Walnut Creek, Calif.: AltaMira, 1998.

Harris-Shapiro, Carol. *Messianic Judaism: A Rabbi's Journey through Religious Change in America*. Boston: Beacon, 1999.

Kesher: A Journal of Messianic Judaism. Online: http://www.kesherjournal.com/.

Kollontai, Pauline. "Between Judaism and Christianity: The Case of Messianic Jews." *Journal of Religion & Society* 8 (2006): 1–9. Online: http://www.mjstudies.com.

———. "Messianic Jews and Jewish Identity." *Journal of Modern Jewish Studies* 3:2 (2004): 195–205.

Messianic Judaism.net. Online: http://www.MessianicJudaism.net. A platform for mainstream Messianic Judaism on the internet.

Michael, Boaz. *Tent of David: Healing the Vision of the Messianic Gentile*. Marshfield, Mo.: First Fruits of Zion, 2012.

Nichol, Richard C. "The Unique Place of Gentiles in Messianic Jewish Congregational Life." Paper presented at the Borough Park Symposium, New York City, NY, 2012. Online: http://www.mjstudies.com.

Rudolph, David J. "Contemporary Judeo-Christian Communities in the Jewish Diaspora." Pages 146–50 in *Encyclopedia of the Jewish Diaspora: Origins, Experiences, and Culture I*. Edited by M. Avrum Ehrlich. Santa Barbara: ABC-CLIO, 2008.

———. *Growing Your Olive Tree Marriage: A Guide for Couples from Two Traditions*. Clarksville, Md.: Lederer, 2003.

———. "Paul's 'Rule in All the Churches' (1 Cor 7:17–24) and Torah-Defined Ecclesiological Variegation." *Studies in Christian-Jewish Relations* 5 (2010): 1–23. Online: http://www.mjstudies.com.

Saal, Paul L. "Messianic Jewish Communities by Design: Open Doors and Reserved Seating." Paper presented at the annual Hashivenu Forum. Beverly Hills, Calif., 2012. Online: http://www.mjstudies.com.

Stern, David H. *Messianic Judaism: A Modern Movement with an Ancient Past*. Clarksville, Md.: Lederer, 2007.

Stokes, H. Bruce. "Messianic Judaism: Ethnicity in Revitalization." PhD diss., University of California, Riverside, 1994.

Wasserman, Jeffrey S. *Messianic Jewish Congregations: Who Sold This Business to the Gentiles?* Lanham: University Press of America, 2000.

CHAPTER 3

Messianic Jewish Worship and Prayer

Seth N. Klayman

Once one of Yeshua's disciples approached him with a request: "Lord, teach us to pray."[1] The request reveals the disciples' drive to learn from their rabbi. They wanted to understand the essence of prayer according to Yeshua, and to find out how, on a practical level, prayer should be expressed. Yeshua's response is called by some Messianic Jews "the Prayer to 'Avinu" ("*Pater Noster*," "Our Father," "The Lord's Prayer").[2] It was apparently formulated in Aramaic or Hebrew, and bears many structural, thematic, and linguistic characteristics found in Jewish prayers that already existed in some form during the first century CE.[3] Consequently, many scholars agree that the prayer is rightly considered "a beautifully simple expression of Jewish prayer."[4] At the same time, the specific wording of the prayer is uniquely shaped by Yeshua himself, and, in its historical and literary context, it is given to his Jewish disciples who would follow him as the promised Messiah. The result is a prayer that is at once Messianic and Jewish.

From Antiquity to Modernity

The last seventeen centuries have not prepared the modern Messianic Jewish community to worship and pray in a way that is at once Messianic and Jewish. From our vantage point, tragic forces of history have intervened to separate Jewish believers in Jesus from modes, forms, and expressions of worship and prayer that uniquely articulate the faith conviction that Yeshua is Messiah and Lord in a way that is faithfully Jewish. For the most part, Messianic Jewish worship and prayer reemerged in the latter part of the twentieth century out of "a vacuum of expression."[5] At the beginning of the twenty-first century, Messianic Jewish worship and prayer is maturing in the quest to restore, through its modes, forms, and expressions, "the perspective of New Covenant faith as understood by the apostles."[6] It has risen again over the horizon of history as an application of "the kind of intentionality shown by Jesus and the Apostles, but for a new day and context."[7]

---

1. Luke 11:1.
2. Matt 6:9–14; Luke 11:2–4.
3. Seth Klayman, "*Tephillat HaAdon* in *Mattityahu* 6:9–13 and Luke 11:2–4: A Linguistic Approach with Historical Implications," *Kesher: A Journal of Messianic Judaism* 15 (2003): 22–61.
4. John Nolland, *Luke 9:21–18:34* (Dallas: Word, 1993), 619.
5. Daniel C. Juster, *A Messianic Jewish Worship Book* (Gaithersburg, Md.: Beth Messiah Congregation, 1988), 4.
6. Juster, *A Messianic Jewish Worship Book*, 3.
7. Stuart Dauermann, *Christians and Jews Together* (Los Angeles: Messianic Jewish Theological Institute, 2009), 19.

When the Messianic Jewish movement emerged in the late 1960s and early 1970s, Messianic Jews could have adopted *in toto* forms of worship and prayer from the Jewish or Christian traditions. As Jews, Messianic Jews could have relied exclusively upon the *Siddur* (Prayer Book), *Machzor* (Cycle of Prayers for the High Holy Days), and *Haggadah* (Passover Telling). Despite the historic, regional, and modern variations among these compilations, they contain the time-honored order of Jewish prayers for Shabbat (Sabbath) and holy days. The overwhelming majority of the prayers, hymns, and texts found within these works are either direct quotations from the Tanakh (Hebrew Bible) or rooted in scriptural themes. As believers in Jesus, Messianic Jews could have turned exclusively to one of the myriads of worship expressions within Christianity. Liturgies within the Catholic, Orthodox, and Anglican churches, the rich tradition of hymnody, and the more contemporary evangelical and charismatic worship styles are but a few of the manifold options Messianic Jews could have chosen.

However, Messianic Jews did not find the existing Jewish and Christian modes of worship and prayer to be fully reflective of the totality of their own Messianic Jewish identity and faith. Recalling the state of affairs in the late 1960s, Stuart Dauermann remarks, "At that time, there was nothing available to us that reflected the praise in our hearts to Jesus and sounded like something a Jew could recognize as being religious."[8] On the one hand, when these Messianic Jews looked to traditional Jewish worship, they did not find there Yeshua, their Messiah and Lord, through whom they had experienced spiritual rebirth. Sadly, in a few instances, they even encountered in the *Siddur* vestiges of historic Jewish reactions against Yeshua-faith.[9] On the other hand, when they looked to Christian worship, they were hard-pressed to find affirmation of God's enduring covenant with the Jewish people. The styles, sounds, and terminology employed were, at best, foreign to Jewish ears and, at worst, outright offensive to Jewish sensitivities. Tragically, in some instances, Christian "worship" was even associated with some of the most heinous crimes ever perpetrated against the Jewish people.[10]

Music

In the late 1960s and early 1970s, some Messianic Jews spontaneously and independently became acutely aware of the need to learn how to worship and pray in a way that is at once Messianic and Jewish. Out of this awareness, and along with the rise of the Messianic Jewish movement, came the birth of a unique type of worshipful music that has come to be known as "Messianic Music." This music was popularized by such groups as The Liberated Wailing Wall, Lamb, Kol Simcha, and later Israel's Hope (led by Paul Wilbur), Marty Goetz, and many others. By the late 1970s and 1980s,

---

8. Stuart Dauermann, introduction to *Avodat Y'shua* (San Francisco: Purple Pomegranate, 1991), i.

9. For example, the thirteenth blessing of the *'Amidah* ("Standing Prayer") includes a benediction against the "*minim*" ("sectarians" or "heretics"). When this benediction was added, probably in the late first century CE, "*minim*" included Jewish believers in Jesus (cf. Nosson Scherman, ed., *The Complete ArtScroll Siddur: Nusach Ashkenaz* [Brooklyn: Mesorah, 1997], 106–7).

10. For example, it is reported that during the First Crusade (1096–99), Crusaders set fire to a synagogue in Jerusalem and then encircled "the screaming, flame-tortured humanity singing 'Christ We Adore Thee!'" (David Rausch, *Legacy of Hatred: Why Christians Must Not Forget the Holocaust* [Chicago: Moody, 1984], 27).

Messianic Music had become one of the primary traits of the worship services in the rapidly increasing number of Messianic Jewish congregations. Indeed, Messianic Music served as fuel for the burgeoning movement; at the same time, Messianic Music proliferated as a result of the movement's growth.

Dauermann has defined Messianic Music in a general sense as "that music which is identifiably Jewish in character and/or perspective and which is apostolic in doctrine."[11] The content of "classic" Messianic Music bears a number of common characteristics. Messianic songs are often direct scriptural quotations or derived directly from passages of Scripture that contain the following themes: biblical psalms of praise, affirmation of God's covenant loyalty to Israel, prophecies in the Tanakh concerning the past and future work of the Messiah, and the coming fullness of the messianic kingdom. Many Messianic songs employ Hebrew in order to deepen the connection of the worshiper to the words of the Tanakh, the historic Jewish experience, and the land of Israel. The lyrics often express worship in communal terms rather than individual terms ("we" rather than "I"). Moreover, Messianic songs frequently have an overt outreach orientation, seeking to communicate the messiahship of Yeshua among Jewish people.

The "classic" Messianic sound is often in minor keys and includes distinctive Jewish rhythms and instrumentation. The chordal patterns and melodies often draw from traditional liturgical prayers and poems, as well as Klezmer sounds rooted in celebratory Jewish folk music.[12] Some Messianic songs bear marks of influence from progressive and renewal streams within Judaism. Contemporary evangelical and charismatic worship music has also influenced some Messianic artists. Trademark Messianic songs are often upbeat and jubilant, inspiring the worshiper to hand clapping and raised hands.

Dance

"Messianic Dance" (sometimes called "Davidic Dance" because it is done in the spirit of David's worshipful dancing before the Lord)[13] emerged in concert with Messianic Music. Messianic Dance involves the interpretation and application of Jewish dance styles as an expression of the joy of intimacy with God available in Yeshua. It has been called a "hallmark of the Messianic expression"[14] and has been described as "prayer in motion."[15] Corporate dancing is one way that unbridled joy was concretized in ancient Israel's worship, especially in the context of pilgrimage to the Temple.[16] The primary influences upon Messianic Dance are Israeli folk dance, Yemenite dance, and Hasidic dance.[17] Messianic Dance, a feature of the worship services in a number of

---

11. Stuart Dauermann, "Toward a Philosophy of Music Ministry," *Kesher: A Journal of Messianic Judaism* 3 (1995–96): 118.

12. See Steve McConnell et al., "Resources for Worship," *Kesher: A Journal of Messianic Judaism* 7 (1998): 74.

13. 2 Sam 6:16.

14. Murray Silberling, *Dancing for Joy: A Biblical Approach to Praise and Worship* (Baltimore: Lederer, 1995), 3.

15. Silberling, *Dancing for Joy*, 42.

16. Silberling, *Dancing for Joy*, 5–6.

17. Silberling, *Dancing for Joy*, 49–52.

congregations, is usually done in the form of a circle or line, and generally employs from these Jewish dance forms simple choreographed steps, making the dances egalitarian and accessible.

Holy Days, Rituals, and Observances

Messianic Jewish worship and prayer in the home and synagogue generally follows the cycle of the Jewish calendar, highlighting the fullness of each holy day's meaning in light of the past and future work of Messiah Yeshua.[18] The cycle commences with the weekly celebration of Shabbat, a day of rest, remembrance of creation and the Exodus, and, for Messianic Jews, a day of exalting Yeshua, mediator of creation and redemption, in whom is found eternal rest.[19] Messianic Jewish families commonly welcome Shabbat with the traditional Friday night meal, including such elements as candle lighting, traditional songs, blessing of the children, reading of Proverbs 31:10 – 31, hand washing, blessings for wine and *challah* (traditional braided bread), spontaneous prayers, and Messianic songs. Messianic Jewish congregations hold at least one corporate worship service on Shabbat. These services, often gatherings of Jewish people together with people from diverse backgrounds, are usually characterized by a fusion of Messianic songs, dance, liturgy, spontaneous prayer, a Torah service, *B'rit Chadashah* (New Testament) reading, *drash* (an address similar to a sermon) often relating the weekly Torah portion to Yeshua-faith, and an *'oneg* (literally "delight"; a Shabbat fellowship meal). The goal of the service is to impart "God's story, Messiah's story, and our story as his children."[20]

The annual festival cycle begins in the spring with the celebration of *Pesach/Hag HaMatzot* (Passover/Festival of Unleavened Bread).[21] Messianic Jews employ the use of a *haggadah*, often one of the many published or unpublished Messianic *haggadot*. Passover meals — expounding Israel's redemption from Egyptian bondage and, for Messianic Jews, spiritual redemption from the bondage of sin through Messiah, our Passover lamb[22] — are shared in the home and/or congregational setting. During Passover (and in many communities more frequently), Messianic Jews observe what they sometimes call *Shulchan Adonai* (Messiah's Table; "Communion"), a Passover ritual that Yeshua infused with Messianic significance in the context of the Passover meal he shared with his disciples just prior to his crucifixion.[23] Messianic Jews observe this rite in a way that seeks to restore its inherent Jewishness and reinsert it into a Jewish context. They emphasize that Yeshua's identification with the broken *matzah* and wine is most effectively illuminated through an understanding of the redemption imagery and symbolism that the Scriptures and Jewish tradition assign to the *matzah* and wine of the Passover meal. Though symbolic, these elements of the Passover meal are

---

18. See Barney Kasdan, *God's Appointed Times: A Practical Guide for Understanding and Celebrating the Biblical Holidays* (Clarksville, Md.: Messianic Jewish Publishers, 1993).

19. Lev 23:3; Exod 20:11; Deut 5:15; Matt 11:29; Luke 1:68; John 1:3; 1 Tim 2:5.

20. Richard Nichol, "Shabbat Services as Sacred Drama," *Kesher: A Journal of Messianic Judaism* 3 (1995 – 96): 9.

21. Lev 23:4 – 8.

22. 1 Cor 5:7.

23. Matt 26:17 – 30; Luke 22:14 – 19; 1 Cor 11:23 – 26.

to bring the participant into an experiential reality.[24] By partaking of these elements together, Messianic Jews affirm their faith in, and identification with, the broken body and shed blood of the Messiah, which bring redemption and bind Messianic Jews together with the multinational Body of Messiah throughout the ages.

The period of the 'Omer begins during Passover with Bikkurim (Festival of First Fruits),[25] in which a grain offering was waved in the Temple, and which for Messianic Jews points to Yeshua's resurrection on Bikkurim.[26] Hag HaShavu'ot (Festival of Weeks, Pentecost), which traditionally marks the giving of the Torah at Sinai, also marks for Messianic Jews the giving of the Holy Spirit in Jerusalem, which took place on Shavu'ot.[27] Traditionally, the autumn holy days of Yom Teruah (Day of Trumpet Blasts; Rosh HaShanah [Head of the Year]),[28] Yom Kippur (Day of Atonement),[29] and Hag HaSukkot (Festival of Booths)[30] respectively awaken the worshiper to spiritual introspection, emphasize the need for atonement to be effectuated, and inspire rejoicing in God's eternal kingship. For Messianic Jews, Yom Teruah points toward the eschatological great trumpet blast,[31] Yom Kippur points to Yeshua's sacrifice on our behalf as well as the fountain of cleansing to come at his return,[32] and Sukkot points to the fullness of the kingdom of Messiah on this earth.[33]

Messianic Jews generally observe some or all minor ancient Jewish holidays. Hanukkah (Dedication)[34] in the late fall/early winter and Purim (Lots),[35] both of which celebrate God's faithfulness in protecting and preserving his people through times of persecution, are the most widely celebrated of the ancient minor observances. Some Messianic Jews acknowledge or observe minor fast days, such as Tisha b'Av (the ninth day of the Hebrew month of Av), which commemorates the destruction of the First and Second Temples in Jerusalem, as well as other tragedies that have befallen the Jewish people throughout history. Some Messianic Jews participate in modern Jewish and/or Israeli observances such as Yom HaShoah (Holocaust Remembrance Day), Yom HaZikkaron (Israel Day of Remembrance), and Yom HaAtzma'ut (Israel Independence Day). Observance of the minor fasts and modern commemorations varies among Messianic Jews from corporate gatherings in Messianic Jewish congregations to joining wider Jewish community observances.

---

24. Barney Kasdan, "Zachor — In Remembrance of Me," Kesher: A Journal of Messianic Judaism 3 (1995 – 96): 61.

25. Lev 23:9 – 14.

26. E.g., Matt 28:1; 1 Cor 15:19 – 24.

27. Lev 23:15 – 22; Exod 19 – 20; Acts 2.

28. Lev 23:23 – 25.

29. Lev 23:26 – 32.

30. Lev 23:33 – 43.

31. 1 Cor 15:51 – 53.

32. Heb 2:17; Zech 13:1.

33. Zech 14:16; Rev 7:9 – 17; Rev 21:2 – 4.

34. John 10:22 – 23. Messianic Jewish communities generally do not hold Christmas celebrations or observances. In the context of Hanukkah, popularly referred to as "the Festival of Lights," Messianic Jews honor Yeshua as the light of the world (John 8:12) and the greatest servant (shammash) of humanity (Matt 20:28; Mark 10:45). Shammash is also the name of the candle on the Hanukkiyah (nine-branched Hanukkah candelabrum) that "serves" or lights the eight Hanukkah candles. See First Fruits of Zion, Light: A Hanukkah Anthology (Marshfield, Mo.: First Fruits of Zion, 2011), 1 – 80.

35. Esth 9:20 – 32.

Prayer

Published Messianic Jewish *Siddurim* (Prayer Books) for Shabbat and festivals presently used in Messianic synagogues in the United States adhere, to a greater or lesser extent, to the traditional times, structure, and wording of Jewish prayers for appropriate occasions. For instance, the published prayer books generally follow the structure of the traditional Shabbat service, which for the morning service includes (1) *Birchot HaShachar* (Morning Blessings); (2) *Pesukei d'Zimra* (Verses of Song); (3) *Shema* (Hear, O Israel!) and Its Blessings; (4) *'Amidah* (Standing Prayer); (5) Torah Service (Reading and Exposition of Scripture); and (6) Concluding Hymns and Prayers. In Judaism, the standardized formulation of the services and prayers is called *keva* ("fixity"). Published Messianic Jewish worship resources, therefore, advocate prayer in, and as a part of, *klal Yisrael* (all Israel). Such identification is done after the example of Yeshua, and in the spirit of the apostles, who, even after Yeshua's death, resurrection, and ascension, evidently continued to engage in traditional Jewish prayer practices,[36] frequented the Temple during traditional worship times,[37] and regularly attended synagogues.[38]

In Judaism, *kavannah* ("intentionality," "inner directedness of the heart") refers to the heart orientation of the worshiper and the resulting spontaneous prayers that may be inspired by the fixed prayers. For Messianic Jews, all prayers are offered (explicitly or implicitly) in Messiah Yeshua, and on the merit of his death and resurrection. In fact, for many Messianic Jews, it is faith in Yeshua that has brought them back to Jewish worship forms. They have found the traditional elements of the worship services to be "entirely bathed in the bright light of Yeshua's revelation."[39] For example, a Messianic Jew finds the summons of the *V'ahavtah* (Deut 6:5 – 9) to wholehearted love and obedience to God as only possible in and through Yeshua, for it is Yeshua's perfect living out of this *mitzvah* (commandment) that inspires the worshiper to wholehearted obedience and makes such obedience possible since the Messianic Jew is in him.[40]

Published Messianic Jewish prayer books make Yeshua-faith explicit in the context of traditional prayer in at least four ways. First, these prayer books contain *uniquely Messianic prayers and blessings*, often placed at climactic moments in the service. For example, just after the *'Amidah*, which is traditionally the central prayer of the service and the height of intimate worship, the *Siddur for Messianic Jews* includes (in Hebrew and English) the Prayer to *'Avinu*,[41] and "The [Blessing of] Messiah Yeshua," a lengthy blessing recounting the past work of Messiah, which begins with the words, "Blessed

---

36. Acts 2:42. Luke's notice of the apostles' devotion to prayer (literally "the prayers") likely indicates their engagement in formal Jewish prayer together (Richard N. Longenecker, *John-Acts* [Grand Rapids: Zondervan, 1981], 290).

37. Acts 2:46; 3:1.

38. E.g., Acts 13:5, 14; 14:1; 17:1, 10; 18:4, 26; 19:8.

39. Mark S. Kinzer, "Prayer in Yeshua, Prayer in Israel: The Shema in Messianic Perspective" (paper presented at the annual Hashivenu Forum, Pasadena, Calif., January 2008). Online: http://www.mjstudies.com.

40. See Kinzer, "Prayer in Yeshua, Prayer in Israel," 9 – 11.

41. John Fischer and David Bronstein, *Siddur for Messianic Jews* (Palm Harbor, Fla.: Menorah Ministries, 1988), 86 – 87; cf. Jeremiah Greenberg, *Messianic Shabbat Siddur* (Gaithersburg, Md.: Messianic Liturgical Resources, 2000), 139 – 40.

are you, O Lord, who has given us the way of salvation in Messiah Yeshua."[42] In this way, Yeshua is overtly granted central place in this Messianic Jewish *Siddur*.

Second, these resources contain readings from the *B'rit Chadashah* woven into the flow of the service. The readings are intended to align with the themes of the prayers surrounding them, so as to highlight the compatibility of Yeshua-faith with the particular thrust of the traditional prayer or declaration. For example, just prior to the recitation of the Shema (Deut 6:4), *A Messianic Jewish Siddur for Shabbat* contains the reading of Mark 12:28 – 34,[43] in which Yeshua affirms the Shema as the foremost commandment. After the recitation of the Shema, there is a reading from 1 Corinthians 8:4 – 6,[44] which reaffirms the declaration of God's oneness, while also declaring that "there is one Lord, Yeshua the Messiah." For Messianic Jews, who hold to Yeshua's full deity (as well as full humanity), the declaration of Yeshua's Lordship is especially appropriate in the context of the Hebrew word *echad*, employed in Deuteronomy 6:4, to refer to God's oneness. For, that word opens the door for the Messianic Jewish understanding of God as a composite unity.[45]

The third way in which published Messianic Jewish prayer books make Yeshua-faith explicit is through *Messianic alterations of traditional prayers*. For example, in its traditional formulation, the first blessing of the *'Amidah* contains the phrase, "and [God] brings [*umevi'*] a redeemer to their [Israel's] children's children."[46] *A Messianic Jewish Siddur for Shabbat* alters this prayer to communicate that God has "*brought and brings* [*asher hevi'u*] a redeemer to their children's children" (emphasis added).[47] In this way, an explicit assertion that the Messiah has already come enters into the very text of the prayer.

Fourth, published Messianic Jewish prayer books may include *Messianic addenda to traditional prayers* in order to prompt the worshiper to relate the prayer or hymn to faith in Yeshua. For example, at the end of *L'cha Dodi* (Come My Beloved), a medieval liturgical poem recited upon welcoming the Sabbath, the *Siddur for Messianic Jews* adds the words "Sabbath peace in Yeshua, Sabbath peace, Sabbath peace."[48] This addendum stresses that it is in and through Yeshua, the Lord of Shabbat, that the peace of Shabbat can be enjoyed in fullest measure.

The foregoing discussion should not obscure the present reality that there exists exceedingly great diversity among the various prayer books and Messianic Jewish

---

42. Fischer and Bronstein, *Siddur for Messianic Jews*, 82 – 85. See also an abbreviated form of this blessing in Greenberg, *Messianic Shabbat Siddur*, 13 – 14.

43. Barry A. Budoff, trans., *A Messianic Jewish Siddur for Shabbat* (ed. Kirk Gliebe; Skokie: Devar Emet Messianic Publications, 2006), 80 – 81.

44. Budoff, *A Messianic Jewish Siddur for Shabbat*, 80 – 81.

45. See also the alterations to *Yigdal* in Fischer and Bronstein, *Siddur for Messianic Jews*, 108 – 9, which eschew the word *yachid* (because it can connote an absolute singularity as opposed to a composite unity) in the traditional formulation of the prayer, replacing it with *echad*. For comparisons between the Messianic Jewish understanding of God's oneness and Jewish mystical conceptions of God's oneness, see Mark S. Kinzer, "Finding Our Way through Nicaea: The Deity of Yeshua, Bilateral Ecclesiology, and Redemptive Encounter with the Living God" (paper presented at the annual Hashivenu Forum, Los Angeles, Calif., January 2010, 20 – 23). Online: http://www.mjstudies.com.

46. Scherman, *Complete ArtScroll Siddur*, 420 – 21.

47. Budoff, *A Messianic Jewish Siddur for Shabbat*, 86 – 87.

48. Fischer and Bronstein, *Siddur for Messianic Jews*, 25.

prayer practices in general. In the home setting, some Messianic Jews *daven* (pray) regularly in a traditional Jewish manner, while the personal prayer lives of others are more akin to the practices of evangelical Christians. And many heartily engage in both expressions. Within the congregational setting, as Dan Cohn-Sherbok observes, "Congregations do not rigidly follow the patterns recommended in the various prayer books produced by the movement; instead they modify their observance in accordance with their own spiritual needs."[49] Many congregations do not use prayer books, or have devised their own. The structure of the service differs widely among congregations.

The framers of the worship services in all congregations seek to prioritize the leading of the *Ruach HaKodesh* (Holy Spirit) in their worship services. The way this priority is applied accounts for much of the diversity that exists among congregations. For many, this priority means openness in certain worship contexts to spontaneous expressions of the *charismata* (sometimes described in a narrow sense as the "manifestational gifts of the Spirit").[50] Those congregations that promote the exercise of the *charismata* seek to do so in the spirit of the apostles, through whom prophecy, healing, and other supernatural signs of God's power regularly buttressed exhortative preaching so as to draw Jews especially, as well as Gentiles, to the Messiah.[51]

In the view of some, there is a unique intercessory dimension to Messianic Jewish prayer. In praying for the multinational Body of Messiah to enter into its fullness, and for the good news (gospel) to be proclaimed in all the nations, the Messianic Jew intercedes from within the covenant people whose prophetic destiny is to be "a light to the nations."[52] Because Messianic Jews have embraced Yeshua, "the light of the world,"[53] they are uniquely positioned to intercede out of the fullness of Israel's calling to be a light to the nations. In praying for the redemption of Israel, Messianic Jews can intercede out of a place of intimate relationship with Israel's redeemer, through whom that redemption will be accomplished. Moreover, when Messianic Jews pray for their fellow Jewish people, they can pray out of the extraordinary depth of heartfelt burden that one bears for kin.[54]

Conclusion: From Modernity to the Future

In the latter half of the twentieth century, scholars convincingly restored Yeshua and the early Yeshua movement to their thoroughly Jewish context.[55] Messianic Jewish worship and prayer is an audible and visible outworking of the implications of this historical truth for Jewish believers in Yeshua today. It is one of the primary ways the remnant of Israel, though preserved in every age, has once again become identifi-

---

49. Dan Cohn-Sherbok, *Messianic Judaism* (London: Cassell, 2000), 87.
50. See 1 Cor 12:1–11.
51. E.g., Acts 2–3; 13:1; 1 Cor 1:22.
52. Isa 60:3.
53. John 8:12.
54. Rom 9:1–2; 10:1.
55. See, for example, the *Time* magazine article that highlighted this contribution, calling it an "idea that is changing the world" (David Van Biema, "Re-Judaizing Jesus," *Time*, March 13, 2008. Cited 6 March 2012. Online: http://www.time.com/time/specials/2007/article/0,28804,1720049_1720050_1721663,00.html).

able.[56] This reemergence has occurred seemingly against all odds, only to continue to grow and flourish. At the most basic level, Messianic Jewish worship and prayer challenges the uncritical yet commonly held assumption that "Jews don't believe in Jesus." Messianic Jewish worship and prayer challenges Jewish people to reconsider the centuries-old misconceptions that Yeshua does not belong among his Jewish people, and that his Jewish people do not belong in him. Messianic Jewish worship and prayer challenges Christians to come to terms with Christianity's centuries-old distance from its own Jewish roots, as well as with Christian theology's historically pervasive supersessionism, which has so effectively served to perpetuate the error that Yeshua-faith must be irrelevant, undesirable, or destructive for Jewish people.

What does the future hold? Some are fervently pursuing deeper understanding of traditional Jewish prayer, relating it critically, and in thoughtful detail, to Yeshua-faith.[57] Mark Kinzer has proffered that the presence of Yeshua, though veiled, may be found in the structure and prayers of the *Siddur* — a view that is provocative, if not controversial.[58] Some are moving forward practically with the vision of bringing together riches culled from traditional Jewish worship, and the treasures of apostolic teachings, in original sounds and artistic expressions relevant to a new generation of Messianic Jews. Some even have the audacity to suggest that, given Israel's coming redemptive encounter with Messiah Yeshua,[59] and the coming participation of the nations of the earth in Israel's worship,[60] modern Messianic Jewish worship and prayer is a prolepsis of worship and prayer in the messianic kingdom. To borrow from the words of the prayer that Yeshua taught his inquisitive disciples long ago, may that kingdom come, may his will be done, right here on earth as it is in heaven.

For Further Reading

Budoff, Barry, trans. *A Messianic Jewish Siddur for Shabbat*. Edited by Kirk Gliebe. Skokie, Ill.: Devar Emet Messianic Publications, 2006.

Dauermann, Stuart. "The Importance of Jewish Liturgy." Pages 1 – 9 in *Voices of Messianic Judaism: Confronting Critical Issues Facing a Maturing Movement*. Baltimore: Lederer, 2001.

———. "Toward a Philosophy of Messianic Music Ministry." *Kesher: A Journal of Messianic Judaism* 3 (1995 – 96): 111 – 25.

Eby, Aaron, trans. *Vine of David Haggadah: Messianic Jewish Passover Seder*. Marshfield, Mo.: Vine of David, 2011.

———. *We Thank You: Blessings of Thanks Before and After Meals*. Marshfield, Mo.: Vine of David, 2011.

Fischer, John, and David Bronstein. *Messianic Services for Shabbat and Holy Days*. Palm Harbor, Fla.: Menorah Ministries, 1992.

———. *Siddur for Messianic Jews*. Palm Harbor, Fla.: Menorah Ministries, 1988.

Greenberg, Jeremiah. *Messianic High Holiday Machzor*. Gaithersburg, Md.: Messianic Liturgical Resources, 2001.

---

56. Rom 11:1 – 5.

57. See Jonathan Kaplan, "A Divine Tapestry: Reading the Siddur, Reading Redemption, Reading Yeshua" (paper presented at the annual Hashivenu Forum, Pasadena, Calif., February 1 – 3, 2004). Online: http://www.mjstudies .com.

58. Kinzer, "Prayer in Yeshua, Prayer in Israel," 7, 21 – 22.

59. Zech 12:10; Rom 11:24 – 26.

60. Zech 14:16; Isa 66:23.

————. *Messianic Shabbat Siddur*. Gaithersburg, Md.: Messianic Liturgical Resources, 2000.

Juster, Daniel C. "Authenticity in Messianic Jewish Worship." *Messianic Jewish Life* 73, no. 3 (2000): 4–5, 33.

Kasdan, Barney. *God's Appointed Times: A Practical Guide for Understanding and Celebrating the Biblical Holidays*. Clarksville, Md.: Messianic Jewish Publishers, 1993.

Nichol, Richard C. "Shabbat Services as Sacred Drama." *Kesher: A Journal of Messianic Judaism* 3 (1995–96): 9–20.

Rudolph, David J., ed. *The Voice of the Lord Messianic Jewish Daily Devotional*. Baltimore: Lederer, 1998.

Silberling, Murray. *Dancing for Joy: A Biblical Approach to Praise and Worship*. Baltimore: Lederer, 1995.

Van de Poll, Evert W. *Sacred Times for Chosen People: Development, Analysis and Missiological Significance of Messianic Jewish Holiday Practice*. Missiological Research in the Netherlands 46. Zoetermeer: Boekencentrum, 2008.

CHAPTER 4

Messianic Jews and Scripture

CARL KINBAR

Messianic Jews accord Scripture a unique status as the inspired and authoritative Word of God. They study it, use it liturgically, and base their life and practice on it. However, Messianic Jews grapple with certain issues involved in biblical interpretation that are particularly relevant to Jewish followers of Yeshua. In the first two parts of this essay I will focus on how Messianic Jewish interpretation of Scripture is affected by interpretive traditions and how this leads to the task of shaping a post-supersessionist canonical narrative. In the third part I will focus on unique uses of Scripture in Messianic Judaism.

Scripture and Traditions of Interpretation

Messianic Jewish views of the inspiration and authority of Scripture are expressed in the various statements of faith of Messianic Jewish national organizations. The Messianic Jewish Alliance of America (MJAA), an organization of individual Messianic Jews, states in their foundational documents, "We recognize [the Bible's] divine inspiration, and accept its teachings as our final authority in all matters of faith and practice."[1] The Union of Messianic Jewish Congregations (UMJC) affirms, "The writings of Tanakh and Brit Hadasha [the Scriptures] are divinely inspired and fully trustworthy (true), a gift given by God to His people, provided to impart life and to form, nurture, and guide them in the ways of truth. They are of supreme and final authority in all matters of faith and practice."[2] The basic line of thought reflected in these statements is that *the Bible is divinely inspired, infallible, and authoritative*. This represents the consensus of Messianic Jewish leadership and laity.

Because Scripture is of such great importance in Messianic Jewish life and thought, Messianic Jewish thinkers seek to clarify how its teachings may be understood. Daniel Juster explains that a grasp "of the basic thrusts of much biblical teaching is available to the average reader who is seeking the truth with the help of the Holy Spirit. This is called *the doctrine of the perspicuity of Scripture*. However, it is not always easy to know what the biblical author is teaching. Many tools have to be applied to obtain an accurate understanding."[3] While most Messianic Jews are unfamiliar with critical

---

1. Messianic Jewish Alliance of America, "Statement of Faith." Cited 13 February 2012. Online: http://www.mjaa.org/site/PageServer?pagename=n_about_us_statement_of_faith.

2. Union of Messianic Jewish Congregations, "Statement of Faith," July 19, 2012. Online: http://www.mjstudies.com.

3. Daniel Juster, "Biblical Authority," in *Voices of Messianic Judaism: Confronting Critical Issues Facing a Maturing Movement* (ed. Dan Cohn-Sherbok; Baltimore: Lederer, 2001), 23.

Scripture study methods, Juster sees their judicious use as required in order to bridge the linguistic and cultural gaps that separate interpreters from the authorial intent of Scripture.

Mark Kinzer, another Messianic Jewish thinker, approaches the interpretation of Scripture from a different direction. He argues that the Bible must be interpreted in the context of interpretive traditions, which consist of "the accumulated insights of a community transmitted from one generation to the next. In a Messianic Jewish context, tradition represents the understanding of Scripture preserved through the generations among the communities — Jewish and Christian — within which Scripture itself has been preserved. If we are connected to these communities, then we are also heirs of their traditions."[4]

Kinzer explains that, at its most formative and often unrecognized levels, tradition is reflected in scribal transmission and clarification of the texts including, for example, the interpretive practices underlying Masoretic vocalization of the Tanakh (Old Testament).[5] Arguably the most significant of these unrecognized traditions are the differing arrangements of the Jewish "Tanakh" and the Christian "Old Testament." All these arrangements include the same thirty-nine writings but in different orders and therefore telling different stories.[6] Kinzer argues that our current reading and thinking about Scripture already embodies an acceptance of these traditions, however unrecognized; he argues that recognized tradition must also be employed in our approach to Scripture.

Kinzer qualifies his emphasis on tradition by pointing out that "if the distinction between Scripture and tradition is problematic, it is nonetheless necessary. An appreciation for tradition and a serious engagement with it in our reading of Scripture need not imply an obliteration of the line separating biblical traditions from post-biblical tradition or an elevating of the latter over the former."[7] Communities that read Scripture through the lens of tradition often restrict interpretive options. For example, Jewish tradition does not allow interpretations of Scripture that directly support the claim that Yeshua is the Messiah, while Christian tradition does not generally allow for a reading of Scripture that supports the ongoing covenant responsibility of Messianic Jews to observe the Torah. Messianic Jews argue that Scripture requires these disallowed readings and therefore also requires a critical reading of tradition, even as tradition can help to inform our reading of Scripture more generally.

Juster argues for a more cautious approach toward Jewish tradition, asserting that "only biblical teaching is fully binding, whereas other authorities might be fol-

---

4. Mark S. Kinzer, "Scripture and Tradition," in *Voices of Messianic Judaism*, 30.

5. Tanakh is a Hebrew acronym for Torah, Prophets, and Writings.

6. John W. Miller, *How the Bible Came to Be: Exploring the Narrative and the Message* (New York: Paulist, 2004), 77–94. Miller, a canon historian, argues that "The Bible as presently published, with its stark bifurcation into 'Old and New Testaments' and the peculiar rearrangement of its books, is the result of far-reaching social and theological changes that were entrenched during the fourth and fifth centuries when the church (after Constantine) triumphed as an exclusively Gentile church cut off from its Jewish roots" (96). When the books of the Tanakh, for example, are returned to their ancient order concluding with Ezra-Nehemiah and Chronicles (which is still found in Jewish Bibles today), the additional Scriptures beginning with Matthew then describe an extension of Israel's vocation that they had already begun to fulfill in the restoration and renewal that began following the return from Babylonian captivity.

7. Kinzer, "Scripture and Tradition," 35.

lowed because we perceive wise application or respect community practices."[8] In other words, Scripture is the measure of tradition, never the reverse. Juster does not address the claim of traditionalists that the cumulative weight of centuries of interpretation is necessarily of greater weight than the judgment of an individual.

The positions of Juster and Kinzer on the place of tradition in the interpretation of Scripture represent the views of two branches of Messianic Judaism and are emblematic of broader disagreements in the movement over the place of traditional practices in Messianic Jewish life.[9]

Scripture and the Canonical Narrative

Messianic Jewish theologians and laity recognize the need to tie together the diverse elements of Scripture into a coherent and theologically sound narrative. For the most part, they object to the overall canonical narrative of the majority of Christian theologians and commentators, which they regard as failing to account for the realities and significance of God's ongoing relationship with Israel. Messianic Jews object strenuously to narratives and interpretations in which Israel's place in God's economy is taken over by the Church. They find the standard canonical narrative, which reduces Israel's history to a narrative of sin and rejection by God, to be insufficient to explain the Scriptural data and account for their own existence as a movement of Jewish followers of Yeshua.

R. Kendall Soulen's *The God of Israel and Christian Theology* is a foundational work in the effort to develop post-supersessionist approaches to the canonical narrative, which Soulen defines as "a framework for *interpreting* the biblical canon ... reflect[ing] a fundamental decision about how the Bible 'hangs together' as a whole. The need for a canonical narrative arises because the Bible is an extraordinarily complex text whose unity and coherence are subject to debate."[10] Soulen argues that in the standard (Christian) canonical narrative, forged in the late second century, the history and prophecies described in the Hebrew Scriptures are important primarily because they foretell the coming and work of Christ. This clears the way for Jesus to redeem humanity and ultimately bring all things to their originally intended consummation. Soulen asserts that in the process of reducing God's relationship with Israel to foreshadowing and failure, the standard narrative inserts the Church in place of the now-rejected Israel, thereby undermining God's identity as the God of Israel.

Soulen explains that in the standard canonical narrative, the consummation of all things only reflects what has already been achieved in the death and resurrection of Yeshua. He argues that the death and resurrection of Yeshua should rather be seen as an anticipation of what will be achieved more substantially in the consummation of all things.[11] In this model, Israel continues to fulfill her vocation, begun in Abraham and continued in Yeshua, of blessing the nations, a task that will be fully realized only in that consummation.

8. Juster, "Biblical Authority," 23.
9. See Carl Kinbar, "Messianic Jews and Jewish Tradition," chapter 5 of this volume.
10. R. Kendall Soulen, *The God of Israel and Christian Theology* (Minneapolis: Fortress, 1996), 13.
11. Soulen, *God of Israel and Christian Theology*, 166.

Soulen's articulation of the problems in the standard narrative has stimulated important responses by several Messianic Jewish thinkers. Against the background of a general Messianic Jewish consensus that Israel's history and ongoing relationship with God must be included in any summary narrative of Scripture, a Messianic Jewish conference was convened in 2002 in order to reflect on Soulen's work. Stuart Dauermann, Paul Saal, and Mark Kinzer responded to Soulen's analysis and suggested approaches to the development of a distinctly Messianic Jewish canonical narrative. Their approaches are particularly salient because they are attuned not only to the Scripture but also to existing Jewish approaches to canonical narrative.

Dauermann addresses the issue of canonical narrative as part of a broad narrative construal of Jewish identity that also includes continuing Jewish history, liturgy, ritual, and family elements. For Dauermann, such a communal narrative is indispensable to community formation, identity, and continuity. Concerning the Jewish story, Dauermann argues that Israel should not be viewed as the Parcel Post People of God that delivers the package of salvation to the Church and then recedes from the scene. The traditional Christian narrative "presents the Bible as fundamentally the story of the Church.... Israel's story has simply become the Church's story, and ethnic Israel is most often reduced to the status of a vestigial organ that was once useful but now unnecessary."[12] Insofar as Messianic Jews have internalized the traditional Christian perspective, they suppress their own narrative and compromise their identity. Dauermann contends that a Messianic Jewish canonical narrative is based on "the continuing story of God's faithful engagement with the descendants of Abraham, Isaac and Jacob for the sake of the world."[13]

Paul Saal recounts the standard Jewish canonical narrative, in which the accounts of creation are the prologue and background to the call, identity, and vocation of Israel. Most of Saal's paper concerns the first period of this narrative, the Genesis 1–11 account, and focuses on the progress from chaos to order. He discusses the ongoing place of the Abrahamic and Mosaic covenant in facilitating the restoration of the created order: "As the individual and personal embodiment of the entire people of Israel, Yeshua calls Israel and, by association, all humanity into an active state of grace, whereby they are to fulfill their responsibility for imaging the sovereignty and service of God in the re-created world. This can only be accomplished if the fragile distinction between Israel and the nations is preserved."[14] Saal views the process of ordering or reordering the created realm as the constant thread of the Messianic Jewish canonical narrative in which the Church does not replace Israel but works alongside her.

Mark Kinzer's paper concerns "how the Bible's eschatological vision shapes the entire biblical narrative, and is shaped by it."[15] He discusses how the vocation of Israel

---

12. Stuart Dauermann, "Making Israel's Story Our Own: Toward a Messianic Jewish Canonical Narrative" (paper presented at the annual Hashivenu Forum, Pasadena, Calif., February 2002), 4–5. Online: http://www.mjstudies.com.

13. Dauermann, "Making Israel's Story Our Own," 5.

14. Paul L. Saal, "Origins and Destiny: Israel, Creation and the Messianic Jewish Canonical Narrative" (paper presented at the annual Hashivenu Forum, Pasadena, Calif., February 2002), 39. Online: http://www.mjstudies.com.

15. Mark S. Kinzer, "Beginning with the End: The Place of Eschatology in the Messianic Jewish Canonical Narrative" (paper presented at the annual Hashivenu Forum, Pasadena, Calif., 2002), 1. Online: http://www.mjstudies.com.

as a holy nation in this world anticipates the realities of the world to come. This consists of a body of holy practices that concretize the future reality in the here and now. Jewish tradition builds on this biblical truth and extends it in a variety of ways, for example by emphasizing the eschatological dimensions of Shabbat and the daily liturgy. Kinzer argues that the Messianic Jewish canonical narrative must maintain the significance of Israel's vocation of embodying a foretaste of the future in holy actions now.

Kinzer remarks that Christian theology generally ignores the eschatological character of Israel's holiness and accentuates the "discontinuity between Israel's covenant existence before Yeshua's coming and the eschatological newness that Yeshua brings. Messiah is thus exalted by the lowering of Moses and Israel."[16] To the contrary, God's presence with Israel is an ongoing reality that always anticipates the time of consummation. Kinzer agrees with Soulen's argument that the death and resurrection of Yeshua anticipates what will be achieved for Israel and the nations at the time of the consummation of all things. The anticipatory quality of Yeshua's death and resurrection aligns seamlessly with the anticipatory quality of Israel's holy practices. Israel's vocation is thus not occluded but brought to a new height in Yeshua, the one-man Israel. The person and work of Yeshua may thereby be seen in the context of Israel's ongoing life and vocation and not as its replacement.

In the final essay of *Introduction to Messianic Judaism*, Soulen argues, contrary to his critique in *The God of Israel and Christian Theology*, that the standard canonical narrative may be rehabilitated. He writes that *"even if* one interprets the Bible in light of a canonical narrative that privileges the story of creation, fall, redemption, and consummation (as the standard canonical narrative does), *one is continuously faced with scriptural testimony to the Divine Name and the primordial mystery of divine uniqueness to which it points."*[17] He argues that by foregrounding the Divine Name, the standard canonical narrative will demarginalize the God of Israel and avoid structural supersessionism. This is because the Divine Name connects with Israel's history and vocation from Abraham through the consummation of all things. Of particular interest is the way in which the Torah, given by the Divine Name on Sinai, is the basis for Israel's anticipatory holy practices, which continue until the eschaton. Since the Torah and these practices are given specifically to Israel, the integration of Torah into the narrative ensures the ongoing identity of Israel and guards against the idea that it has been replaced in any way by the Church.

Scripture and Community

In Judaism, and therefore in Messianic Jewish communities, the properly inscribed text of Scripture is considered particularly holy, as explained by the following portion from the Mishnah (ca. 225 CE): "A sheet of a scroll whereon are written eighty-five letters (as many as in the portion *And it came to pass, when the ark set forward* [Numbers

---

16. Kinzer, "Beginning with the End," 12.

17. R. Kendall Soulen, "The Standard Canonical Narrative and the Problem of Supersessionism," chapter 27, emphasis original.

The UMJC Statement of Faith (2012)[*]

We affirm the following:

There is one God, who has revealed Himself as Father, Son, and Holy Spirit. Every divine action in the world is accomplished by the Father working through the Son and in the power of the Spirit. This God has revealed Himself in creation and in the history of Israel as transmitted in Scripture. (Gen. 1:1; 1 Cor. 8:6; Eph. 4:4 – 6)

God is the Creator of the heavens and the earth. He created humanity in the divine image to serve as creation's priest and ruler. God's intention for creation involves an order of differentiation, interdependence, and mutual blessing. (Gen. 1:26 – 28; 2:15; Eph. 1:4 – 6)

Through the exercise of free will, human beings disobeyed God, tarnished the divine image, and abandoned their privileged vocation. As a result, God's consummating purpose for creation met with initial frustration, and all relationships within creation became subject to violence and disorder. (Gen. 4:8; 6:5 – 7; Rom. 8:20 – 22)

God chose Israel, the Jewish people, and entered into an everlasting covenant with them so they might be the firstfruits of a renewed humanity, who would mediate blessing and restoration to all the nations of the world. In gracious love, God gave to Israel the holy Torah as a covenantal way of life, and the holy Land of Israel as an inheritance and pledge of the blessing of the World to Come. (Gen. 12:1 – 3; Jer. 31:34 – 36, 35 – 37; Rom. 11:28 – 29)

In the fullness of time, the Divine Son became a human being — Yeshua the Messiah, born of a Jewish virgin, a true and perfect Israelite, a fitting representative and one-man embodiment of the entire nation. He lived as a holy *tzaddik*, fulfilling without blemish the *mitzvot* of the Torah. He brings to perfection the human expression of the divine image (Isa. 7:14; John 1:14; Gal. 4:4; Heb. 1:1 – 4; 4:15)

Yeshua died as an atonement for the sins of Israel and of the entire world. He was raised bodily from the dead, as the firstfruits of the resurrection promised to Israel as its glorification. He ascended to heaven and was there enthroned at God's right hand as Israel's Messiah, with authority extending to the ends of creation. (Isa. 53:4 – 6; Ps. 110:1; Matt. 28:18; Mk. 14:61 – 62; 1 Cor. 15:3 – 8; Phil. 2:9 – 11)

God poured out the Divine Spirit on the community of Yeshua's followers, so that they might be joined intimately to the Messiah as His Body and become the preliminary representation of the New Covenant fullness promised to Israel. To this early Jewish community God added partners from among the nations, who heard the news of God's work in Yeshua and responded to the good news with faith. (Isa. 66:20 – 21; Acts 2:1 – 21; 10:44 – 48; 15:8 – 9; Eph. 1:13; 2:11 – 22)

Messiah's community is a single community expressed in diverse forms within the Jewish community and among the nations. All are called to a dedicated life of worship, neighborly service, and public testimony to Yeshua. Unity and love

[*]Union of Messianic Jewish Congregations, "Statement of Faith," July 19, 2012. Online: http://www.mjstudies.com.

throughout the entire community confirm Yeshua's role, as the One sent by the Father, and God's purpose in Messiah for Israel and the Nations. (John 17:20 – 21; Acts 21:20; Gal. 2:7 – 8)

Spiritual life is grounded in godly family units within the relational framework of congregations, whereby persons are to be encouraged, trained, and disciplined. Families in Messianic Jewish congregations should be strengthened and established in their Jewish calling to covenant life. Messianic Jewish congregations are called to connect in Messianic Jewish associations, where they will find mutual enrichment and accountability. (Matt. 18:15 – 18; Gal. 6:1 – 2; Rom. 9:1 – 5; 1 Cor. 7:17 – 20)

The Torah is God's gift to Israel. It serves as the constitution of the Jewish people and thus also of the Messianic Jewish community, which comprises Israel's eschatological firstfruits. The Torah does not have the same role for Messianic communities from the nations, though it does provide spiritual nourishment as a witness to the Messiah. The Torah also provides universal norms of behavior and practical life teaching for all. The Torah is to be applied anew in every generation, and in this age as is fitting to the New Covenant order. (Matt. 5:17 – 20; 2 Tim. 3:16 – 17; 1 Cor. 7:17 – 20)

Forgiveness of sins, spiritual renewal, union with Messiah, the empowering and sanctifying presence of the indwelling *Ruach Ha Kodesh*, and the confident hope of eternal life and a glorious resurrection are now available to all, Jews and Gentiles, who put their faith in Yeshua, the Risen Lord, and in obedience to His word are joined to Him and His Body through immersion and sustained in that union through Messiah's remembrance meal. Yeshua is the Mediator between God and all creation, and no one can come to the Father except through Him. (Matt. 28:19 – 20; Lk. 24:46 – 48; Jn. 14:6; Rom. 6:22, 23; 1 Cor. 11:23 – 27)

Messiah Yeshua will return to Jerusalem in glory at the end of this age, to rule forever on David's throne. He will effect the restoration of Israel in fullness, raise the dead, save all who belong to Him, judge the wicked not written in the Book of Life who are separated from His presence, and accomplish the final *Tikkun Olam* in which Israel and the nations will be united under Messiah's rule forever. This restoration will bring everlasting joy for those who belong to Him. They will live forever in an order of mutual blessing and fellowship with God, in a cosmos perfected beyond description. (Isa. 9:4 – 5/5 – 6; Rom. 8:18 – 19; Rev. 20:11 – 15; 21:1 – 4)

The writings of Tanakh and Brit Hadasha are divinely inspired and fully trustworthy (true), a gift given by God to His people, provided to impart life and to form, nurture, and guide them in the ways of truth. They are of supreme and final authority in all matters of faith and practice. (2 Tim. 3:16, 17; 2 Pet. 1:19 – 21)

The Jewish tradition serves as the living link that connects us as contemporary Jews to our biblical past and provides resources needed to develop a Messianic Jewish way of life and thought. Furthermore, the Christian theological tradition offers riches of insight into the revelation of the Messiah and His will, and Messianic Jews need to draw upon this wealth. (1 Thess. 2:15; Rom. 13:7; Jude 3)

10:35, 36, which contains 85 letters] renders the hands ritually unclean. All the Holy Writings render the hands ritually unclean" (*m. Yad.* 3.5).

The phrase "renders the hands ritually unclean" is often understood in Judaism as the equivalent of "is canonical." In fact, it refers to the status and effect of Holy Writings when they are written to exacting standards on parchment scrolls. Even a single mistake or smudged letter disqualifies a scroll, changing its status so that it no longer "renders the hands ritually unclean." A full explanation of ritual purity is beyond the scope of this essay; suffice it to say that ritual uncleanness (1) has nothing to do with physical cleanliness; (2) has nothing to do with sin; and (3) is conveyed by contact with material that is associated with certain key issues of life and death (such as the act of giving birth or contact with a corpse). The properly inscribed text of Holy Writings is considered to be such an issue of life and therefore it renders ritually unclean whoever touches it. Although the method of removing ritual uncleanness has not been in effect since before the Mishnah's time, the status of properly inscribed scrolls remains holy in Jewish thought and, when written properly in every respect, they render the hands ritually unclean.

In Judaism, the only writings that "render the hands ritually unclean" are the thirty-nine writings that make up the Tanakh. Other writings of Jewish tradition, however important a role they may play in the process of biblical interpretation and Jewish practice, do not share this unique status of holiness.

The Torah scroll is accorded great respect and handled with care in Messianic synagogues. The congregation rises when the Torah is taken out of the ark (the synagogue cabinet in which the scrolls are stored) and later when it is returned. Before the Torah is chanted using accent marks that are over a millennium old, it is carried throughout the synagogue so that everyone can touch it indirectly with an object such as the corner of a prayer garment or a Bible (which does not render the hands ritually unclean), to indicate their respect and affection for the Torah.

Handwritten extracts from the Torah have a unique place in Jewish prayer and the sanctity of the Jewish home. Participants in designated prayer services strap small boxes called tefillin (phylacteries) on one arm and on their forehead.[18] These boxes each contain four portions of Scripture: the Shema (Deut 6:4 – 9), which declares the One God; Deuteronomy 11:13 – 21, expressing the rewards for obeying and punishments for disobeying the Torah; Exodus 13:1 – 10, which concerns the duty of Jews always to remember the redemption from Egyptian bondage; and Exodus 13:11 – 16, concerning the obligation of Jews to inform their children of these things. The Jewish home is sanctified by the use of a small written scroll called a *mezuzah* on which the first two paragraphs of the Shema are written, then placed in a small box and affixed to the doorposts of Messianic Jewish homes just as they are found on the doorposts of traditional Jews.[19] The *mezuzah* is a reminder of the Exodus from Egypt, when the

---

18. Toby Janicki, *Tefillin: A Study on the Commandment of Tefillin* (Mayim Chayim Series; Marshfield, Mo.: First Fruits of Zion, 2010), 1 – 68. Cf. Toby Janicki, *Tzitzit: You Shall Make Yourself Tassels on the Four Corners of the Garment* (Mayim Chayim Series; Marshfield, Mo.: First Fruits of Zion, 2011), 1 – 67.

19. Toby Janicki, *Mezuzah: You Shall Write Them upon the Doorposts of Your House and upon Your Gates* (Mayim Chayim Series; Marshfield, Mo.: First Fruits of Zion, 2007), 1 – 37.

lamb's blood smeared on the doorpost marked the Jewish homes that the angel passed over during the plague of the firstborn.

The Messianic Jewish canon consists of the Tanakh and the B'rit Chadashah (the New Testament). The Tanakh is written in an ancient form of Hebrew, the "Holy Language." Sections of the Torah and Prophets are chanted publicly in Hebrew during weekly synagogue services. Portions of the Writings, the third part of the Jewish canon, are chanted in Hebrew on certain festival days. Later forms of Hebrew are found in rabbinic writings, Jewish liturgy and songs, and modern Israeli Hebrew. Hebrew is the unique language of the Jews and therefore of Messianic Jews, who appreciate the importance of Hebrew language proficiency and are increasingly involved in studying biblical, rabbinic, and modern Hebrew. One of the practical outcomes of this study is the increasing ability of a cadre of Messianic Jews to read the texts of the Tanakh and Jewish tradition in their original Hebrew. Another exciting development in Messianic Judaism is the increasing number of formal and informal programs that involve Hebrew text study.

Among the Scriptures, the Torah (the five books of Moses) holds a primary place in the history and affections of the Jewish people as the record of the progenitors of Israel and the formation of Israel as a community bound to God by the commandments (also called collectively "the Torah"). Mainstream Messianic Jews, especially those who adhere to Jewish tradition, depart from the classic Christian teaching that the Torah was made obsolete in Messiah. Rather, they see that Yeshua has affirmed the Torah as the basis for a life of covenant faithfulness in keeping with their calling as Jews (Matt 5:17 – 19).[20]

The Torah is divided into weekly portions (parashot) that form a primary object of Messianic Jewish study and preaching. As in the broader Jewish community, Messianic Jews celebrate Simchat Torah (Rejoicing of the Torah) at the end of the annual cycle of Torah readings with singing and dancing. Messianic Jews accord the Prophets and Psalms special attention as the source of a great number of passages used in the B'rit Chadashah to explain the life, teaching, and work of Yeshua and the apostles. Messianic Jewish lectionaries[21] include material from the Gospels, Acts, Epistles, and Revelation that are read publicly along with the Torah and Prophets on the Sabbath.

Current Trends

The number of Messianic Jewish commentaries on Scripture is small but growing. In English, the foremost of these is David Stern's Jewish New Testament Commentary.[22]

---

20. Richard Harvey, *Mapping Messianic Jewish Theology: A Constructive Approach* (Milton Keynes, UK: Paternoster, 2009), 140 – 222; John Fischer, "Yes, We Do Need Messianic Congregations!" in *How Jewish Is Christianity? 2 Views on the Messianic Movement* (ed. Louis Goldberg; Grand Rapids: Zondervan, 2003), 50 – 65; John Fischer, "Messianic Congregations Should Exist and Should Be Very Jewish," in *How Jewish Is Christianity?* 129 – 39.

21. See Mark S. Kinzer and Jonathan Kaplan, "Chayyei Yeshua Three-Year Besora Reading Cycle." Cited 20 February 2012. Online: http://www.umjc.org/torah-mainmenu-28/chayyei-yeshua-reading-list; Jeffrey E. Feinberg, "Flame Foundation Reading Cycle." Cited 20 February 2012. Online: http://www.flamefoundation.org/parashiot .html.

22. David H. Stern, *Jewish New Testament Commentary* (Clarksville, Md.: Jewish New Testament Publications, 1996); Hilary Le Cornu with Joseph Shulam, *A Commentary on the Jewish Roots of Galatians* (Clarksville, Md.:

It is to be expected that Messianic Jewish scholars will write additional commentaries in the coming decades. Messianic Jews are now contributing to the fields of Hebrew Bible and New Testament scholarship through the publication of monographs and journal articles informed by a Messianic Jewish perspective.[23]

The Messianic Jewish construal of the relationship between Scripture and tradition is in flux. Messianic Judaism is still in need of a canonical narrative that is clear and comprehensive, accounting for Israel's ongoing vocation as a holy people. Saal's work on the place of creation in the canonical narrative and Kinzer's work on the place of consummation are important contributions in this regard. However, like the standard narrative, a Messianic Jewish canonical narrative must also be simple enough to ensure its effectiveness among Messianic Jewish laity. In light of the intense movement-wide interest in combating supersessionism, Messianic Jewish thinkers will likely develop such a narrative in the coming decades. Given the unique status Messianic Jews accord to Scripture and the profound role it has in their thought and practice, Scripture-based reflection and writing will continue to play central roles in the future of Messianic Judaism.

Messianic Jewish Resources International, 2008); Hilary Le Cornu with Joseph Shulam, *A Commentary on the Jewish Roots of Acts* (Clarksville, Md.: Messianic Jewish Resources International, 2009); D. Thomas Lancaster, *The Holy Epistle to the Galatians* (Marshfield, Mo.: First Fruits of Zion, 2011); David B. Friedman, *Bereshit: The Book of Beginnings* (Eugene, Oreg.: Wipf and Stock, 2010); Michael L. Brown, *Jeremiah* (Expositor's Bible Commentary 7; Grand Rapids: Zondervan, 2010). The most popular Messianic Jewish Bible translation is David H. Stern, *Complete Jewish Bible* (Clarksville, Md.: Jewish New Testament Publications, 1998). Cf. *The Delitzsch Hebrew Gospels: A Hebrew/English Translation* (Marshfield, Mo.: Vine of David, 2011).

23. E.g., David J. Rudolph, *A Jew to the Jews: Jewish Contours of Pauline Flexibility in 1 Corinthians 9:19–23* (Tübingen: Mohr Siebeck, 2011); David J. Rudolph, "Paul's 'Rule in All the Churches' (1 Cor 7:17–24) and Torah-Defined Ecclesiological Variegation," *Studies in Christian-Jewish Relations* 5 (2010): 1–23. Online: http://www.mjstudies.com; David J. Rudolph, "Festivals in Genesis 1:14," *Tyndale Bulletin* 54, no. 2 (2003): 23–40. Online: http://www.mjstudies.com; David J. Rudolph, "Jesus and the Food Laws: A Reassessment of Mark 7:19b," *Evangelical Quarterly* 74, no. 4 (2002): 291–311. Online: http://www.mjstudies.com; David Rudolph et al., *The Jewish New Testament: An Introduction to Its Jewish Social and Conceptual Context* (Grand Rapids: Eerdmans, forthcoming); David Rudolph et al., eds., *New Testament after Supersessionism* (18 vols.; Eugene, Oreg.: Cascade, forthcoming); Noel Rabinowitz, "Matthew 23:2–4: Does Jesus Recognize the Authority of the Pharisees and Does He Endorse Their Halakhah?" *Journal of the Evangelical Theological Society* 46, no. 3 (September 2003): 423–47. Online: http://www.mjstudies.com; Vered Hillel et al., *Noah and His Book(s)* (Atlanta: Society of Biblical Literature, 2010); Vered Hillel, "Why *Not* Naphtali?" in *Things Revealed: Studies in Early Jewish and Christian Literature in Honor of Michael E. Stone* (ed. Esther G. Chazon et al.; Leiden, Netherlands: Brill, 2004), 279–88; Akiva Cohen, *Matthew and the Mishnah: Redefining Identity and Ethos in the Shadow of the Second Temple's Destruction* (Tübingen: Mohr Siebeck, forthcoming); Isaac W. Oliver, "Torah Praxis after 70 CE: Reading Matthew and Luke-Acts as Jewish Texts" (PhD diss., University of Michigan, forthcoming).

For Further Reading

Feinberg, Jeffrey E. "A Messianic Jewish Reading Cycle." *Kesher: A Journal of Messianic Judaism* 8 (Winter 1999): 65–88.

———. *Walk: A Messianic Jewish Devotional Commentary for Readers of the Torah, Haftarah, and B'rit Chadashah.* 5 vols. Clarksville, Md.: Lederer, 1998–2003.

First Fruits of Zion. Online: http://www.torahclub.org. A subscription-based, Messianic Jewish Bible-study program.

Friedman, David. *They Loved the Torah: What Yeshua's First Followers Really Thought about the Law.* Baltimore: Lederer, 2001.

Kinzer, Mark S. "Beginning with the End: The Place of Eschatology in the Messianic Jewish Canonical Narrative." Pages 91–125 in *Israel's Messiah and the People of God: A Vision for Messianic Jewish Covenant Fidelity.* Edited by Jennifer M. Rosner. Eugene, Oreg.: Cascade, 2011. Online: http://www.mjstudies.com.

———. "Scripture as Inspired, Canonical Tradition." Paper presented at the Hashivenu Forum, Pasadena, Calif., 2001. Online: http://www.mjstudies.com.

MJ Studies. Online: http://www.mjstudies.com. A gateway to scholarship that makes a cogent case for post-supersessionist interpretation of the New Testament and Messianic Judaism.

Nichol, Richard C. "Messianic Jewish Preaching: Handling the Sacred Text in Light of Sacred Relationships." *Kesher: A Journal of Messianic Judaism* 8 (Winter 1999): 3–38.

Resnik, Russell. *Creation to Completion: A Guide to Life's Journey from the Five Books of Moses.* Clarksville, Md.: Lederer, 2006.

———. *Gateways to Torah: Joining the Ancient Conversation on the Weekly Portion.* Baltimore: Lederer, 2000.

Rudolph, David, Joel Willitts, Justin K. Hardin, and J. Brian Tucker, eds. *New Testament after Supersessionism.* 18 vols. Eugene, Oreg.: Cascade, forthcoming.

Rudolph, David J. "Paul and the Torah according to Luke." *Kesher: A Journal of Messianic Judaism* 14, no. 1 (2002): 61–73. Online: http://www.mjstudies.com.

———. "Scripture Memory in the Jewish Tradition." *Kesher: A Journal of Messianic Judaism* 8 (1999): 102–11.

Saal, Paul. "Re-Imagining of the Canonical Text." Paper presented at the Hashivenu Forum, Pasadena, Calif., February 2001. Online: http://www.mjstudies.com.

Willitts, Joel, David Rudolph, and Justin K. Hardin. *The Jewish New Testament: An Introduction to Its Jewish Social and Conceptual Context.* Grand Rapids: Eerdmans, forthcoming.

CHAPTER 5

Messianic Jews and Jewish Tradition

Carl Kinbar

Jewish tradition is a network of interrelated practices, texts, and concepts that has been developed and passed down in Jewish communities from generation to generation. These include, for example, the conduct and content of prayer; norms of ethical behavior; texts such as the Scriptures, Talmud, and midrash[1] collections; ritual items; lifestyle; and lifecycle events. These practices, texts, and concepts are carried forward in the context of the ongoing interpretation, debate, and modeling that are the glue of Jewish tradition.

All forms of Messianic Judaism have at least these three characteristics in common: they embrace the unique status of the person, words, and work of Yeshua the Messiah; they view the Scriptures as normative; and they observe some level of traditional Jewish practice. However, while the status of Yeshua and the Scriptures is normative, there are differing views on the value of Jewish tradition and its place in Messianic Jewish life.[2] This variety is most evident in the widely divergent practices that can be observed from one Messianic Jewish congregation to the next. Even within congregations, there is often uncertainty or tension about the role of tradition. Messianic Jewish celebration of Passover is a case in point.

Passover

The Scriptures, which are the central texts of Messianic Judaism, specify that a certain day must be set aside each year for the celebration of Passover, followed by the seven-day Feast of Unleavened Bread. After certain preparations at home, all Jews must go up to Jerusalem where a Passover lamb is sacrificed in the Temple for each family and then cooked and eaten according to Scriptural protocols. Even while the Second Temple stood, traditions about the manner in which Passover is observed began to develop.

When the Second Temple was destroyed, Jews could no longer go up to Jerusalem to sacrifice and eat the Passover lamb; therefore it was no longer possible to observe all the commandments related to Passover. Over time, the remaining commandments to eat unleavened bread and bitter herbs, along with related traditions that had developed over time, were fashioned into an elaborate Passover observance, including a

---

1. Midrash is a genre of early rabbinic interpretation of Scripture.
2. The relationship of Messianic Judaism to Christian tradition deserves separate treatment and is not addressed in this essay.

celebration (called a *seder*, or "order" of service) with an accompanying written or printed script (the Haggadah).

The great majority of Messianic Jews follow these traditions loosely (like other non-Orthodox Jews) when celebrating Passover in their own congregations and homes. Their approach is eclectic, incorporating elements that are considered necessary to make the observance truly Jewish, including those customs found in Scripture. They do not consider the entirety of the Passover tradition to be normative. These Messianic Jews tend to omit traditions they consider strange, irrelevant, or too lengthy. At the same time, in order to ensure that their celebration of Passover is centered on Yeshua, Messianic Jews introduce New Covenant passages, especially the New Covenant identification of Yeshua as the Passover lamb (1 Cor 5:7).

During the past twenty years, some Messianic Jewish leaders have advocated for close adherence to Jewish tradition. These leaders consider the body of Passover traditions to be normative. They consider it their obligation and pleasure as Jews to observe Passover in an entirely traditional manner. The majority of Messianic Jewish leaders have remained unconvinced, retaining their eclectic approach. These disparate approaches have occasioned much heated debate and a significant level of stress in Messianic Judaism.

The relationship of Messianic Judaism to Jewish tradition is also expressed in attitudes toward texts such as the Talmud and toward Jewish prayer, both of which lie at the core of traditional Jewish life.

The Talmud

The Babylonian Talmud consists primarily of detailed discussions concerning the Scripture-based norms of Jewish life. The discussions in the Talmud, which took place over a period of several centuries in the early Common Era, investigate the nature and underlying principles of these norms and seek to define them in practical terms. The Talmud enjoys a status among traditional Jews that is surpassed only by the Scriptures and their center, the Torah (the Pentateuch).

While the Talmud is the main object of traditional Jewish study, most Messianic Jews have never seen, much less studied, a page of Talmud. Despite this lack of firsthand knowledge, they are generally wary of the Talmud, or even antagonistic toward it. A small minority have a more positive stance toward the Talmud as a source of Jewish norms that they consider to be essential to Jewish, and therefore Messianic Jewish, identity.

Jewish Prayer

Messianic Jews have a more positive attitude toward Jewish prayer and the Siddur, the traditional Jewish prayer book. Although they may object to certain passages in the Siddur that they consider inconsistent with the Scriptures, every Messianic Jewish service includes at least one or two selections from the Siddur. A modest number of congregations use a substantial amount of material from the Siddur. A small number consider it a normative text that may not be altered by addition or abbreviation.

Messianic Jewish attitudes toward Passover practices, the Talmud, and Jewish prayer reflect an underlying divide concerning the relevance and authority of Jewish tradition. While some Messianic Jews regard Jewish tradition in a positive light and consider it to have some level of inherent authority, most regard tradition with considerable caution and consider only its biblically justified practices to be authoritative. The former assert that Jewish tradition should be a formative influence in Messianic Judaism; the latter argue that selected traditions may serve as valuable practices that may be adapted to Messianic Jewish culture. These different approaches do not reflect mere preference for one set of practices versus another; they are rooted in differing underlying theological stances that are expressed in Messianic Jewish theological writings.

Among Messianic Jewish leaders, there is a consensus that the Scriptures are the central and primary (or even the only) Messianic Jewish sacred texts. While it is also evident to most of these leaders that the Scriptures do not function alone but in concert with tradition, the precise nature and outworking of this relationship is a matter of contention. Thus Messianic Jewish leaders hold a wide variety of views on the extent to which Jewish tradition should provide context and practical guidance for contemporary Messianic Jewish life. A discussion of these views is beyond the scope of this essay and has been dealt with elsewhere.[3] Suffice it to say that the practical and theological tensions existing in Messianic Judaism over this issue are present at every level.

Since the eclectic approach has been advanced from the perspective that Jews are not bound in any way by Jewish tradition, it entails no clear guidelines for what Messianic Jewish practice should look like. However, three Messianic Jewish organizations have published official documents that understand Jewish tradition as binding in some way. To varying degrees, these documents describe what Messianic Jews should do and how Messianic Jewish practice should look. These organizations are Hashivenu, the Union of Messianic Jewish Congregations (UMJC), and the Messianic Jewish Rabbinical Council (MJRC).[4] Their official documents represent a Messianic Judaism that has engaged more seriously with Jewish tradition, and is more positive toward it, than the general body of Messianic Jewish writings.

Hashivenu Core Values

Hashivenu is a board-run organization founded in 1997 by several UMJC-ordained rabbis to promote "an authentic expression of Jewish life maintaining substantial continuity with Jewish tradition."[5] Hashivenu is programmatically simple: it hosts an annual theological forum and has a website. Although it has no membership,

3. See Richard Harvey, *Mapping Messianic Jewish Theology: A Constructive Approach* (Carlisle, UK: Paternoster, 2009), 140–222.

4. The author of this essay volunteers with the UMJC and is a member of the MJRC. He participated in committee work on parts of the MJRC document under discussion, but was not involved in the genesis or overall architecture of the document.

5. Hashivenu, "We Cry Hashivenu!" Cited 6 March 2012. Online: http://www.hashivenu.org.

Hashivenu has come to represent the sentiments of many tradition-oriented Messianic Jews.

The Hashivenu paper "Values and Convictions of Hashivenu" (1999)[6] expresses the principles that have guided Hashivenu since its inception. It articulates a fully positive view of Jewish tradition and its importance for Messianic Jewish thought and practice, describing the tradition as a heritage that informs and transforms Messianic Jews and Messianic Judaism.

In its fifth core value, the paper outlines the relationship of Torah (or, more broadly, the Scriptures), rabbinic tradition, and community: "The richness of the rabbinic tradition is a valuable part of our heritage as Jewish people.... The Bible cannot be understood apart from a community context which helps one understand its deepest meanings. In this way, obedience might become incarnate in daily life." The paper thus construes rabbinic tradition as embedded in a community that exists over time. The way Torah has been understood and practiced by the community over the generations serves as the context for Jews today (including Messianic Jews) to understand and practice it.

The fifth core value is expressed largely in narrative form, giving the sense that the convictions it expresses were clarified and developed gradually by members of Hashivenu:

> We also began to appreciate how our own spiritual lives stood to benefit from the fruit of thousands of years of Jewish struggle for understanding.... We began to lean upon these structural pillars [the three pillars of Torah, liturgical worship, and deeds of kindness] which stabilize Jewish religious life, understanding that they could help strengthen us and the Messianic Jewish community as well.... In all these ways and more, we have become informed and transformed by our own heritage.

The thought here is that Jewish tradition not only informs the thought and practice of the Jewish community in a general way; it also strengthens the spiritual lives of individual Jews.

Perhaps because it is written as a journal of discovery of the richness of Jewish tradition, the Hashivenu paper extols the virtues of Jewish tradition in only a general way. It does not offer concrete guidance or discuss specific factors involved in "maintaining substantial continuity with Jewish tradition" in a twenty-first-century Messianic Jewish context.

The UMJC Statement

The UMJC, an association of Messianic Jewish congregations, was formed in 1979. It is a "big tent" organization that includes congregations with varied approaches to Jewish tradition. In 2002, its delegate body affirmed the "Defining Messianic Judaism"

---

6. Hashivenu, "Values and Convictions of Hashivenu." Cited 6 March 2012. Online: http://www.hashivenu.org/index.php?option=com_content&view=article&id=47:principles&catid=35:principles&Itemid=54.

statement,[7] written by Mark Kinzer and Dan Juster, two prominent leaders in the Messianic Jewish movement and members of the UMJC Theology Committee. The statement discusses the relationship between Messianic Judaism and Jewish tradition in its Basic Statement and at the conclusion of its Expanded Statement. The Basic Statement begins with this sentence:

> The Union of Messianic Jewish Congregations (UMJC) envisions Messianic Judaism as a movement of Jewish congregations and groups committed to Yeshua the Messiah that embrace the covenantal responsibility of Jewish life and identity rooted in Torah, expressed in tradition, and renewed and applied in the context of the New Covenant.

To my knowledge, this is the first statement by a Messianic Jewish national organization that accorded such status to Jewish tradition. Placed between the soil of Torah and the New Covenant context, tradition is the expressive mode of Messianic Jewish life and identity. By implication, traditional Jewish practices, texts, and concepts are neither stigmatized nor marginalized, but considered significant for Messianic Judaism.

The approach expressed in the Basic Statement precludes treating Messianic Judaism and Jewish tradition as disconnected entities. Messianic Judaism does not merely dabble in Jewish tradition, but renews and applies it in a New Covenant context.

The concluding paragraphs of the Expanded Statement address the place of traditional halakhah (the portion of Jewish tradition that defines Jewish practice) in Messianic Jewish life:

> Messianic Jewish halakhah is rooted in Scripture (Tanakh and the New Covenant writings), which is of unique sanctity and authority. It also draws upon Jewish tradition, especially those practices and concepts that have won near-universal acceptance by devout Jews through the centuries. Furthermore, as is common within Judaism, Messianic Judaism recognizes that halakhah is and must be dynamic, involving the application of the Torah to a wide variety of changing situations and circumstances.
>
> Messianic Judaism embraces the fullness of New Covenant realities available through Yeshua, and seeks to express them in forms drawn from Jewish experience and accessible to Jewish people.

The phrase "draws upon Jewish tradition" appears to circumscribe the role of Jewish tradition as a resource rather than a full expression of Jewish life.[8] This description seems to be in tension with the Basic Statement's description of Jewish life as "rooted in Torah, expressed in tradition [and] renewed and applied in the context of the New Covenant." The body of tradition is further restricted by privileging "prac-

---

7. Union of Messianic Jewish Congregations, "Defining Messianic Judaism," 2005. Cited 6 March 2012. Online: http://www.umjc.org/home-mainmenu-1/global-vision-mainmenu-42/13-vision/225-defining-messianic-judaism.

8. Cf. the UMJC's "Statement of Faith," which affirms: "The Jewish tradition serves as the living link that connects us as contemporary Jews to our biblical past and provides resources needed to develop a Messianic Jewish way of life and thought" (Union of Messianic Jewish Congregations, "Statement of Faith," July 19, 2012. Online: http://www.mjstudies.com.

tices and concepts that have won near-universal acceptance by devout Jews through the centuries," since the number of such accepted practices and concepts has diminished considerably in the past two centuries. In fact, the standard of "near-universal acceptance by devout Jews" is itself a modern innovation. Before modernity, by far the most important factor in the formation of Jewish tradition was the body of normative practices as defined by generations of rabbis. The theoretical basis for the shift to acceptance by devout Jews is not explained.

To summarize, the UMJC statement acknowledges the distinct and valuable place of Jewish tradition in Messianic Jewish life and identity. However, it also limits the role of tradition. Finally, by substituting "experience" for "tradition," the UMJC statement obscures the relationship between Messianic Judaism and Jewish tradition. Like the Hashivenu paper, and perhaps in part because of its brevity, the statement does not discuss in detail the factors that come into play as Messianic Judaism adopts (or draws from) Jewish tradition.

MJRC "Standards of Observance"

In 2006, a group of Messianic Jewish rabbis (all UMJC-ordained) and associates formally incorporated as the Messianic Jewish Rabbinical Council. For the MJRC, "Messianic Jewish practice [is] rooted in Torah, instructed by Tradition, and faithful to Messiah Yeshua in the twenty-first century."[9] This description is similar to the one found in the UMJC's "Defining Messianic Judaism" statement.[10] However, where the UMJC statement configures tradition as an expression of Jewish life and Torah on the one hand and subject to renewal and application in the New Covenant on the other, the MJRC document depicts tradition in the role of an instructor who "helps us to identify the shape of obedience, so that we might retrace with the stylus of our own lives patterns of holiness worn deep by generations of our forebears."[11]

The MJRC "Standards" document describes factors involved in the development of Messianic Jewish halakhah in the twenty-first century. The document notes that the norms found in Scripture do not stand alone:

While all Halakhah is rooted in Scripture, the text usually provides limited information on how the mitzvot [commandments] are to be lived out and how they are to be adapted to new circumstances. In order to add concrete substance to Halakhic decision making, we must have recourse to the way the mitzvot have been understood and observed by Jews throughout history and in the present.... Thus, while we may critique traditional rulings, and argue for alternative positions, we should be reluctant to depart from Halakhic rulings accepted by Jews throughout the centuries and held today by most of the branches of Judaism and most committed Jews.[12]

---

9. Messianic Jewish Rabbinical Council, "Standards of Observance" (West Haven, Conn.: MJRC, 2011), 1. Cited 6 March 2012. Online: http://ourrabbis.org/main/documents/MJRC_Standards_Aug2011.pdf.
10. The similarities in wording between the two documents can be explained in part by the participation of Mark Kinzer in the writing of both.
11. Messianic Jewish Rabbinical Council, "Standards of Observance," 30.
12. Messianic Jewish Rabbinical Council, "Standards of Observance," 5.

Like the UMJC's "near-universal acceptance" principle, the standard articulated here rests on a modern innovation that implicitly accepts a certain shrinkage of tradition that has taken place in the past two centuries. And yet, the inclusion of the term "Halakhic rulings" implies the generative activity of the rabbis who have been responsible for these rulings (and without whom there would be no commonly accepted practices). As the document states in numerous places, what we have called "Jewish tradition" in this essay is actually rabbinic tradition. Thus, the document proposes a Messianic Judaism that is oriented toward a form of tradition that originates with the rabbis and Jewish communities of the past and also engages with the Jewish consensus of the present.

The MJRC "Standards" document also speaks of the changed circumstance of Jewish communities that are no longer isolated from their surrounding cultures but are now deeply embedded in modern life. The document recognizes that the non-Orthodox branches of Judaism have already responded to some of these changes (for example, by elevating the status and halakhic obligations of women). The document urges that Messianic Judaism look to these branches of Judaism for guidance:[13]

> Like Conservative, Reform, and Reconstructionist branches of Judaism, we recognize that the new circumstances of the modern world require adaptation in traditional practices. Our Halakhic decision making will require thoughtful reflection on these new circumstances, and the changes they may require. In this process, we should pay special attention to the Halakhic analysis and rulings of these branches of Judaism, and learn from them.[14]

Despite this recommendation, the document does not often refer to the halakhic analyses or rulings of these other branches. In the portion dealing with specific standards,[15] the vast majority of authoritative sources are found in the Hebrew Scriptures and traditional writings such as the Babylonian Talmud and later compendiums of halakhah. The rulings of Conservative and Reform Judaism are occasionally cited as precedents.[16] Contemporary Orthodox and Conservative books are also used to clarify halakhic practice.

The MJRC "Standards" document also discusses the contribution of the New Covenant writings to the formation of Messianic Jewish halakhah. In the Gospels, Yeshua did not focus on issuing halakhic rulings but functioned primarily as "a prophetic teacher who illumined the purpose of the Torah and the inner orientation we should have in fulfilling [it]." Nevertheless, "his example and his instruction are definitive for us in matters of Halakhah as in every other sphere." The remainder of the New Covenant writings shows us "how the early Jewish believers in Yeshua combined a

---

13. Orthodox Judaism has resisted these adaptations.

14. Messianic Jewish Rabbinical Council, "Standards of Observance," 6.

15. Messianic Jewish Rabbinical Council, "Standards of Observance," 7 – 35.

16. Conservative halakhic rulings are used as precedents on four occasions — the most significant being the ruling that driving is permissible on the Sabbath under certain circumstances — and in supporting roles three times. Reform halakhic rulings are used as precedents twice, the most significant being the legitimacy of patrilineal descent to determine Jewish status under certain circumstances. No Reconstructionist rulings are offered as precedents.

concern for Israel's distinctive calling according to the Torah with a recognition of the new relationship with God and Israel available to Gentiles in the Messiah. They also provide guidelines relevant to other areas of Messianic Jewish Halakhah."[17]

Given the unique status of Yeshua's example and teaching, and of the models provided in the remainder of the New Covenant writings, one might expect the specific practices described in this document to reflect them more overtly than they do. While the New Covenant writings are referenced a number of times to support analyses and rulings derived from other sources, they do not seem to determine individual norms. Instead, Yeshua's example of reaching out to those on the margins shapes the MJRC "Standards of Observance" as a whole in a highly innovative and pervasive manner.

> We recognize that the Messianic Jewish movement consists mainly of people unaccustomed to or uncomfortable with traditional Jewish religious life, and those we are seeking to reach for Yeshua generally have a similar background. In large part this results from the high rate of secularization and assimilation among twenty-first century Jews. However, this profile also fits our calling as a movement for Yeshua within the Jewish world. Just as he came to seek and save the lost, and devoted his energy especially to reaching the disenfranchised among the Jewish people, so our mission is directed primarily to Jews who have little knowledge of or attachment to traditional Jewish practice.[18]

In this statement, it is clear that the MJRC desires not only to bring the knowledge of Yeshua to the wider Jewish world, but also to return disaffected and assimilated Jews to a more traditional orientation. The council therefore decided not to formulate a fully orbed Messianic Jewish halakhah but "to presume the basic teaching of the halakhic tradition, especially as understood by contemporary authorities who appreciate the dynamic nature of that tradition and the need for its wise development in a rapidly changing world."[19] They fleshed out this approach in a set of "Basic" and commended "Expanded" practices that are more reachable for most Jews today. These levels of practice do not substitute for halakhah but represent and point toward it.

The MJRC "Standards" document continues, "We want to set out on a journey with Yeshua that will lead us all, in diverse ways, to a richer and fuller life as Jews obedient to the Torah through Messiah Yeshua, and obedient to Yeshua through the Torah."[20] This sentence depicts a Messianic Judaism that is rooted in Yeshua and embedded in Jewish tradition. However, it also recognizes that Jewish tradition is not synonymous with today's Orthodox Judaism but is amenable to a diversity of practices within a dynamic tradition.

As the MJRC "Standards of Observance" is expanded to cover other areas, particularly the role of Gentiles in Messianic synagogues, distinctly Messianic Jewish practices may become more prominent. Nevertheless, in its current form, the "Standards" document as a whole is clearly an innovative expression of Jewish tradition, not only

17. Messianic Jewish Rabbinical Council, "Standards of Observance," 4.
18. Messianic Jewish Rabbinical Council, "Standards of Observance," 1.
19. Messianic Jewish Rabbinical Council, "Standards of Observance," 2.
20. Messianic Jewish Rabbinical Council, "Standards of Observance," 2.

because of its Messianic Jewish framework but because its very substance is informed by the example and teaching of Yeshua in reaching out to the disenfranchised. It does not represent an "Orthodox" version of Messianic Judaism but the beginnings of a distinctly Messianic Jewish expression of traditional Jewish life.

Conclusion

All forms of Messianic Judaism engage in traditional Jewish practices. On one end of the spectrum, even the most nontraditional forms of Messianic Judaism connect with the tradition by adapting elements of traditional Jewish prayer and ways of celebrating the festival days such as Passover.[21] On the other end of the spectrum, tradition-oriented Messianic Judaism views Jewish tradition as a formative influence in personal and communal Messianic Jewish life. The tension between these positions is apparent, focusing on whether, and in what way, Jewish tradition is normative for Messianic Jews. It remains to be seen whether this tension will be resolved in some way or if it will result in two different versions of Messianic Judaism.

For Further Reading

Brown, Michael L. *Answering Jewish Objections to Jesus: Traditional Jewish Objections*. Vol. 5. San Francisco: Purple Pomegranate, 2009.

Cohn-Sherbok, Dan. "Messianic Jewish Observance." Pages 87 – 166 in *Messianic Judaism*. London: Cassell, 2000.

Dauermann, Stuart. "Transmitting Tradition: The Biblical and Jewish Mandate." *Kesher: A Journal of Messianic Judaism* 1 (1994): 155 – 79.

Eby, Aaron. *Biblically Kosher: A Messianic Jewish Perspective on Kashrut*. Marshfield, Mo.: First Fruits of Zion, 2012.

Fischer, John. "The Place of Rabbinic Tradition in a Messianic Jewish Lifestyle." Pages 145 – 70 in *The Enduring Paradox: Exploratory Essays in Messianic Judaism*. Edited by John Fischer. Baltimore: Lederer, 2000.

Juster, Daniel C. "The Value of Tradition." Paper presented at the Hashivenu Forum, Pasadena, Calif., 2003. Online: http://www.mjstudies.com.

Kinbar, Carl. "Israel, Torah, and the Knowledge of God: Engaging the Jewish Conversation." *Kesher: A Journal of Messianic Judaism* 24 (2010): 1 – 28. Cited 10 October 2011. Online: http://www.kesherjournal.com/Issue-24/Israel-Torah-and-the-Knowledge-of-God-Engaging-the-Jewish-Conversation.

Kinzer, Mark S. "Messianic Judaism and Jewish Tradition in the Twenty-First Century: A Biblical Defense of Oral Torah." Pages 29 – 61 in *Israel's Messiah and the People of God: A Vision for Messianic Jewish Covenant Fidelity*. Edited by Jennifer M. Rosner. Eugene, Oreg.: Cascade, 2011. Online: http://www.mjstudies.com.

———. "Scripture and Tradition." Pages 29 – 37 in *Voices of Messianic Judaism: Confronting Critical Issues Facing a Maturing Movement*. Edited by Dan Cohn-Sherbok. Baltimore: Lederer, 2001.

Kinzer, Mark S., John Fieldsend, Tsvi Sadan, and Barney Kasdan. "Forum: Authority Old and New." *Kesher: A Journal of Messianic Judaism* 5 (1997): 96 – 116.

21. These practices are often used in ways that call into question the group's depth of understanding of the tradition.

Messianic Jewish Rabbinical Council. "Standards of Observance." West Haven, Conn.: Messianic Jewish Rabbinical Council, 2011. Cited 6 March 2012. Online: http://ourrabbis.org/main/documents/MJRC_Standards_Aug2011.pdf.

Resnik, Russell. "Halakhic Responsibility." Pages 39–46 in *Voices of Messianic Judaism: Confronting Critical Issues Facing a Maturing Movement*. Edited by Dan Cohn-Sherbok. Baltimore: Lederer, 2001.

Schiffman, Michael H. "Messianic Judaism and Jewish Tradition in the Twenty-First Century: A Historical Perspective on 'Oral Torah.'" Paper presented at the Hashivenu Forum, Pasadena, Calif., 2003. Online: http://www.mjstudies.com.

Silberling, Kay, Paul Saal, Elazar Brandt, and David J. Rudolph, "Forum: Oral Tradition and New Covenant Scripture." *Kesher: A Journal of Messianic Judaism* 8 (1999): 39–59.

Stern, David H. "Halakhic Issues in Messianic Judaism." Pages 158–87 in *Messianic Judaism: A Modern Movement with an Ancient Past*. Clarksville, Md.: Lederer, 2007.

CHAPTER 6

Messianic Jewish Ethics

Russ Resnik

A Jewish reclamation of Jesus has been in process for decades, reclaiming Jesus not as the Messiah promised in the Hebrew Scriptures, but as a great Jewish teacher and moral example — perhaps the greatest of all. At the close of World War II, for example, novelist Sholem Asch wrote, "No one before him and no one after him has bound our world with the fetters of law, of justice, and of love, and brought it to the feet of the one living Almighty God as effectively as did this personage who came to an Israelite house in Nazareth of Galilee — and this he did, not by the might of the sword, of fire and steel, like the lawgivers of other nations, but by the power of his mighty spirit and his teachings."[1]

A generation later, the Orthodox Jewish scholar Pinchas Lapide commented on the Sermon on the Mount, "In all this messianic urgency toward the humanization God wills for all the children of Adam and toward the humanization of this earth, in the deathless power of hope that finds in reliance on 'the above' the courage to go 'forward,' Jesus of Nazareth was 'the central Jew,' as Martin Buber called him, the one who spurs us all to emulation."[2]

Such quotations could be multiplied many times, and most would reflect the same emphasis on Jesus' "spirit and teachings." The Jewish reclamation of Jesus tends to focus above all on his ethical teachings and example, rather than on the questions of his messianic identity and mission that fascinate the Christian world.

More recently, the Christian world, which of course recognizes Jesus as Messiah, has entered its own process of reclamation of Jesus as a Jew, who can be fully understood only within the Jewish context of his message and life work. Lapide quotes a line made famous by Pope John Paul II: "Whoever meets Jesus Christ meets Judaism."[3] Numerous Christian writers have expanded on this idea. Brad Young, for example, writes, "Jesus is Jewish both in his ethnic background and in his religious thought and practice.... The teachings of Jesus are intimately connected to his Jewish background, which runs deeper than flesh and blood. The Judaism of Jesus is represented in his profound theology of God and the inestimable value of each person created in the divine image. Jesus is Jewish."[4]

---

1. Scholem Asch, *One Destiny: An Epistle to the Christians* (New York: G. P. Putnam's Sons, 1945), 5.
2. Pinchas Lapide, *The Sermon on the Mount: Utopia or Program for Action?* (Eugene, Oreg.: Wipf and Stock, 1999), 8.
3. Lapide, *Sermon on the Mount*, 8.
4. Brad H. Young, *Jesus the Jewish Theologian* (Peabody, Mass.: Hendrickson, 1995), xxxiv – xxxv.

Like the Jewish reclamation, the Christian reclamation often emphasizes the ethics of Jesus. Thus, New Testament scholar Richard Hays writes, "This is first and foremost the way in which the historical Jesus should be understood: he was a prophet in the tradition of the prophets of Israel, warning of God's judgment on Israel, calling Israel to repentance and acknowledgement of God's justice in human affairs."[5]

Hays goes on to say that, if his portrayal of the historical Jesus is sound, "the continuity of the gospel with Israel's heritage would be highlighted" in any discussion of New Testament ethics. In other words, for Hays, Jesus' Jewishness is most evident in his prophetic call to ethical living, and his Jewishness in turn is essential to understanding that call.

A 2008 article in *Time* magazine listed "Re-Judaizing Jesus" as one of "Ten Ideas That Are Changing the World." "The shift [in Christian thinking] came in stages: first a brute acceptance that Jesus was born a Jew and did Jewish things; then admission that he and his interpreter Paul saw themselves as Jews even while founding what became another faith; and today, recognition of what the Rev. Bruce Chilton, author of *Rabbi Jesus*, calls Jesus' passionate dedication 'to Jewish ideas of his day' on everything from ritual purity to the ideal of the kingdom of God — ideas he rewove but did not abandon."[6]

This dual Jewish-Christian reclamation of Jesus helps to define what we mean by our title, "Messianic Jewish Ethics." Yeshua's ethical message is profoundly Jewish as well as profoundly significant for Christians. Messianic Jewish ethics understands this message in ways that build upon both Jewish and Christian readings, but that are distinct from both and unique to the Messianic Jewish community.

One of the fruits of the Jewish reclamation of Yeshua is the realization that the ethics of Yeshua are indeed *Jewish* ethics brought to their highest point. Messianic Jewish ethics carry this vital truth a step further, to see Yeshua not just as teaching ethics, but as embodying his ethics to reveal the character of God himself. Indeed, in Yeshua, the God of Israel expresses the very core of all Jewish ethical teaching and provides the model toward which all ethical behavior strives. Yeshua's ethics are *revelatory*, uniquely displaying the character and presence of the God of Israel.

Yeshua's revelatory ethics give rise to two corollaries for Messianic Jewish ethics: First, they entail *Jewish loyalty*. Just as Yeshua lived his ethics among, and as part of, the Jewish people, so should his Jewish followers. Second, this Jewish loyalty should lead Messianic Jews to *embrace their marginalization* within the wider Jewish community as a unique opportunity for testimony and service. Acceptance of this position is essential to countering the accusation that Messianic Judaism is unethical in identifying itself as a form of Judaism while affirming Yeshua as Messiah.

Yeshua's unique ethical message and these two corollaries are foundational to Messianic Jewish ethics.

---

5. Richard B. Hays, *The Moral Vision of the New Testament* (New York: HarperOne, 1996), 164.
6. David Van Biema, "Re-Judaizing Jesus," *Time*, March 13, 2008. Cited 6 March 2012. Online: http://www.time.com/time/specials/2007/article/0,28804,1720049_1720050_1721663,00.html.

Yeshua's Revelatory Ethics

Yeshua fully embodies the image of God, which is placed upon humankind from the beginning: "God created mankind in *his own image*" (Gen 1:27, emphasis added). As the divine image-bearers, the first man and woman are immediately given an assignment: "Be fruitful and increase in number; fill the earth and subdue it. Rule over the fish in the sea and the birds in the sky and over every living creature that moves on the ground" (Gen 1:28). In other words, the divine image is obviously not a physical resemblance, but neither is it an abstract spiritual resemblance. Rather, it entails representing God through active engagement with the creation. This understanding of the image of God gives rise to the Jewish idea that God does ethics before we do, that our ethical behavior is not just a matter of obedience, or even of pleasing God, but of reflecting God and his nature, fulfilling the assignment to bear the divine image. It is beyond the scope of this essay to consider the historic roots of this idea, or whether it was in place in the first century, when Messiah appeared. Rather, my point is that this idea has been inherent in Judaism throughout most of its history and is part of the Jewish ethos.

A famous passage in the Talmud reflects this idea:

> What does it mean, "You shall walk after the Lord your God"? Is it possible for a person to walk and follow in God's presence? Does not the Torah also say "For the Lord your God is a consuming fire"? (Deut 4:24). But it means to walk after the attributes of the Holy One, Blessed be He. Just as He clothed the naked, so you too clothe the naked, as it says "And the Lord made the man and his wife leather coverings and clothed them" (Gen 3:21). The Holy One, Blessed be He, visits the ill, as it says, "And God visited him in Elonei Mamreh" (Gen 18:1); so you shall visit the ill. The Holy One, Blessed be He, comforts the bereaved, as it says, "And it was after Abraham died that God blessed his son Isaac …" (Gen 25:11), so too shall you comfort the bereaved. The Holy One, Blessed be He, buries the dead, as it says, "And He buried him in the valley" (Deut 34:6), so you too bury the dead. (b. Sotah 14a)

By seeing God as the first one to exemplify such acts of kindness, Judaism roots its ethics in deep theological soil. God visiting the sick and burying the dead is not so much anthropomorphism — God pictured in human form — as a yearning to see the divine image reflected in human deeds. The Talmudic passage recognizes that the Torah itself portrays a God who is not above practical compassion and ethical behavior. Messianic Jewish ethics, therefore, embraces Yeshua's ethical teachings not as mere embellishments to his core mission, as they are sometimes understood in Christian thought, but as essential to his mission, the channel through which he reveals deity to and among humankind. Indeed, Yeshua's atoning work upon the cross and his subsequent resurrection are of the same fabric as his teachings in the Sermon on the Mount, or his instructions to his apostles in Matthew 10 — all are about self-sacrificial love that displays the character of God. Thus, Yeshua tells his followers not to resist evil, but to overcome evil with good, to turn the other cheek to the aggressor. Then he demonstrates this teaching in his response to his betrayal, trial, and crucifixion to reveal the very character of God. In Mark's account, Yeshua is finally recognized as Son of God at the moment of his death, ironically by a Gentile, the Roman centurion attending the crucifixion. John deliberately uses the ambiguous phrase "lifted up" to describe the crucifixion, by which Yeshua is literally lifted up on the cross and figuratively lifted up in glory (John 3:14 – 15; 8:28; 12:30 – 33).

Messianic Jewish ethics understands Yeshua's teachings and his deity as inseparable. Indeed, Messianic Jewish ethics sees the God of Israel revealed most fully in the concrete, sacrificial acts of Yeshua the Messiah and calls upon his followers to emulate these acts. The Jewish reclamation of Yeshua as the great ethical teacher and exemplar inevitably points to a reclamation of Yeshua as the divine Messiah.

Corollary 1: Jewish Loyalty

If Yeshua's ethics are rooted in Jewish ethics and bring them to fulfillment, following Yeshua is certainly not incompatible with loyalty to the Jewish people and their way of life. First, Yeshua said he came to restore Israel to God through sacrificing himself on their behalf — a most powerful expression of Jewish loyalty. Indeed this loyalty can help us understand more fully Yeshua's entire messianic strategy. Readers of the Gospels tend to highlight Yeshua's opposition to the religious gatekeepers of his day, who of course were Jewish, and to overlook his impassioned loyalty to the Jewish people as a whole. Thus, for example, Yeshua declares that he is sent only to the lost sheep of the house of Israel (Matt 15:24). But before Yeshua speaks of his fellow Jews as lost sheep, he has gone about "all [their] cities and villages, teaching in their synagogues, preaching the gospel of the kingdom, and healing every sickness and every disease among the people." Then Matthew adds, "But when He saw the multitudes, He was moved with compassion for them, because they were weary and scattered, like sheep having no shepherd" (Matt 9:35 – 36 NKJV). Gentile readers of the Gospels tend to emphasize the lostness of the sheep and forget that the sheep metaphor also implies Israel's chosenness. It originates with the Hebrew prophets who declare that Israel is the Lord's flock (Jer 23:1 – 2; Ezek 34:6), so precious that he will seek them out himself (Ezek 34:11 – 16), and who rebuke not the sheep so much as the shepherds who have failed them (Jer 50:6; Ezek 34:2 – 10).

Yeshua's reference to the lost sheep, then, embodies an intense loyalty to Israel that reflects God's passion for his people, his desire to restore them to himself. Other sayings of the Master hint at this same passionate loyalty, including Yeshua's longing over Jerusalem near the end of his earthly ministry, "O Jerusalem, Jerusalem, the one who kills the prophets and stones those who are sent to her! How often I wanted to gather your children together, as a hen gathers her chicks under her wings, but you were not willing!" (Matt 23:37 NKJV). *Ahavat Yisrael* — love for Israel as a people — fuels Yeshua's entire ministry among his people and indeed his entire earthly ministry among humankind.

Yeshua modeled such loyalty not only in word, but also in his own practice at key junctures. He was open to Jewish tradition because he was open to the living, breathing Jewish people, not just to an idealized image of them. For example, baptism, which Messianic Jews often translate more literally as "immersion," or *tevilah* in Hebrew, reflects Jewish practices of purification based on Leviticus. In the Second Temple period the use of the *mikveh*, or immersion pool, had expanded to include general spiritual purification or dedication, rather than just purification after specific defilement. John took this custom, which already involved tradition as well as direct biblical command, and developed it into the immersion of repentance that he urged upon everyone — not exactly what Leviticus commanded. Again, at his last Passover, Yeshua incorporated a Jewish tradition not mentioned in Scripture at all — drinking wine during the meal — and made that central to the meaning of his last supper.

It is significant that these two sacramental acts draw so heavily upon Jewish tradition rather than on the Jewish Scriptures alone. One implication is that respect for Jewish tradition is inherent to the ethics of Yeshua as an aspect of Jewish loyalty. We can also reverse this statement: it would be unethical to claim to be a Messianic *Jewish* movement and to foster anti-Jewish or anti-Semitic attitudes, including an overriding negativity toward Jewish tradition. Messianic Jewish ethics require an interpretation of Scripture that honors Jewish identity and supports its continuity, without ignoring the criticisms of some aspects of Jewish life and practice that also appear in Scripture.

Furthermore, Jewish tradition is rooted in Torah and is in general faithful to its teachings. Yeshua came not to destroy Torah and the Prophets, but to fulfill them (Matt 5:17). Jewish loyalty, then, which has historically been framed and expressed through loyalty to Torah, is by no means incompatible with loyalty to the Messiah promised in the Jewish Scriptures. Indeed, Yeshua's example suggests that a positive regard for Torah and its claims upon Jewish people is essential to his message.

Corollary 2: The Ethics of the Margins

The Jewish reclamation of Yeshua is attracted to his ethics in part because Yeshua's ethics seem like the most Jewish aspect of his whole story. Christian scholar John Howard Yoder claims that, "If Jewish historians find a new interest in Jesus as a figure in first-century history, that is certainly partly because that Jesus is more like what Jews have always been like than he is like the Christians Jews have known, especially their Constantines or their crusaders."[7]

Yeshua maintained Jewish loyalty despite his rejection by the Jewish authorities and sometimes even by his Jewish peers and friends. He accepted his undeserved marginalization and transformed it into a position of service and prophetic testimony. This quality must become part of the ethical stance of those who claim to follow Yeshua, particularly as Jews.

A Messianic Jewish colleague in South Africa recently had the opportunity to display this unique aspect of our ethical assignment. He described this opportunity in an email to his colleagues, noting that he had attended a synagogue service on the festival of Shavuot. Because he was the only *cohen* (descendant of the priestly line)

---

7. John Howard Yoder, "Jesus the Jewish Pacifist," in *The Jewish-Christian Schism Revisited* (ed. Michael G. Cartwright and Peter Ochs; Grand Rapids: Eerdmans, 2003), 87.

present, my friend was asked if he would be willing to make an *aliyah*.[8] He concurred and got ready to go up when, in front of the whole synagogue, the rabbi waved his finger and said no! My friend explained, "Somehow, although he [the rabbi] was new to the community, my reputation had preceded me. And let me tell you, I keep *shtum* [quiet, low-key]. I'm not out on the streets wearing 'Jesus made me kosher' t-shirts. But, in such a small community, everyone knows everything about another! I had to leave the congregation for a few moments so that they could announce *'eyn cohen'* [no priest is here]. Only then could I reenter and continue with the service. This, ten days after my father's burial."[9] My South African friend accepted his humiliating marginalization with no attempt to marginalize the synagogue in return. Instead, he left the service so that the gatekeepers could announce that there was no *cohen* present and move on with the service without him. Then, when the presence of a *cohen* was no longer an issue, he rejoined the congregation for the rest of the service.[10]

My friend was displaying ethics on the margins, which is the distinctive quality of Yeshua's ethics — even though Yeshua is rejected by some of his people, he never rejects his people in turn. Rather, he employs his place on the margins to display the undeserved love and favor of God. These ethics on the margins are inherent to following a Messiah who spent so much of his time among those on the margins and clashed so radically with those at the centers of power.

Stuart Dauermann applies this ethical stance to our circumstances today: "Even in contexts where other Jews might seek to exclude us and discount us for our Yeshua faith, we must never be confused about our solidarity with them. We must continue to contribute to Jewish institutions, support Jewish causes, and labor for the wellbeing of all Jews everywhere."[11]

As I mention above, Messianic Judaism is often accused of unethical behavior simply because it identifies itself as a form of Judaism while affirming Yeshua as Messiah. Rabbi Carol Harris-Shapiro writes that not believing in Jesus is a "crucial boundary marker for American Jews." Therefore, "Jews who cross the boundaries are seen to be traitors, almost violating a law of nature."[12] In response to such perceptions, we Messianic Jews must accept our place on the margins and practice loyalty to the wider Jewish community and its values from that place. At the same time, Messianic Jews must clearly identify themselves as believers in Yeshua, so that their Jewish loyalty can never be abused as a disguise or cover for evangelistic activity.[13] This self-disclosure doesn't need to be done immediately, as if a Messianic Jew needs to wear a Yeshua badge whenever he or she interacts with other Jews, but faith in Yeshua should not be

8. *Aliyah* refers to "going up" to read from the Torah portion for the week. A *cohen*, or descendant of the priestly line, is called up first, then a descendant of the Levites, then an ordinary Israelite.

9. Russell Resnik, "Hesed and Hospitality: Embracing Our Place on the Margins," *Kesher: A Journal of Messianic Judaism* 23 (2009): 7.

10. Resnik, "Hesed and Hospitality," 7 – 8.

11. Stuart Dauermann, *Son of David: Healing the Vision of the Messianic Jewish Movement* (Eugene, Oreg.: Wipf & Stock, 2010), 33.

12. Carol Harris-Shapiro, *Messianic Judaism: A Rabbi's Journey through Religious Change in America* (Boston: Beacon, 1999), 2.

13. See Jay Alan Sekulow and Joel Thornton, "Ethics in Evangelism," *Kesher: A Journal of Messianic Judaism* 2 (1995): 27 – 31.

hidden indefinitely, especially when a Messianic Jew becomes involved in significant Jewish communal activities or relationships.

A Concluding Midrash

I began writing this essay as the Jewish world was concluding its annual cycle of Torah readings. The Torah ends, of course, with the death of Moses, a story that sheds light on the three main strands of this essay.

Moses must die outside the Promised Land, but the Lord allows him a glimpse of the land, reminding him, "I have let you see it with your own eyes, but you will not cross over into it. And Moses the servant of the LORD died there in Moab, as the LORD had said. He buried him in Moab, in the valley opposite Beth Peor" (Deut 34:4 – 6). God himself buries Moses, a compassionate act that the Talmud cites, as we have seen, as an example of the loving-kindness that Jews are to practice in imitation of God.

The rabbinic sages read the Hebrew text here literally — "And Moses died at the mouth of the Lord" — indicating that Moses died by a divine kiss, as if to compensate him for the harshness of his death sentence: "Thereupon God kissed Moses and took away his soul with a kiss of the mouth, and God, if one might say so, wept,"[14] then God himself buried Moses. Both of these deeds, the kiss and the burial, display a tender humanity that the rabbis found hard to square with God's transcendence. Thus, the great medieval commentator Rashi reports, "Rabbi Ishmael said: [Moses] buried himself," based on a variant interpretation of the Hebrew.[15] But undoubtedly, in this scene, God is revealing himself through his ethics, through deeds of loving-kindness that are the essence of ideal humanness.

This portrayal underscores my first point: ethics are revelatory of God's nature. God buries Moses because he is "the compassionate and gracious God, slow to anger, abounding in love and faithfulness, maintaining love to thousands" (Exod 34:6 – 7). These divine qualities, part of what Jewish tradition calls the thirteen attributes, are not primarily theological, at least in the abstract sense, but ethical. When the Messiah appears as the self-revelation of the God of Israel, he displays those ethical qualities to the fullest, and it is the same ethic toward which Jewish discussions of the Torah consistently yearn. Messianic Jewish ethics are rooted in this understanding of God's nature as revealed in Yeshua of Nazareth.

Furthermore, in burying Moses, God supports Jewish loyalty. He not only models the importance of care for the dead, but in doing so honors a specific person, Moses the lawgiver, the one who established the norms of Jewish practice from that point on, so that Jewish loyalty is inextricable from Torah loyalty. One might think that Moses is discredited at the end of his story because he must die outside the Promised Land, but God honors him in a way that highlights and preserves his unique status. In the Jewish reading of Torah, the death of Moses is a new beginning, immediately followed by the opening chapter of Joshua. The legacy of Moses is not superseded but continued on in

---

14. J. Rabinowitz, trans., *Midrash Rabbah Deuteronomy* (New York: Soncino, 1983), 187. See also *b. B. Bat.* 17a.

15. Y. I. Z. Herczeg, trans., *Sapirstein Edition Rashi: The Torah with Rashi's Commentary Translated, Annotated and Elucidated* (Brooklyn: Mesorah, 1998), 401.

the Promised Land and throughout Israel's history, beginning with the life of Joshua. In the same way, Joshua's namesake Yeshua does not supersede the legacy of Moses, but fulfills it, revealing its depth and impact in ways that are altogether new, and yet altogether consistent with Moses' instruction.

Finally, this divine self-revelation takes place on the margins, at the extreme of death itself, when Moses is utterly alone with God. He dies not only outside the Promised Land, but even outside the encampment of Israel, so that no one knows the place of his burial. So, Jewish followers of Yeshua will often find opportunity to embody God's ethical standards, to show loyalty to God's chosen people, of which they are a part, *on the margins*. For us as Jews, it is there for the time being that we must meet our Messiah, and it is there that we may most effectively mirror his ways.

For Further Reading

Fischer, John. "Foundations of Messianic Theology: Following in Jesus' Footsteps?" *Mishkan: A Forum on the Gospel and the Jewish People* 22 (1995): 65 – 89.

Friedman, David. "Yeshua's Teaching on Divorce in Light of Hillel and Shammai." *Kesher: A Journal of Messianic Judaism* 9 (1999): 3 – 31.

Juster, Daniel. *Due Process: A Plea for Biblical Justice among God's People.* Shippensburg, Pa.: Destiny Image, 1992.

Leman, Derek. *Proverbial Wisdom & Common Sense: A Messianic Jewish Approach to Today's Issues from the Proverbs.* Clarksville, Md.: Messianic Jewish Publishers, 1999.

Levertoff, Paul Philip. *Love and the Messianic Age.* Marshfield, Mo.: Vine of David, 2009. Reprint of *Love and the Messianic Age.* London: Episcopal Hebrew Christian Church, 1923. Also Janicki, Toby, and D. Thomas Lancaster, eds. *Love and the Messianic Age: Study Guide and Commentary.* Marshfield, Mo.: Vine of David, 2009.

Resnik, Russell.———. *Divine Reversal: The Transforming Ethics of Jesus.* Clarksville, Md.: Messianic Jewish Publishers, 2010.

———. "Hesed and Hospitality: Embracing Our Place on the Margins," *Kesher: A Journal of Messianic Judaism* 23 (2009): 1 – 24. Cited 25 March 2012. Online: http://www.kesherjournal.com/Issue-23/Hesed-And-Hospitality-Embracing-Our-Place-on-the-Margins.

Riverton Mussar: A Wellspring for Ethical Change. Online: http://www.rivertonmussar.org.

Rudolph, David J. "Bilateral (Jew-Gentile) Ecclesiology and Ethics." *Verge* 1, no. 2 (2009): 4. Online: http://www.mjstudies.com.

———. *A Jew to the Jews: Jewish Contours of Pauline Flexibility in 1 Corinthians 9:19 – 23.* Tübingen: Mohr Siebeck, 2011.

Saul, Paul L. "Toward a Messianic Jewish Moral Vision." Paper presented at the annual Hashivenu Forum, Pasadena, Calif., 2005. Online: http://www.mjstudies.com.

Silberling, Kay. "Jewish Life as Sacrament." Paper presented at the annual Hashivenu Forum, Pasadena, Calif., 2005. Online: http://www.mjstudies.com.

CHAPTER 7

Messianic Jewish Outreach

Stuart Dauermann

This chapter summarizes the outreach paradigm prevalent in nineteenth- and twentieth-century Jewish missions and Hebrew Christianity, and compares it to outreach practiced in the Messianic Jewish congregational context since the early 1970s. It then examines an alternative paradigm that is increasingly finding acceptance in the Messianic Jewish movement. These outreach paradigms will be compared in three respects: the good news *message* that is communicated, the intended *milieu* where the life of faith is to be lived out, and the *methods* used to communicate the good news to Jewish people.

Hebrew Christian Outreach: Its Message and Milieu

For nineteenth- and twentieth-century missionaries to the Jews, whether Gentile or Hebrew Christian,[1] outreach was evangelism, the heart of their calling. David Rausch makes this clear, speaking of the founding of the Hebrew Christian Alliance of America (HCAA) in 1915, "The driving motive of the Jewish Christian was to be evangelism, ... [and responsibility for this] fell squarely on the shoulders of Hebrew Christians."[2]

Attacked by churchmen who were disturbed by the idea that Jewish believers in Jesus continued to share an affinity with each other and other Jews, the HCAA clarified its goals in 1920, indicating that the group was neither a church nor a denomination and had no intention of disrupting the unity of the church. Rather, their aim was to evangelize Jews and to bring them to "the true faith."[3]

Here we find in seed form the message and milieu of Hebrew Christianity. The message was the gospel of individual salvation through faith in the work of Jesus Christ, the true faith (as opposed to Judaism), and the milieu where that faith was to be lived out was the church rather than the synagogue.

Hebrew Christian Outreach: Its Methods

The missional methods employed among European Jews in the nineteenth and twentieth centuries varied as a result of local conditions and denominational factors. Yet

---

1. Hebrew Christians were church-affiliated Jewish believers in Jesus. See chapter 1 ("Messianic Judaism in Antiquity and in the Modern Era").

2. David R. Rausch, *Messianic Judaism: Its History, Theology, and Polity* (Lewiston: Edwin Mellen, 1982), 31. In his quotation, the terms "Jewish Christian" and "Hebrew Christian" are synonymous.

3. *Organ of the New York Evangelization Society* 11, no. 124 (1920): 75–78, paraphrased in Dan Cohn-Sherbok, *Messianic Judaism* (London: Continuum, 2000), 31.

in each context, the heart of the method was "the center approach." Mitch Glaser describes center activities in pre – World War II Poland, presenting a typical portrait that was replicated not only throughout Europe but also in the New World and the modern State of Israel:

> The center usually included a building with a hall for gospel meetings, a reading room for Bible study and discussion, as well as residences for the missionaries and new believers who were either newcomers into the area or had been forced from their homes for their faith. In some instances, medical and educational services were provided at these centers.
>
> Missionaries and converts also distributed tracts, held street meetings, and did personal visitation and engaged in Scripture distribution. Many of them convened children's meetings.... Some missionaries were particularly effective in reaching the destitute among the Jewish community.
>
> All missions conducted special meetings for the Jewish holidays as well as followed the pattern of regular Sabbath services and Bible studies. Unbelievers were invited to these meetings and many became believers. In Poland, generally speaking, such mercy ministries as medical work, children's education and poverty relief appeared to be less needed than in some of the other European countries.[4]

Such activities were especially aimed at addressing the social needs of poor Jews and immigrants while sharing with them the missionary's gospel. Variations on this approach are still in use today, especially where Jewish mission agencies are working with immigrants.[5] Modern center activities include distribution of literature (not only on the street but also over the internet), street meetings, personal visitation, holy day and Shabbat (Sabbath) services, Bible studies, and social services of various kinds. And just as European lay and professional missionaries itinerated in the surrounding areas, so this too remains central to the mission enterprise.

Where and Why the Messianic Jewish Congregational Outreach Approach Differs

In its methods, the Messianic Jewish movement adapts approaches used in the missions and Hebrew Christian movements, with the exception of certain confrontational approaches that are alien to its ethos. While the methods employed are similar, the message, milieu, and underlying commitments of Messianic Judaism differ from those of the Hebrew Christian/missions culture.

The reasons for these differences are rooted in underlying presuppositions. First, the Messianic Jewish ethos affirms the importance of ongoing covenantal participation with the Jewish people past, present, and future, while the Hebrew Christian/missions paradigm is individualistic. Agents of the latter message often fail to take

---

4. Mitch L. Glaser, "A Survey of Missions to the Jews in Continental Europe 1900 – 1950" (PhD diss., Fuller Seminary School of Intercultural Studies, 1998), 73 – 74.

5. Barry Yeoman, "Evangelical Movement on the Rise," *Jewish Telegraphic Agency*, November 15, 2007. Cited 12 August 2012. Online: http://www.jta.org/news/article/2007/11/15/104639/evangelicalpartI.

practical steps to preserve Jews as members of a covenant community with responsibilities to be honored.

Second, while the Messianic Jewish congregational movement relates to the Jewish community as its own community, forming synagogues mirroring those of the wider Jewish world, missionaries and Hebrew Christians generally see themselves as rooted in the church world and encourage the Jews whom they reach to affiliate with "Bible-believing churches," adopting the Gentile Christian world as their primary community of reference.[6]

Congregations within the Messianic Jewish movement have always sought to prevent communal assimilation and to fortify Jewish life and intergenerational Jewish communal cohesion.[7] Along these lines, Messianic Jews are increasingly thinking of outreach from an eschatological perspective, which highlights the communal consummation of the Jewish people.[8]

Concerning an Eschatologically Driven Messianic Jewish Outreach

That Messianic Jewish outreach may be driven by eschatological motives is nothing new, which is why the first chapter of Yaakov Ariel's sociological study of American missions to the Jews is titled "Eschatology and Mission."[9] The apostle Paul himself viewed Jewish mission/outreach to Jews within an eschatological framework in Romans 9–11. There he contemplates Israel's destiny against the background of the eschatological fullness of the nations and the fullness of Israel, neither of which he equates with or collapses into the other.

In Paul's view, God has a discrete purpose for Israel coordinate with but not identical to his purpose for the nations. He indicates that the fullness of Israel is greater than the fullness of the nations, even stating why: whereas the fullness of the nations results in "the reconciliation of the world," the fullness of Israel leads to "life from the dead"

---

6. "If Messianic Jews are to represent national Israel within the multinational *ekklesia*, they must participate actively in Israel's national life. If they do not, they will eventually either assimilate to the Gentile majority in the *ekklesia* ... or become a fossilized and irrelevant sect.... So, we find that to be itself the multinational *ekklesia* requires Messianic Jews with their Messianic Judaism, and to be themselves Messianic Jews with their Messianic Judaism requires full involvement in Israel's national life and way of holiness. Thus, we reach the paradoxical conclusion that it is in the best interests of the *ekklesia* as a whole to expect its Jewish members to root their lives deeply in Jewish soil" (Mark Kinzer, *The Nature of Messianic Judaism: Judaism as Genus, Messianic as Species* [West Hartford: Hashivenu Archives, 2000], 34–35).

7. Leaders in the Union of Messianic Jewish Congregations (UMJC) have done much to strengthen Jewish communal cohesion and intergenerational continuity. Among these contributions are the definitional statement adopted by the UMJC in 2002 and revised in 2005, and "Introducing Messianic Judaism and the UMJC" (2010), available online at http://www.mjstudies.com. Other noteworthy efforts in communal self-definition are the halakhic documents and ritual innovations of the Messianic Jewish Rabbinical Council, the core values of Hashivenu, together with papers from its leadership forums (http://www.hashivenu.org), and articles in *Kesher: A Journal of Messianic Judaism* (http://www.kesherjournal.com/).

8. For what unique purpose did God raise up the Messianic Jewish movement? My answer to this question is this: God raised up the Messianic Jewish movement to be a sign, demonstration, and catalyst preparing the way for the fullness of Israel.

9. Yaakov Ariel, *Evangelizing the Chosen People: Missions to the Jews in America, 1880–2000* (Chapel Hill: University of North Carolina Press, 2000), 4–19.

(Rom 11:12, 15, 25 – 27). This seems to suggest that Israel entering her fullness will trigger the general resurrection and the consummation of all things. Echoing Paul's perspective, the alternative paradigm presented here places great weight on linking Messianic Jewish outreach to preparing for Israel's prophesied fullness.

What will this fullness look like? Ezekiel 37:21 – 28 provides a helpful sketch. Synthesizing a large body of biblical data, the text describes seven aspects of God's consummating purposes for Israel — her fullness:

1. God will gather Israel to the land.
2. God will unify the Jewish people.
3. God will bring this people to repentance and spiritual renewal.
4. God will cause them to serve the Son of David, their Messianic King.
5. God will cause them to walk in his statutes and ordinances — Torah living.
6. God will cause this people to communally experience the Divine Presence.
7. God will thus vindicate himself as their God and them as his people.

Seen in this prophetic context, the good news of Yeshua is indeed good news for the Jewish people. As the Son of David, the Messiah plays a central role in the fulfillment of all these aspects. Yeshua's Davidic identity is central for Paul as well. Of the three times he summarizes the gospel he preaches (Rom 1:1 – 6; 1 Cor 15:3 – 8; 2 Tim 2:8), twice Paul highlights Yeshua's identity as the Son of David, highlighting not simply Yeshua's genealogy, but rather his office. While he is the head of the church, as the Son of David, Yeshua is also the one through whom all of God's consummating purposes for Israel are to be realized.

One ought not miss how these seven aspects of God's final purposes for Israel entail core aspects of the missional/Hebrew Christian paradigm, but in a Jewish communal and covenantal context. For example, the third point speaks of repentance from sins, and the fourth of faith in Yeshua the Messiah, while the sixth speaks of the Holy Spirit corresponding to themes found in Ezekiel 36 and 37. These texts underlie much preaching in the early chapters of Acts and surface in Paul's epistles.[10] The gospel preached to Jewish audiences in the book of Acts was the good news of God's covenant faithfulness to *a people* who were being called to respond in faith and obedience ("Therefore let the entire house of Israel know with certainty that God has made him both Lord and Messiah"; Acts 2:36 NRSV). From its inception, the gospel was preached not as a benefit for faith-gifted individuals, but as good news for Zion.[11] The eschatologically driven Messianic Jewish outreach paradigm returns the gospel to a Jewish covenantal/communal context.

---

10. On the linkage between the sermons in the early chapters of Acts and Ezek 36 – 37, see Richard N. Longenecker, "The Acts of the Apostles," in *The Expositor's Bible Commentary* (vol. 9; ed. F. E. Gaebelein; Grand Rapids: Zondervan, 1981), 66 – 67. For further exploration of the connection between Pauline language and Ezek 36 – 37, see Stuart Dauermann, *Son of David: Healing the Vision of the Messianic Jewish Movement* (Eugene, Oreg.: Wipf and Stock, 2010), 20 – 21.

11. Cf. Isa 52:1 – 12, where Zion and Jerusalem are each five times named as recipients of the good news of redemption. Also Luke 2:10, where Messiah's coming is declared good news for all the people of Israel. See Stuart Dauermann, *Christians and Jews Together* (Eugene, Oreg.: Wipf and Stock, 2009).

Messianic Jewish Outreach:
Not Simply Another Term for Evangelism

While many would reflexively say that "outreach" is simply the Messianic Jewish term for "evangelism," it is not so simple. There are at least three notable differences in how the terms are generally understood.

First, how evangelization is to be conducted is contingent upon how one defines the good news being proclaimed. The Lausanne Consultation on World Evangelization defines evangelization as follows:

> To evangelize is to spread the Good News that Jesus Christ died for our sins and was raised from the dead according to the Scriptures, and that as the reigning Lord he now offers the forgiveness of sins and the liberating gift of the Spirit to all who repent and believe.... Evangelism ... is the proclamation of the historical, biblical Christ as Saviour and Lord, with a view to persuading people to come to him personally and so be reconciled to God. In issuing the gospel invitation we have no liberty to conceal the cost of discipleship. Jesus still calls all who would follow him to deny themselves, take up their cross, and identify themselves with his new community. The results of evangelism include obedience to Christ, incorporation into his church and responsible service in the world.[12]

Evangelism as defined here is not the same as Messianic Jewish outreach, although the two inextricably overlap. While proclaiming Yeshua as Messiah and Lord is essential and central to Messianic Judaism's message, the implications of Yeshua's messianic office go far beyond matters of personal destiny to encompass a wider communal covenantal context amply testified to in Scripture and summarized by Ezekiel.

Second, the term "outreach" is borrowed from the wider Jewish world and has its own connotations and valence that influence the meaning of the term for Messianic Jews. In the Jewish world, outreach is termed *kiruv* (drawing near), from the phrase *kiruv rechokim* (drawing near those who are far off). In the Jewish community, the term "those who are far off" is most commonly used to describe Jews who are as yet nonaffiliated, nonobservant, or both.[13]

While the missional and Hebrew Christian paradigm is a bounded set model, seeing the "us" as Christians and the "them" as non-Christians being sought to become one of "us," the Jewish model is more a centered set model, seeking to draw nearer to the center those who are already regarded as "us." In the missional/Hebrew Christian paradigm, the evidence of having been evangelized is most often subscription to a declaration of faith and testimony to an inward spiritual experience. In the Jewish world, outreach is judged effective by communal and covenantal behavioral criteria.

In this alternative paradigm, Messianic Jewish outreach assumes and values

12. *Lausanne Covenant*, Section 4. Cited 25 March 2012. Online: http://www.lausanne.org/covenant.
13. For example, the transdenominational Jewish Outreach Institute defines and evaluates outreach as a wide variety of initiatives aimed at educating and attracting unaffiliated and intermarried Jews so that they become more deeply engaged with Jewish life. The criteria for success are the attraction of individuals with little or no affiliation with the community and the deepening of their Jewish identity. Online: http://www.joi.org/JewishConnectionPartnership/introduction.shtml.

covenantal relationship between those reached and those reaching out, seeking not simply doctrinal affirmation and personal testimony but also deepened and even transformed communal and covenantal behavioral markers as evidences of new allegiance to Yeshua the Son of David, in the power of the Spirit, and in anticipation of the fullness of Israel. This is what it means to make Jewish disciples of Yeshua: not disciples of Yeshua who happen to be Jewish, but Jewish disciples who follow Yeshua in the context of a renewed vision of Jewish community, covenant, and consummation.

This brings us to a third difference between Messianic Jewish outreach and evangelism that is often neglected: Jewish repentance is not the same as repentance for Gentiles. R. Kendall Soulen highlights a pivotal distinction intrinsic to the Bible but almost entirely ignored by the church:

Christians should recover the biblical habit of seeing the world as peopled, not by Christians and Jews, but by Jews and gentiles, by Israel and the nations.... The Bible, including the Apostolic Witness, presents the distinction as an enduring mark of the one human family, still visible in the church and even in the consummated reign of God.[14]

Human sin is never merely the sin of the creature against the Creator-Consummator. Human sin is also always the sin of Jew and Gentile, of Israel and the nations.[15]

This insight has profound implications for our understanding of Jewish repentance. If departure from Torah living is the measure of Jewish sin, should not a return to paths of Torah be a sign of Jewish repentance?

As shocking as this proposition may be for many, Scripture provides ample support. In Nehemiah 9:26, 29 (CJB), notice how Jewish sin and Jewish repentance are described:

They disobeyed and rebelled against you, throwing your Torah behind their backs. They killed your prophets for warning them that they should return to you and committed other gross provocations.... You warned them, in order to bring them back to your Torah; yet they were arrogant. They paid no attention to your mitzvot, but sinned against your rulings.

Two aspects of sin are underscored here: Throwing the Torah behind our backs — that is, not paying attention to the *mitzvot* (commandments) — and rejection/killing of God's chosen messengers.[16]

The New Testament confirms this perspective. Just prior to his martyrdom, Stephen defines Jewish sin as rejecting God's messengers and disobeying his *mitzvot*:

Stiffnecked people, with uncircumcised hearts and ears! You continually oppose the Ruach HaKodesh [Holy Spirit]! You do the same things your fathers did!

<hr>

14. R. Kendall Soulen, "The Grammar of the Christian Story," *The Institute* 10 (Autumn 2000).
15. R. Kendall Soulen, *The God of Israel and Christian Theology* (Minneapolis: Fortress, 1996), 153. Online: http://www.icjs.org/publications/inaword/.
16. Confirming this perspective, the passage equates the pathway of return to God with a return to Torah obedience. Notice the parallelism in verses 26 and 29: "warning them that they should return to you ... You warned them, in order to bring them back to your Torah."

Which of the prophets did your fathers not persecute? They killed those who told in advance about the coming of the Tzaddik [Righteous One], and now you have become his betrayers and murderers! — you! — who receive the Torah as having been delivered by angels — but do not keep it! (Acts 7:51 – 53 CJB)

Paul himself underscores the Torah living aspect of Jewish repentance when he teaches in Romans 2:12 (CJB) that "All who have sinned outside the framework of Torah [the Gentiles] will die outside the framework of Torah; and all who have sinned within the framework of Torah [the Jews] will be judged by Torah." The point: as Jewish sin is measured by violation of Torah, Jewish repentance includes a return to obeying God's commands.

While Hebrew Christians and missionaries have long emphasized the need to repent for rejecting God's messengers, a return to paths of Torah has not generally been part of the message presented in outreach to Jewish people. In this, the message proclaimed has been un-Jewish and incomplete. Messianic Jewish outreach fills this gap.

Conclusion

This chapter has compared the message, milieu, and methods of the nineteenth- and twentieth-century Jewish missions and Hebrew Christian contexts with those employed in the twentieth- and twenty-first-century Messianic Jewish world. For the Hebrew Christian and missionary movement, the message is a call to individuals to repent and to "receive Christ as your personal Savior," and the Gentile Christian world is the milieu in which the life of faith is to be lived out. For the modern Messianic Jewish movement, the message of personal repentance includes not only the call to faith in Yeshua, but also an eschatologically driven return to Jewish communal and covenantal living, those paths of righteousness from which one had departed. In contrast to the Hebrew Christian and mission model of the local Gentile Christian church as one's social and spiritual home, the Messianic Jewish movement, while positive about the local church, favors a return to Jewish life and community through the vehicle of Messianic Jewish congregations.

For Further Reading

Ariel, Yaakov. *Evangelizing the Chosen People: Missions to the Jews in America, 1880–2000*. Chapel Hill: University of North Carolina Press, 2000.

Bock, Darrell L., and Mitch Glaser. *To the Jew First: The Case for Jewish Evangelism in Scripture and History*. Grand Rapids: Kregel, 2008.

Brown, Michael L. *Answering Jewish Objections to Jesus*. 5 vols. Grand Rapids: Baker, 2000–2009.

Brumbach, Joshua. "Messianic Jewish Outreach: Reaching Out or Reaching In?" *Kesher: A Journal of Messianic Judaism* 21 (2006): 93–100.

Congdon, Jim, ed. *Jews and the Gospel: At the End of History*. Grand Rapids: Kregel, 2009.

Evearitt, Daniel Joseph. "Jewish-Christian Missions to Jews, 1820–1935." PhD diss., Drew University, 1988.

Glaser, Mitch L. "Outreach and Jewish Missions in the Twenty-First Century." *Kesher: A Journal of Messianic Judaism* 21 (2006): 32–48.

———. "A Survey of Missions to the Jews in Continental Europe 1900–1950." PhD diss., Fuller Theological Seminary, 1998.

———. "The Traditional Jewish Mission as a Model." Pages 169–76 in *Voices of Messianic Judaism: Confronting Critical Issues Facing a Maturing Movement*. Edited by Dan Cohn-Sherbok. Clarksville, Md.: Lederer, 2001.

Kaplan, Jonathan. "Say to the Cities of Judah, 'Behold Your God.'" *Kesher: A Journal of Messianic Judaism* 21 (2006): 7–18.

Kinbar, Carl. "Communal Aspects of the Besorah." Paper presented at the Hashivenu Forum, Pasadena, Calif., 2004. Online: http://www.mjstudies.com.

Parker, David, ed. *Jesus, Salvation and the Jewish People: The Uniqueness of Jesus and Jewish Evangelism*. Milton Keynes, UK: Paternoster, 2011.

Rudolph, David J. "Abraham the Proselytizer *Par Excellence* in Jewish Antiquity." Paper presented at the Young Messianic Jewish Scholars Conference, New York City, 2006. Online: http://www.mjstudies.com.

———. *A Jew to the Jews: Jewish Contours of Pauline Flexibility in 1 Corinthians 9:19–23*. Tübingen: Mohr Siebeck, 2011.

Silberling, Kay. "Messianic Keruv: Gathering In, Reaching Out." Pages 177–84 in *Voices of Messianic Judaism: Confronting Critical Issues Facing a Maturing Movement*. Edited by Dan Cohn-Sherbok. Clarksville, Md.: Lederer, 2001.

CHAPTER 8

Messianic Judaism and Women

Rachel Wolf

There are two characteristics that most Messianic Jewish women share.

First, Messianic Jewish women feel they are pioneers. This pioneering spirit has been compared to the pioneers who built the modern nation of Israel in the early twentieth century. Messianic Jewish women understand their individual calling as part of the larger picture of God's ongoing fulfillment of His prophetic purposes for the Jewish people.

After the worst tragedy of Jewish history, and after two millennia of exile, we saw the reestablishment of a sovereign Jewish state in 1948 and the restoration of Jerusalem in 1967. God was bringing back His people to the Land, but also, now, back to Himself in fulfillment of promises in Scripture. All but a handful of Messianic Jewish women at the beginning of the modern movement were baby boomers and the first in their families to believe in Yeshua. They saw themselves both as the fruit of this prophetic move of God, and, now, as Yeshua followers, as agents in God's redemptive actions for Israel. Messianic Jewish women understand themselves, whether in family life or community, to be serving God within a framework of prophetic destiny. This is expressed by confidently pioneering a new way of life, built upon ancient texts and traditions.

Second, Messianic Jewish women struggle to find an integrated cultural identity, as we endeavor to navigate a sea of disparate voices coming from traditional Judaism, contemporary Judaism, and conservative Christianity. These voices have very different things to say about the meaning of Jewishness and about our female identity and social roles as women.

My life can serve as an example to further explain these two characteristics. I grew up in an observant Jewish family strongly connected to the large and active Jewish community in our city. I attended a Jewish day school, learning history through Jewish eyes, understanding myself to be part of a Jewish continuum going back to Abraham and particularly to Moses and Sinai. My postwar Jewish world, though very traditional in many respects, became increasingly progressive with respect to the role of women in the synagogue. As a thirteen-year-old I stood before the congregation and read from the Torah scroll at my bat mitzvah. I saw women participating in the synagogue service, women teaching religious subjects to children and adults, and women active in leadership in Jewish organizations. As a child I did not know of any women rabbis, but when women began to be ordained in the Reform movement, though it was controversial, most in my circle believed this to be a good thing.

Spiritual Calling

When I told God while walking in a park in 1971 that if Yeshua was indeed the Jewish Messiah I wanted him in my life, it was not in any way connected to the idea of joining a church or becoming a Christian, nor did it have anything to do with securing my eternal future in heaven — a thought far from my mind. Two foundational concepts formed the basis of my faith. To begin with, when I read the book of Matthew for the first time, the Spirit of God showed me how Yeshua's life and death were intimately connected to the Jewish holidays I had grown up with, filling them with a deeper spiritual and personal meaning than I had known. I intuitively understood that Yeshua's life acted out the prophetic meaning of Passover and Yom Kippur. Second, after hearing a teacher speak about the State of Israel, I understood for the first time that it was God's hand guiding our history. My sense of living within the flow and continuum of Jewish history now had an added spiritual dimension.

Finding Direction

After briefly encountering various forms of conservative Christianity and becoming acquainted with nascent Messianic Judaism (which derived many of its forms from a somewhat charismatic evangelicalism), I felt pulled in many directions and did not know what was right. I did not know how to act in the Messianic synagogue, and I did not know how to raise my children. I wanted my children to have a Jewish identity and did not want to emulate the children's training I saw in evangelical churches. Yet there was no model for raising children as Jews in a Yeshua-following community. I did not see any reason I shouldn't teach men in the congregation, and I wanted my views to be heard. The conservative Christian teachings on women's roles that I heard did not seem warranted by Scripture, nor did they fit my experience.

Though my story is mine alone, many Messianic Jewish women have had similar experiences. Other Messianic Jewish women's voices are heard in this essay; some are from a written survey sent to forty-seven Messianic Jewish women who currently serve in leadership capacities. Together, we as Messianic Jewish women have built something new on traditional foundations.

Pioneering

Within this pioneer movement that breaks many religious stereotypes, Messianic Jewish women have had tremendous impact. Without titles and often without recognition, women have accomplished much of the foundational work of the movement. Couples working together built up most of the early congregations, often with only a few others. Just as women worked alongside men in the early pioneer days of the modern State of Israel, Messianic Jewish women have labored with strength and vision, alongside men, to lay the foundations for today's Messianic Judaism.

Many women have been innovators, especially within the local congregation, but also on a broader national level. Women educators were, and continue to be, leaders in the development of Messianic Jewish day schools and synagogue children's education programs. Women have played a visible and central role in the development of Messianic Jewish music: writing worship songs, developing synagogue worship styles, producing albums and liturgical music. In the 1980s, women were instrumental in instituting more traditional Jewish forms of worship in Messianic synagogues. Today, many Messianic synagogues have an egalitarian policy when it comes to liturgical prayer and worship, so many women serve as cantors, Torah readers, and in other traditionally male roles. In Israeli Messianic Jewish congregations, "views range from [women taking] absolutely no administrative or teaching responsibilities, except for teaching women and children, to full administrative and teaching/preaching responsibilities. Some women teach the Torah portion and also preach and teach the main sermon."[1]

Based on my discussions with Messianic Jewish rabbis' wives, these women are involved in the following activities: Most lead local prayer groups, retreats, Bible studies, and other women's events on a regular basis. Some co-founded and co-lead their congregation with their husbands, though nearly all would agree that the rabbi (husband) holds the head leadership role. Many women work as congregational administrators or sit on the board of the congregation; some serve as president of their synagogue. Women sit on the boards of national organizations; the Messianic Jewish Alliance of America (MJAA) had a female president for two terms. Young women have been visibly represented in the youth arms of the two major national Messianic Jewish organizations in the United States — the Young Messianic Jewish Alliance and the Union of Messianic Jewish Congregations Youth, holding top positions.

Organizations

Messianic Jewish women have started a number of organizations. Some of these are specifically for women and women's needs; others have a more general focus:

The mission statement for Achot, the Sisterhood of the Union of Messianic Jewish Congregations (UMJC), reads:

> As a sisterhood, we will act in unison to help enhance our love of Torah, and our witness to the world of the power and love of Yeshua, the Messiah of Israel. Our sisterhood will provide an arena where the women of the UMJC will be able to create stronger bonds with one another and encourage each other in our strengths. It will also provide an opportunity for women of all ages to participate in an edifying and fulfilling role in the Union [i.e., UMJC]. *Achot* will offer an ongoing menu of educational forums, discussion groups and a national/international *tzedakah* (humanitarian) project.[2]

---

1. Vered Hillel, survey response. An informal email survey was sent to forty-seven Messianic Jewish women in December 2010. The list was compiled from email addresses obtained at a women's session of the Rabbis conference of the Messianic Jewish Alliance of America (MJAA) in January 2010, as well as email addresses of others I knew and that were suggested to me by David Rudolph. These others for the most part represented the Union of Messianic Jewish Congregations (UMJC). The survey asked five questions about women's roles and identity, as well as three questions that were more theological in nature. Approximately 30 percent responded to the survey.

2. Extracted from the Achot page of the UMJC website. Cited 8 June 2011. Online: http://umjc.org/achot/.

The MJAA offers an annual half-day "For Women Only" class and prayer time as part of its annual Messiah Conference. Most MJAA congregations have a local sisterhood or other women's group. There is also an annual retreat in northern New Jersey started by an MJAA rabbi's wife that has drawn women from all over the country. "The retreat gives women a voice. We try to give as many [women] as possible the opportunity to have a public role.... Women attend year after year because it is inclusive."[3]

Be'ad Chaim (pro life) is an Israeli organization for women started and run by Messianic Jewish women. It is a nonprofit that helps, free of cost, women with unplanned pregnancies by providing confidential counseling, education, monthly support groups, and medical and practical assistance through a special project called "Operation Moses" that provides an entire baby room and monthly deliveries of diapers to needy mothers.

The Messianic Jewish Israel Fund (MJIF) is an arm of the MJAA. It is the brainchild of a rabbi's wife who leads the organization and serves as its spokesperson. MJIF raises significant funds to support Messianic Jews in Israel who are in financial need.

Identity Issues

Most of the established female leaders in the Messianic Jewish community grew up in Jewish contexts that valued independent thinking. Early Messianic synagogues tended to adopt conservative Christian views, and though some Messianic Jewish women embraced this outlook on women's roles, others looked to Jewish sources as models. There is tension when it comes to identity because Messianic Jewish women come from a variety of backgrounds, and we find ourselves within a developing Messianic Jewish culture that includes many Gentiles. Messianic Judaism is in some ways foreign to everyone: it is not what most of us grew up with. "We come from varied [Jewish] backgrounds — and, for many, no Jewish background at all.... While we share the most important bond — our faith in Messiah Yeshua — we do not share a common way of living as Messianic Jews."[4]

Even in Israel, where the majority culture is Jewish, "Messianic Jewish women struggle with this question [of identity].... The younger generation of Israeli believers is really grappling with what it means to be a believing Jewish woman.... Younger Israeli believers actually discover or understand their identity as Jews and Israelis after they come to faith in Yeshua. The question is how to walk this out in daily life. Women want to be Israelis, Jews, want to relate to their neighbors and want to be part of the nation as a whole, but they want to base this on the Bible and not rabbinic tradition, culture and *halacha* [Jewish religious law]."[5]

Messianic Jewish women as a whole, not only Israelis, struggle with the question of how to relate to *halacha*. Those in more traditional Messianic synagogues are more

3. Marlene Rosenberg, survey response.
4. Roz Kinzer, "Women's Roles in the Jewish World: Our Relationship to Covenant, Commitment, Community" (paper presented at the UMJC Northeast Messianic Jewish Congregations Women's Retreat, Enfield, Conn., March 1, 2009), 1.
5. Vered Hillel, survey response.

likely to live a traditional Jewish lifestyle. Other "Messianic Jewish women understand their identity based on the evangelical models because this is what congregations still offer them.... I have seen some parts of the messianic movement where women are embracing their Jewish inheritance and returning to traditional Jewish lives, i.e., observing traditional Jewish law, but it is not the norm."[6]

But the identity struggle is not limited to the questions of Jewish law and tradition:

> Messianic Jewish women find themselves continually caught between the contra-dictory messages being issued by the wider Jewish and Christian communities, especially the two segments of these communities with which Messianic Judaism overlaps. While liberal Judaism ... encourages egalitarian gender roles and leader-ship positions, conservative Christianity has tended to perpetuate a complemen-tarian view of both familial and ecclesial roles.... These opposing messages pose a difficult situation for the movement's women in particular. This is one of the many ways in which Messianic Jewish identity requires consistent navigation of often contradictory messages from communities to whom we consider ourselves related.[7]

Community

The vibrant discussion challenging traditional women's roles in the Orthodox Jewish community[8] runs parallel in many ways to that of the Messianic Jewish community. Though the discussion in Orthodox Judaism is still in process, many take the view that women can serve in any role except for congregational rabbi.[9] Similarly, nei-ther the MJAA nor the UMJC ordain women as rabbis. Both organizations recognize female teachers and women in other roles of authority, and will recognize as congrega-tional leaders women who come into the organization already leading congregations. In some unusual cases the MJAA may issue rabbinical ordination to a woman who is already leading a congregation, but the UMJC, though recognizing her leadership, would not give her the title of rabbi. In her 2009 study of the roles of women in Mes-sianic Judaism, Pauline Kollontai writes, "Compared to Orthodox Judaism, the range and diversity of roles which women can play in the Messianic community are much greater. Yet, women are unable to undertake full leadership responsibilities in decision making and governance."[10]

Among women in Messianic Judaism one can find views that span the spectrum from strongly egalitarian to very conservative. The majority of women today would agree with the position cited above on ordination and lean toward what may be termed a "progressive conservative" position. Most want to see a man leading a congregation

---

6. Deborah Pardo-Kaplan, survey response.

7. Jen Rosner, survey response.

8. Rachel Barenblat, "Sara Hurwitz's 'Rabba' Title Sparks Orthodox Jewish Condemnation," *Religion Dispatches*, March 10, 2010.

9. Jonathan Mark, "The Dirty Truth about Orthodox Women Rabbis," *Jewish Week*, April 28, 2010. Cited 2 Janu-ary 2012. Online: http://www.thejewishweek.com/blogs/route_17/dirty_truth_about_orthodox_women_rabbis.

10. Pauline Kollontai, "Women as Leaders: Contemporary Perspectives on the Roles of Women in Messianic Judaism," *Women in Judaism: A Multidisciplinary Journal* 6, no. 1 (2009): 28 – 29.

in the rabbi's position, but would like to see women represented more evenly in other roles of teaching and decision making. Younger women tend in greater numbers to advocate for the egalitarian model they see in more liberal forms of Judaism, including ordaining female rabbis.

A number of baby-boomer women are also strong advocates for greater female involvement in top positions at Messianic Jewish conferences. The MJAA and UMJC each sponsor an annual national conference, as well as regional conferences, where many gather for teaching, worship, fellowship and concerts. "I've found a healthy dose of frustration among boomer women who feel that their voices have been ignored for too long within the major Messianic Jewish organizations. It seems their job is to organize the conferences and make everything happen, and then step back into the shadows when the men take the stage."[11] The national organizations are "primarily male-dominated, but they are growing [in female involvement]."[12] The visibility of women at the front is increasing at conferences. Women have always been prevalent leading music and in other creative and performing arts. In recent years, more women have had the opportunity to teach and give presentations from the front at national conferences; however, except for guest speakers from the outside, I am not aware of a woman who has ever presented one of the keynote evening messages. Women are very involved behind the scenes running the conferences, but rarely at the highest levels of decision making.

"Many Messianic Jewish women happily inherit more traditional roles"[13] in the community, such as hospitality, the nursery, children's education, music, worship dance, and other service-oriented roles. All surveyed, even those who want to see additional opportunities emerge, feel that these traditional roles remain very important to the functioning of the congregation.

Theology

As Messianic Jewish women look for direction in the Hebrew Scriptures, in the Apostolic Writings, in Jewish and Christian tradition, each through the lens of their own experience, it is easy to find many contradictory messages. Thus there are a variety of opinions on the question of women's roles, and there is no recognized Messianic Jewish standard. Kollontai observes that each side of the debate in the Messianic Jewish community cites Scripture to support their views and claims that the other side is being unduly influenced by culture — by secular culture on the one hand, and patriarchal Christian or Jewish culture on the other.[14]

Indeed, there is enough seemingly contradictory evidence in Scripture to support either side of the argument, but some feel that traditional role models have been overemphasized. "All of the current role models have been women in a supportive role under their husband's leadership. But roles [that we should also emulate] come from

---

11. Monique Brumbach, survey response.
12. Marlene Rosenberg, survey response.
13. Jen Rosner, survey response.
14. Kollontai, "Women as Leaders," 28.

women like Deborah and Yael in the scriptures who followed God in conviction and were leaders in Israel. We have to carve out new leadership roles for our children.... The next generation will not have as hard of a time accepting women in leadership roles as the last generation."[15]

Most women in the Messianic Jewish movement recognize that Scripture presents norms of behavior for women that fall within traditional lines, but these are not necessarily presented as prescriptive or limiting. Scripture also describes exceptional women who are called by God to fill traditionally male roles. "[Torah] recognizes the important contribution of women who played a public role such as Deborah the judge, Miriam the prophet and Yael and Judith who were military combatants."[16]

Despite this complexity, Messianic Judaism can be a fruitful vantage point from which to view the issue of women's roles in the body of Messiah. A central theological tenet of Messianic Judaism is that God desires Jews and Gentiles to retain their distinctive identities. This is in stark contrast to the standard view in New Testament studies that Paul taught the collapse or elimination of difference, creating a new order of social equality (Gal 3:28).[17] If Jews and Gentiles are called to maintain their distinctive identities, perhaps men and women are likewise called to reveal the image of God in distinct ways. Exploring what it means for women to be co-heirs "in Messiah," equally bearing the image of God yet retaining a distinct female identity, has the potential to be an important contribution of Messianic Judaism to Christian theology. As Paul and the other apostles did not require Gentiles to become Jews to be members of God's people, neither should women have to become like men to be full participating members of our communities. The women I have spoken with in the Messianic Jewish movement are eager to discover, along with the men in our movement, how to walk this out heuristically with patience, humility, and mutual respect.

Home and Motherhood

Messianic Jewish women, whether more traditional or more progressive, strongly emphasize the importance of setting an example for the sake of future generations. Even for the most progressive this starts in the home: "One clear calling for Messianic Jewish women is to perpetuate Messianic Jewish values in the home and raise children who embrace these values."[18]

God chose Jerusalem as the place to establish his Name; this unique city and its Temple became the center of sacred ritual. But for many centuries since the destruction of the Temple in 70 CE, the center of sacred Jewish ritual has been the home. From the Passover *seder* to the decorating of the *sukkah*, to the weekly Shabbat meal and its accompanying rituals, the Jewish home has been a sacred space — the place where the family shares in the ancient rituals that mark and remember God's eternal

---

15. Helene Rosenberg, survey response.
16. Kollontai, "Women as Leaders," 15.
17. Pamela Eisenbaum, "Is Paul the Father of Misogyny and Antisemitism?" *Cross Currents* 50, no. 4 (Winter 2000–2001): 511.
18. Jen Rosner, survey response.

covenant with the Jewish people. By acting out these rituals, many of which revolve around special foods, the family participates in the covenant and fulfills the command to "teach them diligently to your children." In this setting, Jewish women are blessed by their husbands every Shabbat as part of the Shabbat liturgy. In their preparations for meals and traditions, Jewish women have lived out the sacred responsibility of assuring future generations of Israel, the covenant people. "We are called to maintain Jewish identity and not assimilate into the larger Christian world. We are called to raise our children to be aware of their Jewishness and to have a sense of belonging to the Jewish people."[19] There is profound spiritual significance in the effort to sustain our people generation after generation. It is a foundational way of expressing covenantal faithfulness, and this has been largely accomplished by mothers.

"Some feminist critics are inclined to see motherhood in the Bible solely in patriarchal terms, as a role to which women are ... serving the interests of husbands and fathers in patrilineal descent."[20] But this view concedes to the patriarchal structure the right to dictate the meaning of arguably the most powerful and uniquely feminine potential. In fact, in the case of key women in the story of Israel, such as Hannah and Miryam the mother of Yeshua, "motherhood is exalted as the decisive role of an agent of God in the salvation of his people."[21]

The role of women in our sacred texts is clearly not limited to motherhood. But motherhood has a dimension of creative power in Scripture and Jewish tradition that is often overlooked in Christian feminist literature — but which many Messianic Jewish women intuitively recognize. As we rightly lift up women like Deborah and Yael as role models, we should at the same time acknowledge the power of the traditional role of motherhood. Our heritage includes mothers in Israel who "confidently act out their parts, fully aware of their significance in the divine plan for Israel."[22]

Our current culture makes a clear distinction between public and private life and attaches great value to public achievements in traditionally male roles. Because of this it is easy to overlook the enormous power of roles that in our culture are considered feminine and private, and that do not receive significant cultural recognition. While it is important for women in Messianic Judaism to press for more voice in all aspects of community life, feminism has often overlooked the power in what is most uniquely feminine: "We change the world by raising our children and by pioneering in the congregations. We are creating the trends that will be observed later."[23] Hannah's, Ruth's, and Naomi's decisions about motherhood, made as free agents and servants of God, are understood in our tradition as crucial acts of public service to the people of God and to God's divine plan for Israel.

Messianic Jewish women see themselves as changing the world through the example of their lives, lived out in the public eye, faithful to Israel our people and to the

19. Merrill Lasko, survey response.
20. Richard Bauckham, *Gospel Women: Studies of the Named Women in the Gospels* (Grand Rapids: Eerdmans, 2002), 64.
21. Bauckham, *Gospel Women*, 65.
22. Bauckham, *Gospel Women*, 57.
23. Marlene Rosenberg, survey response.

Messiah Yeshua. The struggle to understand and walk in our identity as Jewish women who follow Yeshua is ongoing and has the potential to add an important perspective to discussions on gender roles in broader Christian and Jewish circles. Through some-times quiet, sometimes strongly vocal, influence — at home, in local and national or international community settings — Messianic Jewish women understand themselves as pioneering a new way of life in faithfulness to the God who has ever been faithful to his people Israel.

For Further Reading

Bauckham, Richard. *Gospel Women: Studies of the Named Women in the Gospels*. Grand Rapids: Eerdmans, 2002.

Bloesch, Donald G. *Is the Bible Sexist? Beyond Feminism and Patriarchalism*. Westchester: Crossway, 1982.

Brooten, Bernadette J. *Women Leaders in the Ancient Synagogue*. Atlanta: Scholars, 1982.

Brumbach, Joshua. "Women Rabbis and Messianic Judaism." Paper presented at the Messianic Jewish Rabbinical Council, Windsor Locks, Conn., 2011.

Eisenbaum, Pamela. "Is Paul the Father of Misogyny and Antisemitism?" *Cross Currents* 50, no. 4 (Winter 2000 – 2001): 506 – 24.

Hogan, Pauline Nigh. *No Longer Male and Female: Interpreting Galatians 3:28 in Early Christianity*. New York: T&T Clark, 2008.

Hove, Richard W. *Equality in Christ? Galatians 3:28 and the Gender Dispute*. Wheaton: Crossway, 1999.

Juster, Daniel. "Does the Bible Prescribe Different Roles for Men and Women in Regard to Leadership?" *Messianic Outreach* 17, no. 3 (1998): 13 – 21.

Kinzer, Roz. "Women's Roles in the Jewish World: Our Relationship to Covenant, Commitment, Community." Paper presented at the UMJC Northeast Messianic Jewish Congregations Women's Retreat, Enfield, Conn., March 1, 2009.

Kollontai, Pauline. "Women as Leaders: Contemporary Perspectives on the Roles of Women in Messianic Judaism." *Women in Judaism: A Multidisciplinary Journal* 6, no. 1 (2009): 1 – 19.

Nadler, Sam. "Male Leadership and the Role of Women." Pages 159 – 68 in *Voices of Messianic Judaism: Confronting Critical Issues Facing a Maturing Movement*. Edited by Dan Cohn-Sherbok. Baltimore: Lederer, 2001.

Saal, Paul. "No Longer Male or Female? A Case for Leadership Equality for Women in the Messianic Jewish Synagogue." Paper presented at the Messianic Jewish Rabbinical Council, Windsor Locks, Conn., 2011.

Silberling, Kathryn J. "Gender and Ordination." *Kesher: A Journal of Messianic Judaism* 13 (Summer 2001): 68 – 81.

———. "Position Paper Regarding Leadership/Ordination of Women." Presented at the International Alliance of Messianic Congregations and Synagogues, Orlando, Fla., October 15, 1993.

CHAPTER 9

Messianic Jews in the Land of Israel

Akiva Cohen

The appearance of Messianic Jews in *Eretz Yisrael* (the Land of Israel) is an integral part of the modern story of the Messianic Jewish movement and heralds an ecclesial shift — Yeshua's Jewish brothers and sisters returning home spiritually and geographically.[1]

Historical Background

In the late nineteenth century, the Hebrew Christian Prayer Union (1890) paved the way for the Jerusalem Hebrew Christian Association (1898), which consisted of more than fifty members. This effort was linked to Christ Church in Jerusalem.[2] In 1925, two Messianic Jews, Hyman Jacobs and Moshe Immanuel Ben-Meir,[3] attempted to establish an independent Messianic Jewish congregation in Jerusalem. However, they failed due to pressure exerted on them by overseas mission boards who accused them of Judaizing since they desired to observe Jewish customs and Holy Days.[4] Haim Joseph Haimoff, a Messianic Jewish immigrant from Bulgaria, made aliyah[5] in 1928 and was active in Mandatory Palestine as a worker for the Christian and Missionary Alliance. Haimoff, who subsequently changed his family name to Bar-David, held Bible studies in his home and focused on the discipleship of his six sons and daughter during what were austere years of the newly founded State.[6]

Several pioneering congregations of various theological persuasions were established in the decades leading up to 1948 that included Brethren congregations in Haifa, Jerusalem, and Jaffa. In addition, Ze'ev Kofsman, a Jewish immigrant from

---

1. I use the term "Messianic Jews" in its broadest sense to refer to Jewish followers of Yeshua as Messiah, often without regard for earlier self-designations, e.g., Hebrew Christians, Jewish Christians, Christian Jews, Jewish believers in Yeshua, etc. *Hasidei Yeshua* (followers of Yeshua) has recently been suggested as an appropriate term; however, *Yehudim Meshichim* (Messianic Jews) remains the most common self-designation in Israel today.

2. Gershon Nerel, "Attempts to Establish a 'Messianic Jewish Church' in Eretz-Israel," *Mishkan* 28 (1998): 37. See Kelvin Crombie, "Michael Solomon Alexander and the Controversial Jerusalem Bishopric," *Mishkan* 15 (1991): 1–12.

3. Moshe Ben-Meir was an Orthodox Jew born and raised in the Old City of Jerusalem whose great-grandfather had come from Munich to Palestine in 1800. See Moshe Immanuel Ben-Meir, *From Jerusalem to Jerusalem: Auto-biographical Sketches by Moshe Imanuel [sic] Ben-Meir* (Jerusalem: Netivyah, 2006).

4. Nerel, "Attempts to Establish a 'Messianic Jewish Church' in Eretz-Israel," 38–39.

5. Literally, "ascent" and used to denote a Jew's immigration to his or her historic homeland: *Eretz Yisrael*.

6. See Gershon Nerel, "Haim (Haimoff) Bar-David: Apostolic Authority among Yeshua-Believers," *Mishkan* 37 (2002): 59–78. Nerel is married to Haimoff's daughter and lives at *Yad Hashmonah* (Memorial to the Eight), a Messianic Jewish *moshav* (cooperative settlement) named after the eight Finnish Jews who were sent to the death camps during the Holocaust.

France, founded the Messianic Assembly in Jerusalem (1958) with the vision of becoming an umbrella organization for all Messianic Jewish congregations in Israel.[7] Kofsman's aspiration to restore characteristics of the first-century Jerusalem congregation contributed to his refusal to adopt traditional church creeds, emphasizing instead a preference for Hebrew terms based on the Hebrew translation of the New Testament.[8]

There were also several attempts by Messianic Jews to establish settlements. The purchase of a small hen farm in the Judean hills, a purchase of two thousand dunams near Gaza, and a plan to purchase land near Acre (Akko) all failed. These efforts reflected the ethos of these Yeshua-believers to "present a Messianic Jewish alternative to the dominant prototype of secular Zionism."[9]

The mid-1950s to early 1970s were peak years for the arrival of Messianic Jews, the majority of whom emigrated from Eastern Europe.[10] These new immigrants mitigated the previous setback caused by the evacuation of approximately a hundred or so British Yeshua-believers who had been airlifted from Israel during Operation Mercy in 1948.[11] These Messianic Jews "moved into the Land during the massive *aliya* (immigration) waves of the 1950s and 1960s, [and] together formed a new foundation for local believers. They worked strongly to eliminate their minority status within the expatriate minorities of churches and missions in Israel. In fact they did become an independent self-determined ideological minority."[12]

Several fellowships were founded during the 1950s such as the Union of Messianic Jews (1950), which was later replaced by the Israeli Messianic Jewish Alliance (1954). However, due to disagreements over the participation of non-Jewish Christians who were connected to various missions and Christian churches, both the union and the alliance were dissolved.[13]

In 1955, Hebrew Catholics formed the Association of St. James, which is recognized today as a Vicariate within the Roman Catholic Church and part of the Diocese of the Latin Patriarchate of Jerusalem. The Hebrew Catholic members of this society adopted a Hebrew translation of the Latin rite.[14]

---

7. "Facts and Myths about the Messianic Congregation in Israel," *Mishkan* 30–31 (1999): 99–104.

8. Gershon Nerel, "'Messianic Jews' in Eretz-Israel (1917–1967): Trends and Changes in Shaping Self-Identity," *Mishkan* 27 (1997): 19.

9. Nerel, "'Messianic Jews' in Eretz-Israel (1917–1967)," 19.

10. Ole Chr. M. Kvarme, "Hebrew Christianity in the Holy Land from 1948 to the Present," *Mishkan* 28 (1998): 56.

11. Gershon Nerel has described this evacuation of Jewish Yeshua-believers to London at the end of the British Mandate as a kind of "spiritual Dunkirk." The operation resulted from the Jerusalem Anglican authorities' concern that upon the declaration of the Jewish State the Hebrew Christians would be viewed as the "double British enemy" since they were linked to British missionaries and the British government. Nerel also notes the interesting parallel between this evacuation and the tradition of a "first century Jerusalem community 'Exodus' to Pella in Trans-Jordan shortly before the destruction of the Temple in 70 CE." See Nerel, "'Messianic Jews' in Eretz-Israel (1917–1967)," 17. The precise number of Jews evacuated is disputed. All of those evacuated were connected with British mission organizations; however, not all of them were Jewish. Nonetheless, the significance of even a lower estimate of Jewish believers in Yeshua evacuated from a country with less than three hundred Jewish believers in total is immediately apparent. See *Mishkan* 62 and 63 for the most recent discussions.

12. Nerel, "'Messianic Jews' in Eretz-Israel (1917–1967)," 17.

13. Nerel, "'Messianic Jews' in Eretz-Israel (1917–1967)," 18.

14. Nerel, "'Messianic Jews' in Eretz-Israel (1917–1967)," 18. Currently Father David Neuhaus, a Jew by birth, is the Patriarchal Vicar and responsible for the Hebrew-speaking Catholic community in Israel.

Supersessionism (the doctrine that the Church has replaced Israel as God's covenant people) was unanimously denounced by Messianic Jews in the 1950s through the 1970s without negating their commitment to the universal body of Messiah. This notwithstanding, Messianic Jews were often accused of holding "Judaizing tendencies." Nerel interprets this accusation as a reflection of Gentile Christian insecurity that these Jewish Yeshua-believers would establish a "Jewish-Israeli Protestant 'Bishop' in Jerusalem" sitting upon "the See [cathedra, seat] of James."[15]

Contemporary Israeli Messianic Jewish Congregations

While most Israeli Messianic Jewish congregations embrace a *national* Israeli identity, strengthened by the national observance of Jewish festivals, commemoration days, and mandatory army service, few embrace a *traditional* Jewish identity and ethos.[16] One Messianic Jewish leader, Joseph Shulam, embraced the model of Rabbi Daniel Zion[17] and Moshe Immanuel Ben-Meir (with whom he was personally acquainted) in seeking to restore a Messianic Jewish community in Jerusalem similar to the one that existed in the first century. Shulam established Congregation *Roeh Yisrael* (Shepherd of Israel) in Jerusalem in 1972, a somewhat Torah-observant community seeking to be free of Gentile missionary influence.[18]

Another significant pioneer on the contemporary scene, whose theological perspective represents the polar opposite of Shulam's traditional Jewish expression, is Baruch Maoz, the now retired founder of *Kehilat Hesed V'Emet* (Grace and Truth Christian Assembly), established in 1976 in Rehovot and now located in Rishon L'Tzion. Although the congregation does not have an official denominational affiliation, it defines itself as Reformed Baptist, emphasizes the centrality of the ministry of the Word of God, and embraces the celebration of all major Jewish holidays.[19]

New Immigrants and Sabras

Currently there are about one hundred and twenty Messianic Jewish congregations and small groups in Israel, with a conservative estimate of approximately ten thousand self-identified Messianic Jews.[20] Russian and Ethiopian *olim* (immigrants) have

---

15. Nerel, "'Messianic Jews' in Eretz-Israel (1917–1967)," 24.

16. E.g., while one would be hard-pressed to find an image of a cross in an Israeli Messianic Jewish congregation (since the cross is a symbol of persecution in the Jewish world), one would also not normally find Jewish symbols either. Most Israeli Messianic Jewish congregations do not own a *Sefer Torah* (Torah scroll) and would not view it as necessary to conduct a traditional Jewish service in which the weekly *parashah* (Torah portion) is chanted.

17. See Joseph Shulam, "Rabbi Daniel Zion: Chief Rabbi of Bulgarian Jews during World War II," *Mishkan* 15 (1991): 53–57.

18. Other contemporary Israeli Messianic Jewish congregations that embrace more of a Jewish ethos in terms of liturgy are, e.g., Eitan Shishkoff's congregation *Ohalei Rahamim* (Tents of Mercy) in Kiryat Yam and several of his daughter congregations in Haifa, Upper Nazareth, and Akko.

19. Although pioneers other than Shulam and Maoz could have been mentioned, I have sought to focus on a select few who are representative of their generation and illustrative of the two subterranean theological streams that have surfaced at various times throughout the modern Messianic Jewish story: an evangelical stream and a traditional Jewish one.

20. This number is contested by some Messianic Jews who argue that mixed marriages and the Rabbinic definition of a Jew as the child of a Jewish mother would place the number of ethnic Messianic Jews at less than three thousand.

significantly impacted the national congregational movement. A seismic demographic shift took place during the 1990s when approximately one million Russians were absorbed into a country that, at the start of that decade, numbered just under four million Jews.[21] Russian-speaking congregations now number conservatively one-third of all Israeli Messianic Jewish congregations and include over half of all congregants.

Approximately eight thousand Ethiopian Jews were brought to Israel during Operation Moses from November 1984 to January 1985. This was followed by Operation Solomon, in which thirty-four hollowed out planes — mostly El Al jumbo jets — brought fourteen thousand more Ethiopian Jews to Israel in thirty-six hours. The first Ethiopian Amharic-speaking congregations were established in Jerusalem and Netanyah and then Jaffa, Haifa, Nazareth, Rehovot, and Tel Aviv. Ethiopian Messianic Jews make up just over 5 percent of the Yeshua-believing community in Israel.[22] Sabras (native-born Israelis) currently make up about 10 percent of the Messianic Jewish community in Israel. While there is a slow but steady increase in Sabras coming to faith in Yeshua, their growth is mostly the result of children being born to Yeshua-believing families.

Outreach and Discipleship

The National Outreach Committee was established in the early 1980s and has since led many street outreaches. Various organizations share the gospel with Israelis, and Jewish believers in Yeshua increasingly use the internet for outreach. Israeli fascination with Eastern and Jewish mysticism, which includes travel to India, has also provided a favorable context to share the gospel. Israelis who dabble in such mysticism tend to be more open to learning about Yeshua.

Israel has sections in its criminal code that make it illegal to offer anyone material benefits to change their religion. The law regulates the manner in which the religion of minors (persons under eighteen) can be changed, and imposes criminal sanctions on anyone who entices a minor to change their religion. This said, there are no known cases of prosecution as a result of this law and, as I have noted, Israelis freely evangelize in many different ways.[23]

Various training institutes and post-army discipleship programs exist.[24] These are resourced in part by several Messianic Jewish publishers that produce theological, devotional, and outreach literature in Hebrew.

---

21. According to Israel's Central Bureau of Statistics, as of September 2010, there were 5,770,900 Jews in Israel. Many Israelis from the Former Soviet Union became eligible to immigrate based on the "law of return" (see "The Law of Return," below), which guarantees the right of children and grandchildren of Jews to receive Israeli citizenship.

22. See *Mishkan* 30 – 31 (1999) for a list and description of the (then) eighty-one Messianic Jewish Israeli congregations and house groups. I am grateful to Caspari Center in Jerusalem for the following unofficial estimates of the current makeup of the Messianic Jewish community: 10 percent Sabras, 55 percent Russians, 5 to 7 percent Ethiopians, at least 25 percent English, French, Spanish, and German immigrants, and 3 to 5 percent expatriates.

23. See David H. Stern, "Evangelism in Israel, 1979 – 2005," *Mishkan* 46 (2006): 6 – 16.

24. These are generally nonaccredited programs. Israel College of the Bible, a degree-granting institution, is accredited by the Asia Theological Association and the European Evangelical Accrediting Association, but its degrees are not currently recognized by Israel's Ministry of Education.

Current conferences for youth, soldiers, and college students sometimes gather up to a couple hundred participants. There is also an annual music conference that has spawned a steady stream of Hebrew worship songs, which have played a significant role in establishing Messianic Jewish identity.[25]

Leadership

Since 1981, Israeli Messianic Jewish leaders have been gathering together regularly. Their attempt to write a broad statement of faith that would serve the wider congregational movement has ultimately proven unsuccessful.[26] The National Congregational Leaders Conference remains responsible for the leadership of the National Outreach Committee and the Messianic Action Committee. In 1997, an email network for congregational leaders called the Messianic Congregation Leadership Network (MCLN) was established. The MCLN (and a similar network for leaders of Messianic Jewish ministries) continues to be a vital means of disseminating information to local congregations and facilitating intra-community discussion.[27] A growing polarization between more evangelical Messianic Jewish leaders and more Rabbinic/heritage-positive Messianic Jewish leaders has been evident in recent leadership conflicts.

The Law of Return

Hok ha-Shvut (the Law of Return) grants Jews, descendants of Jews, and their spouses the right to immigrate to Israel and receive Israeli citizenship.[28] Several cases involving Messianic Jews have reached Israel's Supreme Court of Justice. Brother Daniel, a Polish-born Jew who converted to Christianity in 1942 and joined the Carmelite Order and the Stella Maris Monastery, submitted an application in 1962 to be registered as a Jew in Israel. His application was rejected by the State; Brother Daniel subsequently lost his appeal to the Supreme Court but was allowed to remain in Israel as a permanent resident.

As a result of the Brother Daniel case and another case in 1968, in 1970 the Knesset (Israeli parliament) amended the Law of Return and added section 4b which states, "For the purpose of this Law, a Jew is one born to a Jewish mother or who converted and is not a member of another religion." The Beresford case in 1989 resulted in the court's ruling that "belief" in any of the basic tenets of Christianity invalidates one's qualification for aliyah under the Law of Return.[29] This case resulted in denying the right of many Messianic Jews to make aliyah.

---

25. See David Loden, "Messianic Music in Modern Israel: A Thirty Year Perspective," *Mishkan* 46 (2006): 32–38. Many of these worship songs are based on biblical texts taken from the Tanakh and the Hebrew version of the New Testament and are put to music with Israeli-style melodies.
26. Lisa Loden, "A Look at Leadership in Israel's Messianic Community," *Mishkan* 46 (2006): 27.
27. Loden, "A Look at Leadership in Israel's Messianic Community," 29.
28. See Marvin S. Kramer, "The Law of Return and Its Application to Messianic Jews," *Mishkan* 63 (2010): 4–12. The entire issue is dedicated to legal challenges of Messianic Jews in Israel.
29. This does not include beliefs that overlap with central Jewish doctrines (e.g., God as Creator) but refers to distinct Christian teachings.

Messianic Jewish lawyers are currently engaged in defending the rights of Messianic Jews. A 1970 amendment to the Law of Return has been successfully applied to individual cases of children of Messianic Jews. However, this does not affect the legal rights of Messianic Jews to claim entitlement to the Law of Return. The reasoning behind the 1970 amendment was the Nuremburg Laws in Nazi Germany, which defined Jewish identity as traceable three generations back. The court concluded that since such individuals would have been sent to the gas chambers, third-generation descendants of Jews should be eligible for Israeli citizenship (even if not considered Jewish by Rabbinic definition).

Identity Issues

Israeli Jewish identity is markedly different than that of its diasporic counterpart. As noted earlier, Israelis have a strong sense of national Jewish identity that is reinforced by mandatory military service. Men are required to serve for three years after high school and participate in reserve duty until age fifty-one. Women serve for twenty-one months after completing high school. Israel's need for a strong civilian standing army in the face of constant military threats, combined with the pride of defending one's historic homeland, contributes to the uniqueness of Israeli identity formation.

The modern State of Israel was founded on a secular (socialist) ethos that shaped the State's nonreligious character. Because most *Haredi* (ultra-Orthodox) Jews do not serve in the army[30] and are carried on the financial backs of their heavily taxed secular counterparts, there is significant tension between secular and religious Jews. There is also a grassroots *ba'alei t'shuvah* (secular "repenters" to traditional Judaism) movement. This trend — returning to one's Jewish heritage — is also evident among a growing number of first-generation Messianic Jews seeking connection with their Jewish spiritual heritage while maintaining their faith in Yeshua as Messiah.

The influence of missionary organizations and Western Christianity has also played a role in the theological perspectives of many Messianic Jews, an influence that has not contributed toward a Judaism-positive ethos. Nevertheless, by living in a Jewish State, speaking Hebrew, and celebrating the Jewish festivals — which are national holidays in Israel — Messianic Jews have a much more consistent and natural connection to the Jewish religious cycle than their diasporic secular (non-Messianic) Jewish counterparts.[31]

---

30. It is important to distinguish between the *Haredi* sector and the National Religious sector (recognized by their knitted head coverings). Many of the latter are known for their sacrificial dedication and exemplary military service.

31. See Keri Zelson Warshawsky, "Returning to Their Own Borders: A Social Anthropological Study of Contemporary Messianic Jewish Identity in Israel" (PhD diss., Hebrew University, Jerusalem, 2008). Cited 25 March 2012. Online: http://shemer.mslib.huji.ac.il/dissertations/W/JWE/001441354.pdf; Gershon Nerel, "'Messianic Jews' in Eretz-Yisrael (1917–1967): Trends and Changes in Shaping Self-Identity" (PhD diss., Hebrew University, Jerusalem, 1997).

Relationship with Arab Israeli Christians and Palestinian Christians

To say that the relationship between Messianic Jews and their Arab Israeli Christian and Palestinian Christian counterparts is a complex subject is an understatement.[32] Few Israeli Messianic Jews have frequent fellowship with their Palestinian Christian brothers and sisters. This notwithstanding, some Messianic Jews and Arab Israeli Christians who live in close proximity (e.g., Galilee and Haifa) enjoy a corporate solidarity, and some are even members of the same local fellowship. There is a minority within the Israeli Messianic Jewish community that actively seeks opportunities for fellowship and dialogue with Palestinian Christians. Several Messianic Jewish leaders and some of their congregants are involved with a ministry called *Musalaha* (Arabic for "Reconciliation"), which seeks to foster dialogue and reconciliation.[33]

Persecution

In general, Israeli Messianic Jews do not suffer from violent persecution, though openly confessing one's faith in Israeli society is normally perceived as a betrayal of Jewish corporate solidarity.[34] There are sporadic and localized attacks against Messianic Jews by ultra-Orthodox Jews and their "anti-missionary" arm, *Yad L'Achim* (Arm of the Brothers).[35] Messianic Jewish immigrants may find resistance in their attempts to make aliyah and, if already citizens, may be discriminated against in the marketplace and experience ostracism by colleagues.

Challenges and Opportunities

Israeli Messianic Jewish youth need training to become better equipped to defend their faith from challenges arising from secular culture on the one hand and traditional Jewish unbelief in Yeshua on the other. In addition, the next generation of Messianic Jews needs to acquire a higher level of education and professional vocational training. This is vital for Messianic Jews to free themselves from financial dependence

---

32. Arab citizens of Israel use a number of self-designations. Some describe themselves as "Israeli Arabs" on the basis of their primary civil identity, whereas others describe themselves as "Palestinian Israelis" on the basis of their primary ethnic identity. Both self-designated groups live in the State of Israel and are Israeli citizens with Israeli passports, but do not normally serve in the Israeli Defense Force (although a few Israeli Arabs choose to serve in the IDF or participate in national service). "Palestinians" live in the West Bank or Gaza and are not citizens of Israel. Many Palestinians hold Palestinian passports (which are not recognized by all countries, as Palestine is not officially recognized by the United Nations as an independent country), and some hold Jordanian passports.

33. See http://www.musalaha.org and the controversial Kairos Palestine Document: http://www.oikoumene .org/gr/resources/documents/other-ecumenical-bodies/kairos-palestine-document.

34. Despite the social stigma attached to Israeli Jews openly professing their faith in Yeshua, it should be noted that this has not prevented the academic study of Yeshua and the New Testament. Some of Israel's pioneers and legendary scholars have expressed fascination with Yeshua and have viewed him as a Second Temple – era Israeli Jew. For the reaction of secular Zionist pioneers to Jesus, see Tsvi Sadan's revised Hebrew University dissertation, "Flesh of Our Flesh: Jesus of Nazareth in Zionist Thought" (Jerusalem: Carmel, 2008 [Hebrew]). For Israeli scholars of the New Testament, see the works of Joseph Klausner and David Flusser. Most Israeli universities currently offer courses on the New Testament and early Christianity and have recently begun publishing (in Hebrew) significant historical and theological studies on these subjects.

35. See http://www.yadlachimusa.org.il.

on foreign mission groups who exert partisan political and theological influences on them. Furthermore, by entering the professional working class, Messianic Jews will be better positioned to impact Israeli national culture in places of influence.

In the congregational context, the Israeli Messianic Jewish movement needs to see a new generation of leaders emerge with formal academic training. This will elevate the current level of biblical and theological understanding and help shape Messianic Jewish identity and ethos. A central challenge remains the development of congregational paradigms that facilitate connection with Israel's culture and national calendar (religious and civil), while maintaining a theologically rich Yeshua-centered identity.

In addition, there is a critical need for Israeli Messianic Jews to learn to engage in respectful theological discourse with one another, diasporic Messianic Jews, their Palestinian-Christian brothers and sisters, and the wider body of Messiah. Finally, the responsibility of Messianic Jewish leaders to maintain "sound doctrine" needs to be carried out without dogmatically basing Messianic Jewish identity on Israeli civil religion, secular Zionist culture, or theologies that include a predisposed resistance to Jewish heritage.[36] Israel's Messianic Jews need to chart their own course in dialogue with historic and contemporary Christianity. This includes affirming unity within a healthy diversity for the sake of the movement's next generation, a unity that will uphold the credibility of the Messiah's body in *Eretz Yisrael*.[37]

For Further Reading

Brown, Wesley H., and Peter F. Penner, eds. *Christian Perspectives on the Israeli-Palestinian Conflict*. Pasadena: William Carey International University Press, 2008.

Kjær-Hansen, Kai, and Bodil F. Skjøtt. "Facts and Myths about the Messianic Congregations in Israel." *Mishkan* 30–31 (1999).

Maoz, Baruch. "Jerusalem and Justice: A Messianic Jewish Perspective." Pages 155–77 in *Jerusalem: Past and Present in the Purposes of God*. Edited by Peter W. L. Walker. Grand Rapids: Baker, 1994. Cited 9 April 2012. Online: http://www.theologicalstudies.org.uk/pdf/jerusalem_maoz.pdf.

Munayer, Salim J., and Lisa Loden, eds. *The Land Cries Out: Theology of the Land in the Israeli-Palestinian Context*. Eugene, Oreg.: Cascade, 2011.

Nerel, Gershon. *Anti-Zionism in the "Electronic Church" of Palestinian Christians.* Analysis of Current Trends in Antisemitism 27. Jerusalem: Vidal Sassoon International Center for the Study of Antisemitism, 2006.

———. "Messianic Jews and the Modern Zionist Movement." Pages 75–84 in *Israel and Yeshua*. Edited by Torleif Elgvin. Jerusalem: Caspari Center, 1993.

———. "'Messianic Jews' in Eretz-Yisrael (1917–1967): Trends and Changes in Shaping Self-Identity." PhD diss., Hebrew University, Jerusalem, 1997 [Hebrew].

Raheb, Mitri. "Biblical Interpretation in the Israeli-Palestinian Context." Pages 109–17 in *Israel and Yeshua*. Edited by Torleif Elgvin. Jerusalem: Caspari Center, 1993.

Rotberg, Robert I. *Israeli and Palestinian Narratives of Conflict: History's Double Helix*. Bloomington: Indiana University Press, 2006.

---

36. See Warshawsky, "Returning to Their Own Borders."

37. I would like to express my appreciation to those who took time to read and comment on this chapter, especially to Gershon Nerel, whose historical research and comments were invaluable.

Smith, Charles D. *Palestine and the Arab-Israeli Conflict: A History with Documents.* Boston: Bedford/St. Martin's, 2009.

Stern, David H. "The People of God, the Promises of God, and the Land of Israel." Pages 73–78 in *The Enduring Paradox: Exploratory Essays in Messianic Judaism.* Edited by John Fischer. Baltimore: Lederer, 2000.

———. "The Significance of Jerusalem for Messianic Jews." Pages 79–94 in *The Enduring Paradox: Exploratory Essays in Messianic Judaism.* Edited by John Fischer. Baltimore: Lederer, 2000.

Warshawsky, Keri Zelson. "Returning to Their Own Borders: A Social Anthropological Study of Contemporary Messianic Jewish Identity in Israel." PhD diss., Hebrew University, Jerusalem, 2008. Cited 25 March 2012. Online: http://shemer.mslib.huji.ac.il/dissertations/W/JWE/001441354.pdf.

CHAPTER 10

Messianic Jewish National Organizations

Mitch Glaser

A number of Messianic Jewish national organizations and Jewish mission agencies have been initiated or renewed since the start of the modern Messianic Jewish movement. This essay examines the Jewish fidelity of a sampling of these organizations on the basis of five criteria: commitment to Israel, concern about assimilation, involvement in the Jewish community, Torah observance and Jewish tradition, and a vision for the next generation.

Messianic Jewish National Organizations

Messianic Jewish national organizations are institutions that bring Messianic Jews and Messianic Jewish congregations together for conferences, fellowship, teaching, and other cooperative activities such as relief and benevolence work in Israel and the former Soviet Union, and various types of pro-Israel activism. These organizations also provide services usually associated with a denomination such as ordination, ongoing educational programs for leadership, and congregational planting.

I will comment on the larger and better-known organizations, but this is not to diminish the importance of others.

Messianic Jewish Alliance of America (MJAA)

The Messianic Jewish Alliance of America was founded in 1915 and is the largest Messianic Jewish national organization. It is affiliated with the International Messianic Jewish Alliance. The alliance is only open to individual membership. The MJAA hosts the annual Messiah Conference in Harrisburg, Pennsylvania, the world's largest conference of Messianic Jews, and it sponsors regional conferences throughout the United States.

International Alliance of Messianic Congregations and Synagogues (IAMCS)

As a subset of the Messianic Jewish Alliance of America, this organization was created to be a fellowship of Messianic Jewish congregations and connects Messianic rabbis who are oriented toward the American Alliance. The IAMCS links about 150 member congregations internationally with over 100 of them in the United States.

Union of Messianic Jewish Congregations (UMJC)

The Union of Messianic Jewish Congregations performs a similar function to the IAMCS. It developed as a network of congregations in the 1980s and has a vision to "establish, strengthen, and multiply congregations for Yeshua within the house of Israel."[1] It is a fellowship of both congregations and Messianic rabbis that allows for congregational membership. It also offers a rabbinical ordination program. The UMJC currently has about eighty congregations in membership, mostly in the United States.

International Messianic Jewish Alliance (IMJA)

The International Messianic Jewish Alliance is an organization that links about twenty national alliances that offer individual membership and provides a global fellowship for their affiliates. One of the larger alliances is centered in Great Britain. The International Hebrew Christian Alliance (now the International Messianic Jewish Alliance) was formed in 1925.

Union of Messianic Believers (UMB)

A subset of the Union of Messianic Jewish Congregations, the Union of Messianic Believers allows for individual membership of those who might not otherwise be affiliated with the UMJC.

Tikkun International

Started by Dan Juster, Tikkun has representatives and congregations in North America and Israel, and works closely with the UMJC. It is a "Messianic Jewish umbrella organization for an apostolic network of leaders, congregations and ministries."[2]

Association of Messianic Congregations (AMC)

The Association of Messianic Congregations is a group of congregations and leaders who meet regularly for prayer, fellowship, and encouragement. They also offer a variety of resources for congregational growth.

Jewish Mission Agencies

Jewish mission agencies are organizations established to proclaim the gospel to Jewish people and to do all that this entails. These agencies are served by professional staff, governed by boards of directors, and are a unique amalgam between a church or Messianic Jewish congregation and nonprofit agency. Many of these missions are global in reach and active in fundraising, and some are associated with a particular "stream" of the body of Messiah, including a variety of Christian denominations, but today the majority of these agencies are independent. Their Jewish character may also vary considerably as some of the Jewish missions were founded by Jewish believers in Yeshua and others were not.

1. Cited 12 August 2012. Online: http://umjc.org/faith-and-values/core-values.
2. Cited 12 August 2012. Online: http://www.tikkunministries.org/aboutus.asp.

The Jewish mission agencies under consideration are based primarily in North America, though there are others around the globe and many smaller organizations that continue to make significant contributions to the modern Messianic Jewish movement.

Ariel Ministries

Ariel Ministries is a Jewish mission agency started in 1977 by Arnold Fruchtenbaum to "evangelize and disciple" Jewish people.

Chosen People Ministries (CPM)

Chosen People Ministries is a Jewish mission agency started in 1894 by Rabbi Leopold Cohn that has representation in the United States and in about a dozen countries around the world. CPM also plants Messianic Jewish congregations.

Friends of Israel (FOI)

Friends of Israel is a Jewish mission agency led to prominence by Victor Buksbazen and Marv Rosenthal. The mission focuses on advocacy for the nation of Israel.

Jewish Voice Ministries International (JVI)

Started in 1967 by Louis Kaplan, Jewish Voice Ministries International is a Jewish mission agency that focuses on proclaiming the gospel through medical clinics, humanitarian aid, media, and music festivals. Jewish Voice also plants Messianic Jewish congregations.

Jews for Jesus (JFJ)

Jews for Jesus is a Jewish mission agency started in 1973 by Moishe Rosen that has representation in the United States and a dozen countries around the world.

Life in Messiah International (LMI)

The former Chicago Hebrew Mission, Life in Messiah International started in 1882 by William Blackstone. LMI has representation in the United States and a half dozen countries around the world.

Five Critical Concerns

For the purpose of this essay, five criteria will be used to evaluate the Jewish fidelity of Messianic Jewish national organizations and Jewish mission agencies under consideration. These criteria will not be limited to traditional Jewish observance since the mainstream Jewish community itself generally does not define Jewish fidelity in such particularized religious terms. We will instead utilize a standard that makes room for Jewishness expressed in commitment also to the national, social, and political concerns of the global Jewish community.

Commitment to Israel

It would be hard to imagine a Jewish group — whether secular, religious, Messianic, or otherwise — not viewing the modern State of Israel as having a special place in the life and mission of their organization. Advocacy on behalf of Israel (whether or not there is political agreement) must be viewed as a sign of an institution's fidelity to the Jewish — and Messianic Jewish — community.

Concern about Assimilation

We live in a post-Holocaust world, and our concern for the ongoing survival of the Jewish community is paramount. Any Messianic Jewish institution or organization that is not concerned with this issue is neglecting one of the critical concerns of most Jewish people.

Involvement in the Jewish Community

One of the primary commitments of any Jewish group is the welfare of the Jewish community. A Messianic Jewish organization should have some level of relationship to the Jewish community that goes beyond evangelism. If not, then the goals of that institution could and perhaps should be viewed as self-serving.

Torah Observance and Jewish Tradition

I previously stated that the level of Torah observance of a Messianic Jewish group or institution should not be the final measure of their Jewish fidelity; however, the role of Torah and Jewish tradition is an important part of the mix. This would include living a more Torah-observant lifestyle and many other concerns related to traditional Jewish life.

A Vision for the Next Generation

Although this criterion is included in all of the above, passing the torch to a new generation of Jews — especially in light of the Holocaust — is of preeminent importance within the Jewish community. Programs like Birthright Israel and day school and summer camp programs are designed to perpetuate the Jewish community. Any organization that does not concern itself with preserving the Jewish people and identity in the next generation is not in sync with the majority of the Jewish community.

Evaluation of Jewish Fidelity

Messianic Jewish National Organizations

These organizations are usually committed to integrating their faith in Yeshua with their Jewish loyalties.

Commitment to Israel

Messianic Jewish national organizations are generally deeply concerned for the State of Israel and provide benevolence and other types of ministries to Israelis. They link their constituents to Israel by encouraging *aliyah*, prayer, giving, and service opportunities as well as congregational planting and education. Many of the Messianic Jewish national organizations have affiliates or representation in Israel. Of particular note is the extensive benevolence work done by the Messianic Jewish Alliance of America and the Union of Messianic Jewish Congregations in the Land.

Concern about Assimilation
Messianic Jewish national organizations promote Jewish continuity on the basis of Israel's irrevocable calling before God to be a distinct and enduring nation (Rom 11:28 – 29). Commitment to Jewish continuity is central to the existence of these organizations.

Involvement in the Jewish Community
Messianic Jewish national organizations promote involvement in the mainstream Jewish community as seen by some of the creative dialogues sponsored by the Messianic Jewish Theological Institute, whose leaders are part of the UMJC. Most of the national organizations connect with the mainstream Jewish community through benevolence programs and Israel-focused activism.

The younger members of Messianic Jewish national organizations are less willing than their parents to accept an "outsiders" position in relationship to the mainstream Jewish community and are finding new ways to join their young Jewish peers in greater Jewish community involvement.

At times, however, the very nature of the Messianic Jewish national organizations creates an unintentional and antithetical relationship with the non-Messianic Jewish community. Fidelity to the Messianic Jewish community — religiously and socially — is at times unknowingly competitive with a deeper involvement in the mainstream Jewish community. Shabbat services and holiday celebrations, for example, occur at the same times as those within the non-Messianic Jewish community.

Torah Observance and Jewish Tradition
Those involved with Messianic Jewish national organizations generally believe that some level of Torah observance is either commanded by God or should be encouraged of Messianic Jews. To be a part of the International Alliance of Messianic Congregations and Synagogues and the Union of Messianic Jewish Congregations, member congregations must meet on the Sabbath, celebrate the Jewish holidays, and worship in a way that incorporates Jewish religious tradition in one way or another. This is also the orientation of Messianic synagogues affiliated with Tikkun and with the Association of Messianic Congregations, though those who are part of the AMC would be less personally observant than members of the UMJC.

Individual members of the MJAA would more often than not also incorporate some degree of traditional Jewish life in their homes and congregations. The level of personal observance (such as daily davening [Jewish prayer], *kashrut* [kosher], Sabbath observance, etc.) would vary considerably. International Messianic Jewish Alliance members in most countries would have less of a commitment to traditional

Jewish observance, at least historically. This is changing today and members are tending toward more observance and not less.

There is a growing discussion within the Messianic Jewish national organizations about the degree to which Gentile believers in Yeshua should be allowed to participate in traditional Jewish observance (e.g., bar/bat mitzvah) and what the role of non-Jews should be in Messianic synagogue life. There are some within the Messianic Jewish national organizations who are calling for their groups to recognize Jews by choice who have undergone a formal conversion process, either Messianic or traditional.

The level of and nature of rabbinic authority with respect to Jewish tradition is also debated within the Messianic Jewish national organizations. Some Messianic Jews who are more observant would say that there is a historic and community-based authority to Jewish tradition; however, very few would accept a purely Orthodox Jewish view of Oral Torah. Torah observance is most often viewed as a matter of covenant loyalty for Jews, especially by those in some way affiliated with the UMJC, whereas there might be a broader range of reasons for Torah observance articulated by congregations associated with the IAMCS. In general, the Messianic Jewish national organizations believe that Torah observance is an important part of expressing Jewish fidelity to the Lord.

A Vision for the Next Generation
Finally, there is a deep commitment on the part of most national Messianic Jewish organizations to the future of the Jewish community and the Messianic Jewish movement. This is demonstrated by the priority they place on various institutions and youth programs, from the Young Messianic Jewish Alliance and the Union of Messianic Jewish Congregations' K20 program, to support for Grassroots and AMF — A Messianic Jewish Music Festival.

In sum, the Messianic Jewish national organizations have championed a consistent and developing theology of Messianic Jewish identity. The books are only now being written for our generation — including this very volume. This theology reflects a desire within the Messianic Jewish national organizations to promote and advance Jewish fidelity on a variety of fronts.

Jewish Mission Agencies

Many who are part of the Messianic Jewish national organizations and the modern Messianic Jewish movement can trace their spiritual roots back to one or more of the Jewish mission agencies. However, there has also developed a certain tension between the modern Messianic Jewish movement — including the Messianic Jewish national organizations — and the Jewish mission agencies.

Commitment to Israel
The majority of Jewish mission agencies have a deep commitment to Israel. They are mostly favorable to modern Zionism and view the State of Israel as the fulfillment of biblical prophecy. The Jewish mission agencies focus on evangelism in Israel, though many are also engaged in benevolence work, publishing, biblical counseling, children's

camps, and theological education. The Jewish missions also encourage their respective governments to be favorable toward Israel. This is made possible by the strong connections that Jewish mission agencies usually have with local churches and leaders of these churches, some of whom have political influence.

Concern about Assimilation
Some who are involved with Messianic Jewish national organizations wonder to what degree Jewish mission agencies care about the ongoing Jewish identity of Messianic Jews. The answer to this question has to do with the theology of the Jewish mission agencies. Those that are more premillennial tend to view ongoing Jewish fidelity as important (though not always defined in terms of Torah observance), and those that minimize God's ongoing covenantal commitment to the Jewish people do not view Jewish fidelity as important.

Many of the Jewish mission agencies, especially in North America, are dispensational, and this theological perspective maintains a positive view of Israel's future. Some within the Messianic Jewish national organizations dislike dispensationalism because its view on the fulfillment of the Law leads to the conclusion that Messianic Jews no longer have a covenantal responsibility to observe distinctively Jewish commandments in the Torah.

Messianic Jewish national organizations, therefore, sometimes hold a negative view of Jewish mission agencies for "not caring about the Jewish identity of the Messianic Jew" and assume that Jewish mission agencies merely "use" the Torah as an evangelistic tool. This might be true of some, but many of those on the staff of mission agencies with a dispensational orientation also encourage the keeping of Torah and Jewish tradition for the purpose of affirming Jewish identity and not simply as an evangelistic tool. Many staff members of Jewish mission agencies attend Messianic synagogues and participate in Messianic Jewish national organizations, though Chosen People Ministries and Jewish Voice Ministries International are the only major Jewish missions today that actively plant Messianic synagogues. The lines between the Messianic Jewish national organizations and the Jewish mission agencies are blurring.

Chosen People Ministries, Jews for Jesus, Life in Messiah International, Ariel, the Christian Jew Foundation, and Friends of Israel are more dispensational in character, though CPM and JFJ are somewhat broader theologically. In missions that are more Jewish in character, like CPM, JVI, JFJ and Ariel, there is a greater emphasis on matters related to the ongoing Jewish identity of Jewish believers in Yeshua.

This does not mean, though, that other Jewish mission agencies do not have a concern for ongoing Jewish identity. They often do for Jews they serve, but not necessarily for the organizations themselves, as quite a few of those who serve with Jewish mission agencies are not Jewish. This is demonstrated in meetings of the Lausanne Consultation on Jewish Evangelism (LCJE), an umbrella group of Jewish mission agencies that focuses on evangelism. At most LCJE conferences, papers are presented that focus on the challenges and importance of encouraging Jewish believers in Yeshua to retain a commitment to Jewish fidelity.

The Jewish mission agencies minister to Jewish believers in Yeshua in local evangelical churches. It is therefore quite important that Messianic Jewish national organizations be supportive of the Jewish mission agencies, or the majority of Jews in churches will be left without options for some type of Jewish involvement; it is unrealistic to believe that every Jewish believer in Yeshua will leave their church and attend a Messianic Jewish congregation. The Jewish mission agencies help Jews in churches to celebrate the Jewish festivals. They bar/bat mitzvah their children, marry them, and bury their loved ones in a Jewish way, which is an important service and testimony.

Involvement in the Jewish Community

Jewish mission agencies are increasingly supporting the Jewish community by way of benevolence programs, from feeding indigent immigrants in Israel to helping with drug and alcohol programs in Brooklyn — something that Chosen People Ministries has been doing actively for a number of years.

The Jewish mission agencies are more intensely connected with evangelical churches on an institutional level than with the Jewish community. One reason for this is that the activities of the Jewish mission agencies are often evangelistically overt, thus making it more difficult to develop relationships with the Jewish community. However, on a personal level, many of those who serve as part of Jewish mission agencies have deep commitments to the mainstream Jewish community on a variety of levels — culturally, politically, and educationally.

It is a misconception that Jewish mission agencies like Jews for Jesus, Life in Messiah International, or Chosen People Ministries simply relate to churches for the sake of financial support. Though raising support from evangelical churches is part of their ministry, there is also an attempt to encourage Christians to pray for the Jewish people. Jewish missions provide Christians with education about the Jewish roots of their faith. They instill in them a concern for Jewish evangelism and help Christians to develop a deeper love for the Jewish people.

Torah Observance and Jewish Tradition

Many individuals serving with Jewish mission agencies are Torah observant in one way or another, though their organizations do not make this a focus of their ministries. Admittedly, a significant number of Jewish mission agencies were not previously supportive of Jewish believers in Yeshua being Torah observant. Yet this seems to be changing. The staff members of Chosen People Ministries, Jewish Voice Ministries International, Jews for Jesus, Life in Messiah International, Church's Ministry Among Jewish People, Christian Witness to Israel, and a number of other ministries regularly live out Jewish observance for nonevangelistic purposes. This said, Jewish mission agencies tend to relegate Jewish observance to the arena of personal preference.

A Vision for the Next Generation

There is a strong concern for the next generation among the Jewish mission agencies. Some of the current leaders of Messianic Jewish national organizations grew up attending summer camps run by Jewish mission agencies. Many received their theological training through scholarships granted by these agencies. There is a genuine concern for the next generation, though this concern might be expressed differently by the Jewish mission agencies than by the Messianic Jewish national organizations and congregations.

The Jewish mission agencies emphasize evangelism, and this is expressed through short-term mission and service opportunities. However, this does not mean that conveying a Messianic Jewish heritage is unimportant. The two are not mutually exclusive. The Muchan Conference, sponsored by Chosen People Ministries, includes many young people from Jewish mission agencies as well as from Messianic Jewish national organizations. The conference focuses on how to live as Jewish young men and women who love Yeshua. CPM and the UMJC have sponsored the Messianic Jewish Young Scholars program and the Borough Park Symposium, which recently brought almost fifty young Messianic Jews to the symposium.

Many within the Jewish missions world believe that it is impossible to teach our next generation to share the good news without emphasizing the need to remain identified as Jews. Shaping the minds and hearts of our next generation is a key area where the Jewish mission agencies and Messianic Jewish national organizations can partner together.

Conclusion

The tension between the Messianic Jewish national organizations and Jewish mission agencies is beginning to ease as the Messianic Jewish congregational movement grows in strength, size, ideology, theology, and self-understanding. The Jewish mission agencies are also beginning to respond with greater respect toward the Messianic Jewish national organizations. Some within the Messianic Jewish national organizations believe the Jewish fidelity of the Jewish mission agencies is at times lacking. The Jewish missions at times suspect that the Messianic Jewish national organizations promote separatism. Despite these perceptions, the Messianic Jewish national organizations and Jewish mission agencies are perhaps closer on these very important issues involving faith and Jewish fidelity than either group imagined.

For Further Reading

Goldberg, Louis, ed. *How Jewish Is Christianity? 2 Views on the Messianic Movement.* Grand Rapids: Zondervan, 2003.

International Alliance of Messianic Congregations and Synagogues. Online: http://www.iamcs.org.

International Messianic Jewish Alliance. Online: http://www.imja.org.

Kesher: A Journal of Messianic Judaism. Online: http://www.kesherjournal.com.

Lausanne Consultation on Jewish Evangelism. Online: http://www.lcje.net.

Messianic Jewish Alliance of America. Online: http://www.mjaa.org.

The Messianic Times. Online: http://www.messianictimes.com.

Mishkan: A Forum on the Gospel and the Jewish People. Online: http://www.mishkanstore.org/store/.

Robinson, Richard A., ed. *God, Torah, Messiah: The Messianic Jewish Theology of Dr. Louis Goldberg.* San Francisco: Purple Pomegranate, 2009.

————. *The Messianic Movement: A Field Guide for Evangelical Christians.* San Francisco: Purple Pomegranate, 2005.

Union of Messianic Jewish Congregations. "Introducing Messianic Judaism and the UMJC." Albuquerque: UMJC, 2010. Online: www.mjstudies.com.

Zaretsky, Tuvya. "Available Resources and Current Practices in Jewish Evangelism." Pages 273–91 in *Jesus, Salvation and the Jewish People: The Uniqueness of Jesus and Jewish Evangelism.* Edited by David Parker. Milton Keynes, UK: Paternoster, 2011.

CHAPTER 11

Messianic Jews and the Jewish World

Mark S. Kinzer

How do Messianic Jews relate to the wider Jewish world? How does that world relate to them?

In this chapter I will summarize the Messianic Jewish attitude toward the wider Jewish world in the twentieth century and the response given by that world. I will focus on the situation in the United States, which was the institutional center for Messianic Judaism in this period. I will then describe a sub-movement that arose at the end of the twentieth century and the way its new approach to the wider Jewish world dominated discussion among Messianic Jews in the first decade of the twenty-first century.

Hebrew Christianity and
Twentieth-Century Messianic Judaism

Messianic Judaism and its antecedent movement, Hebrew Christianity, first emerged as attempts to reconfigure the relationship between the Christian Church and the Jewish people.[1] The Hebrew Christians of the nineteenth and twentieth centuries were for the most part evangelical Protestants who saw the Church as an invisible and universal body of "true believers" that was expressed concretely but imperfectly in the local Christian congregation — a community constituted by the regenerated individuals who voluntarily joined it. In line with the eschatological scenarios stirring the Christian world of their day, but also in line with the rise of Jewish nationalism, Hebrew Christians saw the Jewish people as a political entity singled out to play a crucial role in the end times. In other words, they saw the Church as essentially a collection of saved individuals but the Jewish people as a communal reality — a nation. From this perspective, there was no contradiction in claiming membership in both.

This was a radical shift for Christian Jews. Before the pietist movements of the post-Reformation period, Christians viewed the Church as a divinely established human institution, a spiritual society. One did not become a Christian through a decision or experience and subsequently join the Church, but one became a Christian by joining the Church in baptism. And before the Jewish enlightenment (the *Haskalah*), both Christians and Jews understood the Jewish people to be a religious community whose national component could not be teased out from its religious foundations. To

---

1. On the history of Hebrew Christianity and Messianic Judaism, see Mark S. Kinzer, *Postmissionary Messianic Judaism* (Grand Rapids: Brazos, 2005), 263 – 302; Dan Cohn-Sherbok, *Messianic Judaism* (New York: Cassell, 2000), 1 – 86.

be a Jew was to be part of an extended family whose identity and life were shaped by the Torah in its dual form as a written text and a living tradition. Since the Christian Church as a divine-human institution and the Jewish people as a religious community had agreed that membership in both was forbidden, Hebrew Christianity or Messianic Judaism was inconceivable.

But by the nineteenth century fundamental changes in Christian and Jewish self-identity had made something possible that was previously impossible. The Church was no longer seen by most as a divinely instituted human society, and the communal life of Jews was no longer bound up with the Torah. Just as English, French, or German evangelicals could be patriotic members of the English, French, and German nations while also being Christians, so Hebrew Christians could be patriotic Jews while being faithful believers in Christ. In similar fashion, just as many Zionists claimed to be loyal Jews while disavowing traditional Jewish religion, so Hebrew Christians claimed to be loyal to their people while rejecting the authority of the Torah.

Messianic Judaism emerged in the 1970s as a mutation of Hebrew Christianity. It maintained the same view of the Church as that held by the Hebrew Christians.[2] However, it modified the Hebrew Christian perspective on the Jewish people. Messianic Judaism was no longer willing to draw a strict separation between Jewish nationality and Jewish religion. Central elements of traditional Torah observance, such as Shabbat, the holidays, and the biblical dietary laws, became essential markers of the new movement. Its reclamation of the Torah provided the justification for its change of name: it no longer saw itself as the Jewish nation's version of Christianity, but instead as the Yeshua-version of Judaism.

Nevertheless, most Messianic Jews remained uncomfortable in synagogues of the wider Jewish world. This was because Messianic Jews accepted the authority of the written Torah but not the oral Torah. In keeping with the theological tenets of evangelical Christianity, Messianic Jews, like the Hebrew Christians before them, viewed the Bible as their sole authority. They no longer followed evangelical Christianity in its nullification of the Pentateuch as the enduring constitution of the Jewish people, but they still maintained the evangelical distrust of tradition. In their eyes, Messianic Judaism was biblical Judaism, not rabbinic Judaism.[3] They disagreed with one another on the value of rabbinic tradition — some finding it of great value,[4] some finding it useful but also problematic,[5] and others rejecting it as dangerous.[6] But they all agreed

---

2. The Messianic Jewish thinker of the 1980s who most creatively challenged existing ecclesiological paradigms concerning the Jewish people was David Stern. He and Dan Juster were the two pioneers of Messianic Jewish theology. Yet his understanding of Christian identity was conventionally evangelical: "Protestants tend to define 'Christian' in terms of belief. Only 'genuine believers' are to be counted as Christians.... Roman Catholics and the older Eastern denominations, as well as some mainline Protestants, tend to define being Christian in terms of community. This corresponds more to what most Jewish people understand when talking about a person's religion.... The Church *is* a community, but only of persons saved by faith, which cannot be inherited from parents" (David H. Stern, *Messianic Jewish Manifesto* [Clarksville, Md.: Jewish New Testament, 1988], 18–19).

3. "We can not say too strongly, we ... are Biblical New Covenant Jews, not Rabbinic Jews!" (Daniel C. Juster, *Jewish Roots: A Foundation of Biblical Theology* [Rockville, Md.: Davar, 1986], xii).

4. See Stern, *Messianic Jewish Manifesto*.

5. See Juster, *Jewish Roots*, xi.

6. See Daniel Gruber, *Rabbi Akiba's Messiah* (Hanover: Elijah, 1999).

that Messianic Judaism should not treat Jewish tradition as authoritative — in any sense of the word — for the interpretation and application of the Bible.

Messianic Jewish attitudes toward the wider Jewish community were also shaped by evangelical soteriology. While adopting a positive vision of the biblically-based elements of Jewish observance, they nonetheless saw most if not all non-Messianic Jews as headed for eternal damnation. Messianic Jews continued to employ the language of their Hebrew Christian predecessors by speaking of themselves as "saved" and of their fellow Jews as "unsaved." It was even more natural to speak of themselves as "believers," and of other Jews as "unbelievers." Such language reflected a mentality that distinguished sharply between these two worlds. This mentality expressed itself not only in language, but also in the adoption of Christian missionary strategy and tactics.

These two evangelical theological tenets of biblical and soteriological exclusivism had profound and subtle sociological implications. They alienated Messianic Jews from the universal discourse of the Jewish world and created internal as well as external distance between themselves and their fellow Jews. Because of this, Messianic Jews found themselves in a tense and ambivalent situation. On the one hand, they claimed to be fully part of the Jewish community and demanded that the wider Jewish world recognize their legitimacy. On the other hand, they adopted a form of theological discourse and an attitude toward the spiritual status and destiny of fellow Jews that severed their own connection to the Jewish world and identified themselves not only as Christian, but as a particular type of Christian — namely, as conservative evangelicals.[7]

Response of the Wider Jewish World

As we have seen, Hebrew Christians had no theoretical trouble in reconciling their Christian and Jewish commitments. Christianity involved personal spiritual transformation, whereas Jewish life was national and distinct from traditional Jewish religion. How could Hebrew Christians be denied membership within the Jewish community at a time when adherence to traditional Jewish religious norms was no longer a prerequisite for communal involvement?

But this was not how the wider Jewish world saw the matter. When leaders of the Hebrew Christian Alliance of America sought membership in the Zionist Organization of America in the 1920s, they were rebuffed.[8] This was in keeping with the way Hebrew Christians were treated by Jewish communities on the local level. Once baptized, a Jew had forfeited all the normal privileges of membership in the Jewish people.

This was because the wider Jewish community refused to accept the way Hebrew Christians defined either Christian or Jewish life. From a mainstream Jewish perspective, Christianity was not only a personal faith that transformed individuals, but also — and preeminently — a tight-knit community with its own distinct identity, tradition, rituals, and way of life. In other words, it was a religion, and adherence to that

7. See Yaacov Ariel, *Evangelizing the Chosen People: Missions to the Jews in America, 1880–2000.* (Chapel Hill: University of North Carolina Press, 2000), 226, 235.

8. Ariel, *Evangelizing the Chosen People,* 173–74.

religion inevitably undermined the integrity of Jewish communal life. Similarly, even most secular Jews recognized that Jewish national life could not be totally separated from Jewish religious tradition. They might no longer believe in God or observe the Torah, but they still understood that Jewish community derived its historical substance from a way of life rooted in the Torah — written and oral — and they usually endorsed at least a modest measure of continuity with that life.

In the eyes of the wider Jewish community, Messianic Judaism was simply a more insidious version of Hebrew Christianity. In 1993 the Jewish Community Relations Council of New York issued a statement on Messianic Judaism (which they continued to call "Hebrew Christianity").[9] This declaration, endorsed by all the major branches of American Judaism, denounced Messianic Judaism as deceptive: "Though Hebrew-Christianity claims to be a form of Judaism, it is not. It is nothing more than a disguised effort to missionize Jews and convert them to Christianity. It deceptively uses the sacred symbols of Jewish observance (i.e., community Passover Seders, menorahs, messianic services, etc.) as a cover to convert Jews to Christianity, a belief system antithetical to Judaism."

The statement recognized that Messianic Jews retained their status as Jews but ruled that they had left the Jewish community and had forfeited the privileges of membership in that community (such as membership or honors in synagogues and/or Jewish communal organizations, burial in Jewish cemeteries, and access to Jewish communal facilities). The declaration articulated the reason for this ruling: "Hebrew-Christians are in radical conflict with the communal interests and the destiny of the Jewish people."

From the point of view of the wider Jewish community, Messianic Jews — like the Hebrew Christians before them — were missionary representatives of the Christian community seeking to entice Jews to leave the Jewish community and join their historical rival. In their own eyes they were simply born-again Jews who had adopted the Bible as their only authority and who had been saved from hell by Yeshua, but in the eyes of their fellow Jews such language demonstrated that Messianics had entered another world — that of evangelical Protestantism. In doing so, they had left the Jewish world behind.

The 1993 statement of the Jewish Community Relations Council of New York represented the official policy of Jewish communities in America. If someone was publicly known to be a Messianic Jew, they were not to be counted as part of a Jewish minyan (the quorum of ten Jews required for communal prayer), and they were not eligible for membership in Jewish organizations. Messianic Jews were the only category of Jews so treated by the Jewish community.

---

9. For the text, see http://www.jcrcny.org/library/spiritual-deception/meeting-challenge.html. The text is introduced as follows, "Jewish religious leadership has unequivocally declared 'Hebrew Christians' as completely separate and disassociated from the Jewish community. This has been set out in a statement, 'Meeting the Challenge: Hebrew Christians and the Jewish Community,' written by Dr. Lawrence H. Schiffman in 1993 for the then Task Force on Missionaries and Cults of the Jewish Community Relations Council of New York. This statement has been endorsed by the four major Jewish denominations Orthodox, Conservative, Reform and Reconstructionist as well as national Jewish organizations."

Twenty-First-Century Challenges
to Twentieth-Century Presuppositions

In the final years of the twentieth century a new perspective on relationship to the wider Jewish community began to emerge among a handful of Messianic Jewish leaders in the United States. The questions they raised and the positions they espoused would set much of the theological agenda for Messianic Jews in the first decade of the twenty-first century.[10]

In 1997 – 98 five leaders from the Union of Messianic Jewish Congregations (UMJC) formed a new entity called Hashivenu and articulated its core values.[11] A year later they convened the first Hashivenu Forum — an invitation-only gathering of Messianic Jewish leaders in which participants presented papers that built upon the Hashivenu core values and discussed the future of the Messianic Jewish movement in light of these presentations.

The fundamental concern driving the formation of Hashivenu was the relationship of Messianic Jews to the wider Jewish community. The central Hashivenu core value states the concern with clarity: "The Jewish people are 'us' not 'them.'"[12] In the expanded form of this core value, the Hashivenu board positioned this affirmation in relation to the conservative evangelical world, which most Messianic Jews still inhabited:

> For most of us, experience in evangelical contexts taught us to look at Jews only as people to whom we ought to witness. For us, the subtext of every family gathering became "How can I bring the subject up?" and the objective in our relationships with Jewish family, friends and acquaintances became "How can I witness to them without their closing the door on the Gospel and on me?"... We became church culture chameleons, adept at blending in, showing that even though we were Jews, "we weren't like the other Jews": we were real Christians, too.... One day we discovered that we had become habituated to speaking of the Jewish community in the third person. We awoke with a start.

But this core value was not merely a rejection of the notion that Messianic Judaism should be a subset of evangelical Protestantism. More significantly, it summoned Messianic Jews to find their home among the Jewish people. "In all aspects of life, we want to live in a Jewish neighborhood socially, culturally, conceptually so that we and our children and our children's children will not only call Yeshua Lord but also call the Jewish people 'our people' and Jewish life 'home.'"

According to the Hashivenu core values, adherence to Yeshua should bind Jews to their people, rather than alienate them from it.

While the central Hashivenu core value addressed relationship to the Jewish people, the first core value focused on the Messianic Jewish relationship to the religious heritage of this people: "Messianic Judaism is a Judaism and not a cosmetically

---

10. The remainder of this chapter deals with events in which I have played a significant role. While I seek to be as fair as possible in my treatment of these events, I make no claims to impartiality.

11. Stuart Dauermann, Robert Chenoweth, Paul Saal, Michael Schiffman, and Mark Kinzer.

12. For the text of the Hashivenu core values, see http://www.hashivenu.org.

altered 'Jewish-style' version of what is extant in the wider Christian community." The expanded version of this core value included the following:

> Too often the deep structure of Messianic Jewish religious life is indistinguishable from that of popular evangelicalism and bears little or no resemblance to any form of Judaism, past or present. When the world is easily divided into the classes of "saved" and "unsaved," ... when speculation about the end-times is more natural to us than reciting a *berachah* — then we know that the deep structure of our religious life is Hebrew Christian and has been untouched by the drastic changes in the surface structure of our movement.

Once again, we find an explicit attempt to distinguish Messianic Judaism from evangelical Protestantism and to emphasize its relationship with the rest of Judaism.[13] The expanded core value continues by expressing appreciation for the religious life of the wider Jewish world: "When we say that Messianic Judaism is 'a Judaism,' we are also acknowledging the existence of other 'Judaisms.' We do not deny their existence, their legitimacy, or their value. We are not the sole valid expression of Judaism with all else a counterfeit. We recognize our kinship with other Judaisms and believe that we have much of profound importance to learn from them, as well as something vitally important to share with them."

Never before had a group of Messianic Jewish leaders sought to differentiate their movement so definitively from evangelicalism and to identify it so radically as a branch of Judaism.

In 2000 this new perspective on the relationship of Messianic Jews to the wider Jewish world was elaborated in a forty-four-page booklet, *The Nature of Messianic Judaism*, published by Hashivenu.[14] This booklet provided the topic of discussion at the UMJC Theology Forum in the summer of the same year. It stirred many reactions, as evidenced by the responses to the booklet published the same year in *Kesher*.[15]

In 2002 Gabriela Karabelnik Reason submitted her senior thesis to the Department of Religious Studies at Yale University. The title was "Competing Trends in Messianic Judaism: The Debate over Evangelicalism." In this thesis Reason studied the two leading Messianic Jewish organizations, the UMJC and the Messianic Jewish Alliance of America (MJAA), and mapped their different ways of negotiating relationship to the evangelical and Jewish communities. She concluded that the MJAA identified primarily with the former, and the UMJC with the latter. Her interpretation of the UMJC's position was influenced greatly by interviews conducted with leaders associated with Hashivenu and by reading *The Nature of Messianic Judaism*.

---

13. Hashivenu's critical orientation to evangelical Protestantism was more a critique of Messianic Judaism than of evangelicalism itself. It stemmed from the unspoken assumptions of most Messianic Jews that evangelicalism was the only valid expression of Christianity and that Messianic Judaism was a subset of the evangelical movement. While the founders of Hashivenu challenged these assumptions, they nonetheless valued the spiritual and theological riches of the evangelical tradition.

14. Mark Kinzer, *The Nature of Messianic Judaism: Judaism as Genus, Messianic as Species* (West Hartford, Conn.: Hashivenu Archives, 2000).

15. Derek Leman, Jamie Cowen, Michael Rudolph, and Ralph Finley, "On Mark Kinzer's *The Nature of Messianic Judaism: Judaism as Genus, Messianic as Species*," *Kesher: A Journal of Messianic Judaism* 12 (2000): 98–127. A response from me, "The Nature of Messianic Judaism: Replying to My Respondents," was published in the subsequent issue of the journal (*Kesher* 13 [2001]: 36–67). *Kesher* is a theological journal affiliated with the UMJC.

Normally a senior thesis has little impact on the world. But this was no ordinary thesis. Reason was the first external observer to put her finger on a significant development that was taking place in the Messianic Jewish world, though she exaggerated its influence even within the UMJC. The thesis struck a nerve for some Messianic Jews who were troubled by the new directions they discerned within the UMJC. This was especially the case for Jews for Jesus, a missionary organization closely aligned with evangelical Protestantism but also seeking to have an impact within Messianic Jewish circles through its publication *Havurah*. In 2003 *Havurah* published a two-part article critical of developments taking place in the UMJC.[16] The article quoted from the Reason thesis and cited the Hashivenu core values and *The Nature of Messianic Judaism*. Now the argument was joined by those beyond the limits of the UMJC.

But the controversy was just as lively within the UMJC. Many of its leaders did not identify with Hashivenu and could not see themselves reflected in Reason's depiction of the UMJC. At the beginning of 2005 *Kesher* published an abbreviated version of Reason's thesis, along with five responses to it.[17] The discussion demonstrated the desire of some to blur the distinction between the two "competing trends" and between the UMJC and the MJAA.

The next turning point in the broader discussion occurred at the end of 2005 with the publication of *Postmissionary Messianic Judaism* (*PMJ*).[18] This volume included most of the material previously found in *The Nature of Messianic Judaism*, but set that material within a more ambitious theological argument addressed not only to the Messianic Jewish world but also to the Christian Church. The term "postmissionary" was chosen to make an ecclesiological rather than a missiological point — namely, that Messianic Jews are not called to be representatives of the Christian community operating within another religious community (i.e., the Jewish people) but to be fully part of the Jewish world in both religious and national terms. In fact, they are to represent the Jewish community in relation to the Church, rather than the reverse.

PMJ showed that the Hashivenu perspective included not only a revised Messianic Jewish view of the Jewish people but also a transformed vision of the Church. As noted above, Messianic Jews had inherited from their Hebrew Christian predecessors a pietistic and voluntaristic understanding of the Church. Whereas the Jewish people was understood to be a visible, communal, and national reality, the Church was a collection of saved and regenerated individuals whose identity could never be known with any certainty in this life. The former constituted a people with continuity through history, the latter a spiritual community newly established in every generation. In contrast to this ecclesiology, *PMJ* argued that the Church is an eschatological extension of Israel and as such must be a visible community with continuity through

16. Rich Robinson and Ruth Rosen, "The Challenge of Our Messianic Movement," *Havurah* 6, no. 2 (2003): 1 – 3; *Havurah* 6, no. 3 (2003): 1 – 6. Jews for Jesus continued to participate in the discussion through Rich Robinson's *The Messianic Movement: A Field Guide for Evangelical Christians* (San Francisco: Purple Pomegranate, 2005), which included a chapter on Hashivenu, 109 – 22.

17. Gabriela M. Reason, "Competing Trends in Messianic Judaism: The Debate over Evangelicalism," with responses by Marc H. Ellis, Russell Resnik, Daniel C. Juster, Jamie Cowen, and Murray Silberling, *Kesher* 18 (2005): 7 – 60.

18. Mark S. Kinzer, *Postmissionary Messianic Judaism: Redefining Christian Engagement with the Jewish People* (Grand Rapids: Brazos, 2005).

time. Thus, the Hashivenu perspective called not for a withdrawal from the Church, but for the renewal of the Church as a living community through its reconnection with the Jewish people.

PMJ was the first serious theological volume to emerge from the Messianic Jewish movement and to be published by a mainstream religious publisher. For this reason, and because it continued the trajectory of the discussion begun with the formation of Hashivenu at the end of the twentieth century, the book received an immediate and intense response within the Messianic Jewish movement. In 2006 the journal Mishkan, published in Israel and serving the world of Christian missions to the Jews, devoted an entire issue to PMJ.[19] The same year Kesher likewise featured responses to the book.[20] In the spring of 2007 Michael Brown presented a fiercely critical assessment of PMJ at the North American meeting of the Lausanne Consultation on Jewish Evangelism.[21] But even Brown acknowledged it as a "watershed volume."

In his response to PMJ included in the Kesher volume of 2006, Mitch Glaser — the president of Chosen People Ministries — proposed the convocation of a movement-wide gathering of leaders to discuss the kinds of issues raised by PMJ. This initiative culminated in the Borough Park Symposium of 2007. One of the main issues discussed at Borough Park was soteriology. The radical identification with the wider Jewish world called for by the Hashivenu core values and by PMJ appeared incompatible with the more exclusivist soteriology held by most Messianic Jews.[22] At Borough Park two of the founders of Hashivenu argued for a more inclusivist soteriology in which all salvation comes through Yeshua, though all who receive that salvation may not have confessed Yeshua in this life.[23]

---

19. Mishkan: A Forum on the Gospel and the Jewish People 48 (2006): 3–72. The issue included substantive reviews of the book by Rich Robinson, Richard Harvey, and Eckhard J. Schnabel, a response to the reviews from the author, and then shorter comments on the book from Kai Kjaer-Hansen, Akiva Cohen, Derek Leman, Baruch Maoz, and David Stern.

20. Kesher 20 (2006): 7–64. The issue included a summary of the book by Jonathan Kaplan, responses to the book by David Stern, Daniel Juster, Mitch Glaser, R. Kendall Soulen, Douglas Harink, and Peter Hocken, and a concluding rejoinder from the author.

21. Michael L. Brown, "Is a Post-Missionary, Truly Messianic Judaism Possible?" (paper presented at the North American Lausanne Consultation on Jewish Evangelism, San Antonio, Tex., April 18, 2007). Cited 9 April 2012. Online: http://www.lcje.net/papers/2007.html.

22. E.g., Daniel C. Juster, "The Narrow Wider Hope," Kesher 22 (2008): 14–41. Online: http://www.kesher-journal.com/Issue-22/The-Narrow-Wider-Hope; Michael Rydelnik, "The Jewish People and Salvation," Mishkan: A Forum on the Gospel and the Jewish People 53 (2007): 34–43. Cf. Richard Harvey, "Implicit Universalism in Some Christian Zionism and Messianic Judaism," in Jesus, Salvation and the Jewish People: The Uniqueness of Jesus and Jewish Evangelism (ed. David Parker; Milton Keynes: Paternoster, 2011), 209–34. The UMJC's 2004 "Statement on the Work of Yeshua" affirms that "Yeshua is the Messiah promised to Israel in the Torah and prophets. Through His death, burial, and resurrection, He provided the atoning sacrifice that gives assurance of eternal life to those who genuinely trust in Him. Jewish people, along with all people, need the spiritual redemption that is only available in Messiah Yeshua, and need to put their trust in Him and His sacrificial work. Our role as a union of congregations is to embody the message of life and redemption through Messiah in the context of the larger Jewish community." Cited 1 March 2012. Online: http://www.umjc.org/home-mainmenu-1/faqs-mainmenu-58/14-umjc-faq/19-what-are-the-standards-of-the-umjc.

23. Stuart Dauermann, "What Is the Gospel We Should Be Commending to All Israel in These Times of Transition?" and Mark S. Kinzer, "Final Destinies: Qualifications for Receiving an Eschatological Inheritance," Kesher 22 (2008): 42–78, 87–119. Online: http://www.kesherjournal.com/Issue-22/View-issue. See also Mark S. Kinzer, "Yeshua, the Glory of God and the Glory of Israel: Motives for Postmissionary Messianic Jewish Outreach" (paper presented at the annual conference of the Union of Messianic Jewish Congregations, Chicago, July 2007). Online: http://www.mjstudies.com.

While the question of the Messianic Jewish relationship to the wider Jewish world has been front and center for the movement as a whole in the twenty-first century, few outsiders to the movement have been aware of the intense discussion that has taken place. The new perspectives are far from dominant and have yet to have an impact on attitudes in the wider Jewish community. As far as Jewish communal leaders are concerned, they are still dealing with Hebrew Christianity.

Conclusion

For the first three decades of its existence the Messianic Jewish movement adhered to the presuppositions of traditional evangelical ecclesiology, soteriology, eschatology, and hermeneutics. While it claimed to be a movement internal to the Jewish world, most outsiders — Jewish, Christian, and secular — viewed it as a subset of evangelical Christianity.

In the first decade of the twenty-first century these presuppositions have been challenged. A vocal minority has called for radical identification with the Jewish community and an identity distinct from the evangelical world. This may be a passing current of thought, with little impact on the future of Messianic Judaism, or it may set the stage for the twenty-first-century evolution of the movement. Those who consider Messianic Judaism of any importance will be watching closely as the next chapters of the story unfold.

For Further Reading

Berger, David. *The Rebbe, the Messiah and the Scandal of Orthodox Indifference*. Portland: Littman Library of Jewish Civilization, 2001.

Blecher, Arthur. "Community, Intermarriage and Optimism." Pages 163–91 in *The New American Judaism: The Way Forward on Challenging Issues from Intermarriage to Jewish Identity*. New York: Palgrave Macmillan, 2007.

Boyarin, Daniel. "The Suffering Christ as a Midrash on Daniel." Pages 129–56 in *The Jewish Gospels: The Story of the Jewish Christ*. New York: New Press, 2012.

Cohen, Diane. "Our Relationship as Messianic Jews with the Wider Jewish Community from My Perspective." Paper presented at the Borough Park Symposium, New York City, NY, 2012. Online: http://www.mjstudies.com.

Cohn-Sherbok, Dan. "Models of Messianic Judaism." Pages 203–13 in *Messianic Judaism*. London: Cassell, 2000.

———. "Modern Hebrew Christianity and Messianic Judaism." Pages 287–98 in *The Image of the Judaeo-Christians in Ancient Jewish and Christian Literature*. Edited by Peter J. Tomson and Doris Lambers-Petry. Tübingen: Mohr Siebeck, 2003.

Eisenbaum, Pamela. "They Don't Make Jews Like Jesus Anymore" (review of Daniel Boyarin, *The Jewish Gospels: The Story of the Jewish Christ*). *Moment Magazine Book Reviews* (March/April 2012). Cited 4 April 2012. Online: http://www.momentmag.com/moment/issues/2012/04/Books_Eisenbaum.html.

Harris-Shapiro, Carol. "The Saved *and* the Chosen?" Pages 166–89 in *Messianic Judaism: A Rabbi's Journey through Religious Change in America*. Boston: Beacon, 1999.

Lockshin, Marty. "Judaism, Christianity and Jewish-Christianity: What the Future May Hold." Pages 137–48 in *Cult and Culture: Studies in Cultural Meaning*. Edited by B. Zelechow and D. Paycha. Université de Cergy-Pontoise, 1999.

Novak, David. "When Jews Are Christians." Pages 218–28 in *Talking with Christians: Musings of a Jewish Theologian*. Grand Rapids: Eerdmans, 2005.

Prager, Dennis. "A New Approach to Jews-for-Jesus." *Moment Magazine* (June 2000): 28–29.

Rosenblum, Jonathan. "The Ultimate Jewish Pluralists." *Jerusalem Post*, January 9, 1998. Cited 26 March 2012. Online: http://www.jewishmediaresources.com/141/the-ultimate-jewish-pluralists.

Rudolph, David J. "Contemporary Judeo-Christian Communities in the Jewish Diaspora." Pages 146–50 in *Encyclopedia of the Jewish Diaspora: Origins, Experiences, and Culture*, vol. 1. Edited by M. Avrum Ehrlich. Santa Barbara: ABC-CLIO, 2008.

Shapiro, Faydra. "Jesus for Jews: The Unique Problem of Messianic Judaism." *Journal of Religion & Society* 14 (2012): 1–17. Cited 26 March 2012. Online: http://moses.creighton.edu/JRS/2012/2012-15.pdf.

Wyschogrod, Michael. "A Letter to Cardinal Lustiger." Pages 202–10 in *Abraham's Promise: Judaism and Jewish-Christian Relations*. Edited by R. Kendall Soulen. Grand Rapids: Eerdmans, 2004. Originally published as "Letter to a Friend" in *Modern Theology* 2 (April 1995): 165–71.

———. "Response to the Respondents." *Modern Theology* 2 (April 1995): 229–41.

CHAPTER 12

Messianic Jews and
the Gentile Christian World

Daniel C. Juster

Messianic Jews regard Gentile Christians as their brothers and sisters in the Lord and at the same time experience significant tension with the Gentile Christian world. It is almost impossible for a Jewish person to grow up in a Christian cultural context without being exposed to Christian anti-Judaism and feeling its impact personally. Since the time of Constantine, Jews have been subject to persecution under national powers that claimed to be Christian. This has included the 1492 expulsion of Jews from Spain, the Inquisition, and pogroms initiated by church authorities.[1] Classic Christian theology describes the Church as having replaced Israel as the people of God. Many churches teach that Messianic Jews are not called by God to continue to identify and live as Jews. These historic realities in part shape the Messianic Jewish view of the Gentile Christian world.

The UMJC "Defining Messianic Judaism" Statement

The Union of Messianic Jewish Congregations has developed a statement that helps to clarify the relationship between Messianic Jews and the Gentile Christian world:

Expanded Statement
Jewish life is life in a concrete, historical community. Thus, Messianic Jewish groups must be fully part of the Jewish people, sharing its history and its covenantal responsibility as a people chosen by God. At the same time, faith in Yeshua also has a crucial communal dimension. This faith unites the Messianic Jewish community and the Christian Church, which is the assembly of the faithful from the nations who are joined to Israel through the Messiah. Together the Messianic Jewish community and the Christian Church constitute the *ekklesia*, the one Body of Messiah, a community of Jews and Gentiles who in their ongoing distinction and mutual blessing anticipate the shalom of the world to come.[2]

According to this statement, the Messianic Jewish community is united with the "Christian Church" in forming the *ekklesia*, the Body of Messiah. The term "Chris-

---

1. James Carroll, *Constantine's Sword: The Church and the Jews* (New York: Houghton Mifflin, 2001), 18, 343–62, 365–68.
2. Union of Messianic Jewish Congregations, "Defining Messianic Judaism," 2005. Online: http://www.umjc .org/home-mainmenu-1/global-vision-mainmenu-42/13-vision/225-defining-messianic-judaism.

tian Church" is used here in a more delimited way to describe the "Gentile wing of the Church." This is in keeping with the connotation of the word "Christian" in the wider Jewish world. For Jews, Christian = not Jewish, i.e., Gentile. This is why Messianic Jews do not self-identify as "Christians." It would imply to fellow Jews that they are no longer Jews.

The UMJC definition statement underscores that Messianic Jews are *a distinct part of the Body of Messiah*, a particularity manifest in the continuation of Jewish identity and lifestyle as Jewish followers of Yeshua.[3] Mark Kinzer calls this "bilateral ecclesiology" — there is *one* Body of Messiah, but it exists in two expressions, a Jewish expression and a Gentile expression, with variation existing in both expressions.[4] The Messianic Jewish community is the organic bridge between the Body of Messiah and the Jewish people. We are part of both.

The relationship between the Messianic Jewish community and the Gentile wing of the Church is described in the UMJC statement as one of "mutual blessing."[5] The attainment of our respective goals requires the two wings of the *ekklesia* to be interdependent. Since interdependence can come about only through relationship, Messianic Jews invest themselves in Christian groups and organizations that enable relationship building. In addition to this book project, which reflects Messianic Jewish and Gentile Christian collaboration, two other examples of interdependence and relationship building are the Messianic Jewish – Roman Catholic dialogue and Toward Jerusalem Council II.

The Messianic Jewish – Roman Catholic Dialogue

A Roman Catholic – Messianic Jewish dialogue began in 2000 with a meeting between Cardinal (then Father) George Cottier, the Vatican's papal theologian, seven other Catholic leaders, and seven Messianic Jews. In 2008, Cardinal Christoff Schönborn of Vienna, the editor of the new *Catechism of the Catholic Church*, joined the dialogue. As part of the annual meetings, the Messianic Jewish contingent wrote a response to *Lumen Gentium* (Light of the Nations), the official Roman Catholic statement on the doctrine of the Church. The response, written by Mark Kinzer and subsequently published in *First Things*,[6] claimed that the Roman Catholic doctrine of the Church was inadequate. The Messianic Jewish delegation praised the Catholic Church for its strong stand against replacement theology (supersessionism) and for affirming the continued election of the Jewish people.[7] However, they also expressed concern about the extent to which the Church was defined as a new thing in *Lumen Gentium*.

3. Daniel C. Juster, *Jewish Roots: A Foundation of Biblical Theology* (Shippensburg, Pa.: Destiny Image, 2005), 35, 220 – 23.

4. Mark S. Kinzer, *Postmissionary Messianic Judaism* (Grand Rapids: Brazos, 2005), 151 – 79.

5. See R. Kendall Soulen, *The God of Israel and Christian Theology* (Minneapolis: Fortress, 1996). The creation order of Genesis, including the distinction between Israel and the nations, reflects an interdependence of all parts of creation for mutual blessing.

6. Mark S. Kinzer, "Messianic Gentiles & Messianic Jews," *First Things* 189 (January 2009): 43 – 47. Reprinted in Mark S. Kinzer, "*Lumen Gentium*, through Messianic Jewish Eyes," in *Israel's Messiah and the People of God: A Vision for Messianic Jewish Covenant Fidelity* (ed. Jennifer M. Rosner; Eugene, Oreg.: Cascade, 2011), 156 – 74.

7. Summarized in the *Catechism of the Catholic Church* (New York: Doubleday, 1995), par. 758 – 68.

The statement recognized that the Church was birthed from Israel. Nevertheless, the Church was described in a way that had little connection with Israel today. *Lumen Gentium* described the Church as a completely *separate* reality:

> [The statement] presents "the history of the people of Israel" as a "foreshadowing of the Church," which is "constituted" through Christ's person, life, and work and "made manifest" by the outpouring of the Spirit. This means the Church is an essentially new reality in the world. It shares some features in common with the people of Israel in the old covenant, but it is fundamentally discontinuous. The goal of the divine plan, conceived "before time began," is the establishment of the Church, and God's dealings with the people of Israel in the old covenant were all ordered to prepare for that goal.... The new people — whose membership is determined not by physical but by spiritual birth — is the Israel mentioned by Jeremiah 31 as the recipient of the "new covenant."[8]

The Messianic Jewish response to *Lumen Gentium* continued:

> As Wolfhart Pannenberg has emphasized, Jeremiah 31:31 – 32 "promise[s] the new covenant not to another people but to Israel as the eschatological renewal and fulfillment of its covenant relationship with its God."[9]

> There are two omissions in *Lumen Gentium* that require attention. First, the Church needs to examine the significance and role of the Church for those who come to it "from circumcision." Yeshua is not only *lumen gentium*, a light to the gentiles, but also the "glory of your people Israel" (Luke 2:32). His body should likewise illumine both spheres, but in different ways, as Cardinal Christoph Schönborn has recently emphasized: "St. Paul distinguishes between the two vocations, between those who believed in Jesus as the Messiah who came 'from circumcision' and those who converted to Christ and came 'from the gentiles.' ... These two appeals in the Church reflect the twofold way of the same salvation in Christ, one for Jews and one for gentiles."[10]

Cardinal Schönborn recognized that the Messianic Jewish community organically united the predominantly Gentile Church and the Jewish people. The eschatological destiny of the Gentile wing of the Church is tied to the destiny of Israel. They are inseparable. While the predominantly Gentile Church may be critical of the directions taken by its organically connected partner, she cannot — if she rightly defines herself — be anti-Semitic. To be anti-Semitic is to be against her own identity, an identity that is united with the Jewish people. She must love, honor, and pray for the destiny of the Jewish people. This requires unity with and support for the restored Messianic Jewish community.

In addition to the Messianic Jewish – Roman Catholic dialogue, there has been a concerted effort by Messianic Jewish and Gentile Christian leaders from various communions, denominations, and streams within the Church to work toward a restored Jew-Gentile Body of Messiah.

---

8. Kinzer, "Messianic Gentiles & Messianic Jews," 43 – 44.
9. Kinzer, "Messianic Gentiles & Messianic Jews," 44.
10. Kinzer, "Messianic Gentiles & Messianic Jews," 45.

Toward Jerusalem Council II

In 1996, seven Messianic Jewish leaders from Israel and the Diaspora, and seven Gentile Christian leaders — formed an executive committee to support an initiative that came to be called Toward Jerusalem Council II. TJCII is "an initiative of repentance and reconciliation between the Jewish and Gentile segments of the Church."[11] Its vision is to see the Church formally affirm that Yeshua-believing Jews should continue to live as Jews in keeping with their calling from God:

> Our vision is that one day there will be a second Council of Jerusalem that will be, in an important respect, the inverse of the first Council described in Acts 15. Whereas the first Council was made up of Jewish believers in Yeshua (Jesus), who decided not to impose on the Gentiles the requirements of the Jewish Law, so the second Council would be made up of Gentile church leaders who would recognize and welcome Jewish believers in Yeshua back into the Body of Messiah without requiring them to abandon their Jewish identity and practice.[12]

In order to move toward this goal, the TJCII board sponsored many prayer journeys over a ten-year period. They traveled with groups of intercessors representing many streams of the Church. Acts of intercessory repentance were made at the sites where Church decisions were made rejecting the Jewish people and rejecting Jewish believers in Yeshua in particular. This included several sites in Spain: Elvira near Granada, Alhambra Palace in Granada, and Cordoba. It included Rome, Nicea, Antioch, and Jerusalem.

After ten years, in 2006, leaders and intercessors from thirty-five nations and every major denomination and stream of the Church gathered in Jerusalem. A significant contingent of Messianic Jews from Israel and the Diaspora joined them. Repentance, intercession, and worship characterized the gathering. There was a sense of a great spiritual breakthrough. There has never been such a gathering of representatives from the different streams of the Church in unity with Messianic Jewish leaders. They came together to heal historic wounds and repudiate ancient decisions by the Church against Messianic Jews. The negative attitudes and prejudices, which led the church fathers to exclude and then reject the Messianic Jews in the early centuries of Church history, had never been dealt with in such an international convocation.

The importance of TJCII is highlighted in the works of Peter Hocken.[13] Hocken argues that the Church will remain cursed with division until it deals with its relationship with Israel. Moreover, the Church cannot deal with Israel adequately until it confronts the modern Messianic Jewish movement. Hocken notes that the first Church division came from a rejection of the legitimacy of the early Messianic Jewish community. That decision established the roots of anti-Semitism in the Church and

11. Toward Jerusalem Council II, "What Is TJCII?" Cited 10 April 2012. Online: http://www.tjcii.org/what-is-toward-jerusalem-council-ii.htm.
12. Toward Jerusalem Council II, "What Is TJCII?"
13. Peter Hocken, "The Messianic Jewish Movement: New Current and Old Reality," in *The Challenges of the Pentecostal, Charismatic and Messianic Jewish Movements: The Tensions of the Spirit* (Burlington, Vt.: Ashgate, 2009), 97–115. See also Peter Hocken, *The Glory and the Shame: Reflections on the Twentieth-Century Outpouring of the Holy Spirit* (Guildford, UK: Eagle, 1994), 139, 166.

was repeatedly confirmed by the Church throughout the centuries. The modern Messianic Jewish movement provides churches with an opportunity to change this history by coming alongside and supporting Messianic Jews. Hocken insists that this has to include acts of repentance and reconciliation. He also affirms Messianic Judaism as a self-governing and indigenous movement, which allows it to play a similar role with all denominations and streams of the Church:[14]

> Meeting Messianic Jews confronts Gentile Christians with Jewish believers in Jesus who refuse to be "replaced." It faces Christians not just with a different theology but with an incarnate reality. This encounter requires an unpacking of what it means to switch from a "replacement logic" to an understanding of Israel and the church centred on "the mystery of ingrafting."
>
> This challenge touches Catholics, Orthodox, classical Reformation Protestants, Evangelicals and Pentecostals in their self-understanding and so impinges on the respective Christian identities of all.... The Messianic challenge confronts Catholics and Orthodox with the unfamiliar and disconcerting idea that something went wrong in the earliest period of church history. Maybe not as much was lost as Evangelicals think, but nonetheless something was lost that cannot be dismissed as peripheral. For the idea of divine rejection led inexorably to the inculcation of contempt for an accursed people, the language of deicide (accusations it was necessary for the Second Vatican Council to repudiate) and malicious myths with all the bloodshed and civil disturbance they provoked. But most profoundly this issue is not marginal to Christian faith, because the place of the believing Jews belongs to the nature of the church, the mystery expressed most clearly in Ephesians 2 and 3.... In fact, the challenge from the Messianic Jews directly affects Christian understanding of the church. For the Messianic Jewish claim that they represent a "resurrection" of the Jewish church of the first generations obviously involves an ecclesiological assertion. It is that the one church of our Lord Jesus Christ is made up of Jew and Gentile....
>
> This union of Jew and Gentile is not just the coming together of individuals to form one new entity. It is, as Paul indicates in Romans 11, the ingrafting of wild olive branches (the Gentile believers) into the natural olive tree (Israel renewed in the new covenant through Messiah) that still has its natural branches (the Jewish believers in Yeshua). There is a parallel with the union of man and woman in marriage ("the two become one flesh") without the man ceasing to be a man or the woman ceasing to be a woman. But there is this difference that in the union of Jew and Gentile the Gentile is being drawn into a unity that already existed, the union of the Messiah with his sisters and brothers....
>
> The challenges so far discussed have been at the level of understanding and of theology. However the challenge from the Jewish people and particularly from the Messianic Jews is also a challenge to the heart, a call to repentance. This alone can take us (Gentile Christian and Messianic Jew) beyond our present divisions and limitations.... What distinguishes the TJCII vision from many other church ini-

---

14. Daniel C. Juster, *The Irrevocable Calling: Israel's Role as a Light to the Nations* (Clarksville, Md.: Lederer, 2007), 40–41.

tiatives concerning the Jewish people is: (1) the single focus on the rightness and importance of the corporate Jewish witness to Yeshua and of its recognition by all the Christian churches; (2) the participation of Christians from the full spectrum of churches and ecclesial communities from the Evangelical and the Pentecostal through the historic Reformation churches to the Catholic and the Orthodox; (3) the recognition that this vision can only be carried forward in humility and with a representative confession of the sins of the past against the Jewish people and specifically against a distinctive Jewish witness to Yeshua and (4) the process is always "Toward Jerusalem" because of the place that Jerusalem holds for the Jewish people and in the promises never revoked of the God of Abraham, Isaac and Jacob.[15]

The TJCII committee has been in dialogue with representatives of many different streams within the Gentile Christian world and has encouraged church bodies to adopt the following *Seven Affirmations*:[16]

1. We affirm the election of Israel, its irrevocable nature and God's unfinished work with the Jewish people regarding salvation and the role of Israel as a blessing to the nations.

2. We affirm that Jews who come to faith in the Messiah, Jesus, are called to retain their Jewish identity and live as part of their people in ways consistent with the New Covenant.

3. We affirm the formation of Messianic Jewish congregations as a significant and effective way to express Jewish collective identity (in Jesus) and as a means of witnessing to Jesus before the Jewish community. We also affirm Jewish individuals and groups that are part of churches and encourage them in their commitment to Jewish life and identity.

4. We affirm our willingness as an ecclesiastical body to build bridges to the Messianic Jewish community; to extend the hand of friendship and to pray for their growth and vitality.

5. We affirm our willingness to share our resources with Messianic Jewish congregations, mission organizations and theological training institutes so as to empower them to fulfill their God-given purpose.

6. We affirm our willingness to be a voice within our own ecclesiastical structures and spheres of influence against all forms of anti-Semitism, replacement theology (supersessionism) and teaching that precludes the expression of Jewish identity in Jesus.

7. Finally, we affirm that as Jewish and Gentile expressions of life in Jesus grow organically side by side with distinct identities that God will be glorified; that the Kingdom of Heaven will be advanced and that the vision of "the one new man" in Ephesians 2 will unfold as part of the original Abrahamic blessing to the nations.[17]

---

15. Hocken, "The Messianic Jewish Movement," 104–5, 107, 112.

16. In September 1998, the committee met with Cardinal Joseph Ratizinger, who is today Pope Benedict XVI.

17. Toward Jerusalem Council II, "Toward Jerusalem Council II Articles." Cited 2 January 2012. Online: http://www.tjcii.org/toward-jerusalem-council-ii-articles.htm.

The *Seven Affirmations* statement promotes the same principles articulated in the UMJC "Defining Messianic Judaism" statement and the Messianic Jewish response to *Lumen Gentium*. The second affirmation states that Jews who come to faith in Yeshua are called to maintain Jewish identity and live as Jews. The third affirmation upholds Messianic Jewish congregations and groupings in churches. And the seventh affirmation asserts that a right relationship between the Messianic Jewish community and the Gentile wing of the Church — one characterized by unity with distinction[18] — is a key to the redemption of the nations. Church bodies are beginning to embrace the *Seven Affirmations* statement and are putting their words into practice by building relationships with Messianic Jews.[19]

Conclusion

In looking back over Church history, it would be accurate to say that the Jewish people, through their Messiah and the faithful Jewish apostles who carried his message into the world, gave birth to the Church. So, too, the Church has been called to be the womb of intercession for affecting the rebirth of the Jewish people. However, there is a humbling dilemma: the historic Church has failed abysmally to fulfill her God-ordained role for Israel. The Church has been infected with the very anti-Semitism she was called to battle. The history of the Church's complicity in anti-Semitism and in crimes against the Jewish people is one of the great tragedies of history.[20]

This notwithstanding, the Messianic Jewish community views itself as united with the Gentile wing of the Church in a partnership that is intended by God to reflect interdependence and mutual blessing.[21] Such interdependence and mutual blessing can come about only through close relationship. Therefore, Messianic Jews invest in

---

18. Some people on the fringes of the Messianic Jewish movement hold to a view first attested in Galatians and Acts 15 that Gentile Christians should keep the Torah in the same way as Jewish people. These "One Law" proponents, most of whom are Gentile followers of Yeshua, attack the Gentile wing of the Church, claiming that pagan practices have influenced it, and that Gentile Christian churches should return to the Jewish roots of their faith and essentially become Messianic synagogues. Messianic Jewish national organizations reject this view, which would collapse Jew-Gentile distinction and lead to another type of homogeneity, a Jewish one. See Daniel C. Juster and Russ Resnik, "One Law Movements: A Challenge to the Messianic Jewish Community," Union of Messianic Jewish Congregations, January 28, 2005. Cited 12 August 2012. Online: http://www.mjstudies.com. Also Boaz Michael, *Tent of David: Healing the Vision of the Messianic Gentile* (Marshfield, Mo.: First Fruits of Zion, 2012; First Fruits of Zion, "Divine Invitation: An Apostolic Call to Torah," 2010. Cited 26 February 2012. Online: http://ffoz.org/downloads/white_papers/. Another version of the One Law perspective is the "Two House" or "Ephraimite" movement, which claims that all Christians are assimilated Jews. For a Messianic Jewish response, see Boaz Michael, *Twelve Gates: Where Do the Nations Enter?* (Marshfield, Mo.: First Fruits of Zion, 2012); Kay Silberling, "The Ephraimite Error" (a position paper submitted to the International Messianic Jewish Alliance, July 6, 2007). Cited 12 August 2012. Online: http://www.mjstudies.com.

19. The first larger denomination to embrace the *Seven Affirmations* statement was the Four Square Gospel Church under the leadership of Jack Hayford.

20. Juster, *Irrevocable Calling*, 39.

21. The relationship of mutual blessing between Jew and Gentile in the Body of Messiah is a foreshadowing of the relationship of mutual blessing that will one day exist between Israel and the nations in the *Olam HaBa* (the World to Come). In the Age to Come, Israel and the nations will bring blessing to each other. The prophet Isaiah writes that Israel will take root and blossom and fill the whole world with fruit (Isa 27:6). The nations will in turn bring their riches to Israel (Isa 60:11). This is similar to the picture we see in Rev 21:26, where all the nations bring their riches into the New Jerusalem. Riches should not be thought of in a carnal way. Rather, the nations bring their gifts and creativity to enrich the life of Israel. They are shared in relationships of love and mutual blessing.

Christian groups and organizations that welcome a Messianic Jewish presence, even as Paul wrote, "Welcome one another, therefore, just as Messiah has welcomed you, for the glory of God" (Rom 15:7 JNT).[22]

Christian theology emphasizes that God is unfolding his great plan for the redemption and transformation of the cosmos through the work of the Church.[23] As Messianic Jews, we have added a significant corollary to the traditional Christian narrative: the work of the Gentile Christian world cannot be accomplished without being in right relationship with Israel and the Messianic Jewish community in particular.

For Further Reading

Abraham, William J. "Method in Ecumenism." Paper presented at the annual meeting of the Messianic Judaism and the Church Working Group, Southern Methodist University, Dallas, Texas, June 19, 2012.

Garrigues, Jean-Miguel. "Complementarity between the Vocations of Jews and Gentiles in the Church of Christ." Translation of pages 125–28, 142–45 in Jean-Miguel Garrigues, Le Saint-Esprit sceau de la Trinité: le Filioque et l'originalité trinitaire de l'Esprit dans sa personne et dans sa mission. Paris: du Cerf, 2011. Online: http://www.mjstudies.com.

Glaser, Mitch. "Discovering the Purpose of Our Identity as One New Man." Pages 45–57 in Awakening the One New Man. Edited by Robert F. Wolff. Shippensburg, Pa.: Destiny Image, 2011.

Hayford, Jack W. "Allowing the Spirit to Refocus Our Identity." Pages 17–32 in Awakening the One New Man. Edited by Robert F. Wolff. Shippensburg, Pa.: Destiny Image, 2011.

Hocken, Peter. "The Messianic Jewish Movement: New Current and Old Reality." Pages 97–115 in The Challenges of the Pentecostal, Charismatic and Messianic Jewish Movements: The Tensions of the Spirit. Burlington, Vt.: Ashgate, 2009.

Hoyt, Jane Hansen. "The Master Plan for the One New Man." Pages 139–59 in Awakening the One New Man. Edited by Robert F. Wolff. Shippensburg, Pa.: Destiny Image, 2011.

Juster, Daniel C. "Denominations, Messianic Jews, and the One New Man." Pages 83–105 in Awakening the One New Man. Edited by Robert F. Wolff. Shippensburg, Pa.: Destiny Image, 2011.

———. The Irrevocable Calling: Israel's Role as a Light to the Nations. Clarksville, Md.: Messianic Jewish Publishers, 2007.

———. Passion for Israel: A Short History of the Evangelical Church's Commitment to the Jewish People and Israel. Clarksville, Md.: Messianic Jewish Publishers, 2012.

———. That They May Be One: A Brief Review of Church Restoration Movements and Their Connection to the Jewish People. Clarksville, Md.: Messianic Jewish Publishers, 2009.

Kinzer, Mark S. Postmissionary Messianic Judaism: Redefining Christian Engagement with the Jewish People. Grand Rapids: Brazos, 2005.

Lancaster, D. Thomas. Grafted In: Israel, Gentiles, and the Mystery of the Gospel. Second Edition. Marshfield, Mo.: First Fruits of Zion, 2009.

Levy, Antoine. "Messianic Judaism: The Ecumenical Factor." Kesher: A Journal of Messianic Judaism 25 (2011): 3–14. Online: http://www.kesherjournal.com/Issue-25/Messianic-Judaism-The-Ecumenical-Factor.

---

22. See David Rudolph, "Introduction," in Introduction to Messianic Judaism.
23. N. T. Wright, The New Testament and the People of God (Minneapolis: Fortress, 1992), 321–38, 459–64.

Michael, Boaz. *Tent of David: Healing the Vision of the Messianic Gentile.* Marshfield, Mo.: First Fruits of Zion, 2012.

Rudolph, David J. "Messianic Jews and Christian Theology: Restoring an Historical Voice to the Contemporary Discussion." *Pro Ecclesia* 14, no. 1 (2005): 58–84. Online: http://www.mjstudies.com.

Stern, David H. *Restoring the Jewishness of the Gospel: A Message for Christians.* Clarksville, Md.: Lederer, 2009.

Toward Jerusalem Council II. "Toward Jerusalem Council II: Vision, Origin and Documents." Cited 3 January 2012. Online: http://www.tjcii.org.

Union of Messianic Jewish Congregations. "UMJC Continues Fight against Replacement Theology." Cited 9 April 2012. Online: http://www.umjc.org/home-mainmenu-1/news-mainmenu-40/1-latest/752-umjc-continues-fight-against-replacement-theology.

———. "Will the Presbyterians Support a Divestment Policy of Injustice and Anti-Israelism?" Cited 12 August 2012. Online: http://www.umjc.org/home-mainmenu-1/advocacy/777-ramping-up-against-divestment.

Washington, Raleigh B. "The One New Man in John 17." Pages 33–44 in *Awakening the One New Man.* Edited by Robert F. Wolff. Shippensburg, Pa.: Destiny Image, 2011.

CHAPTER 13

Messianic Jews and Jewish-Christian Dialogue

Jennifer M. Rosner

In an article titled "Salvation Is from the Jews," the late Richard John Neuhaus wrote the following with regard to Jewish-Christian dialogue: "I suggest that we would not be wrong to believe that this dialogue, so closely linked to the American experience, is an essential part of the unfolding of the story of the world."[1] The rivalrous and troubled tale of these two religious communities has been a constant thread in the history of the West, and the need for dialogue and mutual understanding is as urgent as it has ever been. The tumultuous events of the twentieth century have yielded a new chapter in the relationship between Christians and Jews, one that holds great promise for healing, reconciliation, and redemptive partnership.

Beginning with the Catholic document *Nostra Aetate* (1965), the post-Holocaust era has seen a number of significant official Christian statements that chart a new way of relating to other religions, and Judaism in particular.[2] In 2000, an interdenominational group of Jewish scholars drafted the document *Dabru Emet* as a Jewish response to the widespread Christian reassessment of Judaism.[3] These documents represent a new kind of Jewish-Christian encounter, made possible by Christians increasingly recognizing and renouncing the supersessionism that has plagued Christian history, and Jews increasingly acknowledging that Christian theology is not inherently anti-Jewish.

The Established Parameters of Jewish-Christian Dialogue

While the current milieu of Jewish-Christian dialogue ranges from partnering on initiatives of shared interest to rigorous theological engagement, the role of Messianic Jews has continually posed a curious dilemma for proponents of improved Jewish-Christian relations. Both sides have had a difficult time mapping Messianic Jews on the religious landscape, as Messianic Judaism categorically blurs the lines that the dialogue has come to depend upon. According to Edward Kessler, "many involved in Jewish-Christian dialogue view Messianic Judaism as undermining the mutual respect

---

1. Richard John Neuhaus, "Salvation Is from the Jews," *First Things* 117 (November 2001): 19.
2. For examples of such statements, see Michael B. McGarry, *Christology after Auschwitz* (Mahwah, N.J.: Paulist, 1977), and Geoffrey Wigoder, *Jewish-Christian Relations since the Second World War* (Manchester, UK: Manchester University Press, 1988).
3. See Tikva Frymer-Kensky et al., eds., *Christianity in Jewish Terms* (Boulder: Westview, 2000), xv–xviii.

that has been built up in recent years."[4] If the dialogue is about reaching across differences and gaining mutual understanding, those differences must be clearly defined.

This apprehension about Messianic Jewish participation is especially evident from
the Jewish side. David Novak, one of the four authors of *Dabru Emet* and a strong
advocate for Jewish-Christian dialogue, has repeatedly noted the problematic nature
of Messianic Judaism. According to Novak, Messianic Judaism fails to respect the
irreducibly divergent truth claims of Judaism and Christianity, upon which authentic
Jewish-Christian dialogue is built. Novak promotes honest theological engagement
that does not conceal or dilute truth claims for the sake of conciliation. Dialogue on
the basis of "secular agreement," in which "Jews and Christians bracket the historical
character of their respective faiths for the sake of some broader international consensus" in effect replaces faith by something antithetical to it.[5] In the words of Randi
Rashkover, "the Christian is always a Christian and the Jew always a Jew, regardless
of their conversation partners. A Jewish-Christian dialogue relegated to the secular
realm is a contradiction in terms."[6] The respective truth claims of Judaism and Christianity must be brought to the table if true Jewish-Christian dialogue is to take place.

For Novak, upholding these truth claims requires that their differences not be
ignored or minimized. In his words, "the ultimate truth claims of Judaism and Christianity are not only different but mutually exclusive.... One cannot live as a Jew and
a Christian simultaneously."[7] Within the framework of Novak's mutually exclusive
construal of Judaism and Christianity, "the highest form of worship of the Lord God
of Israel is *either* by the Torah and the tradition of the Jewish people *or* by Christ
and the tradition of the Church."[8] While adherents of these two religions can seek to
understand one another, such understanding is grounded in the *distinction between*
the two religions. It is this boundary that, according to Novak, Messianic Judaism
transgresses.

Novak's conclusions regarding Messianic Judaism follow from his understanding
of Judaism and Christianity. Jewish-Christian dialogue must take place "without one
side denying the other's right to independence, and without denying the very real difference between Judaism and Christianity."[9] Because Novak categorically disallows
any overlap between Judaism and Christianity, Messianic Judaism cannot be anything
but a syncretistic aberration that undermines and relativizes the integrity of both.

Rethinking the Relationship between Judaism and Christianity

If we wish to reach a different conclusion with regard to Messianic Judaism and
Jewish-Christian dialogue, we must retrace Novak's steps in defining Judaism and

---

4. Edward Kessler and Neil Wenborn, eds., *A Dictionary of Jewish-Christian Relations* (Cambridge: Cambridge
University Press, 2008), 292.
    5. David Novak, *Jewish-Christian Dialogue: A Jewish Justification* (New York: Oxford University Press, 1989), 11.
    6. Randi Rashkover, "Jewish Responses to Jewish-Christian Dialogue: A Look Ahead to the Twenty-First Cen-
tury," *Cross Currents* 50, no. 1 – 2 (Spring – Summer 2000): 215.
    7. David Novak, *Talking with Christians: Musings of a Jewish Theologian* (Grand Rapids: Eerdmans, 2005), 6.
    8. Novak, *Talking with Christians*, 6.
    9. David Novak, "Jewish-Christian Dialogue: A Jewish Justification," *Review & Expositor* 103, no. 1 (Winter
2006): 267.

Christianity. In the preface of *Jewish-Christian Dialogue*, Novak issues the following disclaimer: "Because this book deals with the relationship between *rabbinic* Judaism and *gentile* Christianity, it will not deal with the whole historical question of the Jewish origins of Christianity, a question about which a huge literature has emerged in the past century especially."[10] In other words, Novak's framework intentionally brackets the overlap that undeniably characterizes the emergence of (rabbinic) Judaism and (Gentile) Christianity. To import a term from canonical criticism, Novak is concerned with the "final form" of these two religious communities.

Undeniably, each tradition has grown up in an atmosphere frequently marked by opposition to the other, and their current self-definitions are a product of this history. However, when speaking about rabbinic Judaism and Gentile Christianity, is it even possible to bracket their shared origin? Can we assess these communities without regard to their formation?

As Novak notes, there is a growing body of literature dedicated to the Jewish origins of Christianity, much of which suggests that we cannot accurately understand these two communities without exploring the history of their emergence.[11] As Robert Jenson reminds us, "the religious life of Israel in the time just before the Roman destruction was a sort of capacious denominational system, united by temple-worship, by Torah … and by allegiance to the land. When land and temple were gone, two denominations survived that could if need be do without land and temple, and it is vital to remember that both were indeed denominations *within* what is often called late second-temple Judaism."[12] These surviving denominations eventually developed into what we now call Judaism and Christianity.

In the absence of land and temple, rabbinic Judaism ("the ethnic-religious community created by the great rabbis in succession of the Pharisees"[13]) found its primary identity in familial descent from Abraham and Sarah and in Torah study and obedience. By contrast, the Christian community found its primary identity in the one in whom it believed the Torah "became flesh and dwelt among us," and whose enduring presence is not spatially limited. Each developing community interpreted their shared scriptural canon (i.e., the Tanakh or Old Testament) differently, and in each case these interpretive traditions themselves became canonical (i.e., the rabbinic writings and the New Testament).

Even as Judaism and Christianity became separate entities, their respective self-understandings were continually hammered out with reference to one another. In fact, the primary identity markers of each community came to be determined by the

---

10. Novak, *Jewish-Christian Dialogue*, ix.

11. See, for example, Daniel Boyarin, *Borderlines: The Partition of Judaeo-Christianity* (Philadelphia: University of Pennsylvania Press, 2004); Paula Fredriksen, *Jesus of Nazareth, King of the Jews* (New York: Vintage, 2000); and Pamela Eisenbaum, *Paul Was Not a Christian* (New York: HarperCollins, 2010).

12. Robert W. Jenson, "Toward a Christian Theology of Judaism," in *Jews and Christians: People of God* (ed. Carl E. Braaten and Robert W. Jenson; Grand Rapids: Eerdmans, 2003), 3.

13. Jenson, "Toward a Christian Theology of Judaism," 3. It should be noted that Jenson's claim of rabbinic Judaism's Pharisaic succession is contested. See, for example, Shaye J. D. Cohen, "The Significance of Yavneh: Pharisees, Rabbis, and the End of Jewish Sectarianism," *Hebrew Union College Annual* 55 (1984): 27–53; Philip S. Alexander, "'The Parting of the Ways' from the Perspective of Rabbinic Judaism," in *Jews and Christians: The Parting of the Ways A.D. 70 to 135* (ed. James D. G. Dunn; Grand Rapids: Eerdmans, 1999), 1–25.

differences that increasingly defined them. As Mark Kinzer explains, "for the Jewish people, the chief community-defining positive commandment was 'You shall observe the Torah' and the chief negative commandment was 'You shall not believe that Jesus is the Son of God.' For the Christian Church, the chief community-defining positive commandment was 'You shall believe that Jesus is the Son of God' and the chief negative commandment was 'You shall not observe the Torah.'"[14]

With regard to the medieval relationship between Judaism and Christianity, historian Amos Funkenstein states that "the conscious rejection of values and claims of the other religion was and remained a constitutive element in the ongoing construction of the respective identities of each of them. Indeed, I know of no other two religions tied to each other with such strong mutual bonds of aversion and fascination, attraction and repulsion."[15] Even in times of mutual hostility, "the synagogue and the church have throughout their histories lived in remarkably paired, if sometimes horrific, lock-step."[16]

The contradictory nature of these communities' truth claims and identity markers *can* lead to a mutually exclusive construal of their relationship, as Novak espouses. But this is not the only possible conclusion. Despite the intervening history that has threatened to obscure the shared origin of Judaism and Christianity, neither community has been able to escape the way in which their emergence continues to inform the reality and identity of each. From this perspective, the challenge becomes to *evaluate* rather than merely observe the mutually exclusive framework Novak describes. If we take their common genesis as our starting point, and bear in mind that the self-understandings of these two communities have remained deeply connected (even if purely negatively), the relationship between Judaism and Christianity begins to look different. It becomes debatable whether either community can fully understand itself without reference to the other.

This model of mutual dependence between Judaism and Christianity is clearly reflected in the thought of Franz Rosenzweig, one of the twentieth century's most influential Jewish thinkers. In his description of Judaism and Christianity, Rosenzweig employs the image of a celestial star, with Judaism representing the star's inner burning core and Christianity representing the rays that emanate outward from the star, carrying its light and heat to its surroundings.[17] While Rosenzweig, like Novak, understands Judaism and Christianity to be two entirely separate realities, he assigns each of them a unique — and complementary — redemptive vocation. Each community's *raison d'être* revolves around the part it plays in redemption; for Rosenzweig, final redemption will be ushered in only through both communities fulfilling their correlative vocations. These paired redemptive tasks effect the preservation (Judaism) and proliferation (Christianity) of revelation, defined by Rosenzweig as God's primary

---

14. Mark Kinzer, "Finding Our Way through Nicaea" (paper presented at the annual Hashivenu Forum, Los Angeles, 2010), 3.

15. Amos Funkenstein, *Perceptions of Jewish History* (Berkeley: University of California Press, 1993), 170.

16. Jenson, "Toward a Christian Theology of Judaism," 3.

17. See Franz Rosenzweig, *The Star of Redemption* (trans. Barbara E. Galli; 1921; repr., Madison: University of Wisconsin Press, 2005), part 3.

and initiatory movement toward humanity. Each community is therefore necessarily defined with reference to the other. While Rosenzweig's thought does not directly challenge the framework Novak provides, Rosenzweig draws an indelible connection between these two communities by suggesting that the relationship between them is integral to the identity (and vocation) of each.

Christian theologian Thomas Torrance goes one step beyond Rosenzweig, positing that Jews and Christians together constitute the one people of God and that the schism between them is one of the greatest tragedies in the history of Western civilization and the root cause of all subsequent ecclesial schisms.[18] In the church's "rebellion against the reconciling purpose of God being worked out through Israel," Christianity suffers detachment from the "creative center of God's providential activity in history."[19] For Torrance, the mutual exclusivity of Judaism and Christianity is not a reality to be accepted but rather a rupture to be healed.

While Torrance focuses on what Christianity loses by severing its connection with Judaism, Jewish theologian Will Herberg understands Christianity to be essentially an expansion of God's covenant with Israel. For Herberg, Christianity bridges the paradox of a divine-human covenant with a universal scope (all of humanity) but a particular referent (the national/ethnic people of Israel).[20] In other words, Christianity is the means by which Judaism's covenant with God attains its final intended telos.

If we follow these thinkers in asserting that Judaism and Christianity essentially share in one overarching covenant and bear complementary redemptive vocations, our assessment of the aim of Jewish-Christian dialogue shifts. We cannot, like Novak, insist that each respect the other's "right to independence." The goal of Jewish-Christian dialogue cannot merely be mutual understanding and esteem; it must in some sense be *interdependence*. If we envision Judaism and Christianity in this light, we might suggest that in discovering one another, each community rediscovers a piece of itself. According to this perspective, the significance of Messianic Judaism becomes a relevant question.

The Role of Messianic Judaism in Jewish-Christian Dialogue

The dawning of the Messianic Jewish movement in the twentieth century represents the reemergence of an overlapping segment of these two communities that has not existed in visible form since the proverbial parting of the ways. Messianic Judaism challenges the nature of the divide that Jews and Christians so often take for granted. According to Richard Harvey, Messianic Jews refuse "to partition Judaism and Christianity into two mutually exclusive theological systems."[21] In other words, Messianic Judaism by definition rejects the strict boundaries that Novak presupposes. By blurring these historically reinforced dividing lines, Messianic Judaism suggests that this

---

18. Thomas Torrance, "The Divine Vocation and Destiny of Israel in World History," in *The Witness of the Jews to God* (ed. David Torrance; Edinburgh: Handsel, 1982), 87, 92.

19. Torrance, "The Divine Vocation and Destiny of Israel in World History," 87.

20. See Will Herberg, "Judaism and Christianity," in *Jewish Perspectives on Christianity* (ed. Fritz A. Rothschild; New York: Crossroad, 1990), 246–47.

21. Richard Harvey, *Mapping Messianic Jewish Theology* (Carlisle: Paternoster, 2009), 96.

divide represents not a value-neutral and perhaps inevitable development, but rather a tragic rupture in the one people of God.

If this is the case, an additional goal of Jewish-Christian dialogue is arguably the healing of a historically entrenched schism. Within this framework, Messianic Judaism need not be statically defined as merely a syncretistic nuisance that transgresses mutually relied upon boundaries. It may instead be viewed as a key component in the bridging of a destructive and distorting chasm.

The emergence of the Messianic Jewish movement in the latter half of the twentieth century coincides with the widespread constructive reengagement between Christians and Jews. The same tumultuous history between Judaism and Christianity that led to the mutually exclusive reality in place today has also disallowed for the existence of Messianic Judaism. In an atmosphere in which the relationship between Judaism and Christianity is being thoroughly reconsidered and reconceived, the role of Messianic Judaism requires to be similarly reevaluated.

There are indications that such a reevaluation is beginning to take place, and Messianic Judaism is slowly establishing a seat for itself at the table of Jewish-Christian dialogue. As we explore this development and the contributions Messianic Judaism has to offer, three distinct areas of interest emerge: intra – Messianic Jewish dialogue, Messianic Jewish – Christian dialogue, and Messianic Jewish – mainstream Jewish dialogue. In recent years, there have been signs of significant development on all three fronts.

Intra – Messianic Jewish Dialogue

With regard to intra – Messianic Jewish dialogue, June 2010 marked an historic milestone. The first ecumenical conference of Jewish believers in Jesus in modern times took place in Helsinki, Finland, where a group of Catholic, Orthodox, Protestant, and Messianic scholars — all of them Jews — met to affirm their Jewish identity and their desire for unity.[22] The group issued a statement affirming Jewish continuity in the body of Messiah and plans to meet annually.[23]

---

22. While not all of the participants in the Helsinki Consultation self-identify as "Messianic Jews," this designation is used to indicate that this conference represents dialogical engagement from different perspectives *within* the world of Jewish believers in Jesus.

23. The Helsinki Consultation on Jewish Identity in the Body of Messiah, June 14 – 15, 2010, issued the following statement: "We thank God for bringing us as Jews to the knowledge of Jesus the Messiah, and we express a debt of gratitude to those from the Nations who have transmitted the knowledge of Christ from generation to generation.... There are many Jewish people in the body of Christ. We believe that this reality reflects God's intention that Israel and the Nations live as mutual blessings to one another. In fact, the Church in its essence is the communion of Jews and those from the Nations called to faith in Christ. In light of this truth, we think that the life of Jews in the body of Christ has theological significance for that body as a whole. Their presence serves as a constant reminder to the body that its existence is rooted in the ongoing story of the people of Israel. This story resounds throughout the celebration of the liturgical life of the community. We believe that this story finds its center in Israel's Messiah. We believe that Jews within the body are a living bond between the Church and the people of Israel. Accordingly, we would like to explore concrete ways in which Jewish people may live out their distinctive calling in the body of Christ. Finally, we wish to express to our Jewish brothers and sisters who do not share our faith in Jesus the Messiah that we consider ourselves to be part of the Jewish people and are committed to its welfare." Cited 12 March 2012. Online: http://www.helsinkiconsultation.com. The second annual Helsinki Consultation was held in Paris, France, in June 2011, during which a new statement that builds on the 2010 Helsinki Statement was drafted. The group met again in Berlin, Germany, in June 2012 and issued a third statement.

Also noteworthy with regard to intra–Messianic Jewish dialogue is the Borough Park Symposium, which convened for the first time in October 2007 and again in April 2010, both in New York City. The symposium provides a forum for leaders in the broader Messianic Jewish community to dialogue about movement-wide issues and respectfully address key theological and ideological differences.[24] The first gathering focused on soteriology, and the second addressed the deity of Messiah; both topics constitute core and contentious issues for the Messianic Jewish movement. The symposium will convene again in October 2012 to address the topic "How Jewish Should the Messianic Jewish Community Be?"

In its short history of existence, the Messianic Jewish movement has developed into many distinct streams, which range from self-identification and existence adjacent to (or within) the Christian church to tight affiliation with the Jewish people and practices of Judaism. As a movement that bridges Judaism and Christianity, the identities of Messianic Jewish individuals and groups dot the entire spectrum that stretches between these two religious traditions. If Messianic Judaism is to have an impact upon Jewish-Christian dialogue, the movement's own inner tensions and diversity must be addressed and attended to as part of this process. These conferences represent the precise type of sharpening dialogue that is required.

Messianic Jewish – Christian Dialogue

With regard to Messianic Jewish engagement with Christians, one of the most significant endeavors has been the ongoing Messianic Jewish–Roman Catholic dialogue. This group — which includes the Theologian Emeritus of the Papal Household, the Archbishop of Vienna, and a number of prominent Messianic Jewish theologians — has gathered annually for the past ten years. The publication of Mark Kinzer's Messianic Jewish assessment of the Catholic document *Lumen Gentium* (presented at the group's gathering in 2008) suggests that the fruit of this dialogue group may be gaining more widespread traction.[25] The historic strides this group continues to make will influence those beyond the group itself as additional content from the annual meetings becomes available to wider audiences.

The papers from the last three years of the dialogue will be published in book form in 2013 and, according to Catholic dialogue participant Peter Hocken, this publication "will bring the [Messianic Jewish] movement and the challenges it poses to the attention of Catholic bishops and theologians. These challenges concern the very heart of Christian faith: the identity of Jesus, rereading the New Testament in the light of the irrevocable covenant with Israel, the ongoing validity of the distinction between Israel and the nations, and the recovery of the full Messianic hope."[26]

The Catholic Church has led the way with regard to recent Christian reevaluations

---

24. See http://www.boroughparksymposium.com.

25. Kinzer's paper appeared with a response by Matthew Levering in *First Things* 189 (January 2009), with responses and a rejoinder by Kinzer in *First Things* 193 (May 2009). Kinzer's essay also appears as chapter 7 in Mark S. Kinzer, *Israel's Messiah and the People of God: A Vision for Messianic Jewish Covenant Fidelity* (ed. Jennifer M. Rosner; Eugene, Oreg.: Cascade, 2011).

26. Peter Hocken, email correspondence, November 4, 2010.

of Judaism and the Jewish people, and the Messianic Jewish participants in this ongoing dialogue are recognized as having the unique ability to serve as both insiders and outsiders to the nuances of Christian doctrine. The Preacher of the Papal Household, Raniero Cantalamessa, suggests that the Messianic Jewish movement may be the beginning of the "rejoining of Israel with the Church," and this reunification "will involve a rearrangement in the Church; it will mean a conversion on both sides. It will also be a rejoining of the Church with Israel."[27] The Messianic Jewish – Roman Catholic dialogue could be a key catalyst for the reconciliation Cantalamessa envisions.

June 2011 also marked the inaugural meeting of a group tentatively titled "The Messianic Judaism and the Church Working Group," which convened at Southern Methodist University in Dallas, Texas. This group, comprised of Messianic Jewish, Catholic, and Protestant theologians,[28] engaged together the topics of postmissionary Messianic Judaism,[29] Pauline ecclesiology, Jewish and Gentile complementarity in the body of Christ, the election of Israel, and Jewish and Christian covenant and mission. According to William Abraham, one of the conference organizers, "our work represents the first formal attempt to bring together Messianic Jewish and non-Jewish Protestant and Catholic theologians to face head-on the reality of postmissionary Messianic Judaism. We are now beyond the initial dialogue phase and moving into the kind of serious theological interaction that is sorely needed. I think the results up ahead over many years to come will be dramatic. I am especially interested in the contributions that will eventually make their way into systematic theology."[30] The group's second annual gathering took place in June 2012.

Messianic Jewish – Mainstream Jewish Dialogue

As discussed above, the most sustained resistance to Messianic Jewish participation in Jewish-Christian dialogue has come from Jewish proponents of and participants in the dialogue.

Nonetheless, progress is being made on this front as well. Messianic Jewish Theological Institute's Center for Jewish-Christian Relations plans to host two annual lecture series in Los Angeles, one focusing on "The New Testament and Judaism" and the second exploring "Theology, the Church and the Jewish People."[31]

The inaugural lecture of the first series, titled "Paul, Judaism and Christian-Jewish

27. Raniero Cantalamessa, *The Mystery of Christmas* (New York: Hyperion, 1996), 101.

28. Members of the group include William Abraham, Fr. Jean-Miguel Garrigues, Mark Kinzer, Bruce Marshall, Dan Keating, Tommy Givens, Gerald McDermott, R. Kendall Soulen, Akiva Cohen, Kurt Richardson, and David Rudolph.

29. Mark Kinzer's first book was titled *Postmissionary Messianic Judaism* (Grand Rapids: Brazos, 2005), and this term is now often used to describe the theological paradigm of Kinzer and his like-minded colleagues. Kinzer is one of the leading proponents of a more Torah-observant, tradition-conscious wing within the Messianic Jewish movement.

30. William Abraham, email correspondence, July 16, 2011.

31. Messianic Jewish Theological Institute (MJTI) is a Messianic Jewish graduate and rabbinical school founded by Mark Kinzer in 2002. This institution has continually been a pioneering force in the Messianic Jewish world, not least with regard to Messianic Jewish participation in Jewish-Christian dialogue. The vision for Messianic Judaism offered by Kinzer and MJTI represents a significant shift in the history of Messianic Judaism/Hebrew Christianity. For a detailed explanation of this shift, see chapter 11, above (Kinzer, "Messianic Jews and the Jewish World").

Relations: Revisiting the Evidence from Romans," was delivered by Pauline scholar Mark Nanos in October 2010. Nanos, a Reform Jew whose scholarship argues that Paul was unfalteringly Torah observant before and after his so-called conversion, remains dedicated to investigating the implications of this reading for Jewish-Christian relations. According to Nanos, Messianic Judaism is the concrete embodiment of a first-century reality that provides an important key to understanding Paul's context.

One of the salient features of Nanos's reading of Paul is the attention he draws to Paul's "implicit when not explicit audience, non-Jews."[32] Nanos explains that the emerging school of "Radical New Perspective interpreters,"[33] an informal grouping to which he belongs, consistently distinguishes between "what Paul writes to non-Jews and what he probably upholds to apply to Jews, to whom he does not write, and about whom, for that matter, he seldom directly refers."[34] Nanos's contention that Paul upheld the covenantal requirement of circumcision and Torah observance for Jewish Christ-followers makes his interpretation a natural ally for Messianic Jewish theology. Nanos's work lends support to Messianic Judaism by revealing that Paul himself envisioned and embodied a similar religious identity, though history subsequently erased both the mandate for and the allowance of a Torah-observant Jewish wing of the Christ-believing community.

As for the second lecture series, Jewish theologian Michael Wyschogrod delivered the inaugural lecture (titled "Is Marcion Trying to Sneak Back into the Church?") in March 2011. Wyschogrod, an Orthodox Jew, argues that a Jew's obligation to "labor under the yoke of the commandments"[35] is not washed away by the waters of baptism. Wyschogrod has noted the correlation between evangelism among Jews and Jewish assimilation, a trend that can only lead to the disappearance of visible Israel. Wyschogrod observes that "throughout the centuries, Jews who entered the Church very quickly lost their Jewish identity. Within several generations they intermarried and the Jewish traces disappeared." Accordingly, Wyschogrod infers, "if all Jews in past ages had followed the advice of the Church to become Christians, there would be no more Jews in the world today. The question we must ask is: Does the Church really want a world without Jews?"[36] Wyschogrod's concern that *all* Jews — including baptized Jews — maintain a Torah-observant lifestyle makes him another theological ally of Messianic Judaism's vision.

Both Nanos (from a New Testament perspective) and Wyschogrod (from a theological perspective) are important voices from the mainstream Jewish world whose work buttresses the existence and importance of Messianic Judaism. Their willingness to speak publicly in Messianic Jewish contexts based upon the recognition of

32. Mark D. Nanos, "Locating Paul on a Map of First-Century Judaism" (paper presented at the Paul and Judaism Session at the annual meeting of the Society of Biblical Literature, Atlanta, November 22, 2010), 8. Online: http://www.mjstudies.com.

33. This term was coined by Magnus Zetterholm in his book *Approaches to Paul: A Student's Guide to Recent Scholarship* (Minneapolis: Fortress, 2009), 161.

34. Nanos, "Locating Paul on a Map of First-Century Judaism," 8.

35. Michael Wyschogrod, *Abraham's Promise: Judaism and Jewish-Christian Relations* (Minneapolis: Fortress, 1992), 206.

36. Wyschogrod, *Abraham's Promise*, 207 – 8.

overlapping aims is a hopeful beacon of increased collaboration between mainstream Jews and Messianic Jews in the years to come.

A New Chapter in Jewish-Christian Dialogue?

Could it be that the history of renewed amity between Christians and Jews is entering into yet another new chapter, one in which Messianic Judaism plays an integral role? Only time will tell, though it seems certain that Messianic Judaism is indeed gaining a voice, and one that both the Christian world and the Jewish world are increasingly hearing. In 1988, Messianic Jewish pioneer David Stern wrote the following: "I am confident that the Messianic Jewish community will be a major means for healing the worst schism in the history of the world, the split between the Christians and the Jews, while helping both to fulfill their God-given callings."[37] Perhaps we are just now beginning to see the fulfillment of Stern's prophetic vision.

For Further Reading

Ariel, Yaakov. "A Different Kind of Dialogue? Messianic Judaism and Jewish Christian Relations." *CrossCurrents* 62 (2012): 318 – 27.

Glaser, Mitch L. "Authentic Dialogue between Messianic and Non-Messianic Jews ... A Miracle Could Happen Here!" *Mishkan: A Forum on the Gospel and the Jewish People* 36 (2002): 87 – 96.

———. "Borough Park Symposium Background and Introduction." *Mishkan: A Forum on the Gospel and the Jewish People* 53 (2007): 9 – 12.

Glasser, Arthur F. "Messianic Jews, Dialogue, and the Future." Pages 105 – 17 in *Christians and Jews Together: Voices from the Conversation*. Edited by Donald G. Dawe and Aurelia T. Fule. Louisville: Theology and Worship Ministry Unit, Presbyterian Church USA, 1991.

Kinbar, Carl. "Missing Factors in Jewish-Christian Dialogue." *Princeton Theological Review* 8, no. 2/3 (April 2001): 30 – 37.

Levine, Amy-Jill. "Jesus in Jewish-Christian Dialogue." Pages 175 – 88 in *Soundings in the Religion of Jesus: Perspectives and Methods in Jewish and Christian Scholarship*. Edited by Bruce Chilton, Anthony Le

Donne, and Jacob Neusner. Minneapolis: Fortress, 2012.

McDermott, Gerald. "Covenant, Mission, and Relating to the Other." Pages 19 – 40 in *Covenant and Hope: Christian and Jewish Reflections*. Edited by Robert W. Jenson and Eugene B. Korn. Grand Rapids: Eerdmans, 2012.

Rosner, Jennifer M. "Franz Rosenzweig and Jewish and Christian Communal Boundaries." Paper presented at the annual Hashivenu Forum, Pasadena, Calif., 2009. Online: http://www.mjstudies.com.

———. *Healing the Schism: Barth, Rosenzweig, and the New Jewish-Christian Encounter*. PhD diss., Fuller Theological Seminary, 2012.

———. "'Salvation Is from the Jews': An Assessment and Critique of Karl Barth on Judaism and the Jewish People." *Kesher: A Journal of Messianic Judaism* 25 (2011): 23 – 36. Cited 26 March 2012. Online: http://www.kesherjournal.com/Issue-25/Salvation-is-from-the-Jews-An-Assessment-and-Critique-of-Karl-Barth-on-Judaism-and-the-Jewish-People.

Rottenberg, Isaac C. "Dialogue and Messianic Jews." Pages 177 – 95 in *Christian-Jewish*

---

37. David H. Stern, *Messianic Jewish Manifesto* (Clarksville, Md.: Messianic Jewish Communications, 1988), 4.

Dialogue: Exploring Our Commonalities and Our Differences. Edited by Isaac C. Rottenberg. Atlanta: Hebraic Heritage, 2005.

———. *Jewish Christians in an Age of Christian-Jewish Dialogue*. A collection of essays published in June 1995 "by the family and friends of the author in honor of his 70th birthday for distribution among circles engaged in Christian-Jewish dialogue."

Rudolph, David J. "Guidelines for Healthy Theological Discussion." *Kesher: A Journal of Messianic Judaism* 22 (2008): 1 – 5. Cited 12 March 2012. Online: http://www .kesherjournal.com/Issue-22/Guidelines-for-Healthy-Theological-Discussion.

———. "Messianic Jews and Christian Theology: Restoring an Historical Voice to the Contemporary Discussion." *Pro Ecclesia* 14, no. 1 (2005): 58 – 84. Online: http://www .mjstudies.com.

———. "Reminder on Respectful Theological Discussion." Paper presented at the Borough Park Symposium on the Deity of Messiah and the Mystery of God, New York City, April 12, 2010. Online: http:// www.mjstudies.com.

Wyschogrod, Michael. *Abraham's Promise: Judaism and Jewish-Christian Relations*. Edited by R. Kendall Soulen. Grand Rapids: Eerdmans, 2004.

PART 2

The Church and
Messianic Judaism

CHAPTER 14

Matthew's Christian-Jewish Community

DANIEL J. HARRINGTON

Matthew's gospel is often described as the most Jewish of the four Gospels. The text assumes that its readers have some interest in and familiarity with the Jewish Scriptures, are sensitive to traditional Jewish modes of argument, and can appreciate its portrait of Jesus as a faithful Jew and a teacher in a Jewish setting. Moreover, it appears that Matthew wrote at one of the most painful and crucial moments in Jewish history: in response to the crisis of Jewish identity caused by the destruction of Jerusalem and its temple in CE 70. And yet Matthew's gospel has also been called anti-Jewish and held responsible for fostering negative Christian stereotypes about Jewish legalism, Jewish responsibility for the death of Jesus, and the idea that the Jews are a self-cursed people (27:25).[1]

In my opinion, it is essential to read Matthew's gospel in what seems to have been its original historical context. The Evangelist we call Matthew (see 9:9; 10:3) wrote for a largely Christian-Jewish community in a city where there was a large Jewish population that spoke and read Greek. While he composed in Greek, there is a clear Semitic cast to both his language and thought. The most commonly accepted location is Antioch in Syria, though other eastern Mediterranean cities (Damascus, Caesarea Maritima, etc.) have been suggested. Several passages (21:41; 22:7; 27:25) presume a date of composition after the Roman capture of Jerusalem and the destruction of its Temple.

One of the Evangelist's major goals was to show that after CE 70 the Jewish heritage was best carried on in the community gathered around Jesus of Nazareth, and that Jesus is the authoritative interpreter of the Jewish tradition now that the Temple is in ruins and the Land of Israel is even more firmly under Roman control. But another one of his goals was to remind his fellow Christians about the Jewish origins and roots of their movement.

Matthew's gospel is generally regarded as a revised and expanded version of Mark's gospel. In his new edition, Matthew, besides adding teaching material from the Sayings Source Q and his own special source(s) designated as M, set out to reemphasize the Jewishness of Jesus. And so the presence of his gospel in the Christian canon of Scripture can and should be a perpetual reminder of the Jewish roots and character of Christianity. Thus it performs a function similar to that which Messianic Judaism can

---

1. For earlier treatments of these matters, see the introduction to my commentary *The Gospel of Matthew* (Sacra Pagina 1; 1991; repr., Collegeville, Minn.: Liturgical Press, 2007); and my articles "Matthew as a Jewish Book" and "Matthew as a Christian Gospel," *Priests & People* 7 (1993): 240–44, and 284–88.

and should play in Christian church life today. Both Matthew and Messianic Judaism remind Jews and Christians today that Christianity was and is a Jewish phenomenon, and that a church without a consciousness of its roots in Judaism cannot be the church of Jesus Christ (see Rom 9 – 11).

This essay seeks to call attention to the Christian-Jewish nature of Matthew's gospel by focusing on themes and features that are characteristic of Matthew's program of highlighting the Jewish roots of Jesus and the movement he began. Thus it attempts to offer historical foundations and encouragement for Messianic Jews while enlightening other Christians about the need to attend to their own Jewish roots.[2]

In Response to a Jewish Crisis

The events of CE 70 left all Jews without their religious center and place of sacrifice (the Temple) and without military and political control of the Land of Israel. I regard Matthew's gospel as a Christian-Jewish response to this crisis.

There were other Jewish responses. Two lengthy apocalypses, *4 Ezra* (= 2 Esd 3 – 14) and *2 Baruch*, from the late first century (and so roughly contemporaneous with Matthew's gospel), provided serious theological reflections about why the Temple had been destroyed and about how God's promises to Israel could still be fulfilled. Their solution to the crisis was eschatological: Rome's rule is only temporary; the intervention of God's Messiah will bring about Rome's defeat and the beginning of Israel's vindication; and the final outcome will involve the resurrection of the dead, the divine judgment, and the kingdom of God on earth. Both works seem to envision this intervention and vindication as occurring soon. In the meantime, the best way for Jews to prepare for these events is careful observance of the Law as the revelation of God's will (see esp. *2 Bar.* 85:3 – 4).

Another response was more military and political. Despite their defeat in the First Jewish Revolt of CE 66 – 73, Jewish rebels or insurgents sought to keep alive resistance to Rome and its occupation of their ancestral land by guerrilla warfare and acts of terrorism. This movement erupted in a second full-scale Jewish revolt against Rome in CE 132 – 35 that is known as the Bar Kokhba Revolt. This effort too resulted in defeat and further subjugation to Rome.

A third and much more lasting Jewish response was what is called "formative" or "rabbinic" Judaism. Although the earliest rabbinic writings (Mishnah, Tosefta, etc.) come from around CE 200, the movement that produced them began to take shape after CE 70 under the leadership of Rabban Yohanan Ben Zakkai. The movement combined various currents in first-century Judaism: priestly traditions, halakhic debates, the scribal traditions, and especially the Pharisees. The priestly strand contributed a lively interest in ritual purity, and the scribes brought their traditions

2. For good examples of reading Matthew in its Jewish context, see J. Andrew Overman, *Matthew's Gospel and Formative Judaism: The Social World of the Matthean Community* (Minneapolis: Fortress, 1990); Anthony J. Saldarini, *Matthew's Christian-Jewish Community* (Chicago: University of Chicago Press, 1994); and David C. Sim, *The Gospel of Matthew and Christian Judaism: The History and Social Setting of the Matthean Community* (Edinburgh: T&T Clark, 1998).

of biblical interpretation and records of debates about what Jews should and should not do.[3]

Before CE 70 the Pharisees took special interest in observing Sabbaths and festivals, marriage laws, ritual purity, tithes, rules about raising crops, and other such matters. According to the Gospels and Josephus, they were a powerful religious movement (with great political influence at certain times) seeking to extend their traditions and interpretations to all Israel. Their program was not centered in or dependent on the Temple. Rather, they sought to replicate the Temple cult in their homes and promoted the ideal of all Israel as a priestly people and a holy nation. Thus the Pharisees could provide a firm foundation for an Israel deprived of its Temple and the political control of its land.

While Matthew shared the hopes of the apocalyptists, he identified Jesus as the Messiah and took his teachings and interpretations of the Torah as the guide to proper behavior in the present. Although he shared the practical agenda of early rabbinic Judaism on many points, he rejected many of the Pharisees' traditions and interpretations in favor of Jesus' approaches. In this sense Matthew's gospel was a Christian-Jewish response to the crisis facing all Jews after CE 70.

Jesus as the Fulfillment of the Jewish Scriptures

The earliest Christians took as their Bible the Jewish Scriptures and soon came to see that many previously obscure passages became clear to them when read in the light of Jesus' life, death, and resurrection. In quoting the very early summary of the good news that he had received and handed on to others, Paul insisted that Christ died for our sins and was raised "in accordance with the Scriptures" (1 Cor 15:3 – 4 RSV). While Paul made abundant use of the Jewish Scriptures in writing to the Galatians and the Romans, he did less with them in his other letters. The later Pauline letters (Colossians, Ephesians, Pastorals) did even less. And because of the increasing influence of Gentiles in the church, there was a danger that a fundamental element of early Christian faith might be lost.

Writing for a largely Christian Jewish community in the late first century CE, Matthew sought to retrieve and reemphasize the theme of Jesus as fulfilling the Scriptures of Israel. While Mark viewed Jesus as fulfilling Israel's Scriptures from the beginning of his public activity (Mark 1:2 – 3 = Exod 23:20/Mal 3:1; Isa 40:3) to the moment of his death (Mark 15:34 = Ps 22:1), Matthew decided to develop this theme in an even more extensive and comprehensive way.[4]

In his infancy narrative in chapters 1 – 2, Matthew provides a genealogy of Jesus the Messiah (1:1 – 17) that links him not only with Abraham and David but also with the exile in the sixth century BCE. The unusual presence of four women — Tamar, Rahab, Ruth, and Bathsheba — prepares for the even more unusual virginal conception of Jesus in 1:18 – 25, which is presented as the fulfillment of Isaiah 7:14 ("the

3. Jacob Neusner, *Judaism: The Evidence of the Mishnah* (Atlanta: Scholars, 1988).
4. The classic study is by Krister Stendahl, *The School of St. Matthew and Its Use of the Old Testament* (Philadelphia: Fortress, 1968).

virgin shall conceive," ESV). The perilous journey of the Holy Family in chapter 2 — Bethlehem, Egypt, and Nazareth — serves to fulfill at each step the divine plan set forth in the Jewish Scriptures (see Matt 2:6, 15, 18, 23). It also evokes memories of the dangerous childhood that Moses experienced according to Exodus 1 – 2.

Throughout his narrative of Jesus as an adult, Matthew includes biblical quotations at pivotal points: the passages from Deuteronomy 6 – 8 in the temptation account (4:1 – 11), the use of Isaiah 8:23 – 9:1 to explain why Jesus began his ministry in Galilee (4:15 – 16), the reference to Isaiah 42:1 – 4 to interpret Jesus' healing miracles as the work of the Servant of God (12:18 – 21), the full text of Isaiah 6:9 – 10 to explain why many failed to understand and accept Jesus (13:14 – 15), the appeal to Psalm 78:2 as the rationale for his use of parables (13:35), and so on. In his passion narrative in chapters 26 – 27 Matthew builds upon and adds to the many biblical allusions and echoes (especially of Ps 22 and Isa 53) in Mark 14 – 15.

Jesus as the Herald of the Kingdom of Heaven

In Matthew's gospel the focus of Jesus' preaching and activity is the coming of the kingdom of God. Matthew's summary of his preaching placed at the beginning of his public ministry makes that clear: "Repent, for the kingdom of heaven has come near" (4:17). Thus he stands in line with John the Baptist, whom Matthew has say the very same words (3:2). And Jesus teaches his disciples to pray, "Thy kingdom come" (6:10 RSV).

Matthew customarily uses the phrase "the kingdom of heaven," which is a Jewish variant expression to avoid too frequent and often careless use of the word "God." It may also have been intended to suggest to the Romans that the Jesus movement was not a threat to their political and military hegemony in this world. By prefacing the first great block of Jesus' teachings with the Beatitudes in 5:3 – 12 Matthew gave the Sermon on the Mount (chaps. 5 – 7) an eschatological horizon. His model prayer (6:9 – 13) is a plea for the coming of God's kingdom in its fullness and for physical and spiritual sustenance as we await it. His healing actions in chapters 8 – 9 and his other miracles (11:4 – 5) are signs that God's reign was breaking in through his ministry. While the kingdom's fullness is future, the present dimensions of the kingdom are expressed symbolically in chapter 13 with images of seeds, treasures, and fine pearls. And the kingdom is enough of a present reality to suffer opposition and even violence (11:12).

By basically reproducing Mark 13:1 – 37, Matthew's version of Jesus' eschatological discourse in chapters 24 – 25 first stresses the future aspects of the kingdom's coming. However, the various parables in the second part (24:37 – 25:30) stress the theme of constant vigilance in view of the uncertain timing of the kingdom's coming (24:44) and the certainty of the last judgment (25:31 – 46). Thus Matthew emphasizes Jesus' pivotal role in the kingdom's future coming, its presence in his person and ministry, and the need for preparation and vigilance in the face of it.

A Very Jewish Messiah

In referring to Jesus, Matthew used the common stock of honorific titles that had emerged early in the Jesus movement: Son of David, Servant, Son of God, Messiah, Son of Man, Lord, Wisdom, and Prophet. But he gave them particularly Jewish spins. As the Son of David, Jesus is the royal Messiah sent to Israel to heal those who in society's eyes counted for nothing (20:29 – 34). As God's Servant, Jesus takes upon himself our infirmities and diseases (8:17 = Isa 53:4). As the Son of God, Jesus functions as Israel did (or should have done) in the Jewish Scriptures (2:15; 3:17; 4:1 – 11). As the Messiah, Jesus is a healer and teacher rather than the victorious military commander and political ruler described in *Psalms of Solomon 17*, *4 Ezra*, and *2 Baruch*. As the Son of Man, Jesus is more clearly defined than the "one like a son of man" in Daniel 7:13 – 14 (RSV), and his future coming will usher in the final judgment and the full coming of God's kingdom. As Emmanuel ("God is with us"), Jesus can be properly addressed as Lord, thus displaying an element of his divinity. Matthew's Jesus is also a wisdom teacher or perhaps even the incarnation of Wisdom (11:28 – 30). In the passion narrative Jesus follows the pattern set by the prophet Jeremiah, who suffered for speaking hard truths to the leaders of his people.

Jesus as Interpreter of Torah

The key to understanding the Matthean Jesus' attitude to the Torah is the saying found in 5:17 (RSV), "Think not that I have come to abolish the Law and the Prophets. I have come not to abolish them but to fulfill them." If we take this claim seriously, then fulfillment means going to the root of what the Law and the Prophets teach, sharpening their demands, attending to the internal dispositions from which evil actions proceed, and avoiding situations in which the commandments might be violated.[5]

In the six "antitheses" in 5:21 – 48 Matthew's Jesus does not render the biblical commandments obsolete or useless. Rather, he interprets them in such a way as to lead to their goal and their fullness. The first antithesis (5:21 – 22) attacks anger as the root of murder, and the second (5:27 – 28) identifies lust as the root of adultery. To avoid the divorce procedure outlined in Deuteronomy 24:1 – 4 one might avoid divorce entirely (5:31 – 32), and to avoid swearing falsely one might avoid oaths entirely (5:33 – 37). The unit about nonretaliation in response to evil (5:38 – 39) advises Jesus' followers to forgo seeking revenge through violence. The final unit (5:43 – 48) urges an all-encompassing love after God's own example, a love that includes even one's enemies.

Jesus' summary statements about the Golden Rule ("do unto others ..." [7:12]) and about love of God and neighbor (22:34 – 40) do not abrogate the biblical commandments entirely. Rather, they offer a vantage point from which God's will as it is revealed in the Law and the Prophets might be perceived and put into practice. The Law and the Prophets as understood and practiced by Jesus retain their authority because in him they reach their goal.

5. See Jacob Neusner, *A Rabbi Talks with Jesus: An Intermillennial, Interfaith Exchange* (New York: Doubleday, 1993).

In Debate with Other Jewish Teachers

Matthew often refers to Jewish opponents of Jesus as based in and controlling "their synagogues" (4:23; 9:35; 10:17; 12:9; 13:54; see also 6:2, 5; 23:6, 34). His chief debating partners are the scribes and the Pharisees. Of special interest for both Matthew and his Jewish contemporaries in the late first century were Sabbath observance, ritual purity, and divorce. On these issues Matthew portrays Jesus as standing within the contours of Jewish debate while holding his own distinctive positions.[6]

Two episodes on Sabbath observance appear in Matthew 12:1 – 14. It is likely that Matthew's largely Christian Jewish community observed the Sabbath rest. This is indicated by Matthew's inserting of the hope that the great tribulation might not occur "on a Sabbath" (24:20; cf. Mark 13:19), presumably because it might present a crisis of conscience for Christian Jews. In recasting the episode about the disciples plucking grain on a Sabbath in Mark 2:23 – 28, Matthew in 12:1 – 8 places the episode in the context of Jewish debates about what constitutes "work" on the Sabbath (see *m. Shabbat* 7:2), corrects Mark's version of the high priest's name, strengthens Mark's rather weak account by adding the Temple precedent and the quotation of Hosea 6:6, and omits the radical saying about the Sabbath having been made for humans (Mark 2:27). In 12:9 – 14 (see Mark 3:1 – 6) Matthew gives Jesus' views on the rescue of an animal that had fallen into a pit on the Sabbath. Here Jesus sides with the Pharisees against the more rigorist Essenes (see *Damascus Document* 11:13 – 14). His rationale is that "it is lawful to do good on the Sabbath" (12:12 RSV). However, the Pharisees regarded this healing on the Sabbath as unnecessary and unlawful, since the man with the withered hand was not in danger of death.

In dealing with issues of ritual purity in 15:1 – 20, Matthew preserved the framework he found developed in Mark 7:1 – 23 but placed the episode more squarely within the context of Jewish debate. He avoids Mark's blanket conclusion that Jesus "declared all foods clean" (Mark 7:19 RSV). Rather, Matthew has Jesus engage the traditions surrounding the Law that the Pharisees had developed and accuse them of being "blind guides" more concerned with their own human traditions about external purity than with the moral purity that emanates from within the person.

It appears that Jesus held very strict views about divorce (see Luke 16:18; 1 Cor 7:10 – 11; Mark 10:1 – 12). While not denying Jesus' own view, Matthew places it more explicitly in the context of the current Jewish debate about the grounds for divorce (see *m. Gittin* 9:10) and the interpretation of Deuteronomy 24:1 – 4 by adding to the Pharisees' question, "Is it lawful for a man to divorce his wife *for any cause*?" (Matt 19:3 NRSV, emphasis added). Moreover, in both 5:32 and 19:9 he mentions an apparent exception to Jesus' absolute teaching ("except for unchastity"), thus aligning Jesus more closely with the view of Shammai over against the more "liberal" views of Hillel and Aqiba. Finally, he omits the case of a woman who might seek to divorce her husband (Mark 10:12), presumably since he found it not applicable in a Jewish setting.

---

6. For detailed treatments of these texts, see Sim, *The Gospel of Matthew.*

Jesus' Ethical Teachings

Jesus' teachings according to Matthew are eminently practical and retain the traditional Jewish link between knowing and doing (see esp. 7:13 – 27). The horizon against
which the Matthean ethical teachings are practiced is hope for the coming kingdom.
Since its precise time is uncertain and the coming of the Son of Man has been delayed,
the followers of Jesus should always be on guard and live as if the fullness of God's
kingdom were to arrive at any moment. The content is supplied not only by the Law
and the Prophets as interpreted by Jesus but also by the collections of Jesus' wisdom
teachings gathered in the five great speeches. Among these discourses, the Sermon
on the Mount (chaps. 5 – 7) has pride of place and content as a summary of Jesus'
instructions for God's people. At several points (5:20; 7:21; 18:3; 19:23 – 24; 21:31 – 32)
the link between entering the kingdom of heaven and human action is made explicit.
Those who look forward to God's universal reign must express their hope in practical
action, or risk losing God's gift of the kingdom.

Christian-Jewish Community Life

Those who gather in Jesus' name (18:20) are promised that they will enjoy his presence for all time (28:20), the presence of the one identified as "Emmanuel" or "God
with us" (Isa 7:14 = Matt 1:23). The disciples who carry on Jesus' mission of teaching
and healing possess exemplary significance for the community's life. They carry on
the project of Jesus and show how people can live in conformity with God's will. In
contrast with the disciples in Mark's gospel who regularly misunderstand Jesus and act
badly, the disciples in Matthew do understand him (13:52; 16:12). Though they sometimes exhibit only "little faith" (6:30; 8:26; 14:31; 16:8; 17:20), their faith is nonetheless
real. By calling Jesus' disciples "brothers" and "little ones" Matthew encourages the
identification between Jesus' first followers and the members of his own community.
The honorific titles for teachers being adopted in early rabbinic/formative Judaism
— rabbi, father, and master — are to be avoided, on the grounds that "you have one
instructor, the Messiah" (23:10 NRSV). The task of Jesus' disciples is to "make disciples of all nations" (28:19). The figure of Peter makes concrete Matthew's approach
to discipleship. Though impetuous and often displaying "little faith," Peter comes to
recognize who Jesus really is (16:17 – 19). Through Peter the Rock, the power to bind
and loose is then given to the whole circle of Jesus' disciples in 18:18.

According to Matthew, the followers of Jesus represent the people of God. Through
Jesus the Jew and in response to his command (28:19 – 20), non-Jews too can become
part of God's people. The parable of the vineyard in Matthew 21:33 – 46 is crucial for
understanding the church's place in salvation history. The vineyard is Israel (see Isa
5:1 – 7), the owner is God, the tenants are Israel's leaders, the servants are the prophets,
and the owner's son is Jesus. The owner (God) "will put those wretches to a miserable
death, and let out the vineyard to other tenants who will give him the fruits in their
seasons" (21:41 RSV). Those from whom the vineyard is taken are the contemporary
Jewish political and religious leaders and their allies. Those who "bear fruit" (see 3:8,

10; 7:16 – 20; 12:33; 13:8; etc.) are the faithful followers of Jesus. Matthew probably interpreted the destruction of Jerusalem and its temple in CE 70 as an appropriate judgment on Israel's bad leaders.

Anti-Jewish?

When Matthew is read as a Jewish book, it fits well in the late first-century crisis of Jewish national and religious identity. In this setting its polemical passages are part of a family quarrel within Judaism as various groups tried to establish their claims to continue the tradition of Israel as God's people. However, when they are taken out of their historical context, the internal polemical texts can become dangerous sources of anti-Semitism.

Many of the Matthean parables carry a polemical element. In Matthew 13:1 – 52 a major theme is the acceptance and rejection of the good news preached by Jesus. Likewise the parables in 21:28 – 22:14 (two sons, tenants, invitees to a royal marriage feast) and in 24:45 – 25:30 (two servants, ten bridesmaids, talents) distinguish sharply between those who accept the gospel and are prepared for the coming of God's kingdom and those who reject it and thus are to be judged severely.

The most polemical passage of all appears in chapter 23. It begins in 23:1 – 12 with a severe warning to avoid the religious style of the scribes and Pharisees, especially their public displays of piety in dress, seeking places of honor in public, and use of honorific titles (rabbi, teacher, and father). Then there are seven "woes" in 23:13 – 36 that accuse the scribes and Pharisees of hindering others from entering God's kingdom, harming their own converts, indulging in casuistry, neglecting the major concerns of the Law, and so on. The scribes and Pharisees emerge as "hypocrites," one of Matthew's favorite designations for the opponents of Jesus and (by extension) of the Matthean community.

In the passion narrative Matthew places the burden of responsibility for Jesus' death on the Jewish leaders in Jerusalem. However, the people's cry in Matthew 27:25 ("His blood be on us and on our children," RSV) appears to extend that responsibility. For Matthew, writing after CE 70, the phrase "on our children" most likely referred to the generation that experienced the destruction of the Temple and was now locked in rivalry with the Matthean community. When taken out of its late first-century Jewish context, this statement can become very dangerous, as the history of Christian persecutions of Jews has shown.

Matthew's gospel can and should be a precious resource for the Messianic Jewish movement today. Written by a Christian Jewish evangelist for a largely Christian Jewish community at a pivotal moment in Jewish history, Matthew's gospel reminds all Christians of their Jewish roots and enables them to see more clearly the pivotal role played by Christian Jews in the early history of the church. Matthew's Christian Judaism has been described as a "road not taken." However, the prominence of Matthew's gospel in the Christian canon of Scripture and in Christian history indicates that Matthew's Christian Judaism has been and should be part of the Christian movement in every age. It is the special vocation of Messianic Judaism to help other Christians to recognize how deeply we all are rooted in Judaism and to show how commitment to Jesus as the Messiah and to Judaism are not necessarily contradictory.

For Further Reading

Clooney, Francis X. "Matthew's Christian-Jewish Community and Interreligious Encounter Today." Pages 529–43 in *When Judaism and Christianity Began: Essays in Memory of Anthony J. Saldarini*. Vol. 2. Edited by Alan J. Avery-Peck, Daniel Harrington, and Jacob Neusner. Leiden, Netherlands: Brill, 2004.

Harrington, Daniel J. *The Gospel of Matthew.* Collegeville, Minn.: Liturgical Press, 1991.

Murphy, Frederick J. "The Jewishness of Matthew: Another Look." Pages 377–403 in *When Judaism and Christianity Began: Essays in Memory of Anthony J. Saldarini.* Vol. 2. Edited by Alan J. Avery-Peck, Daniel Harrington, and Jacob Neusner. Leiden, Netherlands: Brill, 2004.

Overman, J. Andrew. *Matthew's Gospel and Formative Judaism: The Social World of the Matthean Community.* Minneapolis: Fortress, 1990.

Rabinowitz, Noel. "Matthew 23:2–4: Does Jesus Recognize the Authority of the Pharisees and Does He Endorse Their Halakhah?" *Journal of the Evangelical Theological Society* 46, no. 3 (September 2003): 423–47. Online: http://www .mjstudies.com.

———. "Matthew's Genealogy: A Paradigm for Israel's Restoration." *Kesher: A Journal of Messianic Judaism* 20 (2006): 84–122.

Runesson, Anders. "From Where? To What? Common Judaism, Pharisees, and the Changing Socio-Religious Location of the Matthean Community." Pages 97–113 in *Common Judaism: Explorations in Second-Temple Judaism.* Edited by W. O. McCready and Adele Reinhartz. Minneapolis: Fortress, 2008.

———. "Judging Gentiles in the Gospel of Matthew: Between 'Othering' and Inclusion." Pages 133–51 in *Jesus, Matthew's Gospel and Early Christianity: Studies in Memory of Graham N. Stanton.* Edited by Daniel M. Gurtner, Joel Willitts, and Richard A. Burridge. London: T&T Clark, 2011.

———. "Re-Thinking Early Jewish-Christian Relations: Matthean Community History as Pharisaic Intragroup Conflict." *Journal of Biblical Literature* 127, no. 1 (2008): 95–132.

Saldarini, Anthony J. *Matthew's Christian-Jewish Community.* Chicago: University of Chicago Press, 1994.

Sigal, Phillip. *The Halakhah of Jesus of Nazareth according to the Gospel of Matthew.* Atlanta: Society of Biblical Literature, 2007.

Sim, David C. *The Gospel of Matthew and Christian Judaism: The History and Social Setting of the Matthean Community.* Edinburgh: T&T Clark, 1998.

Van de Sandt, Huub, and Jurgen K. Zangenberg, eds. *Matthew, James, and Didache: Three Related Documents in Their Jewish and Christian Setting.* Atlanta: Society of Biblical Literature, 2008.

Willitts, Joel. "The Friendship of Matthew and Paul: A Response to a Recent Trend in the Interpretation of Matthew's Gospel." *HTS Theological Studies* 65, no. 1 (2009): 1–8. Cited 27 March 2012. Online: http://www.scielo.org.za/scielo.php?pid=S0259-94222009000100021&script=sci_arttext.

———. *Matthew's Messianic Shepherd-King: In Search of the Lost Sheep of the House of Israel.* Berlin: Walter de Gruyter, 2007.

CHAPTER 15

The Restoration of Israel
in Luke-Acts

DARRELL BOCK

In some New Testament studies circles, it is said that Israel has become the church. In her rejection of Jesus, Israel has lost her place as the people of God. The church is the new Israel.

A good example of this perspective is Gary Burge's book, *Jesus and the Land: The New Testament Challenge to "Holy Land" Theology*.[1] Working through the New Testament, Burge argues for a landless and nationless theology in which the equality of Jew and Gentile in Christ is the key ecclesiological reality. In this view, Jesus as Temple or as forming a new universal Temple community becomes the locus for holy space. Israel is absorbed into the church and hope in the land is spiritualized to refer to a restored earth.[2] There is some truth in this, even a lot of truth, but to get there Burge ignores many texts and misses completely the role of Israel in the biblical story.

This chapter seeks to redress the balance. When I speak of Israel in this essay it is the Jewish people I have in mind as opposed to *a new Israel*. Since most of the texts not treated by Burge appear in Luke-Acts, we will survey these two volumes for Israel's continuing story.[3] These two books comprise almost a third of the New Testament. Is there hope for God's restoration of original Israel in these texts?

Setting the Stage: The Context of Luke-Acts

Luke-Acts was written between CE 60 and 80 in part to legitimate the inclusion of Gentiles in an originally Jewish movement according to God's plan.[4] Theophilus (Luke 1:3; Acts 1:1) is a Jesus-believing Gentile who needs assurance. Luke-Acts pres-

---

1. Gary M. Burge, *Jesus and the Land: The New Testament Challenge to "Holy Land" Theology* (Grand Rapids: Baker, 2010).

2. See esp. Burge, *Jesus and the Land*, 56.

3. For a wider study of this theme, see Richard Bauckham, "The Restoration of Israel in Luke-Acts," in *Restoration: Old Testament, Jewish and Christian Perspectives* (ed. James M. Scott; Leiden, Netherlands: Brill, 2001), 435–87. Bauckham's study focuses on seven themes, while I will address specific passages. His themes are: (1) Elijah restores the people (Luke 1:16–17, 76b–77), (2) Messiah delivers the people from oppression (1:68–73, 78–79), (3) Israel's consolation as light to the nations (2:25–38), (4) the redemption of Jerusalem and return from the diaspora (2:31–32, 38), (5) Messiah reigns forever (1:32–33; 69–71, 78–79), (6) God exalts the lowly and humbles the exalted (1:46–55), and (7) Messiah is opposed and divides Israel (2:34–35). To these we add (1) a look at the Spirit as marker of the new era and (2) the sequencing and cause for Israel being set aside and then renewed. I shall not examine Bauckham's theme 1, but the rest we shall treat to one degree or another.

4. See Darrell L. Bock, *Luke 1:1–9:50* (Grand Rapids: Baker, 1994), 14–18; Darrell L. Bock, *Acts* (Grand Rapids: Baker, 2007), 23–28.

ents Jesus as God's exalted and vindicated bearer of kingdom promise, forgiveness, and life for all who believe, Jew and Gentile. The bestowal of God's Spirit marks the new era's arrival (Luke 3:16; 24:49; Acts 1:4–5; 2:16–36 with Joel 2:28–32 and Ps 110:1; Acts 11:15–17; 13:16–24). This message completes promises made to Abraham and Israel centuries ago.

Luke argues that the church roots its message in ancient promises, a story in continuity with Israel's promised hope found in God's covenantal promises to her. The entire saga involves Israel's restoration. For all that Gentile inclusion and equality in the new community brings, we never lose sight of the fact that it is *Israel's story and Israel's hope* that brings blessing to the world, just as Genesis 12:3 promised.

Luke 1 – 2

Infancy Material as a Whole

Luke's infancy material tells Israel's story. Consider all the references associated with the Jewish nation. John the Baptist is sent to the sons of Israel (Luke 1:16). The child born to Mary is given the throne of David and will reign over the house of Jacob forever (1:31–32). God has helped his servant Israel realize promises spoken to Abraham and to his posterity forever (1:54–55). Zechariah blesses the God of Israel who has raised up a Davidic horn of salvation as the prophets foretold (1:68–70). Jesus is born in David's city because Joseph is a descendant of David (2:4). The angels hail Jesus' birth in the city of David (2:11). Simeon looks for the consolation of Israel (2:25). Jesus is a light of revelation for the Gentiles and a glory for his people Israel (2:32). Jesus causes the rise and fall of many in Israel (2:34). Anna looks for the redemption of Jerusalem (2:38). The pious in Israel are looking for the Jewish Messiah. The themes introduced in this section point to Israel's story. This is confirmed by a closer look at a few of these texts.

Luke 1:32 – 33

Mary is told that the child she will bear will sit on David's throne and rule over Jacob's house (Luke 2:32–33). The Davidic throne reflects the Davidic covenant's promise of a son, a house, and an everlasting rule (2 Sam 7:8–16, esp. vv. 13, 16; on Solomon's accession, 1 Kgs 1:48; 2:24). The promise to David found its initial fulfillment in Solomon. However, the ultimate fulfillment of the everlasting character of this dynasty is realized in Jesus (Luke 1:33). The initial promise to David was reiterated throughout the Old Testament (1 Kgs 2:24, where Solomon is seen as fulfilling the promise; Pss 89:14, 19–29, 35–37 [89:15, 20–30, 36–38 MT[5]]; 132:11–12; Isa 9:6–7 [9:5–6 MT]; 11:1–5, 10; Jer 23:5–6).[6] The announcement in Luke 1:32–33 recalls a deeply held Old Testament hope.

Luke made much of Davidic descent (Luke 1:69; 2:4, 11; 3:31). Jesus' regal Davidic

---

5. MT stands for the Masoretic Text of the Old Testament, the authoritative Hebrew text of the Jewish Bible. Its numbering in some cases differs from that of contemporary English versions.

6. I. Howard Marshall, *The Gospel of Luke: A Commentary on the Greek Text* (Grand Rapids: Eerdmans, 1978), 67.

connection is the basic christological starting point for Luke's Jesus.[7] Luke's theology is rooted in the Davidic son's kingdom rule. The kingdom in Luke includes earthly elements that are not transformed or redefined into something else. As his two volumes will show, Luke's story involves divine history for *this* earth. Nothing in Luke's story points us to deliverance into a new realm. All the language Luke uses when describing the kingdom of God is about this world and its deliverance.

Luke 1:32 – 33 represents a continuation of Israel's story. Jesus not only has a regal position (1:32) but an everlasting reign (1:33). *Basileusei epi* means "to reign over" a people. The phrase "house of Jacob" is another way to refer to the nation of Israel (Exod 19:3; Isa 2:5 – 6; 8:17; 48:1). Some see an allusion here to Jesus gathering a "new Israel."[8] There is, however, nothing in the context to suggest this. In fact, Mary's hymn expresses purely national sentiments (Luke 1:46 – 55), as do Simeon's remarks (2:29, 32, 34 – 35). Jesus, as God's Messiah, is King of the Jews, whether or not they recognize him. The Davidic king comes to his own.

Jesus rules forever. The idea of an eternal rule in the New Testament emerges from the promise of an eternal line of kings or deliverance figures (2 Sam 7:12 – 16; 1 Kgs 8:25; Isa 9:6 – 7 [9:5 – 6 MT]; Pss 110:4; 132:12; Mic 4:7 with 5:1 – 4 [4:14 – 5:3 MT] portrays God's regal rule; esp. Dan 7:14).[9] Second Temple Judaism also reflected this idea (*Pss. Sol.* 17.4; *1 En.* 49.1; 62.14; 4Q174 [= 4QFlor] 1.11; *2 Bar.* 73 [early second century]). The phrase *eis tous aiōnas* (into the ages; i.e., forever) parallels *ouk estai telos* (shall not be an end), emphasizing the everlasting duration of Jesus' rule. Luke-Acts makes clear that neither official Jewish rejection nor crucifixion will stop God's Davidic king. Israel's story will move on and never end.

These two core infancy account verses show how Luke roots Jesus' story in Israel's hope. There is little "Christianized" language here. Even the Greek style of the two chapters echoes the Septuagint (LXX) to evoke the nation's story. The hope operates in continuity with God's promises.

Luke 1:68 – 69

Zechariah declares that the "God of Israel" has raised up a Davidic horn for his people. Zechariah's praise focuses on God's visitation in messianic redemption (Luke 1:68). This opening call to praise points to a praise psalm.[10] The language is that of Israel's national salvation, as the God of Israel is blessed in terms common in the Old Testament (Gen 9:26; 1 Sam 25:32; 1 Kgs 1:48; Pss 41:13 [41:14 MT]; 72:18; 89:52 [89:53 MT]; 106:48) and Second Temple Judaism (Tob 3:11; *Pss. Sol.* 2.37). Such nationalistic features in Luke 1:68 – 69 argue against reading these verses as holding only

---

7. Darrell L. Bock, *Proclamation from Prophecy and Pattern: Lucan Old Testament Christology* (Sheffield, UK: Sheffield Academic Press, 1987); Mark Strauss, *The Davidic Messiah in Luke-Acts: The Promise and Its Fulfilment in Lukan Christology* (Sheffield, UK: Sheffield Academic Press, 1995).

8. Frederick W. Danker, *Jesus and the New Age: A Commentary on Luke* (Philadelphia: Fortress, 1988), 38; Robert F. O'Toole, *The Unity of Luke's Theology: An Analysis of Luke-Acts* (Wilmington, Del.: Michael Glazier, 1984), 18, who says it means Christians.

9. Marshall, *The Gospel of Luke*, 68; Grundmann, *Theological Dictionary of the New Testament* (trans. Geoffrey W. Bromiley; 10 vols.; Grand Rapids: Eerdmans, 1964 – 76), 9:569, n. 483 (hereafter *TDNT*).

10. Beyer, *TDNT* 2:764.

"transferred Christian significance" for Luke. Israel is in view here, as Luke 1:71 – 73 confirms.

The basis of the praise (*hoti*, for) is God's visitation (Luke 1:68b), specifically God's redeeming (*lytrōsin*, setting free) his people. Ravens notes that "on the four occasions when Luke uses these words [for redemption] they always refer to 'Israel', never to Christians or Gentiles (Luke 1:68; 2:38; 24:21; Acts 7:35)."[11]

As the entire hymn will show, God's visitation comes through Messiah's visitation. Though Zechariah speaks in the past tense in part because Messiah is already conceived, his focus is on what is yet to happen through that Messiah (see the future tense verb "shall visit" in Luke 1:78 ESV). For Luke, God's visitation means God's coming salvation in the Messiah Jesus (Luke 1:78; 7:16; 19:44; Acts 15:14).

What Messiah's visitation means for God's people is redemption, a deliverance from enemies, so that God's people are free to serve their God in righteousness and holiness. Luke 1:71 and 1:74 – 75 suggest a political connotation, especially since the God of Israel is addressed in terms parallel to the Psalms. This is restoration language, but is a political deliverance really in view?

Hendriksen argues that the context refers to a spiritual restoration only, citing Luke 2:38 in support.[12] However, Luke 2 refers to Israel's consolation (2:25), to Jesus as a light to the Gentiles and a glory for his people Israel (2:32), and to Jerusalem's redemption (2:38). The latter phrase goes beyond spiritual restoration, as Luke 21:24, 28; 24:21; Acts 1:6; 3:19 – 26 suggest. These Lucan texts show that Jerusalem's redemption includes the Son of Man's rule and judgment on earth. The political connotation is not absent. Rather, political redemption is delayed because of the nation's failure to respond (Luke 13:31 – 35; 19:44).

Thus, redemption involves both political and spiritual elements, nationalistic themes (Luke 1:71, 74) and the offer of forgiveness (1:77 – 78). Zechariah praises God for the expectation of a total deliverance. Such a linkage between spiritual and political blessing is not surprising, since it parallels the blessing-and-curse sections of Deuteronomy. What is new is the division into two distinct phases tied to Jesus' two comings. Of course, Zechariah has no such twofold conception here: he simply presents the total package. Subsequent events explain the division and present a hope split into two parts due to the vindication of Israel's rejected Messiah.

Luke 2:25 – 34

Simeon, an old pious man, is awaiting Israel's consolation (*paraklēsin tou Israēl*; 2:25). Such consolation is a key theme in many strands of Old Testament and Second Temple Jewish eschatology that refer to Israel's deliverance (Isa 40:1; 49:13; 51:3; 57:18; 61:2; 2 Bar. 44.7).

Echoing Isaiah 42:6, Simeon refers to Jesus as light, a revelation for the nations and glory for "your people Israel." In Luke, we do not choose between Israel and the nations. Rather, Israel's story is for the nations as well.

---

11. David Ravens, *Luke and the Restoration of Israel* (Sheffield, UK: Sheffield Academic Press, 1995), 38.
12. Bock, *Luke 1:1 – 9:50*, 123 – 24, 127 – 28, discusses Hendriksen's view.

Luke 3 – 24

Luke 4:16 – 30

At the synagogue in Nazareth, Jesus declares that his Spirit-anointed ministry unfolded Israel's story described in Isaiah 61. Pointing to the time of Elijah and Elisha, and the healing of the widow of Zarephath and Naaman the Syrian, Jesus notes how in times past blessing bypassed Israel and went to the Gentiles. The warning to the nation is that if she rejects God's message, then blessing may not come to her but may go to Gentiles. Israel's story has an obstacle, her own rejecting heart. The question is whether that obstacle is permanent or not. Later texts in Luke answer this question.

Luke 13:34 – 35

When substantial rejection comes out of Israel, Jesus warns the nation about the risk. In Luke 13:6 – 9, Jesus says that the vine that does not produce fruit will be cut down. Again the question surfaces, is this a permanent judgment against Israel?

This leads us into Luke 13:34 – 35, a crucial text. Luke 13 details the nature of the penalty Israel faces for "Know the time of your visitation" (ESV; see Luke 19:41 – 44).

In Luke 13:34, Jesus speaks as a prophet of the Lord's repeated longing to gather the nation as a hen gathers her brood. The image of God as a bird is common in the Old Testament and Second Temple Jewish texts (Deut. 32:11; Ruth 2:12; Pss 17:8; 36:7 [36:8 MT]; 57:1 [57:2 MT]; 61:4 [61:5 MT]; 63:7 [63:8 MT]; 91:4; Isa 31:5; *2 Bar.* 41.3 – 4; 2 Esd [= 4 Ezra] 1:30). The God of Israel's desire is to care for, nurture, and protect his people. The reference to repeated attempts to gather the nation might allude to the many prophets he sent throughout Israel's history. Only one thing stopped God from exercising his parental care: the people did not wish him to do so. As a result, the gathering and its protection could not take place. The same risk applies now to Jesus' offer.

In Luke 13:35, Jesus underscores the situation. Israel is in peril. The language of the empty, desolate house recalls Jeremiah 12:7 and 22:5 (cf. Ps 69:25 [69:26 MT]; Ezek 8:6; 11:23). The parallel in Matthew 23:38 mentions that the house is desolate (*erēmos*), but Luke lacks this term. The Old Testament declared the possibility of exile for the nation if it did not respond to God's call about exercising justice (Jer 22:5 – 6). As such, Jesus' use of "house" (*oikos*) does not allude to the Temple. Jesus is more emphatic than Jeremiah's statement of the nation's potential rejection; a time of abandoning exile has come. Rather than being gathered under God's wings, their house is empty and exposed (Luke 13:6 – 9). But for how long?

Jesus adds a note about the judgment's duration: Israel will not see God's messenger *until* they recognize "the one who comes in the name of the Lord" (*heōs … eipēte, Eulogēmenos ho erchomenos en onomati kyriou*), from Psalm 117:26 LXX [118:26 Eng.] (quoted from the NASB). Luke already made clear that the key term "one who comes" (*ho erchomenos*) means Messiah (Luke 3:15 – 16; 7:19). Israel is to accept Jesus as sent from God. Until the nation accepts him, it stands alone, exposed to the world's dangers. The quotation from Psalm 118 is positive, not negative.[13] It suggests that Israel's judgment is for a time.

Luke 21:24

Luke 21:24 pictures a turnaround in Israel's fate. Near the end of the eschatological discourse, Luke describes Jerusalem being trodden down for a time and refers to this period as the "times of the Gentiles." What does this verse mean? It refers to a period of Gentile domination (Dan 2:44b; 8:13 – 14; 12:5 – 13), while alluding to a subsequent hope for Israel (Ezek 39:24 – 29; Zech 12:4 – 9). There are three reasons to maintain this reading.

First, the city's fall is of limited duration. Why else mention a time limit?

Second, there is a period in God's plan when Gentiles dominate, which implies that the subsequent period will be characterized by Israel's role.[14] Jesus' initial coming and his future eschatological return represent turning points in God's plan.

Third, this view of Israel's judgment now but vindication later suggests what Paul also contends in Romans 11:25 – 26: Israel has a future, grafted back in when the fullness of the Gentiles leads her to respond (see also Rom 11:11 – 12, 15, 30 – 32).[15] These chapters certainly have ethnic Israel in view, not any concept of a spiritual Israel. Romans 9 – 11 develops the temporary period of judgment noted in Luke 13:34 – 35.

Luke 24:21

These two passages (Luke 24:19, 21) describe the hope that seemed to have been blocked by Jesus' death but was revived as a result of resurrection. In Luke 24:21 one of the companions says that he had hoped Jesus would "redeem Israel" (lytrousthai ton Israēl). This is the only time that Luke uses the verb lytroō ("to redeem"). If this hope is the same as what Zechariah expressed (Luke 1:68 – 79), then it included the connotation of a political release (cf. Isa 41:14; 43:14; 44:22 – 24; 1 Macc 4:11; Pss. Sol. 9.1).

Dillon's comment that Israel means broadly "the people of God" and not strictly the Jewish nation fails (1) to note the disappointment expressed here, (2) to take seriously the infancy narrative background, (3) to recall that part of the disappointment was that "our" chief priests and rulers handed Jesus over, and (4) to appreciate the Jewish perspective that pervades the account.[16] The Jewish disciples in Luke 24:21 still think of Israel as a sociopolitical unit. This fits the time period of the remarks, before the church operated as an autonomous unit. The focus on the nation in the early chapters of Acts adds to the weight of this interpretation.[17]

---

13. Bock, Luke 9:51 – 24:53, 1251.

14. E. Earle Ellis, The Gospel of Luke (Greenwood, S.C.: Attic, 1974), 245.

15. James M. Scott, "'And Then All Israel Will Be Saved' (Rom. 11:26)," in Restoration: Old Testament, Jewish and Christian Perspectives (ed. James M. Scott; Leiden, Netherlands: Brill, 2001), 489 – 527.

16. Richard J. Dillon, From Eye-Witnesses to Ministers of the Word: Tradition and Composition in Luke 24 (Rome: Pontifical Biblical Institute, 1978), 129 – 30.

17. Danker, Jesus and the New Age, 392.

Conclusion

So at the end of Luke's gospel, where are we? Israel's story remains and develops. None of the above Lucan texts we have focused on appear in Burge's *Jesus and the Land*. They represent a significant omission.

Acts

Acts 1:4 – 7

On a literary level, the remark in Acts 1:4 – 5 points back to Luke 24:49. Jesus commands the disciples not to depart from Jerusalem but to begin the mission from there, waiting for the "promise of the Father" (*tēn epangelian tou patros*). The disciples perceive this event as an indication of the end's full arrival, which leads to their question in verse 6 about the restoration of the kingdom to Israel. Many Jewish texts expected that Israel would be restored to a place of great blessing (Jer 16:15; 23:8; 31:27 – 34 [where the new covenant is mentioned]; Ezek 34 – 37; Isa 2:2 – 4; 49:6; Amos 9:11 – 15; Sir 48:10; *Pss. Sol.* 17 – 18; *1 En.* 24 – 25; Tob 13 – 14; Eighteen Benedictions 14).[18] The question is a natural one for Jews. Luke 1 – 2 expressed this hope vividly (Luke 1:69 – 74; 2:25, 38). What was debated in Judaism is whether the centrality of Israel would be positive or negative for Gentiles. Would it come with salvation or judgment for the nations? The disciples are not even thinking in mission terms here. Their question reflects a nationalistic concern for vindication. Nothing Jesus did or said in the forty days he was with them after the resurrection dissuaded them from this expectation. Neither does Jesus' answer. Nothing in Luke's story also should dissuade us from holding on to this hope for Israel.

Neither does Jesus' reply in Acts 1:7 – 8 reject the question's restoration premise. This reading following the Luke-Acts story line stands in contrast to interpretations such as that of Stott, who sees the question as full of errors.[19] In Stott's view, they should not have asked about restoration, since that implied a political kingdom; nor about Israel, since that anticipated a national kingdom; nor about "at this time," since that implied the kingdom's immediate establishment. Jesus' reply does not suggest that anything they asked was wrong except that they are excessively concerned about exactly when this will happen, something that is the Father's business.[20] The other major argument Stott makes is that there is no mention of the land in the New Testament. However, the land is not mentioned, since (1) Israel is in its land when most of the New Testament is written,[21] and (2) the rule of Jesus is anticipated to extend over the entire earth, so why focus on the land?

In fact, neither the definition of Israel nor the expectation for Israel changes.

---

18. On *apokathistēmi* ("restore"), see Mal 3:23 LXX (4:6 Eng.), where it is an eschatological technical term, and Dan 4:36 LXX (Dan 4:36 Eng.). Acts 3:21 will return to this idea.

19. John R. W. Stott, *The Message of Acts* (Downers Grove, Ill.: InterVarsity, 1990), 41.

20. Hilary LeCornu and Joseph Shulam, *A Commentary on the Jewish Roots of Acts* (vol. 1; Jerusalem: Academon, 2003), 15.

21. Michael E. Fuller, *The Restoration of Israel: Israel's Re-gathering and the Fate of the Nations in Early Jewish Literature and Luke-Acts* (Berlin: DeGruyter, 2006), 242.

Rather, God's eschatological work is now centered in Jesus. Throughout Acts, Jesus is the blessing's mediator. Throughout Acts, Israel's role remains central to the hope of salvation, including the expectation of national restoration. Acts 10 – 15 works out this story as it extends into all the world.

Jesus does not answer the question about Israel's restoration and its timing. Nor is his response a renunciation of an imminent end.[22] It makes no commitment at all as to when the end comes. These verses show that the disciples are still thinking in terms of Israel's story. Nothing Jesus did or said in these key days altered their ultimate hope for the nation. What was changing was the scope of their assignment and concern. They were to take Messiah's message to the entire world. A global perspective was becoming more important as a part of Israel's story.

Acts 3:18 – 21

In his speech in Acts 3:18 – 21 Peter puts everything together and speaks of Jesus' return.[23] The "times of refreshing" (*kairoi anapsyxeōs*) refers to a future refreshment.[24] *Anapsyxeōs* refers to a "cooling" to relieve trouble or to dry out a wound.[25] In the LXX the only use of "refreshment" is in Exodus 8:11 LXX (= 8:15 Eng.), where it refers to relief from the plague of frogs. The verb *anapsychō* ("to refresh") is used of the Sabbath rest of slaves and animals and the soothing of Saul by David's music (Exod 23:12; 1 Sam 16:23). Peter prophesies a messianic refreshment, the "definitive age of salvation."[26] The idea has parallels in Second Temple Judaism (2 Esd [4 Ezra] 7:75, 91, 95; 11:46; 13:26 – 29; *2 Bar.* 73 – 74; *1 En.* 45.5; 51.4; 96.3). Peter urges his audience to read what God has already said through the prophets. Texts such as Isaiah 65 – 66 are in view, where Israel is restored to fullness (also Isa 34:4; 51:6; Jer 15:18 – 19; 16:15; 23:8; 24:6; Ezek 17:23; Amos 9:11 – 12). Nothing in any of this says that the story already revealed has been changed.

In our narrative sequence, this is a crucial text. It tells us that what is to come was already disclosed. Whatever the expansion of the promise to Gentiles entails, it does not remove nor redefine Israel's story.

Other Key Acts Texts: Acts 10 – 11, Acts 28:20

In the two passages involving Cornelius in Acts 10 – 11, the Spirit's coming shows that Gentiles are equal to Jews in blessing, so that circumcision is not required of Gentiles. The Spirit occupying uncircumcised Gentiles shows they are already cleansed and

---

22. *Pace* Ernst Haenchen, *The Acts of the Apostles: A Commentary* (trans. B. Noble and G. Shinn; Oxford: Blackwell, 1987), 143.

23. Bauckham, "The Restoration of Israel in Luke-Acts," 477, says this speech "is full of restoration terminology."

24. Kremer, *Exegetical Dictionary of the New Testament (EDNT)* (ed. H. Balz and G. Schneider; English translation; Grand Rapids: Eerdmans, 1990 – 93), 1:95.

25. W. Bauer et al., *Greek-English Lexicon of the New Testament and Other Early Christian Literature* (BAGD) (2d ed.; Chicago: University of Chicago Press, 1957), 63; F. W. Danker et al., *Greek-English Lexicon of the New Testament and Other Early Christian Literature* (BDAG) (3d ed.; Chicago: University of Chicago Press, 2000), 75; Schweizer, *TDNT* 9:664.

26. Schweizer, *TDNT* 9:664.

sacred. The new era's sign comes to Gentiles as Gentiles. There is no need for them to become Jews. Israel's story has finally come to bless the nations.

In Acts 28:20, Paul tells the Jews he is in chains for the hope of Israel. Paul is on trial for the hope of the twelve tribes (Acts 26:6 – 7).[27] Hope involves declaring light both to the people of Israel and to Gentiles with a story from the prophets and Moses (Acts 26:22 – 23). Paul says that he worships "the God of the fathers, believing everything laid down by the Law and written in the Prophets, having a hope in God, which these men themselves accept, that there will be a resurrection of both the just and unjust" (Acts 24:14 – 15 ESV). Paul tells Israel's story. Nothing suggests that the story has changed from the one told in the infancy material and the teaching of John, Jesus, and Peter. In Luke-Acts, this is one story.

Conclusion

For Luke-Acts, Israel's story has not changed, and it is a story of hope for the world. This warns us not to rewrite the story that the Torah and the Prophets give us about original Israel. We can add the nations into the promise through Christ, the ultimate seed, but we cannot lose sight of the hope in the promised one that belonged to original Israel and still exists for her.

Some contemporary readings of Paul and the New Testament suggest that we should change this story when we read those ancient texts and think of Israel in a different way that excludes or minimizes original Israel. However, for Luke-Acts, Jesus' story is Israel's story, as well as a story that blesses the world. It anticipates a future time when Israel responds to Jesus and God restores the nation as the prophets promised. Israel and the nations one day will respond to God as one. In the meantime, the gospel goes out into the world for both Jew and Gentile.

---

27. Fuller, *Restoration of Israel*, 239.

For Further Reading

Bauckham, Richard. "The Restoration of Israel in Luke-Acts." Pages 435–87 in *Restoration: Old Testament, Jewish and Christian Perspectives*. Edited by James M. Scott. Leiden, Netherlands: Brill, 2001.

Bock, Darrell L. *A Theology of Luke-Acts*. Grand Rapids: Zondervan, 2012.

Carras, George P. "Observant Jews in the Story of Luke and Acts." Pages 693–708 in *The Unity of Luke-Acts*. Edited by J. Verheyden. Leuven, Belgium: Leuven University Press, 1999.

Edwards, James R. *The Hebrew Gospel and the Development of the Synoptic Tradition*. Grand Rapids: Eerdmans, 2009.

Fuller, Michael E. *The Restoration of Israel: Israel's Regathering and the Fate of the Nations in Early Jewish Literature and Luke-Acts*. Berlin: DeGruyter, 2006.

Hill, Craig C. "Restoring the Kingdom to Israel: Luke-Acts and Christian Supersessionism." Pages 185–200 in *Shadow of Glory: Reading the New Testament after the Holocaust*. Edited by Tod Linafelt. New York: Routledge, 2002.

Jervell, Jacob. *Luke and the People of God*. Minneapolis: Augsburg, 1972.

———. *The Theology of the Acts of the Apostles*. Cambridge: Cambridge University Press, 1996.

LeCornu, Hilary, and Joseph Shulam. *A Commentary on the Jewish Roots of Acts*. 2 vols. Jerusalem: Academon, 2003.

Oliver, Isaac W. "Torah Praxis after 70 CE: Reading Matthew and Luke-Acts as Jewish Texts." PhD diss., University of Michigan, forthcoming.

Ravens, David. *Luke and the Restoration of Israel*. Sheffield, UK: Sheffield Academic Press, 1995.

Spencer, F. Scott. *The Gospel of Luke and Acts of the Apostles*. Nashville: Abingdon, 2008.

Tannehill, Robert C. *The Narrative Unity of Luke-Acts: A Literary Interpretation*. 2 vols. Minneapolis: Fortress, 1990.

———. *The Shape of Luke's Story: Essays on Luke-Acts*. Eugene, Oreg.: Cascade, 2005.

Tyson, Joseph B., ed. *Luke-Acts and the Jewish People: Eight Critical Perspectives*. Minneapolis: Augsburg, 1988.

Wendel, Susan J. *Scriptural Interpretation and Community Self-Definition in Luke-Acts and the Writings of Justin Martyr*. Leiden, Netherlands: Brill, 2011.

CHAPTER 16

James and the Jerusalem Council Decision

RICHARD BAUCKHAM

The most momentous decision the early Christian movement had to make was on the status of Gentiles who wished to join it.[1] That Gentiles should join the movement was not in itself problematic, since there was a widespread Jewish expectation, based on biblical prophecies, that in the last days the restoration of God's own people Israel would be accompanied by the conversion of the other nations to the worship of the God of Israel. Since the early Christians believed that the messianic restoration of Israel was now under way in the form of their own community, it would not have been difficult for them to recognize that the time for the conversion of the nations was also arriving. What was much less clear, however, was whether Gentiles who came to faith in Jesus the Messiah should become Jews, getting circumcised (in the case of men) and adopting the full yoke of the Torah, or whether they could remain Gentiles while enjoying the same blessings of eschatological salvation that Jewish believers in Jesus did. It is not unlikely that in the early days there were Gentiles who joined the Christian movement, at the same time converting to Judaism. At any rate the issue does not seem to have been clearly posed to the leaders of the movement in Jerusalem before the conversion of the God-fearer Cornelius and his household (Acts 10). For Peter, who preached the gospel to them, this was a landmark event, something the narrative of Acts emphasizes by narrating it twice (the second time when Peter tells the story to the other Jerusalem leaders in Acts 11:4 – 17). When this group of Gentiles believed in Jesus, they immediately received the Holy Spirit in so evident a way that Peter could only conclude that God had extended salvation to them as Gentiles, not requiring that they first become Jews. He therefore baptised them, admitting them to the messianic people of God without expecting them to be circumcised or to observe any more of the Torah than they already did (as God-fearers who worshiped the God of Israel and lived by the moral principles of the Torah).

It is very important to understand what preconceptions Peter had to set aside, both when he visited Cornelius in his home and, more important, when he recognized that

---

1. I have explained and justified the argument of this essay at much greater length in three essays: "James and the Jerusalem Church," in *The Book of Acts in Its Palestinian Setting* (ed. Richard Bauckham; Grand Rapids: Eerdmans, 1995), 415 – 80; "James and the Gentiles (Acts 15:13 – 21)," in *History, Literature and Society in the Book of Acts* (ed. Ben Witherington III; Cambridge: Cambridge University Press, 1996), 154 – 84; "James, Peter, and the Gentiles," in *The Missions of James, Peter, and Paul: Tensions in Early Christianity* (ed. Bruce Chilton and Craig Evans; Leiden, Netherlands: Brill, 2004), 91 – 142. Full documentation of my argument will be found in these essays.

God had given these Gentiles, even though they remained Gentiles, the same blessing of eschatological salvation that Peter and other Jewish believers in Jesus had received at Pentecost. The preconceptions Peter had to set aside were those that the Jewish leadership of the Christian movement would finally (in Acts 15) have to set aside in a decision binding on the whole movement. Crucial to the account of Peter and Cornelius are the words "making a distinction" (Acts 10:20;[2] 11:12; 15:9).[3] The Spirit guides Peter to go with Cornelius's messengers, not making the distinction he would usually make between Jews and Gentiles. Such a distinction was one that God himself made in the Torah (Lev 20:24, 26), where it was symbolized by the distinction between clean and unclean animals that Israelites were to make in their diet (Lev 20:25). The message of Peter's dream, in which he was shocked to hear God telling him to break the dietary rules by eating unclean animals (Acts 10:11–16; 11:5–10), accompanied by the declaration, "What God has purified, you must not consider profane" (Acts 10:15; 11:9), was not literally concerned with Jewish diet, but with the separation between Jews and Gentiles. Peter explains this when he meets Cornelius's household: "You yourselves know that it is taboo for a Jew to associate with or to visit a Gentile, but God has shown me that I should not call anyone profane or impure" (10:28).

In Jewish eyes Gentiles were both profane and impure. They were "profane" (i.e., not holy) simply because they were Gentiles and so did not share the holiness of the people of Israel, who alone constituted God's holy people. The sense in which Gentiles were considered "impure" has often been misunderstood. In the later Second Temple period Gentiles were not usually considered impure in the ritual or cultic sense, that is, defiled by the sort of impurity Jews contracted from such sources as corpses, sexual intercourse, childbirth, or scale disease. The rules of cultic purity did not apply to Gentiles. But the Torah and later Jewish thought envisaged another kind of impurity that scholars have tended to neglect. This is the defilement that resulted from certain especially heinous sins, usually idolatry, sexual immorality of many kinds, and murder. It was with this kind of impurity that, paradigmatically, the Canaanites had defiled not only themselves but also the land (Lev 18:24–25, 27), and Israelites were stringently warned against imitating such practices (Lev 18:24–28; 20:1–5; Num 35:33–34). In the later Second Temple period, especially in the land of Israel, where the presence of Gentiles defiling the land was naturally offensive to devout Jews, Gentile society as a whole was generally regarded as morally impure because of the pervasive idolatry and the prevalence of sexual practices abhorrent to Jews. The prohibition on intimate association between Jews and Gentiles, whether in intermarriage or visiting Gentiles in their homes or eating with them, had this basis. The danger was not that Jews would contract ritual impurity through physical contact, but that they would be contaminated by Gentile idolatry and immorality. In the case of idolatry, for example, all the institutions and practices of Gentile life were so implicated in it that Jews could all too easily be unwittingly involved.

---

2. Most translations have "not hesitating" (or similar), but the verb is the same as in 11:12 and 15:9 and makes a much more significant point.

3. All quotations from the New Testament in this chapter are my own translations, unless otherwise indicated. In many cases, I have given a more literal translation than those of most of the English versions.

We might suppose that this would not apply to Cornelius, "an upright and God-fearing man, of whom the whole Jewish nation speaks well" (Acts 10:22), but we should remember that he was a centurion in the Roman army, where participation in idolatry could scarcely be avoided. In any case, even if God-fearers in some diaspora synagogues might escape denunciation as impure, in Jewish Palestine, where Gentile impurity defiled the land and, even more shockingly, Jewish imitation of Gentile ways would defile the land and the sanctuary, there was more reason for suspicious prudence. The common view was that Gentiles could not escape moral impurity without the protection afforded by submission to the whole yoke of the Torah, including, of course, circumcision for males. Therefore it was necessary for Jews to "make a distinction" between themselves and Gentiles, avoiding intimate association. This did not mean avoiding, for example, business dealings or marketplace conversation, but it did mean avoiding table fellowship, which in the ancient world was the closest form of intimacy other than sexual relationships. This is why the whole Jerusalem church was shocked to hear that Peter had entered Cornelius's home and shared meals with uncircumcised men (Acts 11:2–3). It is also why the events in which Paul clashed with Peter in Antioch concerned table fellowship between Jewish and Gentile Christians (Gal 2:11–13). It was not the food or the wine that was the issue (any problems at that level could easily be avoided if the Jewish Christians supplied the food and the wine). The problem was that the Jewish Christians who on this occasion enforced separation (enlisting even Peter against his better knowledge) did not believe that Gentiles could be morally pure without observing Torah.

When Peter later recalled his experience with the household of Cornelius, he said that God "in cleansing their hearts by faith ... made no distinction between them and us" (Acts 15:9). By the cleansing of the heart Peter refers here to the prophetic expectation that in the messianic age God would purify the hearts of his people and enable them to keep his commandments (see Ezek 36:16–36). It was not circumcision and Torah observance but the transformative power of the Spirit that changed the lives of the Jewish Christian community at Pentecost and subsequently. So the gift of the Spirit to the household of Cornelius showed that in the messianic age God was no longer making the distinction between the impure Gentiles and the pure people of God. Both were being cleansed of impurity in the same way — "through the grace of Jesus Christ" (Acts 15:11 NRSV). With the end of this kind of distinction, it was possible also to envisage the end of the distinction between "holy" and "profane" groups of people, that is, between Jews who were God's people and Gentiles who were not. It became possible to envisage the messianic people of God as a community of both Jews and Gentiles, the former observing Torah, the latter not. Of course, neither Peter nor any of the Jerusalem leaders entertained the idea that Jewish believers in Jesus should give up observing Torah. But Torah observance no longer constituted a barrier between Jews and Gentiles, since their fellowship was based not on Torah, but on faith in Jesus the Messiah and experience of the transformative power of the Spirit. Despite his aberrant behaviour at Antioch, Peter had reached much the same position as Paul on this issue, as Paul recognized very well when he reproached Peter for letting himself be bullied into making a show of separation from Gentiles once again (Gal 2:11 – 16).

At what deserves to be called the first Jerusalem conference, immediately after Peter's visit to Cornelius, Peter persuaded the rest of the Jerusalem church, both leaders and other believers, to agree with him (Acts 11:1 – 18). It was in accordance with this decision that Barnabas, as a representative of the Jerusalem leaders, became deeply involved in the first large-scale movement of Gentile conversions at Antioch (Acts 11:20 – 26). From this followed the missionary journey of Barnabas and Paul to the cities of south Galatia, where they established thriving communities of both Jewish and Gentile believers (Acts 13 – 14). But we should not be surprised that the issue of how Gentile believers should relate to the Torah was not yet finally settled. It is normal in human affairs that agreements on really controversial issues have to be negotiated again and again. Perhaps the Jewish believers (former Pharisees, according to Acts 15:5) who began campaigning for Gentile believers to be circumcised were themselves recent converts, not party to the earlier decision of the church. Perhaps they had had doubts all along but were spurred to action by the success of Paul and Barnabas's mission to Gentiles. In any case, according to the narrative of Acts, the debate was such that a full assembly of the apostles, the elders of the Jerusalem church, and all the Jerusalem believers was convened in an attempt to resolve the issue once and for all (Acts 15:6 – 21).

Scholars have long disagreed as to whether the event recounted in Acts 15 is identical with the meeting between Paul, Barnabas, and the three "pillars" of the Jerusalem church that Paul recounts in Galatians 2:1 – 10. The accounts are so different that many who think the same event is being described in both cases also conclude that Luke's account is seriously unreliable as history. My own view (which there is not space to defend here) is that there were two distinct events. Paul's account is of a private consultation that he and Barnabas had with the three senior Jerusalem leaders — James the Lord's brother, Peter, and John — before they set out on their missionary journey to south Galatia. Even then there were believers Paul regards as "false brothers" who infiltrated the meeting (Gal 2:4 NRSV) and plainly took a different view of the matter. When such people stirred up things in Antioch on Paul's return (Gal 2:12; Acts 15:1 – 2), the need was seen for a plenary meeting of the Jerusalem church, involving all the Christian leaders who could attend, with the aim both of debating the matter seriously and of promulgating an official ruling for all the churches.

According to the narrative in Acts 15, it is Peter who opens the proceedings by reminding his audience of the conversion of Cornelius and his household. He makes the points about this that we have already discussed, concluding that Gentile converts should not be required to shoulder the yoke of the Torah. Barnabas and Paul support Peter's argument with the account of their missionary outreach to Gentiles, which God has evidently blessed by doing "signs and wonders" (Acts 15:12). These speakers are all, in effect, offering miraculous interventions of God as proof that God accepts Gentiles into his eschatological people. However, this may not have been sufficient for some of those present. After all, the matter was one of halakah (interpretation of Torah). Later rabbis — and therefore plausibly some of those present at the Jerusalem

council — held that matters of halakah could be decided only from Scripture. There-
fore it is not the speeches of Peter, Barnabas, and Paul, but the speech of James the
Lord's brother (who, by this stage, seems to have reached a preeminent position in the
Jerusalem church) that provides the clinching argument. James argues from Scripture
that the Gentiles who, it depicts, will join the messianic people of God will do so as
Gentiles.

James's quotation from "the prophets" (Acts 15:15 – 18) is in fact a conflated
quotation, combining Amos 9:11 – 12, the main text, with allusions to related texts
that assist the interpretation. In addition, the form of the text has been selected and
adapted to suit the interpretation. These are Jewish exegetical techniques that are
known to us not only from the New Testament but also from the Qumran biblical
commentaries (*pesharim*). Their use is evidence of skilled exegetical work. What
appears to be merely a quotation of a scriptural text turns out to be in fact also an
interpretation of the text.

The interpretation takes "the dwelling of David" in Amos 9:11 to be the eschatological Temple God will build as the place of his eschatological presence in the messianic age when Davidic rule is restored to Israel. He will build this new Temple so
that all the Gentile nations may seek his presence there. Such a reading of the words of
Amos is promoted by the other, related prophetic texts to which allusion is made (Hos
3:5; Jer 12:15 – 16; Isa 45:21), as well as by following the variant form of the Hebrew
text that is represented by the Septuagint Greek translation (i.e., reading "the rest of
humanity will seek" instead of "they will possess the remnant of humanity," as in the
Masoretic Hebrew).

The importance of this text for the issue in question at the Jerusalem council
turns especially on the words: "all the nations over whom my name has been invoked"
(Acts 15:17). This is a Hebrew idiom, frequent in the Hebrew Bible and later Jewish
literature, that denotes YHWH's ownership. It is frequently used of Israel as YHWH's
own people (e.g., Deut 28:10; 2 Chr 7:14; Jer 14:9; Dan 9:19), distinguished from the
Gentiles, who are "those over whom your name has not been invoked" (Isa 63:19).
Its use in Amos 9:12 of "all the nations" is unique and would have been read by early
Christians as strong evidence that Gentiles do not have to become Jews in order to
belong to the messianic people of God. There are few, if any, other prophetic texts
that James could have selected to make this point as decisively as this one. It shows
that in the messianic age, Gentiles, precisely as Gentiles, will no longer be "profane"
but will join the Jews in belonging to God's holy people, those "over whom YHWH's
name has been invoked."

The text says that all the Gentiles will "seek the Lord," and in line with other prophetic texts that envisage the converted nations coming into God's presence in the
Temple (e.g., Isa 2:2 – 3; Zech 14:16), James no doubt takes this to mean that they will
seek the Lord in his Temple, the restored Temple of the messianic age, "the dwelling
of David" mentioned by Amos. But we need also to recall that the early Christians
thought of their own community as the new Temple. When applied to their own situation, the text implies that, whereas Gentiles were prohibited from entering the Temple

built of stone in Jerusalem, they could enter the new Temple of the messianic age, the Christian community.

While Amos 9:11 – 12 provides the exegetical basis for maintaining that Gentile Christians are not obligated to keep the law of Moses, it is not obvious why this conclusion is then qualified in James's speech by the proviso that there are four prohibitions they must observe (Acts 15:20). Luke's summary has obscured the exegetical argument on which the terms of the "apostolic decree," as it has often been called (Acts 15:28 – 29), are based, but it can be uncovered. The four prohibitions correspond to the four things that are prohibited to "the alien who sojourns in your/their midst" in Leviticus 17 – 18 (the phrase occurs in Lev 17:10, 12, 13; 18:26): (1) "things sacrificed to idols" are prohibited in Leviticus 17:8 – 9 (cf. 3 – 7); (2) "blood" (i.e., eating blood) is prohibited in Leviticus 17:10, 12; (3) "things strangled" (i.e., meat which has not been slaughtered in such a way as to drain the blood from it) are prohibited by implication in Leviticus 17:13; and (4) "sexual immorality" refers to Leviticus 18:26 and covers all the prohibited forms of sexual practice in Leviticus 18:6 – 23.

The reason these four are selected from the commandments of the Torah as alone applicable to Gentile members of the messianic people of God is exegetical. They are specifically designated as obliging "the alien who sojourns in your/their midst" as well as Israelites. Applied to the situation of the messianic people of God, this phrase could be seen as referring to Gentiles included in the community along with Jews. But the point is made more precisely by the use of this same phrase in two of the prophecies about the conversion of the Gentiles in the messianic age: Jeremiah 12:16 ("they shall be built in the midst of my people") and Zechariah 2:11 (LXX: "they shall dwell in your midst"). In the light of these exegetical links, the Torah itself can be seen to make specific provision for these Gentile converts, who are not obliged, like Jews, by the commandments of the Torah in general, but are obliged by these specific commandments.

There is yet another feature of these four commandments in Leviticus 17 – 18 that marks them out as meeting the problem the Jerusalem council faced. They can easily be taken to be just the commandments to which reference is made in Leviticus 18:24 – 30 when it exhorts the Israelites not to follow the practices of the Canaanite peoples with which they had defiled themselves and the land. In other words, the offences that are prohibited both in Leviticus 17 – 18 and in the apostolic decree are those most often regarded as constituting the moral impurity of Gentiles. The fit with the situation in Acts 15 is perfect. If God has indeed, as Peter claims, "purified their [the Gentiles] hearts by faith," these are the impurities — the typical Gentile sins — from which they are henceforth to be pure. In formulating the apostolic decree, James does not really add to Peter's position on the matter. He simply spells out a necessary implication of Peter's view: that Gentile members of the messianic people of God are to refrain from the moral impurities in which Gentiles typically indulged. Since they are members of the messianic people *as Gentiles*, they do not require circumcision and other requirements that the Torah makes on Israelites in order to become or to remain morally pure, but they are obliged by these specific prohibitions of the Torah against morally polluting practices.

This also makes clear why, as Peter has known since his vision and its explication, close association, such as sharing meals, between Jewish and Gentile believers is not problematic. It had been taboo in order to protect Jews from the morally polluting influence of Gentile sinners. But Gentile believers in Christ, according to James and the decree, should not be suspected of idolatry and immorality. By explicitly applying the prohibitions of Leviticus 17 – 18 to them it is made unequivocally clear that they are expected to avoid the impurities that would otherwise impede fellowship between Jews and Gentiles in the church.

It is important to note that the reason the apostolic decree facilitates Jewish and Gentile table fellowship is not because three of its four prohibitions concern meat. It would have been easy enough for Jews sharing even a meal provided by Gentiles to observe these prohibitions by simply not eating meat. The first three practices forbidden by the decree, like the fourth, are matters not of ritual but of moral impurity. The danger of table fellowship with Gentiles was of becoming implicated in these idolatrous and immoral practices of the Gentiles. Their prohibition to Gentiles in the apostolic decree, as in Leviticus itself, has the secondary effect of making close association of Jews and Gentiles who observe the prohibition possible. But they are prohibited primarily because they are pollutions of which all the people of God, Jewish and Gentile, must be free.

There is good evidence that observance of the prohibitions in the apostolic decree was widespread for a long period. It is true that the common view that Christians should not eat "things sacrificed to idols" need not presuppose the apostolic decree. But the conjunction of "to eat things sacrificed to idols" and "to practise sexual immorality" in Revelation 2:14, 20, strongly suggests that the decree is in mind. When the Didache advises "concerning food, bear what you are able, but in any case keep strictly away from meat sacrificed to idols, for it is the worship of dead gods" (6:3), it seems likely that it refers, not to Jewish food laws in general, but to the terms of the apostolic decree. While it shows that avoidance of blood was not found practical by all Christians, it also maintains that ideally this is desirable. That Christians abstain from eating blood is taken for granted by the Letter of the Churches of Vienne and Lyons (*ap.* Eusebius, *Hist. eccl.* 5.1.26), Minucius Felix (*Oct.* 30.6 – 7), Tertullian (*Apol.* 9.13; *Pud.* 12.4 – 5; *Mon.* 5), and Clement of Alexandria (*Strom.* 4.15). Origen (*Cels.* 8.29 – 30) refers explicitly to the decree and clearly sees no problem in regarding all three of the first three prohibitions as binding on and actually observed by Christians in his time. None of these writers relate the decree to table fellowship between Jewish and Gentile Christians, which would, in any case, hardly have been a matter of concern in their contexts. Few of them (Origen is an exception) show any sign of knowing the decree from Acts, which is extremely unlikely in several cases. Such wide acknowledgement of the prohibitions in the decree could not have started when Acts became widely known, but must go back to widespread circulation of the terms of the decree from an early period, independently of Acts. Only if the decree came with the authority of the mother church in Jerusalem, as Acts 15 portrays it, can this be plausibly explained.

We have discussed the evidence that the four prohibitions in the apostolic decree were widely acknowledged and observed. But, of course, logically prior to the four prohibitions was the accompanying decision of the Jerusalem council that Gentile Christians did not have to be circumcised (and thereby be obligated to keep the whole law). This decision was, if anything, more influential than the four prohibitions. It is remarkable how little evidence there is, after this decision must have been promulgated by the Jerusalem church, of Christians proposing that Gentile Christians should be circumcised. To attribute this to the influence of Paul is greatly to exaggerate Paul's influence. James in particular should probably be given much of the credit for the policy that had such an extraordinarily determinative influence on the history of early Christianity.

For Further Reading

Bauckham, Richard. "The Final Meeting of James and Paul: Narrative and History in Acts 21, 18–26." Pages 250–59 in *Raconter, interpréter, annoncer: Parcours de Nouveau Testament: Mélanges offerts à Daniel Marguerat pour son 60e anniversaire.* Edited by E. Steffek and Y. Bourquin. Geneva: Labor et Fides, 2003.

———. "James, Peter, and the Gentiles." Pages 91–142 in *The Missions of James, Peter, and Paul: Tensions in Early Christianity.* Edited by Bruce Chilton and Craig Evans; Leiden, Netherlands: Brill, 2004.

———. "James and the Gentiles (Acts 15:13–21)." Pages 154–84 in *History, Literature and Society in the Book of Acts.* Edited by Ben Witherington III. Cambridge: Cambridge University Press, 1996.

———. "James and the Jerusalem Church." Pages 415–80 in *The Book of Acts in Its Palestinian Setting.* Edited by Richard Bauckham. Grand Rapids: Eerdmans, 1995.

Bockmuehl, Markus. *Jewish Law in Gentile Churches: Halakhah and the Beginning of Christian Public Ethics.* Edinburgh: T&T Clark, 2000.

Bryan, Christopher. "A Further Look at Acts 16:1–3." *Journal of Biblical Literature* 107 (1988): 292–94.

Diffenderfer, Margaret Ruth. "Conditions of Membership in the People of God: A Study Based on Acts 15 and Other Relevant Passages in Acts." PhD diss., University of Durham, 1986.

Koet, Bart J. "Why Did Paul Shave His Hair (Acts 18, 18)? Nazirate and Temple in the Book of Acts." Pages 129–42 in *The Centrality of Jerusalem: Historical Perspectives.* Edited by M. Poorthuis and Ch. Safrai. Kampen, Netherlands: Kok Pharos, 1996.

Langston, Scott. "Dividing It Right: Who Is a Jew and What Is a Christian?" Pages 125–34 in *The Missing Jesus: Rabbinic Judaism and the New Testament.* Edited by Bruce Chilton, Craig A. Evans, and Jacob Neusner. Leiden, Netherlands: Brill, 2002.

Marguerat, Daniel. "Paul and the Torah in the Acts of the Apostles." Pages 98–117 in *The Torah in the New Testament: Papers Delivered at the Manchester-Lausanne Seminar of June 2008.* Edited by Michael Tait and Peter Oakes. London: T&T Clark, 2009.

McKnight, Scot. "A Parting within the Way: Jesus and James on Israel and Purity." Pages 83–129 in *James the Just and Christian Origins.* Edited by Bruce Chilton and Craig A. Evans. Leiden, Netherlands: Brill, 1999.

Miller, Chris A. "Did Peter's Vision in Acts 10 Pertain to Men or the Menu?" *Bibliotheca Sacra* 159 (2002): 302–17.

———. "The Relationship of Jewish and Gentile Believers to the Law between A.D. 30 and 70 in the Scripture." PhD diss., Dallas Theological Seminary, 1994.

Nanos, Mark D. "The Apostolic Decree and the 'Obedience of Faith.'" Pages 166–238 in *The Mystery of Romans*. Minneapolis: Fortress, 1996.

Rudolph, David J. *A Jew to the Jews: Jewish Contours of Pauline Flexibility in 1 Corinthians 9:19–23*. Tübingen: Mohr Siebeck, 2011.

Savelle, Charles H. "A Reexamination of the Prohibitions in Acts 15." *Bibliotheca Sacra* 161 (October–December 2004): 449–68.

Van de Sandt, Huub. "An Explanation of Acts 15.6–21 in the Light of Deuteronomy 4.29–35 (LXX)." *Journal for the Study of the New Testament* 46 (1992): 73–97.

Wahlen, Clinton. "Peter's Vision and Conflicting Definitions of Purity." *New Testament Studies* 51 (2005): 505–18.

CHAPTER 17

Interdependence and Mutual Blessing in the Church

Craig Keener

Paul's letter to the Romans offers us a vision and model for Jewish-Gentile reconciliation. This is because Paul deals with the division between Jesus-believing Jews and Gentiles in his own day. Though Gentile believers were probably a majority in the church in Rome, they were theologically marginalized. For most of history that situation has been reversed, yet part of Romans addresses in advance even that problem.

Paul specifically envisioned the Gentile churches becoming a spiritual blessing to his own people. Gentile Christian devotion to the God of Israel was meant to provoke his people's attention, and Gentile Christian care for their Jewish brothers and sisters should have shown the Jewish people that through Christ God's promised plan for all peoples was being fulfilled. During most of history, however, Paul's vision has gone tragically unfulfilled, for against his explicit teaching Gentile believers have exalted themselves against their Jewish siblings.

The Situation in Rome

Although scholars have offered other reasonable proposals, the most widely accepted background for Paul's letter to the believers in Rome involves disagreement between Jesus-believing Jews and Gentiles regarding Jewish customs. When the emperor Claudius expelled some or most of the Jewish community from Rome (Acts 18:2), probably because of debates over Jesus' Messiahship,[1] Gentile Christians were left to fend more for themselves. Some probably began neglecting distinctively Jewish customs that Romans generally disparaged, like Sabbath observance and abstinence from pork. Later, after Claudius's death annulled his edict, some or many of these Jewish believers returned to Rome (as in the case of Aquila and Priscilla [Rom 16:3]).[2]

When Paul writes this letter, Jewish believers in Jesus worshiped in at least some congregations in Rome (Rom 16:3, 7, 11). Nevertheless, the Roman Christian community as a whole apparently was now predominantly Gentile (Rom 1:5, 13; 11:13). One cannot, of course, necessarily infer members' views from their ethnicity. Some Jewish members, like Aquila and Priscilla, probably shared Paul's view that Gentile believers were not obligated to keep Israel-specific customs in the law. Some Gentile

---

1. See Suetonius, *Claud.* 25.4.

2. I summarize my argument and sources in somewhat more detail in Craig Keener, *Romans: A New Covenant Commentary* (Eugene, Oreg.: Cascade, 2009).

members may have remained committed to practices they had earlier inherited from their first Jewish mentors. Whatever the breakdown, Paul had to address the issue of the Gentiles' relationship with Israel (Rom 9 – 11) and divisions among believers regarding food customs and holy days (Rom 14). These are not simply modern observations; ancient readers of Romans like Origen and Ambrosiaster recognized that the conflict between Jesus-believing Jews and Gentiles or tensions over the law provide the background for this letter.[3]

Paul's Plea for Unity

Unity was a frequent topic of exhortation in antiquity,[4] and it is central to Paul's plea for Jewish-Gentile reconciliation in Romans. This is clear not least because he climaxes his larger argument by inviting unity (Rom 15:5 – 6) and inviting believers to welcome one another (Rom 15:7). He underscores this point by showing from Scripture that God's plan includes faithful Gentiles (Rom 15:8 – 12). The letter's final exhortation includes a warning against those who sow division (Rom 16:17).

Almost two-thirds of the letter establishes the requisite theological groundwork: all of us must come to God on the same terms (Rom 1 – 10). In Romans 1 – 3, Paul begins by demonstrating that Jew and Gentile are equally lost apart from Christ (Rom 1:16; 2:9 – 10; 3:9, 29). Jewish people regarded idolatry and homosexual intercourse (Rom 1:21 – 27) as exclusively Gentile sins, but Paul quickly turns to sins that are more universal (Rom 1:28 – 32) or specifically Jewish (Rom 2:17 – 24) and establishes universal lostness from Scripture (Rom 3:9 – 20). God's way of salvation for everyone, he shows, is through relying on God's climactic saving work in Jesus (Rom 3:21 – 31).

Jewish people often appealed to their descent from Abraham to justify their superior salvific situation, but Paul insists that it is sharing Abraham's resurrection faith, rather than ethnic descent from him, that counts for salvation (Rom 4:1 – 5:11). If anyone does wish to appeal to ethnic descent from Abraham, Paul reiterates that *all* of us are descended from Adam (Rom 5:12 – 21). Some Jewish people believed that possession of the written Torah made them spiritually superior to Gentiles (although Gentiles had some revelation in natural law). Paul, however, emphasizes that God's law in any form just makes us morally responsible for our sins (Rom 2:12 – 16). The law teaches right from wrong, but it can transform the heart only if written there by God (cf. Rom 8:2). Thus in Romans 7, Paul depicts the frustration of life under the law apart from the Spirit.

Many Jewish people insisted that they were chosen in Abraham. Without at all denying Israel's special role in God's plan (Rom 3:1 – 2), Paul explains that this role no more saves all Jewish people now than it did in earlier biblical history, when only a remnant kept covenant with God (cf. Rom 11:5). God is so sovereign that he is not obligated to choose on the basis of ethnicity, or to keep covenant with Abraham only through his ethnic descendants (Rom 9:6 – 13).

---

3. See sources in Gerald Bray, ed., *Romans* (Downers Grove, Ill.: InterVarsity, 1998), 337 – 38, 368; Mark Reasoner, *Romans in Full Circle: A History of Interpretation* (Louisville: Westminster John Knox, 2005), xxv.

4. Margaret M. Mitchell, *Paul and the Rhetoric of Reconciliation: An Exegetical Investigation of the Language and Composition of 1 Corinthians* (Louisville: Westminster John Knox, 1991), 60 – 64.

Paul's Warning to Gentile Believers

Paul cared about his people receiving the gospel — so much so that he echoes Moses' willingness to be destroyed on Israel's behalf (Rom 9:3; Exod 32:32). Most of the letter until this point warns against treating Gentile believers as second-class; Paul opposes those who "boast" in their privileges (Rom 2:17, 23). The temptation to envision ourselves superior, however, is not an exclusively Jewish one, and in Romans 11 Paul turns to exhorting Gentile believers not to "boast" or marginalize Jewish believers. Unfortunately, Gentile believers throughout history have tended to embrace the parts of Romans that defended their equal status while neglecting the parts of Romans that challenge their own ethnocentrism.

Anti-Judaism was rife in the ancient Mediterranean world, though it was worse in some places than in others. Most Jewish people were integrated into the lives of their communities in Asia Minor, but anti-Judaism in Egypt and Syria led to genocidal purges. Rome stood somewhere in between: tolerant of peoples practicing their own customs, they nevertheless resented such customs in their own capital. A number of Gentiles converted to Judaism (and this new form of Jewish faith, the Jesus movement), but many others ridiculed these practices.[5] What would happen if Gentiles became numerically dominant in the Roman church and forgot their heritage in Judaism?

Paul seeks to head off such arrogance. Just as he repeatedly warned Jewish believers not to boast or judge Gentile believers for their different customs, so he now warns Gentile believers not to boast against the Jewish people and the heritage from which Gentile believers have received their faith (Rom 11:18). Gentile believers are grafted in like spiritual proselytes, spiritually circumcised members of the covenant (Rom 11:17 – 19; cf. 2:27 – 29; 4:12),[6] but they should remember that the tree into which they have been grafted is the heritage of Israel. Gentiles are no more saved by Gentile merit or identity than Jewish believers are by Jewish merit or identity, and they too can fall if they cease to rely on Christ (Rom 11:20).[7]

Gentile Christians Have Neglected Paul's Warning

Over time, Gentile converts brought their cultural attitudes into the church. Just as nineteenth-century slaveholders brought their slaveholding views into many churches, eventually corrupting them, Gentiles who resented Judaism imported their outlook into the church. Meanwhile, in responding to pagan anti-Jewish prejudices, some Gentile Christian apologists did their best to distance their faith from Judaism. In its most extreme form, this "Christian" anti-Judaism repudiated the so-called Old

---

5. J. N. Sevenster, *The Roots of Pagan Anti-Semitism in the Ancient World* (Leiden, Netherlands: Brill, 1975); John G. Gager, *The Origins of Anti-Semitism: Attitudes toward Judaism in Pagan and Christian Antiquity* (New York: Oxford University Press, 1983).

6. Terence A. Donaldson, *Paul and the Gentiles: Remapping the Apostle's Convictional World* (Minneapolis: Fortress, 1997), 230 – 47.

7. Indeed, the center of the Christian movement shifted from the Middle East to Turkey and North Africa; later to Ethiopia and Europe; and more recently to the global South. See Philip Jenkins, *The Next Christendom: The Coming of Global Christianity* (New York: Oxford, 2002).

Testament and its God (as in some forms of what we call gnosticism). In its milder forms, the church "replaced" or displaced Israel. Even this milder form did exactly the opposite of what Paul commanded in Romans 11: Gentile believers boasted against the Jewish branches.

As Christians went from persecuted sect to political power in the fourth century, their representatives began to repress their opposition in the same way that they had been repressed. Although this was primarily directed against their former pagan persecutors, it also took the form of enforcing and strengthening anti-Jewish laws, reducing their monotheistic competition. Over time, anti-Jewish attitudes hardened on a popular level, providing excuses for more severe outbreaks of persecution, and ultimately the long history of Christian anti-Semitism.[8]

The Inquisition investigated supposed Jewish converts to Christianity to ensure that they repudiated Judaism. Jews were drowned in forced baptisms and killed in pogroms. Although Luther had been more pro-Jewish in his early years, his later pronouncements were more anti-Jewish — statements that Hitler's circle exploited during the Nazi Holocaust. Granted, the Third Reich's fundamental religion was a utilitarian Aryan faith involving old Aryan deities, not Christianity. Yet a liberal German state church already accustomed to distance from Judaism quickly succumbed to the interests of the totalitarian state. Nazis became leaders in the Reich Church, stifling dissenting voices like Dietrich Bonhoeffer's.

When Gentile churches today criticize Jewish believers in Jesus for Jewish dancing or abstaining from pork or other elements of their heritage and culture, Gentile churches impose their own culture as the norm. This prejudice differs little from Paul's rivals in Galatia who wanted to impose traditional Jewish customs on Gentiles. The parallel simply reveals how deep is the challenge of syncretism, of mixing our own cultural values with the gospel and assuming that the mixture represents the gospel. Contextualizing our faith in cultural forms is good; making this contextualization the standard for all cultures represents a fatal misunderstanding of the gospel.

Provoking "Jealousy"

Paul's writings make clear that he loved his Gentile converts and sacrificed for them. In Romans 11, however, we learn another divine strategy in Paul's mission to the Gentiles. Gentiles received mercy through Israel's failure to embrace the gospel; now Gentiles would become a divine vehicle of bringing Jewish people to Christ. What did this reversal involve? Scripture promised that God would restore and exalt his people in the time of their ultimate repentance (e.g., Amos 9:7 – 15; Hos 14:4 – 7). Now it appeared that God was allowing most Jewish people to miss God's saving plan to allow time before their restoration for reaching the Gentiles.

These Gentiles served a purpose in God's plan for the Jewish people. They

8. See Edward H. Flannery, *The Anguish of the Jews: Twenty-Three Centuries of Anti-Semitism* (New York: Macmillan, 1965); James Parkes, *The Conflict of the Church and the Synagogue: A Study in the Origins of Antisemitism* (New York: Atheneum, 1979); Michael L. Brown, *Our Hands Are Stained with Blood: The Tragic Story of the "Church" and the Jewish People* (Shippensburg, Pa.: Destiny Image, 1992).

would in turn help the Jewish people by provoking repentance. In Romans 10:19, Paul quoted Deuteronomy 32:21, about God provoking Israel to envy by welcoming another people; now he emphasizes that God is provoking Israel's jealousy through the Gentile mission led by him and others (Rom 11:11, 14). Based on Scripture, most Jewish people expected God to deal with the Gentiles in the end-time (whether by converting, subjugating, or destroying them).[9] The success of Paul's mission revealed that God was presently converting Gentiles in a miraculous way, revealing that the end-time era had come. Through learning that Jesus' Lordship produces vast multitudes of Gentile converts to biblical faith and submission to the God of Israel, Paul believes his people will recognize that Jesus is the way and turn to him. Paul's tribute from Gentile churches to Jewish congregations (addressed further below) was likely intended to further this strategy.

Yet Paul's vision never came to fruition because Gentile Christians undercut it, boasting against the natural branches. Instead of becoming allies in the worship of Israel's God, we became competitors and then repressers. Christian anti-Semitism became the chief obstacle in Paul's plan for a living witness based on our common allegiance to the God of Israel. The Bonhoeffers and Ten Booms were too few. In the past two generations, a major shift has been taking place, both in Jewish attitudes toward Jesus and in Christian attitudes toward Judaism. Will we repeat the failures of the past, or will we submit to God's plan that now appears to be unfolding?

What I Am Not Saying

I should qualify my argument with some caveats. I am not talking about rejecting or neglecting our mission to Gentiles in order to embrace the Jewish people. God's plan was to expose the disobedience of all and to welcome *all* for salvation (Rom 11:32), and the diversity of Gentiles is also an ultimate blessing for Israel. I am not talking about uncritically affirming every choice by leaders of national Israel (something that God did not do in Scripture). When I speak of "Israel" in Romans, I am speaking of the Jewish people and not the modern State of Israel per se.

I am also not urging all Gentile Christians to join Messianic Jewish congregations. First, they would numerically overwhelm those congregations and their cultural identity. Second, Paul is clear that while Gentile believers in Jesus are spiritual proselytes to Judaism, they are responsible only for the moral heart of the law and not for Israel-distinctive elements.

A Remnant

Lest Gentiles infer from Paul's argument about Gentile inclusion that God is finished with the Jewish people, Paul explicitly emphasizes the opposite. The present situation includes a "remnant" who remain faithful to God's covenant, namely Jewish believers in Jesus (Rom 11:1 – 5).

As in earlier biblical history, the proportion of Israel remaining faithful to the

---

9. For Jewish views on the fate of Gentiles, see Donaldson, *Paul and the Gentiles*, 52 – 74.

covenant could vary (for example, few in Moses' generation but many in Joshua's). In Paul's day the remnant may have included a large number of Jewish people (cf. Acts 21:20), but it was still a remnant. The biggest surprise was that, through the powerful work of the Spirit, massive numbers of Gentiles were being converted.

Because of Gentile Christian anti-Semitism, the remnant of Jesus-believing Jews grew smaller in subsequent history, at some points representing a miniscule proportion of the Jewish people. Only in the past two generations has the Jewish remnant (in the Messianic Jewish community and beyond) mushroomed to a proportion anywhere possibly comparable to the remnant of Paul's own day.

For Paul, the remnant was God's assurance that a time would come when "all Israel" would be saved (Rom 11:26). Scholars debate what Paul means here by "all Israel." Some believe that he refers to all Jewish people who have ever lived, but this interpretation conflicts with Paul's explicit teaching elsewhere in Romans;[10] it also contradicts the Law and the Prophets, where it is clear that not all Jewish people keep God's covenant. Some others believe that Paul refers only to the church in Romans 11:26, so that when the "fullness of the Gentiles" comes in (Rom 11:25 ESV), that is the "all Israel" that will be saved. But everywhere else in this context, "Israel" refers to the Jewish people (Rom 10:19, 21; 11:2, 7); this is especially clear in the immediately preceding verse (Rom 11:25). Paul's point is precisely that the same Israel that now experiences hardening will one day experience salvation. Thus most scholars conclude that "all Israel" refers to the Jewish people at the time of the "fullness of the Gentiles."[11]

God's Plan for the Jewish People

Paul appears to be arguing that when God has finished bringing into the church the Gentiles who will be saved, the Jewish people will recognize that God is with this movement, and they will themselves turn to faith in Jesus.[12] The "fullness of the Gentiles" may mean that the good news reaches all peoples (Matt 24:14; cf. Acts 1:8; 2 Pet 3:9; Rev 5:9). When every people group has had some opportunity, God lifts the blindness from Israel as a whole and brings about the end of the age.[13]

Once the Jewish people turn to Christ, God will fulfill the restoration promises that he has made, so God has arranged it that Israel's full turning will come only after the Gentile peoples have all had their opportunity (Rom 11:11, 15, 19–20, 25, 30–32).

Paul clearly wants everyone to understand God's marvelous plan in history that

---

10. Before Jesus' coming, God saved by grace through faith in the promise (Rom 4:3, 13; 10:6–8). As God inaugurated new acts in salvation history, he also expected compliance with the new revelation (Rom 10:9–10); for example, in Moses' day one could not demur from the law by protesting that Abraham did not have it. For Paul, Jesus is the climax of prior revelation (Rom 10:4), and Abraham's faith prefigures the resurrection faith of Jesus' followers (Rom 4:17–19, 24).

11. The phrase "all Israel" does not necessarily mean every individual Jewish person. Scholars often point to a similar expression in *Mishnah Sanhedrin* 10:1, which announces that "all Israel" will be saved and then goes on to list apostates from Israel who would not be. We might more safely translate it, "Israel as a whole." Paul, like the earlier biblical prophets, expects a massive turning back to the covenant when God restores his people.

12. See discussion in A. Andrew Das, *Paul and the Jews* (Peabody, Mass.: Hendrickson, 2003), 96–106; Donaldson, *Paul and the Gentiles*, 231–34.

13. This may mean that Jewish people will recognize that the biblical promises of the nations submitting to God (e.g., Isa 19:19–25) are fulfilled specifically through the movement of Jesus' followers. See Mark D. Nanos,

requires the interdependence of the Jewish people and the Gentiles. After praising God's unsearchable mind (Rom 11:34), he calls on Jesus believers to make their own minds new (12:2). Instead of boasting against others, we should think humbly in the face of God's glorious plan for all humanity (12:3).

Sharing Resources

Isaiah had promised that resources from the nations would one day flow to Israel (e.g., Isa 60:5 – 10). Eager to demonstrate to his people that the promised ingathering of Gentiles had begun, Paul brings an offering from the Diaspora, from the majority Gentile churches, to Jesus-believing Jews in Jerusalem (Rom 15:25 – 27).[14] Reciprocity was a fundamental characteristic of ancient ethics,[15] and Paul speaks here of reciprocal obligations. Israel profited the Gentiles spiritually; now the Gentile believers must repay their debt to the Jewish people by contributing to their welfare (Rom 15:27). Paul sometimes speaks of his offering for the Jerusalem church especially in terms of caring for the needs of the poor (1 Cor 16:1 – 4; 2 Cor 8 – 9).[16]

How should we apply the principle today? I doubt that Paul would ask Gentile churches around the world to overwhelm the comparatively small number of Jewish believers in Jesus in Jerusalem with their offerings. Yet it is clear that Paul wanted Gentile Christians to demonstrate their kinship with their Jewish siblings in ways more concrete than mere verbal acknowledgements. Indeed, given Paul's motivation, cooperation not only with the Messianic Jewish community but with the Jewish community more widely may help move us toward the reality that Paul envisioned, in which the Jewish people can recognize Gentile Christians as full-fledged worshipers of their God through Jesus. It has long been true that the largest numbers of worshipers of Israel's God in the world are Gentile Christians. Humbling ourselves, remembering the people whose heritage we share and from whom our faith springs (Rom 9:4 – 5), may help us surmount the past barriers of Gentile Christian anti-Semitism.

The Remnant as a Bridge

Jesus' movement was a Jewish movement, claiming, like prophetic movements earlier in Israel's history, to summon God's people to obedience to his plan. The wedge between Jewishness and faith in Jesus is nonsensical: Jesus and all his first followers were Jewish.

The Mystery of Romans: The Jewish Context of Paul's Letter (Minneapolis: Fortress, 1996), 249 – 50. Yet the Jewish people offer a great blessing to the Gentiles as well. In the past, the gospel came through them (Rom 15:27). In the future, when Israel as a whole turns to God, God will consummate his plan for the ages, including the resurrection (Rom 11:15; cf. Ezek 37:7 – 14) and the restoration of all creation (Rom 8:19 – 22; cf. 11:15).

14. Some scholars also approach the passage in view of the Jewish temple tax (e.g., Keith F. Nickle, *The Collection: A Study in Biblical Theology* [Naperville, Ill.: Alec R. Allenson, 1966], 87 – 89) and other models, some of which may be complementary.

15. See Pliny, *Ep.* 6.6.3; James R. Harrison, *Paul's Language of Grace in Its Graeco-Roman Context* (Tübingen: Mohr Siebeck, 2003), 1, 15, 50 – 53.

16. Paul has just noted that Jesus became a minister both to his own people and to the Gentiles (Rom 15:8 – 9). Now he offers himself as a model, a Jewish minister to the Gentiles who brings offerings from partly Gentile churches to the Jerusalem church (Rom 15:25 – 27; cf. Acts 24:17).

Some Jewish believers in Jesus feel comfortable identifying with Gentile churches, and that is their right. Others, however, prefer to preserve more fully their Jewish identity, to raise their children within this identity, and to provide a corporate, continuing witness to their people. The Messianic Jewish movement challenges the arbitrary dichotomy between Jewish identity and faith in Jesus, reminding us, as the apostolic church did, that these are not mutually exclusive options. One friend of mine, an Orthodox rabbi, contends that history has made the two religions mutually exclusive. I respond that if one must rest the argument on subsequent history, the historic shift in our day should welcome the reopening of the case.

Believers in Jesus are obligated to share our faith with all who are willing to hear it. Leaders in the Jewish community fear cultural genocide as Jewish people become Christians and leave behind their Jewish heritage and culture. Messianic Judaism, however, offers a way to maintain continuity with Jewish heritage while also affirming the truth about Jesus. From the perspective of Jesus' followers, what could be more Jewish than following the one we recognize as God's Messiah? Some Jewish scholars have begun to argue that non-Orthodox Jews who welcome as fellow Jews those less halakhically observant and theistic than Messianic Jews are inconsistent to repudiate Messianic Jews.[17]

Conclusion

Paul affirms the Messianic Jewish remnant of his day and looks forward to its fullness in the future. He views Gentile believers in Jesus as spiritual proselytes, spiritually circumcised and grafted into Israel's heritage, sharers with Israel's remnant in the saving covenant. At the same time, Paul was convinced that God remembered his promises to the Jewish people and continued to have a plan for them, a plan that would ultimately reunite them in obedience to Israel's Messiah along with Gentile believers in Jesus. He intended the obedience and success of Gentile Christianity to be a positive witness to the Jewish people and warned against Gentiles assuming the same attitude of spiritual superiority that some of his own people had toward Gentiles. Ignoring Paul's warnings, Gentile Christianity absorbed its culture's anti-Semitism, marring the Gentile Christian witness to the Jewish people. The indigenous witness of Messianic Judaism offers a fresh opportunity. May a new generation of Gentile Christians unite with our Messianic Jewish siblings to praise God through Jesus the Messiah (Rom 15:8 – 11).

17. See Dan Cohn-Sherbok, *Messianic Judaism* (New York: Cassell, 2000), 169 – 213 (esp. 174, 203 – 13); more concisely, Cohn-Sherbok, "Introduction," ix – xx in *Voices of Messianic Judaism: Confronting Critical Issues Facing a Maturing Movement* (ed. Dan Cohn-Sherbok; Baltimore: Lederer, 2001), especially xiii – xiv; slightly earlier, see the evidence in Carol Harris-Shapiro, *Messianic Judaism: A Rabbi's Journey through Religious Change in America* (Boston: Beacon, 1999), 166 – 89.

For Further Reading

Eisenbaum, Pamela. *Paul Was Not a Christian: The Original Message of a Misunderstood Apostle*. New York: HarperOne, 2009.

Donaldson, Terence L. *Paul and the Gentiles: Remapping the Apostle's Convictional World*. Minneapolis: Fortress, 1997.

Hafemann, Scott. "The Salvation of Israel in Romans 11:25 – 32: A Response to Krister Stendahl." *Ex Auditu* 4 (1988): 38 – 58.

Harrington, Daniel J. "Paul's Use of the Old Testament in Romans." *Studies in Christian-Jewish Relations* 4, no. 1 (2009): 1 – 8. Online: http://www.mjstudies.com.

Keener, Craig S. *Romans: A New Covenant Commentary*. NCCS 6. Eugene, Ore.: Cascade, 2009.

Nanos, Mark D. " 'Broken Branches': A Pauline Metaphor Gone Awry? (Romans 11:11 – 24)." Pages 339 – 76 in *Between Gospel and Election: Explorations in the Interpretation of Romans 9 – 11*. Edited by Florian Wilk and J. Ross Wagner. Tübingen: Mohr Siebeck, 2010.

————. " 'Callused,' Not 'Hardened': Paul's Revelation of Temporary Protection until All Israel Can Be Healed." Pages 52 – 73 in *Reading Paul in Context: Explorations in Identity Formation*. Edited by Kathy Ehrensperger and J. Brian Tucker. London: T&T Clark, 2010.

————. "The Myth of the 'Law-Free' Paul Standing between Christians and Jews." *Studies in Christian-Jewish Relations* 4, no. 1 (2009): 1 – 24.

————. "Romans: Introduction and Annotations." Pages 253 – 86 in *The Jewish Annotated New Testament*. Edited by Marc Brettler and Amy Jill Levine. New York: Oxford University Press, 2011.

Rudolph, David J. " 'Weak in Faith' Language (Rom 14)." Pages 35 – 44 in *A Jew to the Jews: Jewish Contours of Pauline Flexibility in 1 Corinthians 9:19 – 23*. Tübingen: Mohr Siebeck, 2011.

Sievers, Joseph. " 'God's Gifts and Call Are Irrevocable': The Reception of Romans 11:29 through the Centuries and Christian Jewish Relations." Pages 127 – 73 in *Reading Israel in Romans: Legitimacy and Plausibility of Divergent Interpretations*. Edited by Cristina Grenholm and Daniel Patte. Harrisburg, Pa.: Trinity Press International, 2000.

Wilk, Florian, J. Ross Wagner, and Frank Schleritt, eds. *Between Gospel and Election: Explorations in the Interpretation of Romans 9 – 11*. Tübingen: Mohr Siebeck, 2010.

CHAPTER 18

The Relationship between Israel and the Church

WILLIAM S. CAMPBELL

The most explicit and significant text dealing with the relationship between Israel and the church is Paul's letter to the Romans, particularly chapters 9 – 11. One of the main problems with the history of interpretation of Romans 9 – 11 is that it has tended to be theological and decontextualized despite the fact that Paul wrote specifically to Christ-followers in Rome. In this essay I will highlight the importance of reading Paul's statements contextually, both within the letter and in relation to the political and social context.

Both in theological content and dialogical style Romans 9 – 11 is an intrinsic part of an ongoing discussion within the letter. Thus it is crucial to determine what Paul's strategy is in putting forward his argument in Romans 9 – 11. We also need to consider why Paul, in writing to the Romans and responding to their situation, included a specific topic such as the future of Israel. In order to investigate this I will look first at the context that Paul addresses, including the gentile audience, and then at the possible reasons why he needs to teach and develop their understanding of God's purposes for Israel.

Contextual Approach

There is no substantial evidence of Jewish opponents being addressed in Romans. Granted there is much about Jews and Judaism, but Jews are not addressed directly. Thus it is not a dialogue *with Jews* but a dialogue *about Jews* with mainly gentile Roman Christ-followers (cf. Rom 11:13 RSV, "Now I am speaking to you Gentiles …").[1] It follows from this that the view that Paul is arguing *polemically* against Jewish opponents, giving a critique of Judaism from the perspective of the Christ-event to justify God's purposes for the gentiles, is not plausible. The content of chapters 9 – 11 can be more appropriately interpreted *apologetically* and pedagogically in relation to the Roman context.

If the nature of the context and the addressees are carefully observed and adhered to, then Paul's letter and especially chapters 9 – 11 cannot be viewed as a polemical attack on Judaism or as a vindication of Paul's mission to the gentiles over against

---

1. My view is that Romans is addressed to gentile Christ-followers who maintained close contact with Jewish Christ-followers in Rome. Cf. William S. Campbell, "The Addressees of Paul's Letter to the Romans: Assemblies of God in House Churches and Synagogues," in *Between Gospel and Election: Explorations in the Interpretation of Romans 9 – 11* (ed. Florian Wilk and J. Ross Wagner; Tübingen: Mohr Siebeck, 2010), 171 – 95.

Judaism. Why should Paul attack Jews or Judaism if his addressees are mainly gentile? A problem in stressing the Jews as Paul's target for condemnation is that the gentiles thus escape censure. From a parenetic or pastoral perspective, it would be incredible that Paul should so openly appeal to, and therefore reinforce, the bias of his intended audience. Chapters 11 – 15 of Romans reveal a distinct tendency already existing among gentile Christ-followers at Rome to view Jewish practices with a degree of contempt from the perspective of a presumed gentile superiority (cf. Rom 14:10). Thus what Paul intends in chapters 9 – 11 should be interpreted as having some significant moral effect on the gentile Christ-followers at Rome.

Paul the Teacher

Paul's relation to these gentile Christ-followers is not such that he can forcefully direct their behavior. He has to acknowledge (Rom 1:10 – 14) and then later explain (15:22 – 29) his long delay in coming to visit them, and also that even as he writes he is preparing to head east to Jerusalem (15:25). His emphasis on not building on "another man's foundation" (15:20 RSV) and his delicate approach in Romans 15:14 – 33 concerning what he expects from the Romans indicates the peculiar problem he faced in having to tread carefully despite his apostolic authority over the gentiles (cf. Rom 1:11 – 12). Paul wishes to influence the Christ-followers at Rome but can do so only if he does not antagonize them or cause them to distrust him. This is why it is preferable not to read these chapters as an apologetic argument for gentile inclusion since this would not necessarily produce the change in attitude that Paul wishes to see in the Roman gentile Christ-followers. Wherever the dialogical or diatribal style is clearly present, as in chapters 9 – 11, it underlines that the content should be perceived as especially appropriate for *pedagogical purposes*.

This leads us to the proposition that Paul approaches the Romans as a *teacher* rather than as a father in Christ. Thus his dialogical style conforms to the diatribe pattern of a teacher who leads his students by means of question and answer to a fresh perspective on the topic discussed. The rhetorical style suggests a reasoned discussion with an interlocutor who is a student or partner in the discussion rather than an opponent.[2] If the teacher is dogmatic and domineering he may win the argument but lose the audience and Paul cannot afford that.[3] Thus as a good teacher he acknowledges commonalities with his audience such as the impartiality of God, who treats both Jew and gentile justly despite their difference. In some such situations the teacher moves the argument forward by discreet, but sometimes also by astounding, questions or proposals such as "Jacob I loved, but Esau I hated," or "Is there injustice on God's part?" (Rom 9:13 – 14 RSV). Educationally, this is a process of drawing

---

2. Paul's dialogue partner or interlocutor has been almost universally interpreted as an opponent who is a Jew partly because of Paul's statement in Romans 2 — "you call yourself a Jew." But this is not necessarily the case since in 9 – 11 Paul's censure is directed to gentiles who are addressed directly about the need to modify their attitude toward Israel. On the diatribe style in Romans, see Stanley Stowers, *The Diatribe and Paul's Letter to the Romans* (Chico, Calif.: Society of Biblical Literature, 1981), 75 – 80.

3. Cf. Kathy Ehrensperger, *Paul and the Dynamics of Power: Communication and Interaction in the Early Christ-Movement* (London: T&T Clark, 2007), 116 – 36.

out the implications of positions people may already hold and thus leading them to see the outcome of their own presuppositions. By driving an argument to its logical conclusions, its inherent weaknesses or strengths are rendered visible. The questions and responses offered in Romans 9 – 11 may not all be those actually raised by the Romans, but they are used by Paul to effect a change in perception of God's relationship to Israel now that the Christ-event has taken place.

Paul perceives the Roman gentiles as demonstrating an arrogant and superior attitude over against Israel (Rom 11:18 – 19, 25; 12:3). What was the origin of this sense of superiority? Most likely it was rooted in the Roman sense of superiority over subject peoples, including the Jews. Roman dominance and power would suggest that there could be no positive future for such people, some of whom had been recently expelled from Rome.[4] Moreover, if it appeared to the gentile Christ-followers in Rome that a majority of Jews rejected their gospel then it could easily be assumed that Israel was rejected by God as well as conquered by the Romans. God's mercy to gentiles could well have been perceived as favoritism by the gods, which implied a sense of superiority for those favored. It seems we have in this instance a syncretism of a simplistic Christology (you were rejected so that we might be grafted in) with the Roman imperial ideology of benefaction, implying that the Jews had failed to receive both Roman clemency and divine mercy.[5]

The Problem of the Gospel's Rejection
by a Majority of Israel

The fact on which Paul and the Romans could readily agree was that a majority of Jews remained unconvinced by Paul's gospel message. Paul commences Romans 9 – 11 by emphasizing his deepest concern about this situation and then proceeds to address differing interpretations of the Jewish lack of response to the gospel. It is likely that some such interpretations were current in Rome and that these may also have been identified (wrongly) as originating with Paul, perceived as the champion of gentiles.[6] First the apostle acknowledges his absolute loyalty to his own people. Then he acknowledges the right of God to deal with all peoples according to his own free (but not arbitrary) choice. The divine freedom could be viewed as a negative statement against Israel implying that God is not tied to Israel or to the provision of future

---

4. See Ian E. Rock, "Another Reason for Romans — A Pastoral Response to Augustan Imperial Theology: Paul's Use of the Song of Moses in Romans 9 – 11 and 14 – 15," in *Reading Paul in Context: Explorations in Identity Formation, Essays in Honour of William S. Campbell* (ed. Kathy Ehrensperger and J. Brian Tucker; London: T&T Clark, 2010), 74 – 89.

5. On the political, social, and theological significance of Paul's exhortation to the Roman gentiles, see Neil Elliott, "Paul's Political Christology: Samples from Romans," in *Reading Paul in Context*, 48 – 51.

6. See William S. Campbell, "Divergent Images of Paul and His Mission," in *Reading Israel in Romans: Legitimacy and Plausibility of Divergent Interpretations* (ed. Cristina Grenholm and Daniel Patte; Harrisburg, Pa.: Trinity Press International, 2000), 187 – 211. The conquest of Israel by succeeding empires such as the Assyrians and the Babylonians meant that this was not a new topic for Jews or for Paul himself. In all of these conquests a rereading of Scripture was necessitated in order to discern the divine purpose for Israel. In Romans 9 – 11, Paul acknowledges the *temporary* function of Rome as an agent of divine power, which unlike Israel has no permanent role in the divine purpose (contrary to Virgil's assertion that Rome was ordained to eternal rule). Israel (Jacob) and not Rome (Esau) is still preferred. Cf. Rock, "Another Reason for Romans," 88.

blessing for her. But Paul argues only for God's freedom, not for a lack of commitment to his own promises, and this implies that God is not bound to reject Israel any more than he is bound to exclude the gentiles. It is possible that some gentiles took the view that God was bound to reject Israel because of her historic failures, yet this is not what Paul affirms but *rather what he rejects*. God's freedom over against human beings means that the future of all of them is still open. Surprisingly, *God's freedom actually means that he is able to be patient with Israel* — "What if God, because he wished to display his wrath and to make known his power endured with much long-suffering vessels ripe for destruction?"(Rom 9:22 – 24, my trans.). To presume therefore that Israel has been rejected by God is a wrong inference even though a majority of Jews may not have been convinced by Paul's gospel. The rejection of Paul's message by whatever numbers of Jewish people is not in itself a sufficient basis for such a presumption.

Another view that may have been current in Rome was that if God is truly impartial then he cannot restore disobedient Israel. But neither an argument based on God's justice nor on his impartiality nor on the limited response to the gospel by Jews is sufficient foundation for the perception that Israel has no future. This is why Paul can confidently introduce these difficult issues in the course of his argument. These can be, and historically have been, frequently used as ammunition in anti-Jewish polemic, but Paul's purpose in introducing them is to demonstrate that they cannot possibly be interpreted to indicate that Israel has no future.

God's Actions toward Israel

How then does Paul deal with these issues? First, he asserts that the word or promise of God has not failed despite appearances to the contrary (Rom 9:6). Paul reviews God's actions toward Israel in history and concludes that despite great loss, and much suffering at times, God's purpose for Israel has been, and still is being, actively maintained. Paul stresses that God has always retained a faithful remnant as the means through which his purposes are achieved (9:27 – 29). Even Pharaoh could not thwart the divine purpose (9:17). The remnant may seem smaller than it really is, as in the time of Elijah, when the prophet had to be reminded that there were still seven thousand who had not bowed the knee to Baal (Rom 11:4).

Paul brings this history up to date by claiming that *even at the present time*, there remains a faithful remnant through God's grace (Rom 11:5 – 6). The size of this remnant is not the issue, but rather the fact of its existence, though we are certainly not thinking in terms of only one Israelite even if that one were Jesus the Christ. It is a "saving" remnant (rather than a saved remnant) pointing to the ongoing divine purpose for Israel in the future. It would be strange, as some interpreters suggest,[7]

---

7. Cf. Dale Martin, "The Promise of Teleology, the Constraints of Epistemology, and the Universal Vision of Paul," in *St. Paul among the Philosophers* (ed. J. D. Caputo and L. M. Alcott; Bloomington: Indiana University Press, 2009), 91 – 108. Support for this view is suggested perhaps by Rom 9:24, where, for the first time in chapters 9 – 11, gentiles enter the scene. But this reference does not specifically relate to the remnant as such, but rather to God's overall purpose that includes the gentiles as well as Jews. Note also that already in Rom 9:11 Paul previously referred to God's call in relation to his purpose of election so that there can be no question of calling being reserved only for those called in Rom 9:24 – 29.

if this remnant includes gentiles, for it then becomes a remnant of both Jewish and gentile Christ-followers who together indicate a positive future for Christ-following Jews and gentiles, *though not necessarily for Israel as a people*. But there is no real evidence in the text of these chapters that Paul views the remnant other than as a faithful *remnant of Israel*, which thus points towards a positive future *for Israel*. This is evident when he refers to "the others" or the rest (Rom 11:7, 23). He cannot mean the rest of gentiles or of all humanity, but rather the rest of Israel. Nor is it warranted to maintain that the honored title "Israel" includes Christ-following gentiles. As with the remnant, Paul is clear that he is referring to his own people and that the distinction between Jew and gentile abides even in Christ.[8]

The Scriptural references in Romans 9:25 – 26 are not meant to assert that the "not my people" were gentiles. It is the northern kingdom of Israel that is referred to in these texts — those "not my people" are to be restored by the Lord, so that their banishment is over. It is only by analogy that gentiles can be envisaged here, and Paul's primary emphasis is on the restoration of the Jewish people, rather than on the inclusion of gentiles, though of course the latter are not thereby excluded.[9]

Temporary "Stumbling" and "Hardening"

Paul notes in Romans 9:30 – 10:4 the surprising outcome that gentiles who "did not pursue righteousness" (9:30) have attained it, that is, through following Christ. But Israel has somehow not succeeded, despite having zeal for God, though it is not "according to knowledge" (Rom 10:2 ESV). Paul uses two images to describe this anomaly. He suggests that Israel has stumbled and thus failed to reach her goal. Later in chapter 11 he also indicates that Israel has been hardened. These are images or metaphors used to explain what to Paul is almost inexplicable. But they are only *images related to a temporary problem and do not denote any final destiny*.[10] Israel has failed to recognize Christ as the righteousness that comes from God and did not submit to him (or to this form of righteousness), but instead sought to establish a righteousness peculiar to Israel that excludes gentiles, who do not come within the sphere of the covenant. This failure can be interpreted as a failure by some Jews to recognize that in the new era that dawns in Christ, according to Paul's gospel, gentiles need no longer be required to become proselytes and to keep the law in order to be righteous. They can now truly become righteous gentiles via Christ. Not to recognize this possibility means in Paul's view an attempt to establish a righteousness for Jews only, something that is foreign to the Shema, which claims that the God of Israel is the God of the whole world.[11]

---

8. Part of the problem is that there is no term for all of God's people, gentile Christ-followers as well as Jews, except "the people of God," but in Paul that is reserved for Israel; he refers to *laos* in citations from the Scriptures only where it is clear that Israel must be meant.

9. See Campbell, "Divergent Images of Paul and His Mission," 198 – 200.

10. Cf. Mark D. Nanos, "'Callused,' Not 'Hardened': Paul's Revelation of Temporary Protection until All Israel Can Be Healed," in *Reading Paul in Context* (ed. Ehrensperger and Tucker), 52 – 73.

11. See Mark D. Nanos, *The Mystery of Israel* (Minneapolis: Fortress, 1996), 184.

Israel's Lack of Understanding and Its Consequence

The gospel that Paul proclaims declares that God is Lord of all and "bestows his riches upon all who call upon him" (Rom 10:12 RSV). But no one can call upon him of whom they have not heard, so Paul asks two questions. First, has Israel not heard the good news of the new era in Christ when gentiles can now be accepted as partners in the kingdom whilst remaining gentiles? Indeed they have, and then Paul asks, but did Israel not understand? To this he gives no clear answer but cites Scripture, which states that God's hands *have been and still are* stretched out "all day long" to a faithless and contrary people (Rom 10:21). Paul could be claiming here that a mission to Israel, that is, that which was entrusted to Peter according to Galatians 2, is still necessary and should not be discontinued. Otherwise, how is Israel to come to understand the new thing that is in the process of happening? But what is clear is that he is not seeking to show that Israel is guilty because she has heard and deliberately and knowingly refused the message of Christ, especially since in Romans 10:3 she is described as being *ignorant* of the divine righteousness in Christ. Paul's purpose is neither to indict Israel, nor to excuse her failings, but to explain God's faithfulness despite these.

If, as seems to be the case, Israel has heard but not understood the new message that has arrived with Jesus Christ, this fact allows Paul to return to his central topic once again: "I ask, then, has God rejected his people?" (Rom 11:1 RSV). His response is a resounding denial — God forbid — and he begins to show the evidence to the contrary, of which he himself is a prime exhibit. "I myself am an Israelite, a descendant of Abraham, a member of the tribe of Benjamin." In Romans 9:1 – 5 he had listed the great advantages that pertain to Israel, but now he adds his own sterling pedigree as one who is proud of his God-given gifts. No one is more Jewish than I am myself, Paul claims, so how can Israel be perceived as rejected? Israel failed to obtain what it sought because of ignorance, but could it be that they were destined for rejection by God himself? Was their stumble designed to cause them to fall out of God's grace? "By no means," says Paul; see what their stumbling has achieved for the gentiles. The implication of Paul's form of argument here is that when a lack of response was met from many Jews, the missionaries turned instead to the gentiles. I am not convinced this outcome was as straightforward as this suggests, but Paul's main point is that even the hardening of the Jews brought blessing to the gentiles. He continues to argue from the lesser to the greater — if their hardening brought blessing, "how much more" will their incoming be and "if their failure means riches for the Gentiles, how much more will their full inclusion mean?" (11:12 RSV).

Now we see the progress of Paul's argument more clearly. Israel has indeed heard the message of the gospel concerning Christ and the changes this involves, but has not understood. However, in the divine economy of salvation, even this failure has resulted in blessings reaching the gentiles. If Israel's failure results in blessing, Paul argues again as he did in Romans 5:8 – 10, 15 – 17, "how much more" can be expected when Israel's full inclusion happens! Now we see where the argument is tending. Not only is Israel not rejected, but Paul expects untold blessings when she is fully included (rather than only partially as is now the case). These blessings will result from Israel's *full inclusion* in parallel to the "full number" of the gentiles (*to pleroma*, 11:25 NRSV), something Paul has been moving toward but which he only now makes explicit! It is fairly obvious that this expectation on the part of Paul is a presupposition of the entire argument up to this point, but something that Paul has carefully had to build up to in order to prevent misunderstanding or alienating his gentile audience.

Interdependence between Jew and Gentile

It is here that Paul's response to the Roman Christ-followers offers guidance to our contemporary understanding of the relation of the church and Israel. If, as Paul has argued, God cannot possibly have rejected Israel and if, as he will go on to argue at the end of chapter 11, Paul's vision is that Israel as a whole will eventually be restored, then there has to be a form of coexistence between the two. If, as the Roman gentile community wrongly assumed, Israel is rejected since the Roman gentiles have been accepted, then Israel has been displaced or replaced by the church of (gentile) Christ-followers.[12] The image Paul uses to demonstrate the perversion of this view is the olive tree. Some branches have been damaged or broken while wild olive shoots have been grafted in. But these have been grafted in amongst the other branches and not "in their place" as the RSV translation wrongly states.

Thus the first image of the relationship between Israel and the church is that of coexistence in light of common roots (on the same stem of a tree). The old tree is not cut down and replaced despite the damaged branches. Moreover, the branches grafted in are warned not to be presumptuous because they come from wild olive stock and have nothing in their background or culture, despite their location in the center of the mighty Roman Empire, that is greater or more spiritual than that of Israel. In chapters 12 – 15, and especially from Romans 14:1 on, Paul draws out the implications of God's positive future for Israel. If Israel had been displaced, then the Roman gentile Christ-followers could have disdainfully tolerated the Jewish customs (which some of their gentile members still retained) until such times as this now "surpassed" form of discipleship would disappear. If gentiles had truly displaced Jews, then Paul would have had no force to his argument to these gentiles to "accept one another" (Rom 15:7) as equals in Christ, since they would not have been equal if Jewish life-patterns have been surpassed. But instead, Paul maintains that there is a place for abiding Jewish life-patterns in the church and that gentiles who differ from one another must voluntarily yield up their freedom in support of the perceived "weaker brother" (see Rom 12:3; 14:13 – 15). Their gentile arrogance is based on mistaken assumptions, and Paul gives no allowance to such misunderstandings of God's purpose according to election (Rom 9:11).[13] It is no accident that in Romans Paul stresses the order of priority, "to the Jew first, and also to the Gentile" (Rom 2:10 KJV; cf. 1:16). This points to the identity of gentile Christ-followers not as an independent entity, but as interdependent

---

12. If Romans does address gentile Christ-followers, then this argument for the displacement of Jews may have originated initially from these Roman gentiles *alone*. It would thus primarily at this stage in history have been a *local* Jew-gentile issue; perhaps it was only in later reception history that the mainly gentile church, while regarding itself as the whole church, perceived the church as a replacement for Israel.

13. Cf. David R. Wallace, *The Gospel of God: Romans as Paul's Aeneid* (Eugene, Oreg.: Pickwick, 2008), 133.

on the call and identity of Israel, to whom as Ephesians 2:13 asserts they "have been brought near." As Ian Rock asserts, "to affirm the lordship of Christ is to simultaneously recognize the preference of Israel. But to recognize the primacy of Israel is also to accept the importance of the Jews."[14]

Shared Blessing between Jew and Gentile

The second emphasis of Paul concerning the relationship between Israel and the church is that of sharing the blessings of God. The statement, "If some of the branches were broken,[15] and you a wild olive were grafted in amongst them to share the richness of the olive tree ..." (Rom 11:17, Nanos's trans.), indicates that instead of taking over "the stem of the tree" or replacing all the former branches, gentiles are called only to *share* in the riches of God's grace. They could not really share if they had taken over Israel's inheritance, as they would then be the sole inheritors. So Paul reminds the gentile Christ-followers, "Do not boast over the branches ... remember it is not you that support the root, but the root that supports you" (Rom 11:18 RSV).

Humility as the Preeminent Virtue

This points to Paul's third emphasis. Instead of the arrogance of a proud-minded imperial nation like Rome,[16] gentiles are called to humility as those who must depend on God's grace. The attitude of humility in light of God's historic purpose is an abiding one that should be typical of all gentiles since they have access to divine riches through Christ. Gentiles cannot possess these exclusively (i.e., apart from Israel), but they can share in them. Their greatest boast must be that to which God has given them access through Christ,[17] and their greatest glory similarly must be to imitate Christ, who "did not please himself" (Rom 15:3).

The Mystery of God's Purposes for Israel

In order to prevent the Roman gentile Christ-followers from becoming "wise in [their] own conceits" (Rom 11:25 RSV; cf. 12:3), that is, puffed up with their own human wisdom and assumptions concerning Roman world domination, Paul reveals a mystery in God's purposes for Israel. Although many Jews are now actively resisting the gospel he proclaims, this opposition is only partial. Paul and most leaders in the Christ-movement are of Jewish descent, as are many of their co-participants. But more surprising still, Paul hopes for "the full inclusion" of Israel (i.e., the reuniting of "the remnant" and "the rest" within God's purposes), encouraged partly by the growing number of gentiles in the movement.[18] Paul reads the words of Isaiah to infer that

14. Cf. Rock, "Another Reason for Romans," 88.
15. See Mark D. Nanos, "'Broken Branches': A Pauline Metaphor Gone Awry," in *Between Gospel and Election*, 339–76.
16. Cf. Neil Elliott, *The Arrogance of Nations: Reading Romans in the Shadow of Empire* (Minneapolis: Fortress, 2008); Robert Jewett, *Romans* (Minneapolis: Fortress, 2007), 742–76.
17. See Ekkehard W. Stegemann, "Coexistence and Transformation: Reading the Politics of Identity in Romans in an Imperial Context," in *Reading Paul in Context*, 18–19.
18. William S. Campbell, *Paul and the Creation of Christian Identity* (London: T&T Clark, 2008), 121–30.

Israel would be positively influenced by a foolish nation (Rom 10:19–20; cf. 9:25–26), that is, by gentiles, and thus find again her purpose in God's plan. The revelation of this mystery is a crowning element in Paul's argument for Israel's positive future in God's plan. By it he has demonstrated what has been part of his ongoing purpose in his letter to the Romans, to maintain that *there can be no totally separate existence for groups who would claim allegiance to the God of Israel.* Their destinies remain inextricably intertwined in the unfolding of God's plan for the world. Israel is not merely a historical antecedent to the church, and the church has not replaced, and cannot displace, her in the divine purpose. Israel belongs to the present and future of the church and not merely to her inception.[19]

Paul cites in conclusion, in Romans 11:33–36, from the words of Job describing the inscrutable wisdom of God. He thus leaves open the future of Israel — he is not precise concerning the how and when of God's restoration of Israel, but he is certain that this will happen. As a true prophet, his knowledge of God leads him to affirm things about which there can be only *prophetic certainty.* If God is truly faithful as he has been to Israel till now, and if, given his freedom, he chooses to work in and through Israel, then, true to character, he will restore Israel in his good time, and this will mean blessing for the entire world, not just for Israel. God's relation to Israel is not purely functional, as if some failure on Israel's part can lead to gentiles taking her place. Only in association with Israel can gentiles share the divine inheritance, not in and by themselves, even as Christ-followers. God's covenant with Israel is more like a true marriage. Even if the longed-for children do not arrive, the wife cannot be divorced because she was childless, and God will not desert the bride of his choice, nor will he allow his purposes to be thwarted by the weakness of human beings — he has the power (*dunamis,* Rom 11:23 RSV, cf. also 1:16; 9:22) and the will (*ekloge prosthesis,* cf. Rom 9:11) to graft them again into their own olive tree.

In his response to a local problem that arose among gentile Christ-followers in Rome, Paul reacts strongly because of their misunderstanding of the Christ-event coupled with their perception based on Roman imperial ideology that the Jews had been rejected by imperial Rome and by God. This perception had resulted in gentile Christ-following assemblies despising local Christ-following Jews and other Jewish groups, and likewise their own gentile members who still wanted to maintain aspects of a Jewish pattern of life. Paul, in prophetic style, gives no fixed schedule as to when and how God will restore Israel, but he affirms that God's faithfulness ensures this. Thus gentile Christ-followers must learn to accept one another even when their patterns of life differ, thereby implying the mutual acceptance also of those Jewish Christ-following groups committed to maintaining their Jewish identity in Christ. Similarly, gentile Christ-followers must remember the roots of their Abrahamic faith and exercise appropriate humility toward those Jews who are not convinced that the Christ-movement is in accordance with God's purposes.

---

19. Cf. R. Kendall Soulen, " 'They are Israelites': The Priority of the Present Tense for Jewish-Christian Relations," in *Between Gospel and Election,* 502–4.

For Further Reading

Badenas, Robert. *Christ the End of the Law: Romans 10:4 in Pauline Perspective.* Sheffield, UK: JSOT, 1985.

Campbell, William S. "The Addressees of Paul's Letter to the Romans: Assemblies of God in House Churches and Synagogues?" Pages 171–95 in *Between Gospel and Election: Explorations in the Interpretation of Romans 9–11.* Edited by Florian Wilk and J. Ross Wagner. Tübingen: Mohr Siebeck, 2010.

———. "'All God's Beloved in Rome!' Jewish Roots and Christian Identity." Pages 67–82 in *Celebrating Romans: Template for Pauline Theology.* Edited by Sheila E. McGinn. Grand Rapids: Eerdmans, 2004.

———. "Church as Israel, People of God." Pages 204–19 in *Dictionary of the Later New Testament and Its Developments.* Edited by Ralph P. Martin and Peter H. Davids. Leicester, UK: InterVarsity, 1997.

———. "Israel." Pages 441–46 in *Dictionary of Paul and His Letters.* Edited by Gerald F. Hawthorne and Ralph P. Martin. Leicester, UK: InterVarsity, 1993.

———. *Paul and the Creation of Christian Identity.* Edinburgh: T&T Clark, 2006.

———. *Paul's Gospel in an Intercultural Context.* New York: Peter Lang, 1992.

Ehrensperger, Kathy. "'Called to be Saints' — The Identity-Shaping Dimension of Paul's Priestly Discourse in Romans." Pages 90–109 in *Reading Paul in Context: Explorations in Identity Formation: Essays in Honour of William S. Campbell.* Edited by Kathy Ehrensperger and J. Brian Tucker. London: T&T Clark, 2010.

Harrington, Daniel J. *Paul on the Mystery of Israel.* Collegeville, Minn.: Michael Glazier, 1992.

Hoehner, Harold. "Israel in Romans 9–11." Pages 145–67 in *Israel the Land and the People: An Evangelical Affirmation of God's Promises.* Edited by H. Wayne House. Grand Rapids: Kregel, 1998.

Rudolph, David J. "'Weak in Faith' Language (Rom 14)." Pages 35–44 in *A Jew to the Jews: Jewish Contours of Pauline Flexibility in 1 Corinthians 9:19–23.* Tübingen: Mohr Siebeck, 2011.

Stowers, Stanley K. *A Rereading of Romans: Justice, Jews, and Gentiles.* New Haven: Yale University Press, 1994.

Thorsteinsson, Runar M. *Paul's Interlocutor in Romans 2: Function and Identity in the Context of Ancient Epistolography.* Stockholm: Almqvist & Wiksell International, 2003.

Zetterholm, Magnus. "Jews, Christians, and Gentiles: Rethinking the Categorization within the Early Jesus Movement." Pages 242–54 in *Reading Paul in Context: Explorations in Identity Formation: Essays in Honour of William S. Campbell.* Edited by Kathy Ehrensperger and J. Brian Tucker. London: T&T Clark, 2010.

Zoccali, Christopher. *Whom God Has Called: The Relationship of Church and Israel in Pauline Interpretation, 1920 to the Present.* Eugene, Oreg.: Pickwick, 2010.

CHAPTER 19

The Redemption of Israel
for the Sake of the Gentiles

Scott J. Hafemann

Beginning with the call of Abraham, the history of redemption is the history of God's election of his chosen people from among the nations. As Paul argues in Romans 15:7–13, God's commitment to Israel for the sake of the nations forms the bedrock of the Church's hope.[1] Viewed from this perspective, Messianic Judaism reminds us not only of God's faithfulness, demonstrated in Israel's history, and of his grace, now magnified in the Messiah, but also of his promises for the future of his people, to be fulfilled in the final redemption of Jews and Gentiles.

The book of Romans, Paul's magisterial defense of his apostolic ministry of the gospel, reflects from beginning to end the significance of this history-of-redemption distinction between Jew and Gentile. The gospel is the power of God for salvation to every one who believes, "first to the Jew, then to the Gentile" (Rom 1:16). Likewise, human sin and divine judgment is a reality "first for the Jew, then for the Gentile" (2:9; cf. 3:9). Since God is the God of both Jews and Gentiles, both the "circumcised" and the "uncircumcised" will be justified "through [the] same faith" (3:29–30), the faith of Abraham, for "he is the father of us all" (4:16). In fulfillment of the prophets, God has created "objects of his mercy, whom he prepared in advance for glory ... not only from the Jews but also from the Gentiles" (9:23–24). And despite the fact that the majority of Jews have not believed in the Messiah Jesus, God has not rejected Israel as his people (11:1), but is now saving "a remnant chosen by grace" (11:5), even as he grafts Gentile believers into the Jewish "olive root" of God's people (11:17; cf. 11:24). So "Israel has experienced a hardening in part until the full number of the Gentiles has come in" (11:25). Paul looks forward to a coming day in which God, in fulfillment of his promises, will redeem a great multitude of Jews in Christ who are "loved on account of the patriarchs" (11:28, cf. 11:23–24, 29–31).

The Main Point of Romans: Eschatology and Ethics

Given the development of this Jew-Gentile theme throughout Romans, it is not surprising, though often overlooked, that it is precisely the relationship between Jews and Gentiles, both in history and within the church, that forms "the climax of the entire

---

1. This essay is based on, and abridges, the detailed arguments of my article, "Eschatology and Ethics: The Future of Israel and the Nations in Romans 15:1–13," *Tyndale Bulletin* 51 (2000): 161–92.

epistle" in Romans 15:7 – 13.[2] The theological development of the gospel in Romans 1 – 8 leads to the history of redemption implications of Romans 9 – 11, which together express themselves in the hortatory section of Romans 12:1 – 15:13. As an embodiment of the gospel, Paul calls the "strong" and "weak" in faith to welcome one another because Christ has welcomed both Jews and Gentiles in fulfillment of the Scriptures' vision of the Gentiles' joining Israel in the worship of the one true God (Rom 15:7).

We must be cautious at 15:7, however. Redemptive history is not over for Jews and Gentiles as Jews and Gentiles. Paul's careful use of the Scriptures in Romans 15:9 – 12 makes clear that the present church, made up of a small remnant of Jews and Gentiles, is not the final fulfillment of Israel's hope for restoration, as if God's covenant promises "climaxed" with the first coming of the Messiah.[3] The Church is not "an anomaly that Paul must explain"; a great "ironic," "eschatological reversal"; "a new reading" of what the Scriptures actually taught concerning Israel's eschatological hopes.[4] Rather, the combination and sequence of Old Testament quotes in Romans 15:9 – 12 demonstrates that Paul's eschatology is Jewish eschatology.

The Promises to Jews for the Sake of Gentiles (Rom 15:7 – 9a)

In Romans 15:7 – 13 Paul turns from eschatology (hope) in general in 15:1 – 6 to its specific contours concerning Jews and Gentiles. In doing so, the same pattern of argument introduced in 15:1 – 6 is repeated in 15:7 – 13. Once again Paul moves from an admonition in verse 7a (cf. vv. 1 – 2), to its Christological support in verses 7b – 9a (cf. v. 3a), to its Scriptural grounding in verses 9b – 12 (cf. vv. 3b – 4), to its corresponding prayer in verse 13 (cf. vv. 5 – 6):

The Call to Please and Welcome Each Other (vv. 1 – 2 and v. 7a)

Its Support from the Example of Christ (v. 3a and vv. 7b – 9a)

Its Support from Scripture (vv. 3b – 4 and vv. 9b – 12)

Its Support in Prayer (vv. 5 – 6 and v. 13)

Following these parallels, Christ's not pleasing himself from Romans 15:3 is interpreted in 15:8 – 9a in light of the fact that "Christ has become a servant of the *Jews* [literally, "circumcision"] on behalf of God's truth in order to confirm the promises made to the patriarchs *so that* the *Gentiles* may glorify God for his mercy" (my trans. and emphasis). Paul's chain of Scripture will therefore focus on the purpose of *Israel's redemptive history with regard to the Gentiles*, rather than referring merely in a general sense to the inclusion of Jews and Gentiles within the church. The Gentiles are

2. See J. R. Wagner, "The Christ, Servant of Jew and Gentile: A Fresh Approach to Romans 15:8 – 9," *Journal of Biblical Literature* 116 (1997): 473 – 85, quote at 473, see esp. nn. 2 – 3, who in support of this conclusion points to the various verbal and conceptual links between 15:7 – 9 and the rest of Romans.
3. This is the main point of N. T. Wright's important and influential work, *The Climax of the Covenant: Christ and the Law in Pauline Theology* (Edinburgh: T&T Clark, 1991). According to Wright, Paul therefore "subverts the Jewish story from within" (235). For an evaluation of Wright's broader program, see my review of *The New Testament and the People of God*, in *Journal of the Evangelical Theological Society* 40 (1997): 305 – 8.
4. Richard B. Hays, *Echoes of Scripture in the Letters of Paul* (New Haven: Yale University Press, 1989), 73, 90, 169.

to glorify God for what he has promised to do for Israel (Rom 15:9a) since the future redemption of the nations, including the resurrection from the dead and redemption of the world (cf. Rom 5:17; 8:19 – 22, 31 – 39), is tied to the rescue of Israel (Rom 15:8; cf. 11:15). The current experience of Jews and Gentiles as distinct but equal identities within the Church therefore takes on significance precisely because it is a foretaste of this consummation yet to come for both Israel and the nations.

The Argument from Scripture (Rom 15:9b – 12)

The fact that Romans 15:3 – 4 is unpacked in 15:9b – 12 with a series of four quotes from the Law, the Prophets, and the Writings (the threefold division of the Scriptures) indicates the comprehensive, canonical sweep of Paul's argument. It is even more important to note that they present a sequence of thought, rather than simply being a fourfold reiteration of the same basic point linked together simply by their common reference to the "Gentiles." An analysis of the content of the quotes within their original contexts leads to the conclusion that the chain of Scripture in verses 9b – 12 presents *one* long argument in support of his call for the Gentiles to glorify God in fulfillment of his promises to the patriarchs (Rom 15:9a).

Psalm 18:49 (17:50 LXX = 2 Sam 22:50)

Paul begins his argument by quoting Psalm 18:49. As one of the undisputed "royal" thanksgiving psalms, the primary speaker is David himself, who praises God in the midst of the Gentiles for having delivered him from his enemies and from death and Sheol (Ps 18:1, 4 – 6, 33 – 49). David speaks as God's "anointed *king*" ("the Christ" in the Greek of Ps 17:50!), who is expressing his *individual* thanksgiving to God for having delivered him in response to David's righteousness (cf. Rom 4:6 – 8). Specifically, David praises God for the "second-exodus" deliverance he has experienced, which, like the Exodus itself, becomes a testimony of God's faithfulness and sovereign glory to the nations (cf. the portrayal of David's deliverance in Ps 18:9 – 19 with Exod 15:1 – 8 and the Sinai revelation of God's presence).[5]

Since David is God's anointed king, however, more is at stake in his rescue than simply his personal safety. In spite of Israel's history of disobedience, David's deliverance entails God's commitment to establish David's dynasty in accord with God's covenant promise in 2 Samuel 7:14. Hence, *David's* being able to praise the Lord in the midst of the nations because of his *own* deliverance (Ps 18:3 – 49) leads the *psalmist* to reaffirm God's mercy to David's "descendants forever" (Ps 18:50). This link between the vindication of David and God's covenant promises to David's descendants allowed Psalm 18:50 to be taken as looking *forward* to the time in which Israel will be vindicated with and by her messiah.

Just as in Romans 15:3 the suffering of the righteous in Psalm 69:9 prefigured Christ's *death*, so too David's deliverance from "the cords of death" (Ps 18:4) becomes a harbinger of Christ's *resurrection*. Like David, Jesus too, as the messianic son of

5. Peter C. Craige, *Psalms 1 – 50* (Waco, Tex.: Word, 1983), 173 – 74.

David, has been delivered from death and vindicated over his enemies. And according to Psalm 18:50, it is the deliverance of the anointed one from his enemies, including those within Israel herself, that establishes God's continuing commitment to David's seed "forever," for which he will praise God in the midst of the nations. Against the backdrop of Psalm 18:50, the resurrection-enthronement of Jesus, the Davidic Messiah, as God's Son (cf. Rom 1:4) reaffirms God's ongoing commitment to Israel.

The Messiah's vindication at his resurrection, for which he will (and already does!) praise God among the nations, points forward to that day when Israel too will share in the Messiah's triumph as a result of having experienced the same steadfast love already experienced by her king. In light of the majority of Israel's continuing rejection of Jesus as the Messiah, which seems to call this word of God into question (cf. Rom 3:3; 9:4–6), such reassurance is absolutely crucial, not only for Israel, but for the nations as well. For as Paul's next quotation reminds his readers, the eventual salvation of the nations is wrapped up with the deliverance of Israel from her history of hard-heartedness.

Deuteronomy 32:43

In view of the significance of the Christ's vindication for the *future* restoration of Israel (Ps 18:49), Deuteronomy 32:43 draws out the implication of this restoration for the nations: they are to rejoice with God's people (following the LXX and NIV rendering of Deut 32:43). Deuteronomy 32:43 is the climactic verse of Moses' prophetic song on behalf of YHWH as Israel's "rock" (cf. Deut 32:4 with Ps 18:2). The song issues Moses' final testimony against Israel for her faithlessness to the covenant and pronounces upon her God's judgment of exile (Deut 32:1–25; cf. 31:29). Nevertheless, God's last word will be not judgment against Israel, but mercy on Israel and judgment against Israel's *enemies*, lest the Gentiles conclude that they have triumphed over Israel and her God in their own strength (Deut 32:26–27). The nations should not presume from God's present wrath against Israel that God has rejected her as his people (cf. Deut 32:20–21, 36, 39 with Rom 11:11a, 15). Nor should the nations conclude that they have gained God's favor despite their own pagan ways (Rom 11:20–22). Rather, as John Sailhamer has observed, "The emphasis on God's judgment of Israel raises the question of God's judgment of all the nations (Deut 32:34–38). The vengeance stored up against Israel (v. 34) is grounded in God's righteous vindication of the iniquity of all peoples (32:35–42)."[6] The present judgment against Israel at the hands of the nations is therefore a foretaste of the coming judgment against the nations at the hand of God himself (Deut 32:40–42). In turn, the coming judgment against the nations will be the means by which God brings about the ultimate "atonement for his land and people" (Deut 32:43).

In view of this coming eschatological judgment, the call for the nations *themselves* to "rejoice with God's people" is best seen as a call for the nations to repent of their own idolatry in order to escape the wrath to come, while they still have the

---

6. John H. Sailhamer, *The Pentateuch as Narrative: A Biblical-Theological Commentary* (Grand Rapids: Zondervan, 1992), 475–76.

opportunity. Moses' call for the nations to rejoice implies that the final, postexilic restoration of Israel will encompass those Gentiles who join the faithful remnant of Israel in praising YHWH, the true "rock" of their salvation, rather than trusting in idols (cf. Deut 32:31, 37).

Deuteronomy 32:43 therefore provides the counterpart to Psalm 18:49. Paul's first quote established that Christ's resurrection confirmed the ongoing validity of God's promises to Israel as a result of his covenant with David. As its history-of-redemption counterpart, Deuteronomy 32:43 points to the Christ's "second coming" as that which will bring these promises, now inaugurated, to their consummation. The Christ whose vindication secured God's promises to Israel must come again to judge the nations as the final step in his redemptive work on behalf of Israel, the prospect of which should lead the Gentiles to rejoice in God alone.

Psalm 117:1 (116:1 LXX)

By linking Psalm 18:49 with Deuteronomy 32:43, Paul made clear the tie between Christ's reaffirmation of God's ongoing commitment to Israel (Rom 15:8) and the Gentiles' call to glorify God (Rom 15:9a). By turning to Psalm 117:1, one of the "Hallel" psalms in praise of God for his deliverance (cf. Pss 111 – 18), Paul now unpacks how the nations are to respond to this confirmation (Ps 18:49) and consummation (Deut 32:43) of God's promises to Israel. In this regard, it is striking that Psalm 117 is the one Hallel psalm that is explicitly directed to the nations. Paul too highlights this emphasis on the nations' response to YHWH's faithfulness to Israel. Stanley rightly argues that Paul's front-loading of "all nations" (the Greek of Rom 15:11 reads, "Praise, all nations, the Lord") over against its position in the LXX of Psalm 117:1 (which reads, "Praise the Lord, all nations") is not simply stylistic, but calls "attention to what was for him the most important part of the citation, its reference to the Gentiles offering praise to the true God."[7]

Psalm 117:1 specifically commands the nations to praise the Lord because of God's great love and because "the faithfulness of the LORD endures forever." In the LXX this reference in Psalm 117 to God's faithfulness is rendered as a reference to God's "mercy" and "truth" remaining into the age to come (see Ps 117:2 = 116:2 LXX). This Greek translation of Psalm 117:2 matches Paul's own introduction of this covenant couplet of "truth" and "mercy" in Romans 15:8 – 9, which shows how Paul's thought throughout these verses is based on that of the psalm. It is also significant that the language of Psalm 117:1 in the LXX alludes back to the revelation of God's glory in Exodus 34:6 LXX, once again calling attention to the way in which God has made himself known through his redemption of Israel. In Exodus 34:6 God shows his glory to Moses by declaring his character as the Lord who is merciful and true to his covenant promises to Israel, a character made clear by the events of the Exodus themselves. By definition, this revelation of God's glory also entails making his "name" known as the one who shows *mercy* to whomever he desires (Exod 33:19), including,

---

7. Christopher D. Stanley, *Paul and the Language of Scripture: Citation Technique in the Pauline Epistles and Contemporary Literature* (Cambridge: Cambridge University Press, 1992), 181 – 82.

as Paul emphasizes, those Gentiles who, by believing in the Christ, have now joined the remnant of the elect within Israel's history (cf. Rom 9:15, 18 – 26).

The allusion to Exodus 33:19 and 34:6 in Romans 15:8 – 9 makes it clear that in view of the faithful *remnant* within Israel, now including Paul himself (Rom 11:1), the nations are to learn that God remains "true" to his promises and that God is to be glorified for his "mercy," since election is by grace, not works (cf. Rom 9:11; 11:5 – 6). Hence, "The scripture says, 'No one who believes in him will be put to shame.' For there is no distinction between Jew and Greek; the same Lord is Lord of all and bestows his riches upon all who call upon him. For 'every one who calls upon the name of the Lord will be saved'" (Rom 10:11 – 13 RSV). These are the lessons of hope from the Scriptures that fill up the time between the first (Ps 18:49) and second (Deut 32:43) comings of the Christ.

Isaiah 11:10

Paul's chain of quotes culminates with Isaiah 11:10 LXX, a text commonly recognized within both Judaism and the early Church to be messianic. Within its original context, this verse provides the transition between the future coming of the Davidic king in Isaiah 11:1 – 9 and the restoration of Israel in Isaiah 11:11 – 16. As the hinge between these two sections, the king's rising up to rule over the nations with justice (Isa 11:10), thereby rescuing the poor and afflicted by slaying the wicked (cf. Isa 11:4 – 5), is the instrument God uses to bring about the restoration of Israel.

In contrast to the salvation of the remnant remaining after Israel's judgment, Assyria, the false hope of Ahaz, will be destroyed for her arrogance, together with all those idolaters in Israel and Judah who trust in kings other than YHWH (cf. Isa 10:1 – 23 with 5:3 – 30; 8:12 – 15). Paul has already referred to this reality in Romans 9:27 – 33. But rather than signaling an end to the nations, the Davidic king's rule over them becomes the "banner for the nations" of their own ultimate redemption (Isa 11:12). This eschatological redemption of Israel and rule of David's descendant over the nations will lead to the reign of peace on the earth, "for the earth will be filled with the knowledge of the Lord as the waters cover the sea" (Isa 11:9). If Isaiah 11:10 is taken in accordance with its original context, its use in Romans 15:12 points not to Christ's resurrection in the past, but to the "Root of Jesse's" future coming in glory as the one having risen up to rule the Gentiles, so that the nations will set their hopes upon him.

Just as Psalm 18:49 grounded the call for the nations to join Israel in praising God by establishing the fact of Christ's final victory, Isaiah 11:10 does so by establishing what will happen when Christ returns in victory. In this way, the two references to Davidic kingship in Psalm 18:49 and Isaiah 11:10 provide the declarations of Christ's reign that frame the commands from Deuteronomy 32:43 and Psalm 117:1. The Gentiles' hope is to be placed in the culmination of the history of redemption to be brought about by Jesus (Rom 15:8) as the "Root of Jesse" (Isa 11:10), in fulfillment of the promise that was established by David's own vindication (Ps 18:49).

In closing his chain of quotes, Paul reminds his readers that their hope, already confirmed and anticipated by Christ's resurrection, is Christ's universal reign of peace over the nations in accordance with his promises to Israel. At that time the nations, having joined with Israel, will glorify God for his mercy to the Gentiles as an extension of his truthfulness to Israel. Until then, the Church, made up of a remnant of Jews and Gentiles who already glorify God, live under the Lordship of Christ in both life and death (cf. Rom 14:7 – 9). For as Deuteronomy 32:43 and Psalm 117:1 make clear, this hope for the future expresses itself in the present through the Gentiles joining Israel in living lives of praise to the one true "God of hope" (Rom 15:13).

Conclusion

There is a logical and chronological progression in the pattern of Paul's quotes in Romans 15:9b – 13, which fulfills the purpose of Scripture outlined in 15:4. Together they create a chiasm in which the two outer indicatives having to do with David's seed, past and future, support the two inner imperatives to the Gentiles in the present, all of which support Christ's ongoing ministry to Israel for the sake of the Gentiles.

> *Because* David's past vindication establishes God's promise to *David's seed* (v. 9b),
>> *therefore* the *Gentiles* should not give up hope, but learn from the experience of disobedient Israel to rejoice in God alone (in the midst of the false security that comes from the nations' current reign in the world) (v. 10);
>> *specifically*, the *Gentiles* should not give up hope, but learn from the experience of the faithful remnant to praise God for his truthfulness and mercy (in the midst of the adversity that comes from being part of God's elect in the world) (v. 11),
> *because* the future vindication of *David's seed* in fulfillment of God's promise is the hope of the nations (v. 12).

The argument from Scripture in 15:9b – 12 unpacks the way in which Christ's ministry reveals God's glory in 15:8 – 9a, which in turn supports the way in which Christ's having accepted both Jew and Gentile is intended to glorify God among his people (15:7b). As a result, Christ's acceptance of Jew and Gentile supports the admonition to the Romans to do likewise for the same purpose of honoring God (15:5 – 7). By accepting one another (15:7a), the Roman Christians live out in advance Christ's final, eschatological acceptance of Jew and Gentile *to the glory of God* (15:7b). Their hope-driven life of mutual acceptance to the praise of God now witnesses to the final redemption and praise of God still to come. Conversely, hope for the eschatological consummation of redemptive history, based on God's salvific acts in the past, is the engine that drives the obedience of faith in the present.

Our passage thus gives no ground for seeing Israel's identity and eschatological hopes reconfigured into Christ and/or the present Church, having been transformed by Paul into exclusively present realities. Redemptive history does not become abstracted into the "Christ-event" or personalized into an eschatological "community," but continues on after Christ's coming and establishment of the Church just as concretely and historically as it did before. The "climax of the covenant" remains Israel's future restoration for the sake of the nations. Moreover, it is precisely this climax to the covenant that secures the believer's salvific hope in the return of Christ. In light of God's promises to the patriarchs (15:8), the Messiah, as the servant to the circumcision, *must* come again to judge the nations in order to restore Israel and save the Gentiles (15:12; cf. 11:29). Messianic Judaism puts flesh on the (Ezekiel-)bones of this crucial conviction.

For Further Reading

Buchanan, George Wesley. *New Testament Eschatology: Historical and Cultural Background.* Lewiston, N.Y.: Edwin Mellen, 1993.

Hafemann, Scott. "Eschatology and Ethics: The Future of Israel and the Nations in Romans 15:1–13." *Tyndale Bulletin* 51, no. 2 (2000): 161–92.

Horbury, William. "Jerusalem in Pre-Pauline and Pauline Hope." Pages 189–26 in *Messianism among Jews and Christians: Twelve Biblical and Historical Studies.* London: T&T Clark, 2003.

———. "Land, Sanctuary and Worship." Pages 207–24 in *Early Christian Thought in Its Jewish Context.* Edited by John Barclay and John Sweet. Cambridge: Cambridge University Press, 1996.

Kirk, J. R. Daniel. "Resurrection, Messiah, and the Justification of God: Romans 1:1–7 and 15:12." Pages 33–55 in *Unlocking Romans, Resurrection and the Justification of God.* Grand Rapids: Eerdmans, 2008.

Kreitzer, L. Joseph. *Jesus and God in Paul's Eschatology.* Sheffield, UK: JSOT, 1987.

Scott, James M., "'And Then All Israel Will Be Saved' (Rom 11:26)." Pages 489–528 in *Restoration: Old Testament, Jewish, and Christian Perspectives.* Edited by James M. Scott. Leiden, Netherlands: Brill, 2001.

———. "Restoration of Israel." Pages 796–805 in *Dictionary of Paul and His Letters.* Edited by Gerald F. Hawthorne and Ralph P. Martin. Downers Grove, Ill.: InterVarsity, 1993.

Toney, Carl N. *Paul's Inclusive Ethic: Resolving Community Conflicts and Promoting Mission in Romans 14–15.* Tübingen: Mohr Siebeck, 2008.

Turner, Seth. "The Interim, Earthly Messianic Kingdom in Paul." *Journal for the Study of the New Testament* 25, no. 3 (2003): 323–42.

Wagner, J. Ross. "The Christ, Servant of Jew and Gentile: A Fresh Approach to Romans 15:8–9." *Journal of Biblical Literature* 116, no. 3 (1997): 473–85.

———. "The Heralds of Isaiah and the Mission of Paul: An Investigation of Paul's Use of Isaiah 51–55 in Romans." Pages 193–222 in *Jesus and the Suffering Servant: Isaiah 53 and Christian Origins.* Edited by William H. Bellinger and William R. Farmer. Harrisburg, Pa.: Trinity Press International, 1998.

———. *Heralds of the Good News: Isaiah and Paul "in Concert" in the Letter to the Romans.* Leiden, Netherlands: Brill, 2002.

CHAPTER 20

Paul's Rule in All the *Ekklēsiai*[1]

ANDERS RUNESSON

1. Introduction: A Centre in Pauline Thought?

The letters of the apostle to the gentiles (e.g., Rom 1:5, 13; 11:13–14; 15:16) have been interpreted in numerous ways through the centuries. For almost two thousand years, one of the key elements in most readings of Paul has been Paul's understanding of the Jewish law and its validity (or not) after the coming of the Christ (as indicated by Acts 21:20–26). This quest for the place of the law, and thus of the Jewish people, in Pauline thought and practice is still a major issue in the scholarly debate.[2] While the majority of interpreters of Paul through the ages have been (non-Jewish) Christians, this has begun to change in the last half-century or so. We are now in a situation in which no clear consensus exists on these matters; Protestants, Catholics, Jews from different denominational backgrounds, including Messianic Jews, agnostics, and atheists, form new patterns of agreement and disagreement across confessional divides.

For the historical study of Paul, therefore, the age-old question of a possible centre in his writings, a hermeneutical hub around which Paul's theology turns as it addresses problems arising in the congregations he directs his correspondence to, becomes crucial. If such a theological core could be identified, we would have access to an interpretive key with which to unlock other ambiguous passages in his letters and so find more common ground on which to build continued discussions. While all agree that we do not find in Paul's writings a systematic theology in the modern sense, opinions differ regarding what exactly would constitute a theological and hermeneutical centre of his thought, if such a centre exists at all.[3] This is where Paul's rule in all the *ekklēsiai* (1 Cor 7:17–24) provides us with a valuable point of entry into the apostle's thought world.[4]

---

1. The Greek is transliterated since the term *church* is a problematic translation for the first-century institution. See section 4, below.

2. Cf. Stephen Westerholm, *Perspectives New and Old on Paul: The Lutheran Paul and His Critics* (Grand Rapids: Eerdmans, 2004), who points to E. P. Sanders's *Paul and Palestinian Judaism* (1977) as a turning point in Pauline scholarship (xvii). On diversity of interpretation within Judaism, see Daniel R. Langton, *The Apostle Paul in the Jewish Imagination: A Study in Modern Jewish-Christian Relations* (Cambridge: Cambridge University Press, 2010). For a discussion of recent scholarship on Paul, see Magnus Zetterholm, *Approaches to Paul: A Student's Guide to Recent Scholarship* (Minneapolis: Fortress, 2009). William S. Campbell, *Paul and the Creation of Christian Identity* (London: T&T Clark, 2008), places the question in the bigger picture by relating the historical Paul to the emergence of what became Christianity.

3. Heikki Räisänen, *Paul and the Law* (Tübingen: Mohr Siebeck, 1983), claims that Paul is inconsistent; any search for a centre of thought is futile. Cf. Westerholm, *Perspectives Old and New*, 164–77.

4. For recent discussion of our passage, see David J. Rudolph, "Paul's 'Rule in All the Churches' (1 Cor 7:17–24)

The rule is, uniquely, said to be universal; if we study what Paul has to say in this passage we may therefore be able to identify some of his core convictions.

Our guiding question in this chapter is thus: What exactly is it that Paul wants to communicate in 1 Corinthians 7:17 – 24 and why is this so important for him? We shall proceed as follows. A brief discussion of the structure of the passage leads to an analysis of the meaning of Paul's rule and the theology behind it in light of other undisputed Pauline letters. Finally, we shall place this theology in its socio-institutional setting in order to extract from that setting additional explanatory information that may assist us in understanding Pauline thought and practice.

2. Structure and Meaning

Emphasis and meaning is indicated to some degree in the structure of a passage. First Corinthians 7:17 – 24 is a carefully formulated pericope, in which the different elements describe a chiastic-like pattern: (A) represents the universal rule, (B) the concrete implications of the universal rule, and (C) theological support adduced to reinforce the legitimacy of the individual rulings.[5]

A   **However that may be, let each of you lead the life that the Lord has assigned, to which God has called you. This is my rule in all the *ekklēsiai*.**

   B$_1$ Was anyone at the time of his call already circumcised? Let him not seek to remove the marks of circumcision. Was anyone at the time of his call uncircumcised? Let him not seek circumcision.

      C$_1$ *Circumcision is nothing, and uncircumcision is nothing; but obeying the commandments of God is everything.*

A   **Let each of you remain in the condition in which you were called.**

   B$_2$ Were you a slave when called? Do not be concerned about it. But if you are able to become free, use instead freedom.[6]

      C$_2$ *For whoever was called in the Lord as a slave is a freed person belonging to the Lord, just as whoever was free when called is a slave of Christ. You were bought with a price; do not become slaves of human masters.*

A   **In whatever condition you were called, brothers and sisters, there remain with God.**

The universal rule (A) is repeated three times in places inhabiting a maximum of rhetorical emphasis. The first repetition of the rule functions as a divider between two examples illustrating how the rule should be implemented socioethnically (B$_1$)

---

and Torah-Defined Ecclesiological Variegation," *Studies in Christian-Jewish Relations* 5, no. 1 (2010). Cited 29 March 2012. Online: http://escholarship.bc.edu/scjr/vol5/iss1/2/; Adam Gregerman, "Response to Papers Presented at the American Academy of Religion Conference," *Studies in Christian-Jewish Relations* 5, no. 1 (2010). Cited 29 March 2012. Online: http://escholarship.bc.edu/scjr/vol5/iss1/5/. See also David J. Rudolph, *A Jew to the Jews: Jewish Contours of Pauline Flexibility in 1 Corinthians 9:19 – 23* (Tübingen: Mohr Siebeck, 2011), 75 – 88.

5. Translation follows New Revised Standard Version with some noted exceptions.

6. Alternative translation: "Even if you can gain your freedom, make use of your present condition now more than ever" (NRSV). For the present translation, cf. J. Albert Harrill, *The Manumission of Slaves in Early Christianity* (Tübingen: Mohr Siebeck, 1995), 68 – 128, esp. 108 – 21. Slaves had, ultimately, no control over their own lives; change may occur with or without their consent.

and socioeconomically (B_2). Each example is followed by theological statements that underpin the behavior endorsed (C_{1-2}).

From this structure we may conclude that, based on an emerging supralocal authority structure for Christ-believing communities,[7] Paul is reinforcing rules he believes to be theologically critical.[8] Circumcision and socioeconomic status function as key carriers for Paul's eschatological convictions; by investigating these carriers of meaning we may be able to access data revealing the hermeneutical hub around which Paul's theology is built.

3. Theology and Socioritual Behavior

The two problems, socioethnic and socioeconomic status, which the universal rule aims at solving, indicate that Paul's thinking is "layered" hierarchically. When he encounters "on the ground" what he perceives to be problematic circumstances, he works from higher (theological) principles, the implications of which are then applied to specific social contexts. The two rules on circumcision and slavery respectively show that some people in Corinth — and elsewhere (7:17) — interpreted the Christ-event as implying that (a) Jewish identity had become insignificant, and (b) slavery was a state in which an individual "in Christ" should not be (cf. Gal 3:28). For Paul, neither (a) nor (b) harmonized well with the acute eschatological reality from within which he understood the present moment.

Circumcision

The rule itself is clear: those who are circumcised must remain so, and those who are not must not seek to become circumcised. What are the theological implications of this ruling? In his letters, Paul uses the word "circumcised" as corresponding to the word "Jew." While he understands both words to refer ultimately to a (positive) spiritual reality (Rom 2:25 – 3:4, 31; 4:9 – 12), which he connects with "faith," he does not reject the physicality of being circumcised or its implications for Jewish religioethnic identity (cf. Rom 3:1 – 4). Circumcision carries with it not only social implications but also spiritual significance. Paul may therefore describe circumcision as a "seal of righteousness."[9] Circumcision is connected to peoplehood, and precisely for this reason it also relates to divine law (cf. Rom 4:16; Gal 5:3).[10] From this follows that when Paul states that the circumcised must not reverse their circumcision, he rules that Jews "in

---

7. With the growing network of interconnected communities of believers in Jesus in the Mediterranean world followed a need for some sort of intercongregational (supralocal) authority structure that could express, or regulate, the basic unity of the many and diverse local expressions of belief in Jesus that had developed.

8. *Contra* Gregerman, "Response," 3. Cf. Joseph Fitzmeyer, *First Corinthians: A New Translation with Introduction and Commentary* (New Haven: Yale University Press, 2008), 306: "it is best to recognize [these verses] as formulating a principle on which the other more specific topics are based."

9. Rom 4:11 – 12, where this is said in relation to Abraham and his faith before and after circumcision. For Paul, this turns Abraham into the ancestor of both circumcised and uncircumcised; both categories are legitimate in Paul's thought, unified by the entity of faith (cf. Rom 15:8 – 9).

10. On the connection between people, land, law, and God in ancient society, see Steve Mason, "Jews, Judaeans, Judaizing, Judaism: Problems of Categorization in Ancient History," *Journal for the Study of Judaism* 38 (2007): 457 – 512.

Christ" must remain Jewish and keep the Jewish law, since keeping the law is inextricably intertwined with circumcision and ethnicity (Gal 5:3).

Conversely, this principle leads to Paul's insistence that the uncircumcised maintain their non-Jewish status; gentiles must not keep the Jewish law, since this law was given only to those who were circumcised.[11] Does this mean that only those who adhere to the law, that is, the Jews, can keep God's commandments? If so, where would that place non-Jews in relation to salvation? Contrary to later developments in (non-Jewish) Christianity, this seems to have been the key question for most of the early Christ-believing communities.

As 7:19 (C_1) implies, "God's commandments" can be fulfilled both by those who adhere to the law *and* by those who do not. How is this possible? It can be achieved only if one adds a higher principle above the law, which can be effective both through the law and beyond it. The fulfilling of the commandments is then made dependent on that entity (cf. Rom 3:21–22). For Paul, this higher "principle" is the Spirit, which has been given both to those of faith who adhere to the law and to those who do not have the law (1 Cor 12:13; cf. Gal 5:5; Acts 10:45; 15:8–9).[12] In addition, Paul refers to love as the essence of the law: "love is the fulfilling of the law" (Rom 13:10 NRSV; cf. Gal 5:14). Then, by connecting the Spirit to love, Paul can state that "God's love has been poured into our hearts through the Holy Spirit that has been given to us" (Rom 5:5 NRSV; cf. 1 Cor 16:14). Therefore, since Paul believes that the Spirit has been given not only to those who abide by the law, but also to those who are not Jewish, it follows that the fulfilling of God's commandments, which in their condensed form is love, is made possible for all, both Jews and non-Jews as distinct groups.

This brings forth another key concept in Paul's thinking: faith. Both Jews and non-Jews may display the faith that enables God to give humans the Spirit, which in turn channels love/law-fulfillment from God to humans, free of cost (1 Cor 7:23; Rom 3:24). Righteousness cannot, therefore, be achieved apart from faith (Rom 1:17; 4:5; 5:21; 10:4; Gal 2:21; 5:5; Phil 3:9; cf. Rom 3:25); the law is, on its own, empty of salvific force. God will "justify the circumcised on the ground of faith and the uncircumcised through that same faith" (Rom 3:30 NRSV). The fact that there is a hierarchy of theological levels — and faith is above the law — does not, therefore, lead to rejection of the law as such. Paul's point is the opposite: the law can now be fulfilled *also* by people who are not Jewish. Different hierarchical levels cannot cancel each other out but rather build on one another. Therefore, Paul explicitly affirms the law's continued validity: "Do we then overthrow the law by this faith? By no means! On the contrary, we uphold the law" (Rom 3:31 NRSV). Love is the salvific substance, since through it the Spirit makes the law happen.[13]

---

11. On the importance of the particular within the universal, see Campbell, *Paul and the Creation of Christian Identity*, 91–93. Cf. Markus Bockmuehl, *Jewish Law in Gentile Churches: Halakhah and the Beginnings of Christian Public Ethics* (Grand Rapids: Baker Academic, 2000), 170–72; J. Brian Tucker, *You Belong to Christ: Paul and the Formation of Social Identity in 1 Corinthians 1–4* (Eugene, Oreg.: Pickwick, 2010), 245, n. 38.

12. Also David Horrell, *An Introduction to the Study of Paul* (London: T&T Clark, 2000), 64; Paula Fredriksen, "Judaizing the Nations: The Ritual Demands of Paul's Gospel," *New Testament Studies* 56 (2010): 232–52, esp. 247–48.

13. Cf. 1 Cor 13. Love is said to be stronger than faith as a redeeming entity in that, on the basis of God's love, Paul extends salvation to Jews who do not share his faith: Rom 11:28–29.

If we draw this pattern of thought as a chart, it may take the form shown in the figure below.

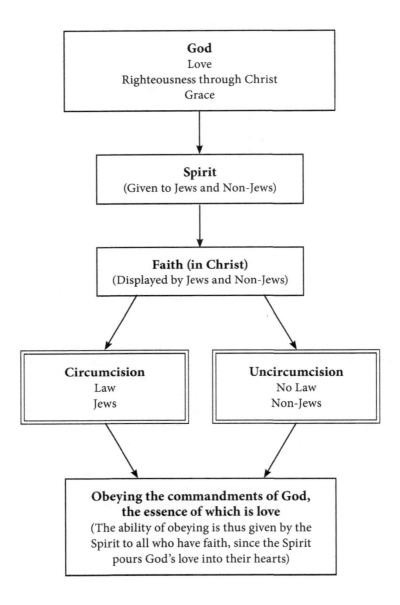

A hierarchical pattern of Paul's thought with special attention to the place of Jews, non-Jews, and the law in relation to obeying the commandments of God and salvation. The double-lined boxes represent the (visible) socioethnic differences between the two groups "in Christ." The single-lined boxes represent theological levels applicable to both groups.

In sum: Being Jewish or non-Jewish means nothing— *in relation to the keeping of the commandments and salvation* (1 Cor 7:19 [C_1]; cf. Gal 5:19–23; Rom 1:32; 13:13; 1 Cor 6:9–11). All that matters is faith, which opens up for the Spirit's salvific outpouring of love, enabling all to fulfill the law. For Paul this does not, however, change the fact that the world still consists of two basic categories: the Jewish people (according to the irrevocable promise; Rom 11:29) and the rest of the world. Paul permitted no conversion between these worlds, since conversion would negate God's acceptance of all regardless of ethnic identity. The unifying elements between the worlds are faith and the outpouring of the Spirit on both.

Slavery

Paul's second example is both similar to and different from the question of Jews and non-Jews. The problem of slavery is a socioeconomic question, not a question about ethnicity and the divine. Further, slavery is disconnected from the hermeneutical mechanisms of the circumcision-uncircumcision problematic in that enslaved individuals were restricted in their ability to make independent choices. What, then, is it that makes Paul think of these as two distinct yet related examples of how his universal principle should be implemented by all local *ekklēsiai*?

Contrary to the Therapeutai, who had withdrawn from society, Paul never challenged the social construct of slavery.[14] The Therapeutai rejected slavery on the basis of the conviction that all human beings were created equal.[15] While Paul doubtless agreed with this sentiment (as implied by 1 Cor 12:13; cf. Gal 3:28), this is not the point of departure for his theological argument. For Paul the key is eschatological— namely, that the Spirit had already been given to people who had faith in Jesus regardless of their socioeconomic status. To be a slave must therefore be irrelevant in relation to salvation (Gal 3:28; Rom 10:12; cf. Acts 2:17–21). Striving to change one's status, however, would call in question God's salvific care for all, as if slaves were inferior by nature. In Paul's theological logic, the rationale for ruling that slaves should not make every effort to become free is precisely that he regarded slaves as equal to the free (B_2; 1 Cor 7:21). By remaining in the condition in which one was when called by God, a person confirmed God's blindness to status constructs as the world was coming to an end (cf. 1 Cor 12:12–14). The Spirit works across borders and turns all into slaves of Christ (C_2; 1 Cor 7:22–23).

How do we, then, explain Paul's theology of ethnic and socioeconomic equality? Theology is never created *ex nihilo*, but emerges in specific social and institutional settings. In order to shed more light on Paul's rule in all the *ekklēsiai* we shall therefore anchor his thought in the Jewish and Roman social reality in which he lived.

---

14. On ancient slavery and manumission, see Raymond F. Collins, *First Corinthians* (Collegeville, Minn.: Liturgical Press, 1999), 278–82. Primary sources are found in Tim G. Parkin and Arthur J. Pomeroy, *Roman Social History: A Source Book* (London: Routledge, 2007), 154–204.

15. Philo, *Contempl.* 70. Cf. the late second-/early third-century Roman writer Florentinus, *Digest.* 1.5.4, who, as also Ulpian (d. 223) did, regarded slavery as being against nature but saw the socioeconomic construct as functioning under the provision of *ius gentium* ("law of nations").

4. Theology and Ecclesial Context

As we have seen above, Paul makes a distinction between the spiritual and the social, so that faith (and therefore also the Spirit) is the only connecting point, which both transforms and preserves the social. Social structures are preserved in that people must remain both socioethnically and socioeconomically where they were when called, giving slaves the option of change only if their masters so decide. Social life is, however, also transformed in that Paul consistently argues that these different social categories are, in relation to ultimate (eschatological) reality, without substance, since all are one "in Christ." This oneness "in Christ" is, to be sure, a theological statement, but as such it cannot exist without social implications, a social frame.

It is clear that Paul envisioned and confirmed theologically the appropriateness of a socio-institutional context in which Jews and non-Jews, slaves and free, men and women, interacted without giving up their respective identities. This context was the *ekklēsia*: a local phenomenon connected via networks and an emerging supralocal authority structure, for which Paul made himself a spokesperson. The question is, what was this *ekklēsia*?

Contrary to our modern translation of *ekklēsiai* as "church," the name itself was used in the first century to refer to both Greco-Roman institutions and Jewish synagogues.[16] Today, "church" indicates an institution separate from the synagogue, which makes this word a misleading translation of *ekklēsiai*. One cannot assume, on the basis of first-century uses of the term, that Pauline *ekklēsiai* were something other than, or disconnected from, the synagogue. How, then, may we understand Paul's theology as related to socioinstitutional contexts in his own time and culture?

Ancient society distinguished between three social spheres, in which what we call "religion" was enacted:[17] the public sphere, the domestic sphere, and the semi-public associations (*collegia* or *thiasoi*).[18] Although Paul certainly aimed at an eschatological transformation of public society on the one hand (cf. Rom 4:13), and believers in Jesus gathered in domestic space on the other (1 Cor 16:19), the social location for Pauline theology of equality matches the association setting quite closely.[19]

In most Greco-Roman associations membership was not restricted, allowing people with (maintained) different ethnic, socioeconomic, and gender identities to interact in ways that they would not have been able to do in the public or domestic spheres of society. While all associations regardless of purpose would include cultic elements among their activities, some associations were dedicated exclusively to the cult of a specific deity.[20] It is not strange, thus, that in the Diaspora the synagogue

---

16. While the Greco-Roman use of the term is well known, its use for synagogue institutions is rarely noted. For sources, see the index in Anders Runesson, Donald D. Binder, and Birger Olsson, *The Ancient Synagogue: From Its Origins to 200 C.E., A Source Book* (Leiden, Netherlands: Brill, 2010).

17. Cf. Hans-Josef Klauck, *The Religious Context of Early Christianity: A Guide to Graeco-Roman Religions* (Minneapolis: Fortress, 2000).

18. On associations, see Philip A. Harland, *Associations, Synagogues, and Congregations: Claiming a Place in Ancient Mediterranean Society* (Minneapolis: Fortress, 2003).

19. Associations could utilise domestic space for their gatherings, especially early on in their existence before they could afford to build separate buildings for this purpose.

20. For a typology of associations, see Harland, *Associations, Synagogues, and Congregations*, 28–53.

was counted among the associations.[21] In such a setting it is entirely predictable that non-Jews would become members or be loosely associated with the synagogue, as is also evidenced by the existence of proselytes and so-called God-Fearers. Patterns of women as leaders in synagogues also find an explanation in such a context.[22]

When Paul refers to ethnic (Jew/Greek), socioeconomic (slave/free), and gender (male/female) categories as he theologizes oneness "in Christ" (Gal 3:28), it is likely that the theology endorsed mirrored the institutional reality of the *ekklēsiai*. This would explain the presence of female leadership in Paul's congregations,[23] Paul's insistence on maintained social identities within a setting of equality,[24] and the general lack of explicit political rhetoric aimed at the public sphere of society. Paul's concern with supralocal networks and universal rules for the *ekklēsiai* also finds a home in the context of association-type institutions, since we have evidence among other cultic associations indicating similar "international" networks.[25]

In sum, the eschatological reality in which Paul was convinced he lived took concrete institutional form in association-like settings, which provided a matrix for a theology of maintained identity within a context of equality. Within such settings, Paul's thinking proceeded from experience to theology to supralocal rulings. Paul's unity-in-diversity theology in 1 Corinthians 7:17–24 is thus best described as the theologized consequence of an experienced situation in a specific type of institutional setting, in which non-Jews as much as Jews, slaves as much as free, expressed faith in Christ and displayed behavior that was interpreted to indicate that they had all, without distinction, been given the Spirit.

5. Conclusion: The Spirit and the Universal Fulfillment of the Law

The fact that Paul maintained a two-category worldview consisting of Jews on the one hand and the rest of the world on the other is essential for the analysis of 1 Corinthians 7:17–24. As he had become convinced by (interpreted) experience that, now at the end of time, the Spirit had made no distinction between people based on socioethnic or socioeconomic identity markers, but that God aimed for the salvation of all, Paul labored to convince Jews and non-Jews, slaves and free (and men and women), that faith — not law in and of itself, or social status or gender — is the universal key to a righteousness given by God for free, based on the Messiah's sacrifice, which had achieved atonement (1 Cor 7:23; Rom 3:25). Faith as key means faith as entrance-point for the Spirit, which pours God's love into human hearts (Rom 5:5) and fulfills the

---

21. The situation was more complex in the land of Israel. See Anders Runesson, *The Origins of the Synagogue: A Socio-Historical Study* (Stockholm: Almqvist and Wiksell International, 2001), 169–235.

22. Runesson et al., *Ancient Synagogue*, 9, n. 19.

23. Cf. Eldon J. Epp, *Junia: The First Woman Apostle* (Minneapolis: Fortress, 2005).

24. Cf. Runesson et al., *Ancient Synagogue*, 13.

25. Harland, *Associations, Synagogues, and Congregations*, 33–36; cf. Martin Goodman, *Mission and Conversion: Proselytizing in the Religious History of the Roman Empire* (Oxford: Clarendon, 1994), 27–28; Anders Runesson, "Was There a Christian Mission before the Fourth Century? Problematizing Common Ideas about Early Christianity and the Beginnings of Modern Mission," in *The Making of Christianity: Conflicts, Contacts, and Constructions* (ed. Magnus Zetterholm and Samuel Byrskog; Winona Lake, Ind.: Eisenbrauns, forthcoming).

essence of God's commandments, which is love and therefore of utmost importance (1 Cor 7:19; Rom 13:10; Gal 5:14; cf. Rom 7:12; 9:31 – 32 and the figure on p. 218).

The law is thus upheld for Jews *and* made available to the rest of the world; this is the eschatological news. Salvation is from God both within *and* apart from the law. In no case, however, can the law be fulfilled — and obeying God's commandments is everything — without the core elements of faith and Spirit. Just as non-Jewish Christ-believers would show lack of faith in the power of the Spirit if they were to convert to Judaism, Jews who had experienced the outpouring of the Spirit as Jews would contra-dict God's grace and promises if they gave up their Jewish identity as they embraced faith in the Messiah. As for slaves, they were not inferior by nature to the free, just as non-Jews and Jews together were part of God's salvific plan. Maintaining the status quo, therefore, would manifest God's borderless grace as the world was about to be completely transformed. This, arguably, would constitute one of Paul's core convic-tions; it surfaces in 1 Corinthians 7:17 – 24 but controls much of the theological argu-ment in other letters as well.

As one ponders the historical Paul as well as his later interpreters through the centuries, it is difficult to escape the conclusion that, contrary to much that has been written, Paul is likely to have applied the universal rule of Jews remaining Jewish "in Christ" also to himself, if we assume that there is at least some consistency between his practice and his belief.[26] A study of Paul's rule in all the *ekklēsiai* seems, therefore, to add a supporting voice — this time Paul's own — to James's and the elders' exhorta-tion in Jerusalem as they instruct a complying Paul in Acts 21:24 (NRSV): "Join these men, go through the rite of purification with them, and pay for the shaving of their heads. Thus all will know that there is nothing in what they have been told about you, but that you yourself observe and guard the law."[27]

---

26. Paul was, after all, also circumcised (Phil 3:5). Cf. Rudolph, *A Jew to the Jews*, 88.

27. See also Acts 28:17. On the representation of Paul in Acts in relation to the portrait that emerges from Paul's letters, see Reidar Hvalvik, "Paul as a Jewish Believer: According to the Book of Acts," in *Jewish Believers in Jesus: The Early Centuries* (ed. Oskar Skarsaune and Reidar Hvalvik; Peabody, Mass.: Hendrickson, 2007), 121 – 53.

For Further Reading

Bockmuehl, Markus. *Jewish Law in Gentile Churches: Halakhah and the Beginnings of Christian Public Ethics.* Grand Rapids: Baker Academic, 2000.

Campbell, William S. *Paul and the Creation of Christian Identity.* London: T&T Clark, 2008.

Dean, Lester. "Jews and Jewish Christians Must Follow Torah." Pages 176–81 in *Bursting the Bonds? A Jewish-Christian Dialogue on Jesus and Paul.* Maryknoll, N.Y.: Orbis, 1990.

Donaldson, Terence L. *Paul and the Gentiles: Remapping the Apostle's Convictional World.* Minneapolis: Fortress, 1997.

Eisenbaum, Pamela. *Paul Was Not a Christian: The Original Message of a Misunderstood Apostle.* New York: HarperOne, 2009.

Fredriksen, Paula. "Judaizing the Nations: The Ritual Demands of Paul's Gospel." *New Testament Studies* 56 (2010), 232–52.

Nanos, Mark D. "A Torah-Observant Paul? What Difference Could It Make for Christian/Jewish Relations Today?" Annual Presentation to the Christian Scholars Group on Christian-Jewish Relations, sponsored by the Center for Christian-Jewish Learning at Boston College, June 4–6, 2005. Online: http://www.mjstudies.com.

Rudolph, David J. *A Jew to the Jews: Jewish Contours of Pauline Flexibility in 1 Corinthians 9:19–23.* Tübingen: Mohr Siebeck, 2011.

———. "Paul's 'Rule in All the Churches' (1 Cor 7:17–24) and Torah-Defined Ecclesiological Variegation." *Studies in Christian-Jewish Relations* 5 (2010): 1–23. Cited 29 March 2012. Online: http://escholarship.bc.edu/scjr/vol5/iss1/5/.

Runesson, Anders. "Inventing Christian Identity: Paul, Ignatius, and Theodotius I." Pages 59–92 in *Exploring Early Christian Identity.* Edited by Bengt Holmberg. Tübingen: Mohr Siebeck, 2008.

Tomson, Peter J. "Paul's Jewish Background in View of His Law Teaching in 1 Cor 7." Pages 251–70 in *Paul and the Mosaic Law.* Edited by James D. G. Dunn. Grand Rapids: Eerdmans, 2001.

Tucker, Brian J. *"Remain in Your Calling": Paul and the Continuation of Social Identities in 1 Corinthians.* Eugene, Oreg.: Pickwick, 2011.

———. *You Belong to Christ: Paul and the Formation of Social Identity in 1 Corinthians 1–4.* Eugene, Oreg.: Pickwick, 2010.

Willitts, Joel. "Weighing the Words of Paul: How Do We Understand Paul's Instructions Today?" *Covenant Companion* 3 (2009): 28–30.

Windsor, Lionel J. "Paul and the Vocation of Israel: How Paul's Jewish Identity Informs His Apostolic Ministry, with Special Reference to Romans." PhD diss., Durham University, 2012. Online: http://etheses.dur.ac.uk/3920/.

Zetterholm, Magnus. *Approaches to Paul: A Student's Guide to Recent Scholarship.* Minneapolis: Fortress, 2009

CHAPTER 21

Equality in the Church

Justin K. Hardin

What does it mean for Jewish and gentile believers to be "one in Christ" (Gal 3:28) or for God to make "one new person out of two" (Eph 2:15)?[1] Do these biblical affirmations imply ethnic equality while maintaining ethnic distinction, or should we understand them as collapsing ethnicity altogether? Admittedly, these passages are often assumed to support the latter — that Jew and gentile have been eclipsed, both groups becoming a *tertius genum* (third race).[2] In this chapter, we will therefore evaluate these two biblical passages afresh, with our sights set on answering this significant question.

Unfortunately, the limits of this study prevent us from undertaking a detailed exegesis of each biblical text. Neither will we be able to discuss other significant issues related to this question, such as the Pauline referent of "the Israel of God" (Gal 6:16), the eschatological question of "Israel" (Rom 11:26), or what Paul precisely meant when he called the Corinthian believers former gentiles (see 1 Cor 12:2). Instead, our aims are much more modest: in this chapter, we will evaluate the meaning of (1) Galatians 3:28 and (2) Ephesians 2:14 – 18, in order to demonstrate that these texts, while clearly affirming full equality between Jew and gentile in the Messiah Jesus, assume an ongoing ethnic distinction between them.

Galatians: Equality through Faith in the Messiah

Paul's letter to the Galatian churches is famous both for its theological density and its firmness of conviction that salvation comes through faith in the Messiah Jesus. Indeed, believers throughout the centuries have heralded this highly charged letter as a *Magna Carta*, as it were, of God's free gift of salvation. But if most interpreters have correctly recognised the weight of Paul's soteriology in this letter, they often tread down the wrong path by assuming Paul thereby diminished Jewish (and, indeed, ethnic) identity. Perhaps at one level this marriage is understandable. After all, in one of the climactic statements in Galatians, Paul pronounced decisively that "There is neither Jew nor Gentile, neither slave nor free, nor is there male and female, for you are all one in Christ Jesus" (Gal 3:28).[3] To be sure, this declaration does not support

---

1. Unless otherwise noted, Scripture translations are my own.

2. This designation was used as early as Tertullian (who opposed this understanding; see *Nat.* 1.3).

3. See also Col 3:11: "Here there is no Gentile or Jew, circumcised or uncircumcised, barbarian, Scythian, slave or free, but Christ is all, and is in all"; and 1 Cor 12:13: "For we were all baptized by one Spirit so as to form one body — whether Jews or Gentiles, slave or free — and we were all given the one Spirit to drink." What is said of Gal 3:28 largely applies to these passages as well, although there are some obvious points of departure in the overall

a collapse of ethnicity any more than it supports the collapse of the male and female genders. (Paul certainly did not think believers were androgynous!) So how precisely are we to understand Paul's statement in Galatians 3:28 that there is neither Jew nor gentile? In order to answer this question, we must place this verse securely within the context of the letter by making two preliminary points.

First, we must bear in mind that Galatians was addressed to gentiles (Gal 4:8 – 9; 5:2) in response to a "crisis" in the churches. In this letter we learn that "agitators" (see 1:7; 5:10) within these communities were demanding that the gentile believers needed to be circumcised to be members of Abraham's family (5:2 – 12; 6:12 – 13).[4] Despite the widespread assumption that the agitators were *legalistic* Jewish believers (a.k.a. "Judaizers"), Paul attributed their Judaizing tactics to practical, not theological, concerns (6:12 – 13).[5] According to Paul, the agitators were preaching circumcision to gentiles simply to avoid persecution.[6] Like Peter at Antioch, who also agreed with Paul's gospel but denied gentiles table fellowship out of fear (2:11 – 21), the agitators in Galatia were distorting the gospel (1:7) out of fear (6:12 – 13; cf. 5:11) and were denying fellowship with the gentiles, until of course they followed through with circumcision (4:17 – 20). As we seek to understand Paul's argument in Galatians, we must therefore remember both the letter's occasion and its gentile recipients.

Second, we must understand correctly Paul's theological aim. In short, Paul sought to demonstrate to his gentile readers that salvation and inclusion as God's people came through faith in Jesus the Messiah, not through circumcision (Gal 3:1 – 9). In doing so, Paul argued that gentiles had been included as Abraham's children though faith (cf. Rom 4). Of course, he did not argue his point by claiming that Abraham's role as father of the Jewish people ceased to exist in the messianic age. Instead, Paul's primary aim was to show that neither gentiles nor Jews are treated differently in God's economy of salvation. In the face of the agitators who were arguing that gentiles needed to be circumcised, Paul averred confidently that gentiles were included as Abraham's children through faith in the Messiah.

Given our understanding both of the occasion and of Paul's aims in the letter, we are now in a better position to understand Paul's broader argument and how Galatians 3:28 functions within it. In 3:1 – 9, Paul began his argument by rebuking these gentiles for the second time,[7] reminding them that faith, not Law keeping (literally: "works of the Law"), makes one a child of Abraham. Thus, Paul prioritized faith over the Law,

---

context in Colossians and 1 Corinthians. For a recent discussion of these three texts on the basis of Paul's vision for social unity in the churches, see Bruce Hansen, *"All of You Are One": The Social Vision of Gal 3.28, 1 Cor 12.13 and Col 3.11* (London: T&T Clark, 2010).

4. It is likely the agitators turned to Gen 17:9 – 14 to make their case that circumcision was for all Abraham's children forever. Paul, of course, also appealed to the Abrahamic narrative but gave priority to the preceding passage in Gen 15:6, where God credited Abraham's faith as righteousness.

5. On the reliability of these statements, see Justin K. Hardin, *Galatians and the Imperial Cult: A Critical Analysis of the First-Century Social Context of Paul's Letter* (Tübingen: Mohr Siebeck, 2008), 94 – 102. For the view that the "agitators" were local, see esp. Mark D. Nanos, *The Irony of Galatians: Paul's Letter in First-Century Context* (Minneapolis: Fortress, 2002), 169 – 99, and Hardin, *Galatians and the Imperial Cult*, 92 – 94.

6. Whether these agitators were seeking to avoid persecution from their own Jewish unbelieving community or from the civil government is hotly debated (see Hardin, *Galatians and the Imperial Cult*, esp. 102 – 15).

7. The first rebuke comes in Gal 1:6 – 9 (cf. also 4:8 – 9 and possibly 5:7 – 11). For an excellent discussion on Galatians as a letter of ironic rebuke, see Mark D. Nanos, *The Irony of Galatians*, 32 – 61.

using Abraham as a key figure in his argument. In the following verses, he then supported this assertion in two primary ways, which we can outline below:

1. The Messiah came under the curse of the Law so that, through faith, the gentiles might receive the blessing of Abraham and so that "we" Jews might receive the promised Holy Spirit (Gal 3:10 – 14).[8]
2. The promise to Abraham and to his "seed" (who is the Messiah Jesus), and thus Abraham's faith, preceded the giving of the Law (Gal 3:15 – 18).

After sketching the priority of the Abrahamic promise/faith, Paul then answered two potential objections with regard to the Law. The first question: Why was the Law added (Gal 3:19a)? Paul replied briefly (and cryptically!) that it was added because of transgressions, even though admittedly it dealt with only one people (Israel) and not the world (Gal 3:19b – 20). The second question was a corollary to the first: Is the Law then contrary to the (Abrahamic) promises (Gal 3:21)? Paul flatly denied this suggestion and argued two basic points in reply:

1. The Law is not able to give life. On the contrary, the Scriptures shut up everything under sin, so that the promise would be given through faith in/of the Messiah Jesus to those who have faith (Gal 3:21b – 22).
2. The Law was a tutor (*pedagogue*) until the Messiah came, so that one would be made righteous from faith (Gal 3:23 – 24).

With these theological rejoinders, Paul had returned to the main thrust of the argument — that Abrahamic faith takes priority over the Law. Indeed, in the concluding verses of this chapter, Paul stressed that because "faith" has come, "we" Jews are no longer under the tutor (i.e., we do not need protection from the deathly consequences of sin) because "you" gentiles are children of God through faith in the Messiah Jesus (Gal 3:25 – 26).[9] In 3:27 – 29, Paul then brought the entire argument to a fitting climax, proclaiming the reason these gentiles were children of God through faith:

for all of you who were baptized into Christ have clothed yourselves with Christ. There is neither Jew nor Gentile, neither slave nor free, nor is there male and female, for you are all one in Christ Jesus. If you belong to Christ, then you are Abraham's seed, and heirs according to the promise.

Given our understanding of Galatians 3, we can observe how Paul's argument requires Jewish particularity, as it is inherently linked with the Abrahamic promise to gentiles (cf. Gen 12:3). Thus, Galatians 3:28 does not assume a deterioration of ethnic distinction; on the contrary, this verse is predicated on ethnic distinctiveness in God's plan of salvation. In the Messiah, God has shown himself to be faithful to redeem both Jews and gentiles, and this reality points to God's "new creation" (Gal 6:15) in which

---

8. Paul's first-person plural pronouns ("we," "us," and "our") most likely refer to Paul along with other Jesus-believing Jews (see the excellent, though rarely known, study of D. W. B. Robinson, "The Distinction between Jewish and Gentile Believers in Galatians," *Australian Biblical Review* 8 [1965]: 29 – 48).

9. With Paul's statement "all of you" (Gal 3:27), perhaps he was including the Jewish agitators along with the gentile readers of this letter. If this is the case, Paul was showing that both groups had equal footing as God's children through faith and must therefore come together in unity.

both groups are members of God's family in the age of the Messiah. For the Galatian gentiles, Paul's discussion would have served as an effective theological antidote to the bewitching tactics of the agitators.

If our interpretation of Galatians 3:28 is correct, we must now clarify two passages elsewhere in Galatians that seem to undercut this understanding. First, what should we make of Paul's assertion that "neither circumcision nor uncircumcision has any value" (Gal 5:6; cf. 6:15)? Does this statement imply that Paul denied any ongoing importance to circumcision for Jewish believers in Jesus?[10] In answering this question, of course, we must remember that Paul's statements in Galatians were directed at gentiles in an effort to affirm that circumcision would not place them any closer to God. In the Messiah, the only thing that matters is the "new creation" (Gal 6:15). Seen in this light, Paul was not devaluing the practice of circumcision. Neither can these statements support the view that Paul was opposed to Jewish observance of the Law more generally or that he thought Jews should stop circumcising their children (1 Cor 7:17–24; cf. Acts 16:3; Acts 21:20–26).[11] Rather, Paul was simply explaining that circumcision was not the means by which the Galatians would be included as Abraham's children. Indeed, to value circumcision above faith was to ignore the age of the Messiah whereby gentiles were grafted into God's people through faith (Gal 5:2–6).

We must now turn to a second passage that may overturn our reading of Galatians 3:28. Does not Galatians 4:1–11 render Jewish practice (and thus identity) in the Messiah an untenable option, since in these verses Paul seems to link observing the Jewish calendar with paganism (Gal 4:3, 9–10)? In response to this question, we should begin by stating that there are good reasons for understanding the calendar in 4:10 as a reference to the pagan calendar, not the Jewish one. The assumption that 4:10 refers to the Jewish calendar runs aground for the following reasons: (1) the faulty strategy of reading the circumcision issue (and Col 2:16) back into the context of Galatians 4:8–11; (2) the distinctly non-Jewish terms "days and months and seasons and years" employed in Galatians 4:10; (3) the evidence elsewhere in the Pauline corpus (and in Acts) that suggests Paul was not at all critical of the Jewish calendar, but even continued to keep it himself (e.g., 1 Cor 16:8; Acts 20:16); and (4) the unlikelihood that observing the Jewish calendar would have appeased the situation in the churches, since the real issue was circumcision (one wonders how uncircumcised gentiles would even be permitted to participate fully in Jewish festivals).[12]

Furthermore, the present tense of the Greek underlying "you are observing" (Gal 4:10) seems to indicate something the Galatians were doing at the time of the letter, whereas the issue of circumcision was a potential action (hence, the warning not to

10. One might add a third passage, Gal 5:2–11, but when we remember these verses were written to gentiles, not Jews, then this passage falls away as a potential obstacle to the reading of Gal 3:28 we have just proposed.

11. For a superb interpretation of 1 Cor 7:17–24 within its context of marriage and celibacy, see David Rudolph, "Paul's 'Rule in All the Churches' (1 Cor 7:17–24) and Torah-Defined Ecclesiological Variegation," *Studies in Christian-Jewish Relations* 5, no. 1 (2010): 1–24.

12. See further the extensive discussion in Hardin, *Galatians and the Imperial Cult*, 116–47, where I argue that Gal 4:10 refers to the pagan calendar, i.e., the civic calendars in the Roman colonies of Galatia, which would have been saturated with imperial festivals and holy days. For similar interpretations see, e.g., Nanos, *The Irony of Galatians*, 267–70; Graham N. Stanton, *Jesus and Gospel* (Cambridge: Cambridge University Press, 2004), 41–46; and Hilary Le Cornu with Joseph Shulam, *A Commentary on the Jewish Roots of Galatians* (Jerusalem: Academon, 2005).

be circumcised in Gal 5:2 – 12). Given the social pressure these gentiles must have experienced for abandoning worship of pagan gods (including the imperial rulers), it is difficult to resist the probability that as they considered the circumcision option, these gentile believers had begun to observe the ubiquitous pagan cults in an attempt to allay their social dislocation. Thus, in Galatians 4:8 – 11 Paul reprimanded these gentile believers for slipping back to their pagan past. Both circumcision and returning to paganism were equal pitfalls for the Galatian gentiles to avoid; they must "stand firm" (Gal 5:1).

But even if we are correct that Galatians 4:10 refers to the pagan calendar, did Paul not consider Judaism to be tantamount to paganism when he claimed that both Jews and gentiles were under the *stoicheia* — that is, the demonic false deities of the world (Gal 4:3, 9)?[13] To answer this question, it is necessary to observe the flow of Paul's argument in Galatians 4:1 – 11. In 4:1 – 3, by means of an analogy of a son who had not yet received his inheritance, Paul argued that before redemption, "we" Jews were enslaved to the *stoicheia* of the world. This statement, of course, was not an attack on either the Law or on Judaism. Rather, Paul was likely pointing to the climax of the Law's curses for disobedience, that is, exile and subjugation to foreign powers and their gods (see esp. Deut 28:36, 64; cf. Gal 3:10 – 14). In Galatians 4:4 – 5, Paul then affirmed that "we" Jews had been redeemed from these curses through Jesus the Messiah. Even more, this deliverance and adoption as children included "you" gentiles (Gal 4:6 – 7). Thus in 4:8 – 11, Paul linked gentile slavery to false gods with the Jewish experience under the Law's curses for disobedience; he was *not* linking Judaism with paganism. With this fresh understanding of Galatians 4:1 – 11, we can observe how Paul maintained that both Jews and gentiles were under the *stoicheia* before the Messiah (see figure).

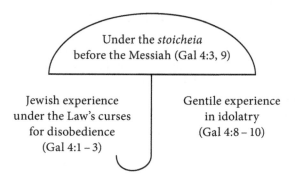

Under the *stoicheia*
before the Messiah (Gal 4:3, 9)

Jewish experience
under the Law's curses
for disobedience
(Gal 4:1 – 3)

Gentile experience
in idolatry
(Gal 4:8 – 10)

If our discussion thus far has been close to the mark, then we can conclude that Paul was neither devaluing circumcision as a practice for Jews nor disparaging the Jewish calendar. We can therefore affirm that Paul's famous declaration "there is neither Jew nor Gentile" (Gal 3:28) was not a clarion call for ethnic collapse. On the contrary, in this verse Paul announced the glorious universal reality that through faith in

---

13. On this understanding of *stoicheia*, see Edward Adams, *Constructing the World: A Study in Paul's Cosmological Language* (Edinburgh: T&T Clark), 230. See also Hardin, *Galatians and the Imperial Cult*, 133 – 34.

the Messiah, there is equality as children of Abraham across ethnic (as well as gender and social) boundaries.

Ephesians 2:14 – 18: One United People in the Messiah

If ethnic distinction is not erased in Galatians 3:28, we must now evaluate Ephesians 2:14 – 18 in order to answer the same question: Does gentile inclusion in the people of God require a dissolution of ethnic identity? Harold Hoehner represents the default position when he states on this passage that "Paul refers to a whole new race that is formed. A new race that is raceless!" and that "they are not Jews or Gentiles but a body of Christians who make up the church."[14] But do these conclusions actually follow from the argument of these verses? To answer this question, we will need first to grasp the context and aims of the broader argument within which 2:14 – 18 is situated.

After explaining in Ephesians 2:1 – 10 how both Jew and gentile have a secure relationship with God through Jesus the Messiah, Paul[15] turned directly to the issue of unity between Jew and gentile (Eph 2:11 – 22). Although it is difficult to determine whether he was addressing a particular pastoral issue in Asia (Ephesus?),[16] one can nevertheless discern that the aim of this section was to illustrate that gentiles had been included along with Israel in the great redeeming work of the one true God.[17] The argument of Ephesians 2:11 – 22 unfolds in three stages, which we can set out below:

1. A command for the (gentile) readers to remember their former life as gentiles in the flesh (Eph 2:11 – 12).
2. A declaration that these gentiles had been brought near to God by the blood of the Messiah, thus creating peace (Eph 2:13 – 18).
3. A conclusion that these gentiles were fellow citizens of the (Jewish) saints, belonged to the household of God, and were being built up together as God's temple (Eph 2:19 – 22).

With this aim and broad outline of the passage in place, we should also note that Paul employed various metaphors of citizenship (Eph 2:11 – 12, 19), of warring parties (Eph 2:14 – 18), and of temple imagery (Eph 2:20 – 22)[18] when explaining how both Jews

---

14. Harold W. Hoehner, *Ephesians: An Exegetical Commentary* (Grand Rapids: Baker Academic, 2002), 279 – 80.

15. For a thorough (and convincing) defence of the Pauline authorship of Ephesians, see Hoehner, *Ephesians*, 2 – 61. We will refer to the author as "Paul" (although of course our conclusion on authorship has no bearing on the interpretation of the passage at hand).

16. See the excellent study on this passage by William S. Campbell, "Unity and Diversity in the Church: Transformed Identities and the Peace of Christ in Ephesians," *Transformation* 25, no. 1 (2008): 21 – 22, who is probably correct to note that the theme of unity is a crucial pastoral issue in this letter. Frank Thielman, *Ephesians* (Grand Rapids: Eerdmans, 2010), 12 – 28, argues that the textual variant "in Ephesus" (1:1) is the original reading and that therefore the letter was written (by Paul) to address a specific pastoral problem in Ephesus.

17. Timothy G. Gombis, "Ephesians 2 as a Narrative of Divine Warfare," *Journal for the Study of the New Testament* 26, no. 4 (2004): 403 – 18, argues convincingly that Eph 2 is linked crucially with the conclusion of Eph 1 in that it explains further how God has set all things under the Messiah's feet (Eph 1:20 – 23): God "announces his victory by proclaiming peace. His people gather to him in unified worship as his temple, which he has founded and is building as a lasting monument to his universal sovereign lordship" (418). What Gombis does not discuss, however, is Paul's view of ethnicity in relation to the Messiah's universal rule.

18. For the temple theme in Ephesians, see Larry J. Kreitzer, "The Messianic Man of Peace as Temple Builder: Solomonic Imagery in Ephesians 2:13 – 22," in *Temple and Worship in Biblical Israel: Proceedings of the Oxford Old Testament Seminar* (ed. John Day; Edinburgh: T&T Clark, 2007), 484 – 512.

and gentiles were unified in the Messiah. Thus, as we come to interpret the text, we must bear in mind how these metaphors were meant to function within Paul's argument.

While the broad scope of Ephesians 2:11 – 22 as set out above is fairly straightforward, the difficulty comes when interpreting the second section of Paul's argument (Eph 2:13 – 18). Before we discuss these verses in detail, however, perhaps it would be best to set out each clause in a sentence flow to highlight the inner logic of this complex argument (see figure).

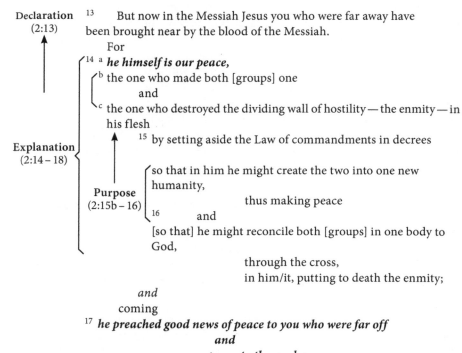

As one can observe in the sentence flow in the figure, in Ephesians 2:13 Paul declared that in the Messiah, God had brought gentiles near to God and to his people (translated "the saints" in some versions of Eph 2:19).[19] In 2:14 – 18, Paul then explained how God had achieved this unity in the Messiah. The section contains two main clauses (see the bold italics in the sentence flow above): (1) the Messiah "is our peace" (Eph 2:14a) and (2) he has "preached good news of peace" to both gentiles and Jews (Eph 2:17).[20] Both clauses highlight the peace gentiles and Jews enjoy in Jesus

19. Thielman, *Ephesians*, 163, correctly points out that 2:14 – 18 was an excursus meant to show how gentiles have been brought near to Jews and to God.

20. Of course, this language of "peace" would have rung bells and whistles for the believers in Asia, who would have been inundated with similar imperial slogans in relation to the peace of the empire.

and serve to frame the entire argument of Ephesians 2:14 – 18. In the two remaining clauses of 2:14, Paul then explained how this peace was achieved: Jesus made "both (i.e., Jew and gentile) one" and "destroyed the dividing wall of hostility."[21] The means by which Jesus had pulled down the dividing wall is then explained in 2:15a with a third participial clause: "by setting aside the Law of commandments in decrees." In Ephesians 2:15b – 16, Paul then provided the twofold purpose for Jesus' demolition work: (a) so that he might create the two into one new humanity (thus making peace) and (b) so that he might reconcile both groups in one body to God.[22]

Now upon first blush, this passage seems to argue decisively that ethnicity has been eradicated in the Messiah. After all, Paul stated quite clearly that "one new humanity" had been created. And yet we must refrain from this understanding of this "oneness" language for at least two reasons. First, we must bear in mind that this language occurs within Paul's metaphor of warring parties, which had come to an armistice through the work of Jesus.[23] As a metaphor, this language of unity thus pointed to a peace in the Messiah where enmity previously existed, where gentiles were formerly "far away" (Eph 2:13, 17). When seen in this way, these statements must be interpreted metaphorically and cannot be interpreted literally to mean that ethnic distinctions have deteriorated.[24]

What is more, we should note that Paul still assumed an ongoing Jewish identity both in the way the broader argument of Ephesians 2:11 – 22 is conducted and how it concludes. In 2:11 – 12, Paul commanded these gentiles to remember that they were formerly excluded from the privileges of being part of God's chosen people of Israel. This same language is then picked up again in the conclusion — namely, that these gentiles were no longer "strangers and aliens" but were included as full members of the household of God and were being built into a holy temple (Eph 2:19 – 22). So as we read 2:14 – 18, we should note that Paul preserved an Israel-centric view of the world, with gentiles being brought into this grand deliverance through the Jewish Messiah.[25] Thus, in 2:18 we should not be surprised to see that Paul still assumed an ongoing distinction between Jew and gentile when he declared that "we both [amphoteroi] have access to the Father by one Spirit," even though he had employed the same term in Ephesians 2:14 to declare that both [amphotera] were made into one. Although it may seem to be a very fine distinction, it is essential to note that "oneness" and "ethnic collapse" are two very different things. Paul clearly declares the former, but not the

21. Campbell, "Unity and Diversity in the Church," 18, along with others, is probably correct to note that the "dividing wall" was metaphorical for the balustrade in the temple that separated the gentiles from the Jews.

22. Note that this peace includes both a horizontal (i.e., between Jew/gentile) and a vertical (i.e., between each group and God) dimension.

23. Tet-Lim N. Yee, *Jew, Gentiles and Ethnic Reconciliation: Paul's Jewish Identity and Ephesians* (Cambridge: Cambridge University Press, 2005), 162, similarly argues that "the notion of 'one new man' can be best understood against the backcloth of ethnic enmity."

24. Campbell, "Unity and Diversity in the Church," 18 – 19, who also points out that this "already" reality contains a "not yet" dimension, hence the command in Eph 4:17 – 24 for the gentiles to put off their old way of walking as gentiles. In this regard, there is clear evidence for gentiles abandoning their former practices in joining the people of God, but no evidence in Ephesians for Jews becoming non-Jews.

25. Of course, this is the language of the prophets as well (e.g., Isa 49:6: "It is too small a thing for you to be my servant to restore the tribes of Jacob and bring back those of Israel I have kept. I will also make you a light for the Gentiles, that my salvation may reach to the ends of the earth").

latter. Indeed, as Campbell notes: "Israelite identity cannot at one and the same time be presented as foundational, and simultaneously undermined, since it is in this direction gentiles are to proceed."[26]

But even if our argument above is convincing, what then are we to make of Paul's affirmation that the dividing wall of hostility was broken down "by setting aside the Law of commandments in decrees" (Eph 2:15a)?[27] Here we will put forth three possible options. First, Paul may have been referring to those laws that were given to the children of Israel in order that they might remain separate from the polytheistic nations around them. Alternatively, perhaps Paul was simply referring to the fact that gentiles were not required to observe the Law (as we saw in Galatians). Third, it may also be possible that Paul was referring specifically to the barrier that separated the court of the Gentiles from the Jews in the Jerusalem temple.[28] In any case, Paul was asserting that in the Messiah, these laws that divided Jews from their gentile neighbors had been set aside. Paul was not maintaining that Torah observance for Jewish Jesus-believers was obsolete; rather, he was declaring how the wall of division between Jew and gentile was eradicated. Thus, Paul was not disparaging the Law in Ephesians 2:15. Rather, his aim was to explain theologically how gentiles had been brought near to God.

In sum, our reading of Ephesians 2:14 – 18 does not support the view that a raceless people has been formed in the Messiah. To be sure, the Jewish Messiah had made everything different: peace had been secured between Jews and gentiles and between each group and God. In particular, gentiles had been brought near as the people of God. But this unity in the Messiah does not simultaneously declare an ethnic collapse. Instead, what is clearly affirmed is a very tangible peace (i.e., equality) between Jew and gentile that has been achieved in Jesus the Messiah. On this aim of reconciliation, Campbell has made the point well:

> The preferred identity which the author seeks to construct is one based on resolution of ethnic enmity by depicting Christ as the peace-maker between those who are alienated from one another due to ethnically significant issues. His solution is not to downplay ethnic awareness or to ignore the hostility usually associated with it, but to seek resolution in that reconciliation and peace with difference, which he presents as the outcome of the Christ-event.[29]

---

26. Campbell, "Unity and Diversity in the Church," 23.

27. Here we must pause to note that some English translations of Eph 2:15 seem to indicate that in the Messiah, the Law was "abolished," thus supporting the view that Paul was pouring scorn on the Mosaic Law (e.g., NIV 1984). But we must resist translating it "by abolishing the Law," and instead use the more neutral term "by setting aside" (NIV 2011). Of course, Paul famously affirmed in Rom 7:12 that the Law was holy, righteous, and good.

28. This view was suggested to me by David Rudolph, who noted (1) that Paul's arrest in Acts 21:27 – 36 was because the gentile Trophimus, *who was from Ephesus,* was thought (wrongly) to have gone beyond this barrier, (2) that Paul employed temple imagery to refer to unity between Jews and Gentiles, and (3) that Paul began Ephesians 3 with "For this reason, as a prisoner of the Messiah Jesus for the sake of you Gentiles," perhaps alluding to his arrest in the temple according to Acts 21.

29. Campbell, "Unity and Diversity in the Church," 24.

Conclusion

In this chapter, we have examined Galatians 3:28 and Ephesians 2:14–18 in order to assess what it means precisely for Jewish and gentile believers to be unified in the Messiah. We have argued that these passages demonstrate full equality between both groups, yet without destroying the ethnic distinctions between them. If this understanding is correct, we can now conclude with two implications of our study.

First, our reading is in agreement with a growing number of scholars who argue that after the Damascus road experience, Paul still lived as a Torah-observant Jew. Of course, there is much more work to be done on this issue, and unfortunately it was beyond the bounds of this essay to discuss other Pauline texts (e.g., 1 Cor 7:17–24; Rom 3:21–31). But at least our conclusions would agree with this understanding of Paul's ongoing Jewish practice according to Acts (Acts 15:1–16:4; 18:18; 21:20–26).

Second, we can suggest that Paul regarded "transformation" to be a necessary obligation for all believers, both for Jews and gentiles, even if this transformation was not to result in stripping away ethnicity.[30] Thus, Paul viewed himself along with other believing Jews as one of the faithful "remnant" (Rom 11:5). On the other hand, gentile believers, who had abandoned their false gods, had been grafted into God's people. As "former gentiles" (see 1 Cor 12:2), they were thus to put off their polytheistic way of living and to put on the new person they had become in the Messiah (Eph 4:17–24). For both groups, the basis of this transformation was found precisely in the equality that had been achieved through the life, death, burial, and resurrection of Jesus the Messiah.

For Further Reading

Bachmann, Michael. *Anti-Judaism in Galatians? Exegetical Studies on a Polemical Letter and on Paul's Theology.* Translated by Robert L. Brawley. Grand Rapids: Eerdmans, 2008.

Campbell, William S. *Paul and the Creation of Christian Identity.* Edinburgh: T&T Clark, 2006.

———. "Unity and Diversity in the Church: Transformed Identities and the Peace of Christ in Ephesians." *Transformation* 25, no. 1 (2008): 15–31.

Eisenbaum, Pamela. "Is Paul the Father of Misogyny and Antisemitism?" *Cross Currents* 50, no. 4 (2000–2001): 506–24. Cited 29 March 2012. Online: http://www.crosscurrents.org/eisenbaum.htm.

Fredriksen, Paula. "Judaizing the Nations: The Ritual Demands of Paul's Gospel." *New Testament Studies* 56 (2010): 232–52.

Gundry-Volf, Judith M. "Beyond Difference? Paul's Vision of a New Humanity in Galatians 3.28." Pages 8–36 in *Gospel and Gender: A Trinitarian Engagement with Being Male and Female in Christ.* Edited by Douglas A. Campbell. London: T&T Clark, 2003.

Hardin, Justin K. *Galatians and the Imperial Cult: A Critical Analysis of the First-Century Social Context of Paul's Letter.* Tübingen: Mohr Siebeck, 2008.

Hodge, Caroline Johnson. *If Sons, Then Heirs: A Study of Kinship and Ethnicity in the Letters of Paul.* Oxford: Oxford University Press, 2007.

---

30. See esp. Campbell, "Unity and Diversity in the Church," 15: "Pauline transformation in Christ does not mean the creation of a new group without ethnic identity but rather the transformation of those who are Greeks into transformed Greeks, and of Judeans into transformed Judeans in Christ."

Hogan, Pauline Nigh. *"No Longer Male and Female": Interpreting Galatians 3.28 in Early Christianity.* London: T&T Clark, 2008.

Kinzer, Mark S. "Yeshua, Israel and the Priestly-Remnant: The Sacramental Vocation of the Messianic Jewish Community." Paper presented at the Roman Catholic – Messianic Jewish Dialogue Group, Rome, Italy, August 2012.

Nanos, Mark D. "Paul and Judaism: Why Not Paul's Judaism?" Pages 117 – 60 in *Paul Unbound: Other Perspectives on the Apostle.* Edited by Mark D. Given. Peabody, Mass.: Hendrickson, 2010.

Rudolph, David J. "Intertextual Issues: Understanding Paul's Jewishness in Relation to Being in Christ." Pages 23 – 89 in *A Jew to the Jews: Jewish Contours of Pauline Flexibility in 1 Corinthians 9:19 – 23.* Tübingen: Mohr Siebeck, 2011.

———. "Paul's 'Rule in All the Churches' (1 Cor 7:17 – 24) and Torah-Defined Ecclesiological Variegation." *Studies in Christian-Jewish Relations* 5, no. 1 (2010): 1 – 24. Online: http://www.mjstudies.com.

Tucker, J. Brian. "The Continuation of Gentile Identity in Ephesians." Paper presented at the annual meeting of the Society of Biblical Literature, Disputed Paulines section, San Francisco, November 2011. Online: http://www.mjstudies.com.

Zetterholm, Magnus. *Approaches to Paul: A Student's Guide to Recent Scholarship.* Minneapolis: Fortress, 2009.

———. "Jews, Christians, and Gentiles: Rethinking the Categorization within the Early Jesus Movement." Pages 242 – 54 in *Reading Paul in Context: Explorations in Identity Formation: Essays in Honour of William S. Campbell.* Edited by Kathy Ehrensperger and J. Brian Tucker. London: T&T Clark, 2010.

CHAPTER 22

The Supersession and Superfluity of the Law? Another Look at Galatians

Todd A. Wilson

The African church father Tertullian (ca. 160–225), often hailed as the Father of Latin theology, is celebrated for his fierce opposition to that arch-heretic of the earliest Christian movement, Marcion (ca. 160), whose central thesis was that the Christian gospel was antithetical to the religious outlook of the Old Testament and thus to a Jewish way of life. Yet despite the vigor of Tertullian's polemic, he did acknowledge one very significant point of agreement with Marcion: "We too claim that the primary epistle against Judaism is that addressed to the Galatians."[1]

Regrettably, Tertullian's essentially Marcionite sentiment about Galatians has not been confined to the early patristic era of the church. Instead, his view has been widely shared; one hears echoes of this from the mouths of leading theologians and scholars down through the centuries of the church and into the modern era. Such a view rests heavily on the conviction that the apostle Paul is at pains in Galatians to persuade his wayward Gentile converts that the law of Moses — that ancient charter of the Jewish people — has now been *superseded with the coming of Christ*. It no longer has a place in redemptive history; its time has passed. But more than that: if the law of Moses has been superseded in God's plan for his covenant people, then when it comes to shaping the behavior of Christ-followers, that same law is of course now *superfluous with the advent of the Spirit*. It is no longer needed and in fact it may not even be useful.

It is this twofold claim with regard to the law of Moses — both its supersession in redemptive history and its superfluity for shaping ethics — that undergirds arguably the vast majority of interpretations of Galatians throughout the history of the church. And it is this particular understanding of Galatians that has given rise over the centuries to the conviction that Galatians is indeed the primary epistle against Judaism.

Obviously, then, anyone interested in a *post-supersessionist* approach to the New Testament, or desirous of creating theological and ecclesial space for Messianic Jewish conviction, will need to deal head-on with this predominant paradigm for reading Galatians. Of course, within the confines of this chapter, I cannot attempt such a full-scale project; nor for that matter am I even able to do justice to the topic of the law in Galatians.

Instead, for the purposes of this volume I will confine myself to a simple sketch of what such a reading of Galatians could be like. It would rest on the following twofold

---

1. Tertullian, *Marc.* 5.2.1.

claim: in Galatians the apostle Paul advocates neither for the supersession of the law with the coming of Christ, nor for its superfluity in shaping the behavior of Christ-followers with the dawning of the Spirit; instead, Paul's chief burden in Galatians is to convince his largely Gentile hearers of the *suspension of the curse of the law* for those who by faith in Messiah Jesus walk by the Spirit and thus fulfill the law of Moses, which by implication still persists into the *post Christum* era.

The Law of Moses Is Not Superseded with the Coming of Christ

The claim that the law of Moses has been superseded with the coming of Christ rests heavily on a particular reading of Galatians 3:23 – 25. This is a key paragraph in Galatians because here we find Paul's first use of the crucial and repeated expression "under the law" (3:23; cf. 4:4 – 5, 4:21; 5:18).[2] Additionally, this phrase appears alongside two similar "under" expressions: "under sin" (3:22, my trans.) and "under a pedagogue" (3:25, my trans.).

In the previous paragraph (Gal 3:19 – 21), Paul denies the possibility that a law was given that could "make alive" (3:21 RSV); and he does so by asserting that Scripture has enclosed all things — indeed the law itself — under sin (3:22). As a prisoner to sin, then, the law was incapable of producing life and therefore unable to provide "righteousness" (3:21; cf. 2:15 – 21; 3:11 – 12).

Therefore, as Paul goes on to say, "we were kept under law, enclosed until faith should be revealed" (3:23, my trans.). Though controversial, this statement likely captures Paul's reflections on *Israel's own experience* with the law under the Sinai covenant (cf. 3:17 – 21).[3] Hence, when Paul says that "we" were kept "under law" by being enclosed "under sin" (3:22 DV), he is probably referring to Israel's inability to escape from *the curse of the law* because of her inability to come out from "under sin" (cf. 3:10 – 12; 4:21 – 27). In other words, sin foiled Israel's best attempts to find liberation from the curse of the law *by means of* the law.

This would then readily explain the metaphor of a pedagogue, which Paul uses to describe Israel's relationship to the law. What does it mean, historically speaking, for Israel to possess the law and yet be imprisoned "under sin" and thus enclosed "under the (curse of the) law" (see 3:22 – 23)? Paul explains by way of a metaphor: "As a result [of being kept under the curse of the law, cf. 3:23], the law became our pedagogue until Christ" (3:24, my trans.). Here Paul employs the metaphor of the pedagogue to describe the peculiar *function* of the law prior to the coming of Christ.

While there has been considerable debate over the precise import of the peda-

---

2. See Todd A. Wilson, "'Under Law' in Galatians: A Pauline Theological Abbreviation," *Journal of Theological Studies* 56, no. 2 (2006): 362 – 92, where I defend the thesis that throughout Galatians Paul uses "under law" as rhetorical shorthand for "under the curse of the law." This present chapter draws heavily on that essay. See also Todd A. Wilson, *The Curse of the Law and the Crisis in Galatia: Reassessing the Purpose of Galatians* (Tübingen: Mohr Siebeck, 2007).

3. Cf. Hans D. Betz, *Galatians: A Commentary on Paul's Letter to the Churches in Galatia* (Philadelphia: Fortress, 1979), 175 – 76; Scott J. Hafemann, "Paul and the Exile of Israel in Galatians 3 – 4," in *Exile: Old Testament, Jewish, and Christian Conceptions* (ed. J. M. Scott; Leiden, Netherlands: Brill, 1997), 329 – 71.

gogue analogy, perhaps Paul's main point is that Israel's confinement under the curse of the law means that the law is not a mediator of the promise, but a mere pedagogue, a household slave whose presence reminds the trustee that he is still a minor and thus unable to have access to his inheritance (cf. 4:1 – 3). Hence, insofar as the law pronounces a curse upon Israel as long as Israel remains "under sin," so the curse of the law serves as a token of Israel's continued estrangement from the inheritance.

In saying this, however, we should note that Paul does not describe the *law itself* as a pedagogue; he only describes the particular historical *function* of the law before the "coming of this faith" (3:23), when the law was itself enclosed "under ... sin" (3:22). Importantly, then, Paul's comparison of the law's function to that of a pedagogue does not necessarily imply that he thought the law itself was of a limited duration. His only point here is that this particular function of the law (i.e., to enclose Israel under a curse) is of a limited duration (i.e., until Christ). The perpetuity of the law *after* the coming of faith is not the point at issue here.

Paul's brief digression in 3:21 – 25 serves, then, not unlike Romans 7:7 – 25, to ward off a possible charge against the law. Given what Paul has said thus far in chapter 3, one might conceivably conclude that the law somehow opposes the promises (3:21). For Paul has denied that the law in any way mediates the *blessing* of Abraham (3:6 – 14), but instead has only brought about the *curse* (3:10 – 14). This grim reading of the law's function is further exacerbated by Paul's intervening claim that the law was secondary to the promises (3:15 – 18) and added only "because of transgressions" (3:19), and that by a "mediator" (3:20). Regardless of the implications one draws from these seemingly disparaging remarks, the question of 3:21 is surely to the point: Is the law against the promises?

Paul's answer to this query, though, is surprisingly straightforward. The law is not ultimately culpable for the curse — sin is. Sin blocks the reception of the promises by interposing, not the law, but the *curse* of the law. This again explains why Paul compares being "under law" (i.e., under the curse of the law) to being "under a pedagogue" (Gal 3:24 – 25 DV). In the Greco-Roman milieu, not only was a pedagogue's role over the life of a child temporary; the very presence of a pedagogue was indicative of the child's *inability to access his inheritance*. Not insignificantly, this latter nuance is precisely the one Paul develops both in 3:23 – 29 (cf. 3:29) and 4:1 – 7 (cf. 4:7).

One of the underlying themes of Galatians 3:10 – 4:7, then, is that while Israel was "under the law" (3:23), Israel was unable to gain access to the promise of the inheritance. As such, Israel was, at least with respect to the inheritance, hardly any different from the nations, despite being rightfully entitled to that inheritance (4:1 – 2). Speaking metaphorically, Israel was "under a pedagogue" during her protracted childhood (3:24 – 25 DV; 4:1 – 2). Alternatively, one could say that for Israel the law, because of its curse, became for a time a pedagogue, which precluded Israel from gaining access to the inheritance. In short, until Christ came to redeem Israel from the curse of the law (3:13; 4:4 – 5), Israel was kept "under the law" — under the law's curse. But now that Christ has come, it is not that the *law itself* has been superseded, but that the *law's curse* has now been suspended for those with faith in Messiah Jesus.

The Law of Moses Is Not Superfluous
with the Dawning of the Spirit

Intriguingly, Paul's fifth and final use of the expression "under law" in Galatians is found in the so-called ethical section of the letter (5:13 – 6:10), "If you are led by the Spirit, you are not under the law" (5:18). In this verse, Paul describes the leading of the Spirit in terms of its consequences for the law; but what does Paul mean when he says that if the Galatians are led by the Spirit, they are not "under the law"? This phrase has been understood to refer to:

1. The "legalistic" system associated with the law.[4]
2. The condemnation or curse of the law.[5]
3. The guiding, restraining influence of the law.[6]

Recently, most scholars have shied away from views (1) and (2), since they are thought to fall foul of Paul's description of Christ as "under the law" (4:4). Many thus opt for view (3), which is not only free of this particular difficulty, but can also make sense of Paul's other four uses of the phrase. On this reading, the point of 5:18 is that for those who are in possession of the Spirit, there is no need for the guiding, restraining influence of the law. Hence, in 5:18 Paul is assuring the Galatians about the *superfluity of the law* for ethical living. According to John Barclay, "This amounts to saying that the Spirit will provide both moral safeguards and moral directives which render the law superfluous."[7]

This particular interpretation of 5:18 serves as an important piece of exegetical support for those who think that one of Paul's major aims in 5:13 – 6:10 is to provide the Galatians with assurances of the sufficiency of the Spirit for Christian living, especially vis-à-vis the threat of the reinstatement of the law for this very purpose. Having demonstrated that the law is superseded with the coming of Christ, Paul now turns his attention to convincing the Galatians that the law is likewise superfluous in light of the advent of the Spirit.

However, doubts about the adequacy of this reading begin to set in upon a closer examination of Paul's actual wording in 5:18. One of the more obvious features of this reading, and perhaps its greatest weakness, is that it depends upon softening the logical link between 5:18a and 5:18b, the protasis and apodosis of Paul's conditional statement.[8] This move was intimated in the previous citation from Barclay, but it finds perhaps its most telling and succinct expression in H. D. Betz's paraphrase of the verse from his highly influential Galatians commentary: "If they are driven by the Spirit,

---

4. Cf. Ernest D. W. Burton, *A Critical and Exegetical Commentary on the Epistle to the Galatians* (Edinburgh: T&T Clark, 1921), 302 – 3; R. A. Cole, *The Letter of Paul to the Galatians* (Grand Rapids: Eerdmans, 1989), 209.

5. Cf. Herman N. Ridderbos, *The Epistle of Paul to the Churches of Galatia* (Grand Rapids: Eerdmans, 1953), 204 – 5; In-Gyu Hong, *The Law in Galatians* (Sheffield, UK: Sheffield Academic Press, 1993), 175.

6. Cf. Betz, *Galatians*, 281; John M. G. Barclay, *Obeying the Truth: A Study of Paul's Ethics in Galatians* (Edinburgh: T&T Clark, 1988), 116; J. Louis Martyn, *Galatians: A New Translation with Introduction and Commentary* (New York: Doubleday, 1997), 496; Richard N. Longenecker, *Galatians* (Waco, Tex.: Word, 1990), 246; James D. G. Dunn, *The Epistle to the Galatians* (Peabody, Mass.: Hendrickson, 1993), 301.

7. Barclay, *Obeying the Truth*, 143; cf. 116: "They do not need the law to marshal their behaviour: in the Spirit-led battle against the flesh they have all the direction they need."

8. Similarly noted by Michael Winger, "The Law of Christ," *New Testament Studies* 46 (2000): 537 – 46, esp. 542.

they *do not need to be* under the Torah."[9] Thus, rather than assuring the Galatians that if they are led by the Spirit, they *are not* under law, instead this verse becomes an assertion about the superfluity or irrelevance of the law for those who are led by the Spirit: they do not *need to be* under the law.

Yet this reading fails to do justice to the syntax of Paul's statement and the contours of his thought. Surely the logical connection between the protasis and apodosis of 5:18 requires that one see an essential *incompatibility* between being led by the Spirit (5:18a) and being "under law" (5:18b). Moreover, at numerous points in Galatians, the thrust of Paul's argument appears in one way or another to make this precise point: life lived in Christ, by the Spirit, is incompatible with existence "under the law" (3:23 – 29; 4:1 – 11, 21 – 31; 5:1 – 6).[10] These are two mutually exclusive alternatives. Furthermore, softening the logical link between 5:18a and 5:18b lessens the rhetorical force of the statement. What was likely intended to be a ringing affirmation of the Spirit's ability to release one from being under law (cf. 5:16) comes out sounding, at least practically speaking, more like a piece of encouraging advice to dispense with the need for law observance. Yet this construal is necessary for the viability of the reading proposed by the majority of Galatians commentators, who must assume the mutual *compatibility* of the leading of the Spirit and existence "under law"; otherwise the point of Paul's statement would be altogether lost. For this reading to succeed, then, one must downplay both the implicit logic and the rhetorical force of 5:18.

But if 5:18 is not about the superfluity of the law for ethics, what is it about? Interpreters rightly suppose that the use of "under law" in 5:18 should correspond, if at all possible, with Paul's other uses of the phrase in Galatians. As I have argued elsewhere and suggested above, there is good reason to think that in Galatians "under the law" serves as shorthand for "under the curse of the law." In addition, it is likely that Paul uses this expression as a way of alluding back to and thus invoking the curse of the law as discussed in 3:10 – 14. On this reading, then, Paul's statement in 5:18 would be rendered as follows: "If you are led by the Spirit, you are not under the *curse* of the law."

Paul would appear, then, to want to assure the Galatians that the leading of the Spirit (5:18a) and love, as the chief mark of the Spirit (5:22), are sufficient to enable one to avoid falling under a curse (5:18b, 23b). The Galatians, in other words, need not fear the curse of the law — as long as they follow the leading of the Spirit. Conversely, if the Galatians continue to succumb to the desires of the flesh (5:16) and its works (5:19 – 21), something to which they appear to be yielding at present (cf. 5:15, 19 – 21, 26), they will assuredly face the ultimate consequence: exclusion from the "kingdom of God" (5:21b), eschatological "destruction" (6:7 – 8). The implication of all of this would appear to be, perhaps somewhat surprisingly, that *in order for the Galatians to obtain their eschatological inheritance, they must avoid the curse of the law.*

---

9. Betz, *Galatians*, 281 (emphasis added).

10. This raises the difficult question of how Christ, who presumably for Paul was "led by the Spirit" (5:18a), could nevertheless come "under the law" (5:18b; 4:4). If one treats Paul's statement in 4:4 about Christ coming "under the law" as a reference back to 3:13 and thus as an allusion to his *crucifixion*, this problem becomes somewhat less acute. With his representative death on the cross, Christ embraced, among other things, the curse of the law that rested upon the Jews — precisely the point he makes in 3:13: "Christ redeemed us from the curse of the law by becoming a curse for us."

The Law of Christ Is the Law of Moses
for Jews and Gentiles

Paul can thus call for the fulfillment of the law within the ethical section of Galatians since the law itself is an expression of God's will for his people and centers upon the love of one's neighbor (5:14; Lev 19:18). As a result, Paul's statement in 5:18 that believers are not under law should be taken to refer to a particular function of the law — not the law *per se*. Similarly, Paul's comment in 5:23 (often translated: "Against such things there is no law") implies that the "fruit of the Spirit" actually meets the requirement of the law.[11] Furthermore, the "law of Christ" in 6:2 is likewise to be taken as a reference either to that aspect of the law of Moses that persists into the new era of salvation or, as I would argue, the law of Moses itself as it was exemplified in the life and teaching of the Messiah and is now fulfilled through the bearing of one another's burdens.[12]

That some aspect of the law of Moses persists into the new era of salvation has been a prominent line of interpretation among patristic and Reformed exegetes, who in one way or another are happy to affirm what in Reformation nomenclature came to be referred to as the "third use" of the law.[13] Augustine was little troubled by Paul's continued references to the law in 5:13 – 6:10, since the law contained both "sacramental works" and "works having to do with good morals," the latter of which, when properly understood, continued to be obligatory for believers.[14] Calvin makes similar sorts of distinctions in order to uphold the moral obligation of the law for the life of the Christian.[15]

A variation of this basic approach can be found among some scholars known as supporters of the New Perspective on Paul. J. D. G. Dunn, for example, insists that Paul's criticisms of the law are carefully targeted, not wholesale, and should not be taken to imply a complete disavowal of the law for the Christian.[16] What has changed is the law's function within the new era of salvation-history: "With the transition to a new epoch, the law's role as guardian of Israel's distinctiveness was at an end. The obligation to walk in a way appropriate to the relationship given by God remained."[17]

---

11. Ridderbos, *Galatians*, 208: "The reference presumably is to the curse, the spoliation, which the law brings upon the disobedient (cf. 3:10, 13). Hence the law is not *against* those who walk by the Spirit because in principle they are fulfilling the law (verse 14). In this again it is evident that the requirement and the strength of the law continue."

12. See further Todd A. Wilson, "The Law of Christ and the Law of Moses: Reflections on a Recent Trend in Interpretation," *Currents in Biblical Research* 5, no. 1 (2006): 129 – 50.

13. Cf. Gerhard Ebeling, "On the Doctrine of the *Triplex Usus Legis* in the Theology of the Reformation," in *Word and Faith* (London: SCM, 1963), 62 – 78.

14. Eric Plumer, *Augustine's Commentary on Galatians: Introduction, Translation (with Facing Latin Text), and Notes* (Oxford: Oxford University Press, 2003), sections 43 – 44 (on 5.13 – 14).

15. John Calvin, *Commentaries on the Epistles of Paul to the Galatians and Ephesians* (trans. W. Pringle; Grand Rapids: Eerdmans, 1993), 164 (on 5:18). While the believer's conscience is not bound by the law for salvation, this does not, Calvin insists, render the law entirely superfluous for Christian living; see esp. Calvin, *Institutes of the Christian Religion* (trans. F. L. Battles; London: SCM, 1960), 3.19.2.

16. James D. G. Dunn, *The Theology of Paul the Apostle* (Grand Rapids: Eerdmans, 1998), 632; cf. E. P. Sanders, *Paul, the Law and the Jewish People* (Philadelphia: Fortress, 1983), 93 – 122.

17. James D. G. Dunn, *The Theology of Paul's Letter to the Galatians* (Cambridge: Cambridge University Press, 1993), 116.

Another variation of this same approach is to argue that Paul, in keeping with many of the other earliest Jewish followers of Jesus, believed that the law was obligatory for Jews and Gentiles in different ways: that is, for Jews *as Jews* and for Gentiles *as Gentiles*.[18] The Jewish theologian Michael Wyschogrod explains this approach:

> Over the centuries, Christian debate about the law has revolved around the before-Jesus and after-Jesus axis. The idea was that the law was in full effect before the coming of Jesus, but that with his coming, large parts of it were suspended. The problem then was which parts were declared inoperative and which not. This question was never answered with the requisite clarity, though not a few Christian authors have tried. There is yet another way of looking at the problem which may be more productive for Jewish-Christian relations. Jews have long believed that the full Mosaic law was binding only on Jews. Non-Jews were duty-bound to obey the Noachide commandments, and if they did so, God was fully pleased.[19]

According to Wyschogrod, the Noachide commandments constitute for Paul, and for much of the early church (cf. Acts 15), the law for Gentiles.[20] While Jews are under obligation to observe, in Paul's terms, the "whole law" (5:3) — that is, to live as Jews — Gentiles are to conform to the basic moral standards of the law, which includes avoiding things such as incest, murder, and robbery. Thus, when Paul refers to Gentiles fulfilling the law, he has in mind the law *as it applies to Gentiles* (cf. 1 Cor 7:19).[21] And when he warns the Galatians that the "works of the flesh" exclude one from the "kingdom of God" (Gal 5:19–21 DV), he identifies behavior that overlaps considerably with those "cardinal" sins proscribed by the law, which Jews, generally speaking, believed even Gentiles were to observe.[22]

On the question of Paul's rationale for continuing to refer to the law in 5:13–6:10,

---

18. See Michael Wyschogrod, "A Jewish Postscript," in *Encountering Jesus: A Debate on Christology* (ed. Stephen T. Davis; Atlanta: Westminster John Knox, 1988), 185–87; Michael Wyschogrod, "Christianity and Mosaic Law," *Pro Ecclesia* 2, no. 4 (1993): 451–59; Michael Wyschogrod, *Abraham's Promise: Judaism and Jewish-Christian Relations* (ed. R. Kendall Soulen; Grand Rapids: Eerdmans, 2004), 160–64, 188–201; Peter J. Tomson, *Paul and the Jewish Law: Halakha in the Letters of the Apostle to the Gentiles* (Minneapolis: Fortress, 1990); Peter J. Tomson, "Paul's Jewish Background in View of His Law Teaching in 1 Cor 7," in *Paul and the Mosaic Law* (ed. James D. G. Dunn; Tübingen: Mohr Siebeck, 1996), 251–70 (cf. 268); Peter J. Tomson, *"If This Be from Heaven ...": Jesus and the New Testament Authors in Their Relationship to Judaism* (Sheffield, UK: Sheffield Academic Press, 2001), esp. 179–90; Markus Bockmuehl, *Jewish Law in Gentile Churches: Halakhah and the Beginning of Christian Public Ethics* (Edinburgh: T&T Clark, 2000), 145–73; Richard Bauckham, *James: Wisdom of James, Disciple of Jesus the Sage* (New York: Routledge, 1999), 148–51; Alan F. Segal, *Paul the Convert: The Apostolate and Apostasy of Saul the Pharisee* (New Haven: Yale University Press, 1990), 187–223; Alan F. Segal, "Universalism in Judaism and Christianity," in *Paul in His Hellenistic Context* (ed. Troels Engberg-Pedersen; Edinburgh: T&T Clark, 1994), 1–29.

19. Wyschogrod, *Abraham's Promise*, 162.

20. It is, of course, somewhat anachronistic to speak of Noachide commandments during the New Testament period, since the earliest explicit formulation of the doctrine comes not until the second century CE. While there are important precursors to this later rabbinic formulation (cf. esp. *Jub.* 7.20–21), probably the most that can be said for Paul is that something like a prerabbinic equivalent of the Noachide commandments may have informed his "halakhic" approach to Gentiles. Cf. Bockmuehl, *Jewish Law in Gentile Churches*, 145–73; see also Huub van de Sandt and David Flusser, *The Didache: Its Jewish Sources and Its Place in Early Judaism and Christianity* (Minneapolis: Fortress, 2002), 238–70 (esp. 265–69).

21. Tomson, *Paul and the Jewish Law*, 175–78.

22. On 5:19–21, see Bockmuehl, *Jewish Law in Gentile Churches*, 168. Jerome H. Neyrey, "Bewitched in Galatia: Paul and Cultural Anthropology," *Catholic Biblical Quarterly* 50 (1988): 72–100, comments in passing that the "works of the flesh" are infractions of "basically the Ten Commandments" (88).

then, each of these approaches comes out looking somewhat similar. While scholars within the Reformed tradition tend to utilize the distinction between various aspects of the law, some of which are now obsolete,[23] those who identify with the New Perspective on Paul tend to mark different priorities within the law, some of which now take precedence over others.[24] The third approach mentioned above — and the one that I believe has the most promise of providing a way forward in debates about Paul and the law — takes a slightly different tack by distinguishing between different aspects of the law along the Jew-Gentile axis; thus, Paul's positive affirmations of the law in 5:14 and 6:2 (and perhaps 5:23) refer to the law as, in some sense, an abiding standard of behavior, while Paul's negative comments in 5:18 and elsewhere should be taken to refer to a particular feature or function of the law (i.e., its curse) that has now been suspended with the coming of Christ.

Conclusion

While it has not been my intention to provide a comprehensive analysis of the law in Galatians, we have discovered that Paul emphasizes in Galatians not so much *the supersession or superfluity of the law with the coming of Christ and the advent of the Spirit*, but *the suspension of the law's curse*. This rests on our exegesis of Galatians 3:23 – 25, where the chronological nature of Paul's argument, which is often assumed to entail the idea of supersession, actually revolves around the cessation of the law's curse for those who participate in redemption in Christ (3:25; cf. 3:13 – 14; 4:4 – 5). Although Paul strongly opposes the circumcision of his Gentile converts (5:1 – 4), it should nonetheless be clear that the thrust of his polemic in Galatians centers upon the law's inability to mediate righteousness (2:15 – 21; 3:21; 5:5 – 6) and its power to curse (1:8 – 9; 3:10, 13), rather than upon it being outmoded or irrelevant now that Christ and the Spirit have come.

This reading of Galatians has, of course, potentially far-reaching implications for how Galatians contributes to discussions about Christian supersessionism, the idea that the church has displaced the Jews as the elect people of God.[25] *For the superfluity of the law is closely related to supersessionist eschatology*. Telling, for example, is F. F. Bruce's interpretative paraphrase of 5:18, "With the coming of Christ and the completion of his redeeming work, the age of the law has been superseded by the age of the Spirit."[26] H. D. Betz is also particularly clear on this point: "If the validity of the Jewish

---

23. Frank Thielman, "The Coherence of Paul's View of the Law: The Evidence of First Corinthians," *New Testament Studies* 38 (1992): 235 – 53, esp. 252: "Paul could distinguish between aspects of the law which were obsolete and aspects of continuing validity."

24. Dunn, *Paul and the Mosaic Law*, 656: "Where the requirements of the law were being interpreted in a way which ran counter to the basic principle of the love command, Paul thought that the requirements could and should be dispensed with."

25. Bruce D. Marshall, "Christ and the Cultures: The Jewish People and Christian Theology," in *Cambridge Companion to Christian Doctrine* (ed. Colin E. Gunton; New York: Cambridge University Press, 1997), 81 – 100, esp. 82.

26. F. F. Bruce, "The Spirit in the Letter to the Galatians," in *Essays on Apostolic Themes: Studies in Honor of Howard M. Ervin Presented to Him by Colleagues and Friends on His Sixty-Fifth Birthday* (ed. P. Elbert; Peabody, Mass.: Hendrickson, 1985), 36 – 48, esp. 44.

Torah ends for the Jew when he becomes a Christian, there is no point or basis for Gentiles *as well as for Jews* to adhere to the Jewish religion."[27]

In other words, the superfluity of the law is a corollary of the supersession of the Jews within God's redemptive purposes. What is more, some advocates of the New Perspective have only reinforced this basic assumption by reading the argument of Galatians 5:13 – 6:10 (and often the rest of the letter) in the following terms: this is what Paul finds wrong with the law of Moses: it is not the Spirit. In other words, the law is not a problem *per se*; it is simply superseded by the dawning of the Spirit.[28]

However, I have argued that Paul's aim in Galatians is not to demonstrate the supersession or the superfluity of the law, but the suspension of its curse. Yet we are admittedly still left with the perennial question of what — *specifically and concretely* — is the role of the law of Moses within the life of Paul's mixed congregations. This is still an unresolved issue in Pauline scholarship, as Stephen Westerholm observes, "Exegetes cannot agree whether or not Paul thought Christians are subject to the law."[29]

Of course, given the aims of this present volume and the limitations of this chapter, I have not tried to engage directly in resolving this difficult issue. In fact, I have intentionally tried to present the argument of this chapter in a way that does not wed my conclusions to a particular solution to this age-old problem. However, that does not negate the fact that what is still needed — and what this present volume seeks to provide in part — is a synthetic, constructive, and exegetically rigorous approach to the question of the place and function of the *law of Moses* in Paul's mixed congregations, a reading that takes seriously his negative polemic against the law and yet does not assume its supersession or superfluity.

For Further Reading

Fredriksen, Paula. "Judaism, the Circumcision of Gentiles, and Apocalyptic Hope: Another Look at Galatians 1 and 2." *Journal of Theological Studies* 42 (1991): 532 – 64.

Howard, George. *Paul: Crisis in Galatia: A Study in Early Christian Theology.* Cambridge: Cambridge University Press, 1979.

Le Cornu, Hilary, with Joseph Shulam. *A Commentary on the Jewish Roots of Galatians.* Jerusalem: Academon, 2005.

Nanos, Mark D. "Galatians." Pages 455 – 74 in *Blackwell's Companion to the New Testament.* Edited by David Aune. Oxford: Blackwell, 2010.

———. *The Galatians Debate: Contemporary Issues in Rhetorical and Historical Interpretation.* Edited by Mark D. Nanos. Peabody, Mass.: Hendrickson, 2002.

———. "Intruding 'Spies' and 'Pseudobrethren': The Jewish Intra-Group Politics of Paul's Jerusalem Meeting (Gal 2:1 – 10)." Pages 59 – 97 in *Paul and His Opponents.* Edited by Stanley E. Porter. Leiden, Netherlands: Brill, 2005.

———. *The Irony of Galatians: Paul's Letter in First-Century Context.* Minneapolis: Fortress, 2002.

Willitts, Joel. "Context Matters: Paul's Use

---

27. Betz, *Galatians,* 179 (emphasis added). Cf. Betz, *Galatians,* 251: "According to Galatians, Judaism is excluded from salvation altogether, so that the Galatians have to choose between Paul and Judaism."

28. I take this to be a fair characterization of the argument in Barclay, *Obeying the Truth.*

29. Stephen Westerholm, *Israel's Law and the Church's Faith: Paul and His Recent Interpreters* (Grand Rapids: Eerdmans, 1988), 198.

of Leviticus 18:5 in Galatians 3:12." *Tyndale Bulletin* 54, no. 2 (2003): 105 – 22. Cited 15 April 2012. Online: http://www.tyndalehouse.com/tynbul/library/TynBull_2003_54_2_08_Willitts_Gal3_LeviticusContext.pdf.

———. "Isa 54,1 in Gal 4,24b – 27: Reading Genesis in Light of Isaiah." *Zeitschrift für die Neutestamentliche Wissenschaft und die Kunde der älteren Kirche* 96, no. 3 – 4 (2005): 188 – 210.

Wilson, Todd A. *The Curse of the Law and the Crisis in Galatia: Reassessing the Purpose of Galatians*. Tübingen: Mohr Siebeck, 2007.

———. "The Law of Christ and the Law of Moses: Reflections on a Recent Trend in Interpretation." *Currents in Biblical Research* 5, no. 1 (2006): 129 – 50.

———. " 'Under Law' in Galatians: A Pauline Theological Abbreviation." *Journal of Theological Studies* 56, no. 2 (2005): 362 – 92.

Zetterholm, Magnus. "A Covenant for Gentiles? Covenantal Nomism and the Incident at Antioch." Pages 168 – 88 in *The Ancient Synagogue from Its Origins until 200 C.E.* Edited by Birger Olsson and Magnus Zetterholm. Stockholm: Almqvist & Wiksell International, 2003.

———. *The Formation of Christianity in Antioch: A Social-Scientific Approach to the Separation between Judaism and Christianity*. London: Routledge, 2003.

———. "Purity and Anger: Gentiles and Idolatry in Antioch." *Interdisciplinary Journal of Research on Religion* 1 (2005): 1 – 24.

CHAPTER 23

The Bride of Messiah and the Israel-ness of the New Heavens and New Earth

Joel Willitts

The fact that experienced readers of the New Testament come away with diametrically opposed interpretations of the same text is today perhaps one of the few universally recognized results of modern historical critical scholarship. I do believe that the meaning of a text resides in what an author intended to communicate, which is now encoded in the written text.[1] The trouble is: the words, phrases, propositions, and arguments in the New Testament are often subject to a variety of valid interpretations. While there may be a number of factors that contribute to this, we are beginning to appreciate more than ever that the differences are often due in large measure to the presuppositions with which readers read. These presuppositions are often the most determinative factor in an interpretation.[2]

One section of the New Testament that has perennially been subject to vastly different, and yet legitimate, interpretations is the last four chapters of the New Testament, Revelation 19–22. This passage and its "bride" imagery is the focus of this essay. My purpose, however, is not to argue for the only valid interpretation of the image of the bride. Rather I intend to present a *fresh* interpretation by approaching it from a different frame of reference.[3]

My approach is to read Revelation in general, and chapters 19–22 in particular, from a first-century *Jewish perspective*.[4] Within this broad framework, I assume that (1) the book of Revelation is a first-century Jewish document, (2) written by a Jesus-believing Jewish author for (3) a primarily, although not exclusively, Jesus-believing Jewish Diaspora audience. This is not to minimize the ethnic diversity that existed within the assemblies of Jesus in Asia Minor, but to recognize their *principal* Jewish social location. This approach is not, however, simply an arbitrary

---

1. For a defense of this position, see Kevin J. Vanhoozer, *Is There a Meaning in This Text? The Bible, the Reader, and the Morality of Literary Knowledge* (Grand Rapids: Zondervan, 1998).

2. This is nowhere more evident than with readings of Paul. One can, for example, find interpreters who think that Paul abandoned his Jewish identity after his encounter with the resurrected Jesus on the road to Damascus, while also finding others who claim that Paul remained firmly within the bounds of first-century Judaism. For a recent study of this topic, see Magnus Zetterholm, *Approaches to Paul: A Student's Guide to Recent Scholarship* (Minneapolis: Fortress, 2009).

3. For a discussion of the difficulties involved in interpreting Revelation, see the introduction by David Rhoads in *From Every People and Nation: The Book of Revelation in Intercultural Perspective* (ed. David Rhoads; Minneapolis: Fortress, 2005), 9–17.

4. For an excellent introduction to the book of Revelation, see David A. deSilva, *Seeing Things John's Way: The Rhetoric of the Book of Revelation* (Louisville: Westminster John Knox, 2009).

"shot in the dark"; rather it is a reasonable starting point for the study of Revelation because, for much of its first half-century of existence, the early Church in Asia Minor lived and thrived within the social space of the Jewish Diaspora. All three of the stated assumptions, not to mention the general framework, are of course subject to rigorous debate. Nevertheless, here, I am taking them as the starting point for understanding the image of the bride of Messiah.

This concrete Jewish approach is not that original, although one will be hard-pressed to find it in any commentaries on Revelation written by Gentile Christians, whether past or present. For the church fathers (e.g., Origen), such an approach would be deemed too "carnal." Almost three decades ago Albert Geyser published an article on Revelation in which he read the imagery of the twelve tribes within a similar set of Jewish assumptions that I am using.[5] Geyser makes the significant observation that such a concrete Jewish message would have been lost on Gentile ears,[6] and regarded as repugnant. Even today, unawareness of the Jewish context of Revelation is one of the primary reasons that an approach like the one taken here will appear strange to many readers.[7]

Yet, if, upon reflection, the concrete Jewish approach I am taking is deemed a more historically accurate scenario for the original setting of Revelation, then the interpretation offered might begin to reclaim the message of Revelation as it was heard and appropriated in its Jewish first-century social location. This, I hope, will be the contribution of this chapter.

It is fair to say that among the various approaches to the book of Revelation, the consensus view is that *in the new heavens and new earth, ethnic Israel's distinctive function in God's administration of creation is terminated.* While with amillennialism Israel's role is superseded by the church, in most scenarios of premillennialism Israel's function is superseded by the eternal state. Israel's distinctive political purposes come to their completion and are supplanted.[8]

---

5. See Albert Geyser, "The Twelve Tribes in Revelation: Judean and Judeo Christian Apocalypticism," *New Testament Studies* 28 (1982): 389. I am in general agreement with his view that "the book's predominant concern is with the restoration of the twelve tribes of Israel, their restoration as a twelve-tribe kingdom, in a renewed and purified city of David, under the rule of the victorious 'Lion of the Tribe of Judah, the Root of David' (5.5; 22.16)." See also Poul F. Guttesen, *Leaning into the Future: The Kingdom of God in the Theology of Jürgen Moltmann* (Eugene, Oreg.: Pickwick, 2009). Guttesen argues that the occasion for writing Revelation had much to do with the absence of "any geopolitical manifestation of the divine rule on earth" (112). The answer John offers his first-century readers is a vision of the future when "God and his Christ will assume the position of geopolitical authority that is now in the hands of the beastly order" (122).

6. "The belief in a future restoration of the twelve tribe Kingdom of David could have had very little attraction for Gentile believers" (Geyser, "Twelve Tribes in Revelation," 390–91).

7. For recent attempts to read Revelation through Jewish eyes, albeit with differing assumptions and results, see Daniel F. Stramara, *God's Timetable: The Book of Revelation and the Feast of Seven Weeks* (Eugene, Oreg.: Pickwick, 2011); David Frankfurter, "Jews or Not? Reconstructing the 'Other' in Rev 2:9 and 3:9," *Harvard Theological Review* 94 (2001): 403–25; John W. Marshall, *Parables of War: Reading John's Jewish Apocalypse* (Waterloo, Ontario: Wilfrid Laurier University Press, 2001). As an example, Marshall makes a distinction between reading Revelation *from* a Jewish matrix and reading it *within* one: "Scholars are quick to say that the Apocalypse proceeds *from* a Jewish matrix; I argue that it moves *within* a Jewish matrix. The difference is full of meaning," and "what I have pictured here is … an author and a community deeply invested in one of the Judaisms of its time" (69, 192). A significant difference between my interpretation of Revelation and Marshall's is that he maintains a "two-covenants" view, i.e., that there are two separate ways to salvation, one for Jews (through the Mosaic covenant) and one for Gentiles (through Jesus Christ).

8. It interesting to note that most Messianic Jewish theologies of Israel's future are largely dependent on Gentile Christian eschatological schemes. See Richard Harvey, *Mapping Messianic Jewish Theology: A Constructive Approach* (Milton Keynes, UK: Paternoster, 2009), 223–61.

By contrast, in the concrete Jewish approach to Revelation, the last four chapters present the end of the story of God's redemption of creation with an abiding *Israel-centric vision of an earthly city of David*; in this way, the eschaton is in the shape of a Davidic city.

As it turns out, Israel's historically distinctive function *continues eternally*. In the eternal state, Israel's history and Israel's kingdom *encompass* the history and kingdoms of the new world. At the end, the picture is not simply a return to Eden as many assume, but the coming of an Edenic and Davidic city — a political capital city where the throne of God *and* Messiah, the Lamb, resides.

From this perspective, Israel's uniqueness in God's administration of his creation appears *never* to be superseded. Instead, in fulfillment of Old Testament prophecy and in line with Second Temple Jewish tradition, the kingdom of Israel, with the New Jerusalem at its center, is the locus of God's glory and the infrastructure of God's eternal kingdom on earth.

In this brief chapter, I will address just one of the several images in the scene painted by John in Revelation 19 – 22 that point in this direction, namely "the bride, the wife of the Lamb" (Rev 21:9).[9]

The Bride of Messiah

John uses the image of a bride first in Revelation 19:6 – 9 and then again in 21:1 – 3, 9 – 10, where it is the headline image for the section introducing the New Jerusalem and the new heavens and new earth. It appears once more in 22:17.

Revelation 19:6 – 9

⁶ Then I heard what sounded like a great multitude, like the roar of rushing waters and like loud peals of thunder, shouting:

"Hallelujah!
 For our Lord God Almighty reigns.
⁷ Let us rejoice and be glad
 and give him glory!
For the wedding of the Lamb has come,
 and *his bride* has made herself ready.
⁸ Fine linen, bright and clean,
 was given her to wear."

(Fine linen stands for the righteous acts of God's holy people.)
⁹ Then the angel said to me, "Write this: Blessed are *those who are invited to the wedding supper of the Lamb!*" And he added, "These are the true words of God."

Revelation 21:1 – 3, 9 – 10

¹ Then I saw "a new heaven and a new earth," for the first heaven and the first earth had passed away, and there was no longer any sea. ² I saw *the Holy City, the new Jerusalem,* coming down out of heaven from God, *prepared as a bride* beautifully

---

9. Other images that also point in a similar direction are: (1) "holy city, the New Jerusalem" (Rev 21:2), (2) "the twelve tribes" and "the twelve apostles" (21:12, 14), and (3) "the nations" and "the kings of the earth" (21:24).

dressed for her husband. [3] And I heard a loud voice from the throne saying, "Look! God's dwelling place is now among the people, and he will dwell with them. They will be his people, and God himself will be with them and be their God."

[9] One of the seven angels who had the seven bowls full of the seven last plagues came and said to me, "Come, I will show you *the bride, the wife of the Lamb*." [10] And he ... showed me the *Holy City, Jerusalem*, coming down out of heaven from God.

Revelation 22:17
The Spirit and the *bride* say, "Come!"[10]

John, rather abruptly it seems, introduces into his vision in Revelation 19 a bridal image with a reference to the "the wedding of the Lamb." Within the first eighteen chapters, John has nowhere hinted at such an event. Nevertheless, this initial reference sets in motion a wedding drama, which unfolds through chapters 19, 21, and 22.

In Revelation 19:6 – 9, the hearers are told that the Lamb's "bride" has made herself ready (19:7), although John is quick to qualify that the preparation itself is in fact a *gift* (19:8a). These are not preparations she herself has earned or acquired; these are divine gifts. The image begins to stretch like a carnival mirror when John tells listeners that the bride is clothed not with garments but with *deeds*: "the righteous deeds of the saints" (19:8b ESV). In chapter 19 as well, John mentions a group of invited guests to the wedding reception. This detail is couched in a beatitude, "Blessed are those who are invited to the marriage supper of the Lamb" (19:9 ESV).

Skipping over chapter 20, the drama continues in chapter 21, and here, direct associations are made. John associates the Lamb's bride directly with a city, the New Jerusalem, which the hearers are told comes down from heaven (Rev 21:2, 9 – 10). Again, he tells his hearers that this bride is "prepared" in an appropriate manner for the occasion (21:1 – 3). Much of the content in chapter 21 is given to describing the prepared bride's jeweled appearance, bedecked with precious stones (21:18 – 21). In chapter 21, it is clear that the bride is a metaphor for a new city of Jerusalem.

In the final reference to the bride in Revelation 22:17, she is heard with the Spirit summoning the "Root and the Offspring of David" (22:16), her groom, to come.

When we summarize what John says about the bride in this brief *bride drama*, we have the following: the Lamb, who is the Root and Offspring of David, is marrying a bride, who represents the New Jerusalem. The details given about the bride's apparel fluctuate between person and place, creating an ambiguity surrounding the identity of the bride. This bride, both person and place, nevertheless, has been beautifully prepared in heaven for the wedding day. The invitations to the wedding guests have been sent, and a blessing was announced on those who will be attending. The *bride drama* comes to a premature conclusion as the hearers are left with the bride impatiently awaiting the arrival of her groom. The hearers, then, stand waiting too!

Assuming we know the identity of the Lamb (Rev 5:5 – 7; 13:8), the primary question remains: To whom or to what does the image of the bride, the New Jerusalem, refer? Most commentators think the image represents the church in view of other

---

10. For all quotes, emphasis mine.

New Testament texts that use marriage imagery to describe the church's relationship to Christ (2 Cor 11:2; Eph 5:25 – 33). However, we should not assume that John means the same thing as Paul. Notably, Paul does not actually use the term "bride" when describing the church. Second, as we will see, marriage imagery has a rich biblical background and can be used to express a variety of ideas. Thus, Paul may use it for one purpose, while John another.

To address the question of John's particular interest in using the bride imagery and what it represents for him, we need to see (1) the connection with two earlier texts in Revelation and (2) the biblical background of the imagery in Isaiah, which all agree is John's primary source material for this section of his letter. When this evidence is considered together within the concrete Jewish framework of our approach, it becomes clear that John's conception of the eternal state, as depicted by the image of the bride, includes a continuing distinctive role for ethnic Israel.

Revelation

There are two important texts in the earlier sections of Revelation that inform our understanding of John's image of the bride. The first is Revelation 11:15. Here John describes the seventh trumpet and the announcement of the culmination of God's kingdom purposes:

> The seventh angel sounded his trumpet, and there were loud voices in heaven, which said:
>
>> "The kingdom of the world has become
>> the kingdom of our Lord and of his Messiah,
>> and he will reign for ever and ever."

This statement is the heart of John's apocalyptic letter. It sums up John's vision of the end. Guttesen concurs, "Revelation 11:15 – 19 is the most succinct statement of the book's eschatological hope … containing the fulfillment of God's final eschatological purpose."[11] The message of the verse is "a regime change in which 'our Lord and his Messiah' will replace the powers that now occupy the central position of geopolitical authority on earth."[12]

The rest of Revelation is merely commentary on this regime change. So when we come to Revelation 19:6 and read, "For the Lord our God, the Almighty, reigns" (NASB), we should immediately think of 11:15. John is describing *again*, albeit in a new way, what he has already stated: God's and Messiah's kingdom is replacing the present devilish empire. Even the structure of Revelation 17 – 22 suggests this with the overt replacement of Babylon, depicted as a harlot, with the New Jerusalem, imagined as a pure bride.[13]

---

11. Guttesen, *Leaning into the Future*, 123 – 24.

12. Guttesen, *Leaning into the Future*, 124.

13. Guttesen notes the structural and lexical parallels between 11:15 – 18 and 19:5 – 6: "This reign is here symbolized as the marriage supper of the Lamb for which the bride has made herself ready which in return anticipates the fuller depiction of the New Jerusalem in 21:1 – 22:5" (Guttesen, *Leaning into the Future*, 137 – 38; also 142 – 54). Cf. Greg K. Beale, *The Book of Revelation: A Commentary on the Greek Text* (Grand Rapids: Eerdmans, 1999), 931.

The wedding imagery is a depiction of the coming of the kingdom of God and Messiah. In the final act of the age, God will reveal his kingdom and the kingdom of Messiah (Rev 11:15; 19:6). The kingdom of the world is replaced by God's reign through the *Davidic Messiah's earthly* reign. Since the Old Testament often equates David's kingdom with Israel's (cf. 1 Chr 28: 5; 2 Chr 6:10; 13:5, 8), and biblical and postbiblical writers expected Israel's restoration (cf. Ezek 34; 36; *Pss. Sol.* 17), it seems reasonable to suppose that first-century Jewish readers would have understood the wedding imagery to refer to the eschatological restoration of Israel's twelve-tribe political kingdom. God's eternal reign on earth, in and through the Messiah, is represented by the bride, the New Jerusalem in the eternal state, which is the renewed kingdom of Israel.

The second important text that informs our understanding of the bride imagery in the final chapters of Revelation is Revelation 12.[14] The text follows on the heels of Revelation 11:15 – 19, discussed above. The relationship between the two texts is best understood as moving from a general statement of ultimate outcome (regime change) to the specific means by which that outcome will be realized. One figurative expression of this means, as John sees it, is a woman adorned with the sun, moon, and a "crown of twelve stars" (12:1), who, under great distress, births a male child who will "rule all the nations with a rod of iron" (12:5 ESV). After the birth of the child, he is taken up to God and to his throne, while the woman flees into the wilderness (12:6). Following a war in heaven, Satan, symbolized as a dragon, is cast down to the earth and he begins to pursue the woman, seeking to destroy her. During this persecution, God supernaturally protects the woman from the dragon. In response, the dragon sets off to attack the "rest of her offspring" who are defined as "those who keep the commandments of God and hold to the testimony of Jesus" (12:17 ESV).

The vision is highly symbolic and open to various interpretations. However, taking cues given from Old Testament allusions and the story of Jesus, one can make a solid case that the woman represents the remnant of corporate-national Israel[15] and that the "rest of her offspring" (12:17) are Jesus-believing Jews who both keep the Torah[16] and worship Jesus.[17] These exist and live on for "1260 days," which is likely a poetic way of representing the whole period between Jesus' first and second comings.[18]

In sum, the two precursors to the bride imagery in Revelation, when read within a concrete Jewish framework, suggest that the bride image represents Israel's eschato-

---

14. Beale calls the "bridal woman" of 19:7 – 8 the "resumption of the 'woman' of ch. 12" (Beale, *Book of Revelation*, 939).

15. See also Charles H. Talbert, *The Apocalypse: A Reading of the Revelation of John* (Louisville: Westminster John Knox, 1994), 48, 51. I think Talbert gets this right until he equates "her offspring" with "Christians" in general (51). More likely, in context, they are Jesus-believing Jews.

16. See Marshall, *Parables of War*, 148.

17. Beale in my opinion overgeneralizes the specific reference to Israel symbolized by the sun, moon, and stars (Gen 37:9; *T. Naph.* 5:3; *T. Ab.* B 7:4 – 16; Philo, *On Dreams* 2.113) when he states that "this woman is a picture of the faithful community" (Beale, *Book of Revelation*, 625). He adds later, "This then is another example of the church being equated with the twelve tribes of Israel (see on 7:4 – 8). Ch. 12 presents the woman as incorporating the people of God living both before and after Christ's coming" (627). This conclusion is certainly possible and popular, but not a necessary conclusion from the text itself.

18. Michael Wilcock, *The Message of Revelation: I Saw Heaven Opened* (Downers Grove, Ill.: InterVarsity, 1975), 119.

logical twelve-tribe kingdom. This conclusion will be confirmed by a brief look at the prophetic background of the bride image in Isaiah.

Isaiah

Now we turn to Isaiah, where Jerusalem and the people of Israel are regularly depicted as God's promiscuous wife, and the remnant of Israel who is redeemed in the future is portrayed as God's bride. This is particularly evident in the latter part of Isaiah, Isaiah 49, 54, and 61 – 62.[19]

In Isaiah 49:18 (ESV), the prophet states that when God regathers the exiles to Jerusalem at the end of the age, Jerusalem will "put them on as an ornament; you shall bind them on as a bride does." This text provides us with two important insights. First, the bride imagery is used of Israel's concrete restoration envisaged as the regathering of the twelve tribes. Second, there is an amalgamation of people and city: the conditions of Jerusalem are one and the same with Israel's faithful remnant. Both of these points are unpacked in the later passages.

In Isaiah 54, the prophet again uses the imagery of a bride to speak of Israel's end-time restoration. Isaiah speaks of God's future *remarriage* with his abandoned wife, Zion. Isaiah 54 is a story about an abandoned wife who is for this reason barren, but who will be freed from both desolation and barrenness when she is again wedded.[20] The woman is Zion, the city of Jerusalem. This reversal will result in Jerusalem bedecked with precious stones.

In Isaiah 61 – 62, the prophet again uses the bride image for the same reason. Isaiah announces:

> I delight greatly in the LORD;
>   my soul rejoices in my God.
> For he has clothed me with garments of salvation
>   and arrayed me in a robe of his righteousness,
> as a bridegroom adorns his head like a priest,
>   and as a bride adorns herself with her jewels.
> — ISAIAH 61:10

> For Zion's sake I will not keep silent,
>   for Jerusalem's sake I will not remain quiet,
> till her vindication shines out like the dawn,
>   her salvation like a blazing torch.
> The nations will see your vindication,
>   and all kings your glory;
> you will be called by a new name
>   that the mouth of the LORD will bestow.
> You will be a crown of splendor in the LORD's hand,

---

19. The imagery can be found elsewhere in the Prophets, e.g., Jer 2:2; 31:32; Ezek 16:8 – 14; Hos 2:5.
20. For a detailed exegetical discussion of Isa 54:1, see "Isa 54,1 in Gal 4,24b – 27: Reading Genesis in Light of Isaiah," *Zeitschrift für die Neutestamentliche Wissenschaft und die Kunde der älteren Kirche* 96, no. 3 – 4 (2005): 188 – 210.

> a royal diadem in the hand of your God.
> No longer will they call you Deserted,
>   or name your land Desolate.
> But you will be called Hephzibah,
>   and your land Beulah;
> for the LORD will take delight in you,
>   and your land will be married.
> As a young man marries a young woman,
>   so will your Builder marry you;
> as a bridegroom rejoices over his bride,
>   so will your God rejoice over you.
>   — ISAIAH 62:1 – 5

What does all of this add up to? Isaiah presents the eschatological Jerusalem, which represented both the people of Israel and the city, as the new bride of God with a twist. The bride is none other than God's former wife whom he abandoned because of her unfaithfulness. God remarries his wife! This imagery then is used to represent Israel's restoration in the eschatological day of salvation.

One additional observation that is important for our understanding of Revelation is the role of the Gentile nations in the restoration. According to Isaiah's prophecy (66:19 – 21), the nations will bring Israel back from exile:

> "I will set a sign among them, and I will send some of those who survive to the nations — to Tarshish, to the Libyans and Lydians (famous as archers), to Tubal and Greece, and to the distant islands that have not heard of my fame or seen my glory. They will proclaim my glory among the nations. And they will bring all your people, from all the nations, to my holy mountain in Jerusalem as an offering to the LORD — on horses, in chariots and wagons, and on mules and camels," says the LORD. "They will bring them, as the Israelites bring their grain offerings, to the temple of the LORD in ceremonially clean vessels. And I will select some of them also to be priests and Levites," says the LORD.[21]

The Gentile nations are the bearers of scattered Israel. They too are present at the wedding of God and his bride Israel. They celebrate the restoration of God's people and his city.

The Israel-ness of the New Heavens and New Earth

With the Scripture as a background, we can now clarify John's use of the bride imagery in Revelation 19 – 22. First, since for John the Lamb is divine, it presents little problem for him to correlate Israel's God with the Lamb — what was attributed to the God of Israel in Isaiah is now associated also with the Lamb.[22] Thus, what was once God's bride is now the bride of Messiah.

---

21. See also Isa 49:22 – 23.
22. See Richard Bauckham, *Jesus and the God of Israel: God Crucified and Other Studies on the New Testament's Christology of Divine Identity* (Grand Rapids: Eerdmans, 2008).

The Lamb's bride is the New Jerusalem, both the people of Israel and the place where God will dwell. Israel, who was unfaithful, now is not. At the end of the age, the Lamb will remarry his bride; he will fulfill his promise. The divine Messiah will redeem his people from captivity and clothe them with righteous deeds because they will be "taught by the LORD" (Isa. 54:13).[23]

It seems most reasonable to see a distinction between the bride and the guests in Revelation 19:6 – 9. More often than not, however, commentators are not willing to recognize this, so they are forced to explain how the bride becomes the wedding guests within the same paragraph, just two verses later. D. Aune rightly calls this reading of the metaphor "somewhat awkward," since, on this reading, "the bride mentioned in 19:7 represents faithful Christians, [and thus] the bride and those invited must be identical."[24] On my reading, however, the two entities are easily differentiated: the bride is Israel and the wedding guests are the nations who will participate in the eschatological kingdom.

At the wedding, a multitude from among the nations who have assisted in the regathering of the exiles will be present. Thus, the New Jerusalem, the bride of the Lamb, is God's restored Israel around which and within which the righteous Gentiles gather.[25]

With the use of the bride imagery, John teaches that Israel's distinctive role in God's administration of creation continues eternally. This interpretation is based on evidence in Revelation and the Isaianic background of John's bride imagery read within a concrete Jewish approach. The covenants God made with Israel through servants like Abraham, Moses, David, *and Jesus* are realized perfectly and completely in the kingdom of God and his Messiah in the eschatological age. The particularity of Jewish flesh crosses the threshold into the eternal state.

To sum up, putting it negatively first, John does *not* supersede Israel's historical role when he describes the coming of the new heavens and new earth. Put positively, in the eternal state, Israel *remains* at the very center of God's work *within* the history of the world. Eternal life is not ethnicity-less or *Israel-less*. As Karl Barth wrote, "The King *of Israel* is the King of the world."[26]

---

23. There is an interesting parallel here with the important Second Temple text *Pss. Sol.* 17.32: "He [the Davidic Messiah] will be a righteous king over them, taught by God, there will be no unrighteousness among them during his reign."

24. David E. Aune, *Revelation 17 – 22* (Nashville: Thomas Nelson, 1997), 1034. See also Talbert, *The Apocalypse*, 89; Stephen S. Smalley, *The Revelation to John: A Commentary on the Greek Text of the Apocalypse* (Downers Grove, Ill.: InterVarsity, 2005), 485; Brian K. Blount, *Revelation: A Commentary* (Louisville: Westminster John Knox, 2009), 347.

25. For a recent and similar presentation of the climax of Revelation see Allan J. McNicol, *The Conversion of the Nations in Revelation* (London: T&T Clark, 2011), 83, 137 – 38.

26. Karl Barth, *Church Dogmatics* (ed. T. F. Torrance and G. W. Bromiley; Edinburgh: T&T Clark, 1936 – 69), III/3, 176 – 77, emphasis added.

For Further Reading

Bauckham, Richard. *Jesus and the God of Israel:* God Crucified *and Other Studies on the New Testament's Christology of Divine Identity.* Grand Rapids: Eerdmans, 2008.

Blount, Brian K. *Revelation: A Commentary.* Louisville: Westminster John Knox, 2009.

DeSilva, David A. *Seeing Things John's Way: The Rhetoric of the Book of Revelation.* Louisville: Westminster John Knox, 2009.

Frankfurter, David. "Revelation: Introduction and Annotations." Pages 463–98 in *The Jewish Annotated New Testament.* Edited by Amy-Jill Levine and Marc Zvi Brettler. Oxford: Oxford University Press, 2011.

Geyser, Albert. "The Twelve Tribes in Revelation: Judean and Judeo Christian Apocalypticism." *New Testament Studies* 28 (1982): 388–99.

Guttesen, Poul F. *Leaning into the Future: The Kingdom of God in the Theology of Jürgen Moltmann.* Eugene, Oreg.: Pickwick, 2009.

Harvey, Richard. *Mapping Messianic Jewish Theology: A Constructive Approach.* Milton Keynes, UK: Paternoster, 2009.

Hirschberg, Peter. "Jewish Believers in Asia Minor according to the Book of Revelation and the Gospel of John." Pages 217–38 in *Jewish Believers in Jesus: The Early Centuries.* Peabody, Mass.: Hendrickson, 2007.

Lee, Pilchan. *The New Jerusalem in the Book of Revelation: A Study of Revelation 21–22 in Light of Its Background in Jewish Tradition.* Tübingen: Mohr Siebeck, 2001.

Marshall, John W. *Parables of War: Reading John's Jewish Apocalypse.* Waterloo, Ontario: Wilfrid Laurier University Press, 2001.

McNicol, Allan J. *The Conversion of the Nations in Revelation.* London: T&T Clark, 2011.

Rhoads, David, ed. *From Every People and Nation: The Book of Revelation in Intercultural Perspective.* Minneapolis: Fortress, 2005.

Stramara, Daniel F., Jr. *God's Timetable: The Book of Revelation and the Feast of Seven Weeks.* Eugene, Oreg.: Pickwick, 2011.

Talbert, Charles H. *The Apocalypse: A Reading of the Revelation of John.* Louisville: Westminster John Knox, 1994.

Wilcock, Michael. *The Message of Revelation: I Saw Heaven Opened.* Downers Grove, Ill.: InterVarsity, 1975.

CHAPTER 24

Mission-Commitment in Second Temple Judaism and the New Testament

JOHN DICKSON

Jewish and Christian scholars alike have argued that Jews of the pre-Christian era had little or no interest in converting Gentiles to the worship of Israel's God. The nations would of course bend the knee to the Almighty at the end of history — in the so-called pilgrimage of the nations — but, before then, Jews were happy to leave the pagans to their own ways. On this reading, it was the Christians who provide us with the first clear evidence of missionizing, and the reasons for this development have little or nothing to do with any historical precedent in Judaism.

This chapter challenges this recent scholarly consensus, demonstrating that the eschatological hope for Gentile conversion found tangible expression in the deliberate "missionary" activities of *some* Second Temple Jews. Christian mission has Jewish roots.

Martin Goodman, professor of Jewish Studies at Oxford University, has argued that the proselytizing mission we observe in early Christianity, and in Paul in particular, was "a shocking novelty in the ancient world."[1] In his important book *Mission and Conversion* he strongly denied that Jews before AD 100 had any interest in seeking converts. A similar conclusion has been reached by Christian scholars Scot McKnight[2] and Eckhard Schnabel; Schnabel concludes, "There was no missionary activity by Jews in the centuries before and in the first centuries after Jesus' and his followers' ministry."[3]

The most recent volume on the subject, *Crossing Over Sea and Land* by Michael

---

1. Martin Goodman, *Mission and Conversion: Proselytizing in the Religious History of the Roman Empire* (Oxford: Clarendon, 1994), 105.

2. Scot McKnight, *Light among the Gentiles: Jewish Missionary Activity in the Second Temple Period* (Minneapolis: Fortress, 1991).

3. Eckhard Schnabel, *Christian Mission I: Jesus and the Twelve* (Downers Grove, Ill.: InterVarsity, 2004), 172 – 73. Other scholars who deny Jewish mission include: John J. Collins, *Between Athens and Jerusalem: Jewish Identity in the Hellenistic Diaspora* (Grand Rapids: Eerdmans, 2000), 261 – 72; Rainer Riesner, "A Pre-Christian Jewish Mission?" in *The Mission of the Early Church to Jews and Gentiles* (ed. J. Ådna and H. Kvalbein; Tübingen: Mohr Siebeck, 2000), 211 – 50; Shaye J. D. Cohen, "Was Judaism in Antiquity a Missionary Religion?" in *Jewish Assimilation, Acculturation, and Accommodation: Past Traditions, Current Issues and Future Prospects* (ed. Menachem Mor; New York: University Press of America, 1992), 14 – 23. Those who affirm the presence of "mission" in ancient Judaism include: Louis Feldman, *Jew and Gentile in the Ancient World* (Princeton: Princeton University Press, 1993), 288 – 415; Joachim Jeremias, *Jesus' Promise to the Nations* (London: SCM, 1958), 11 – 19; James Carleton Paget, "Jewish Proselytism at the Time of Christian Origins: Chimera or Reality?" *Journal for the Study of the New Testament* 62 (1996): 65 – 103; John P. Dickson, *Mission-Commitment in Ancient Judaism and in the Pauline Communities* (Tübingen: Mohr Siebeck, 2003).

F. Bird, provides, on the one the hand, an impressive confirmation of this consensus and yet, on the other, some reason to question that the Christian mission was pure *nova*, let alone a "shocking novelty." Was there an "aggressive," "organized" attempt on the part of Second Temple Jews to convert the Gentile world? No, says Bird. However, there is enough scattered information in our sources, he says, to believe that *some* Jews did engage in *some* proselytizing of non-Jews. Hence, "the origins of the Christian Gentile missions and subsequent intra-Christian disputes about the admission of Gentiles into the church are all explicable within a Jewish framework."[4] Bird is quick to point out the real differences between Christian mission and Jewish missionizing activity of the period, but his concession is consonant with those who have previously argued that early Christian understandings of mission "owed their decisive shape (if not their peculiar fervor) to the particular patterns of mission-commitment current in some strands of ancient Judaism."[5]

What Is "Mission"?

McKnight and Goodman define "mission" as "universal proselytism," the attempt to convert anyone and everyone through explicit means of persuasion.[6] Suppose, however, we were to broaden our definition beyond that of mere personal persuasion to include any activity that aims to move outsiders toward embracing one's religion. Instantly, the admissible evidence becomes more plentiful — and more reflective of the real-life experience of religious adherents. A Christian who prays for the conversion of a non-Christian, for instance, is not explicitly proselytizing, but she imagines she is helping draw others to her faith. To exclude this sort of evidence from our picture of mission is to miss something fundamental to the missionary impulse. Why should it be any different in assessing evidence for Jewish mission?

Our question, then, is not, Was Judaism a missionary religion? Rather it is, What evidence is there that Jews of the Second Temple period sought, in any way, to move Gentiles toward worshiping the God of Israel?

1. Eschatological Conversion

Many Jews in our period *looked forward* to the conversion of Gentiles. Clear evidence of this is found in the widespread theme of the eschatological pilgrimage of the nations. At the climax of history Gentiles would stream to Jerusalem as pilgrims eager to worship the one true God.[7] The theme first appears in the Scriptures themselves (Zech 8:21 – 23; Isa 25:6 – 8; 45:20 – 24; 60:11; Ps 47:9). It is also found in numerous postbiblical Jewish texts, including the pre-Maccabean Tobit, in which we read, "A bright light will shine to all the ends of the earth; many nations will come to you from

---

4. Michael F. Bird, *Crossing Over Sea and Land: Jewish Missionary Activity in the Second Temple Period* (Peabody, Mass.: Hendrickson, 2010), 152.

5. Dickson, *Mission-Commitment in Ancient Judaism and in the Pauline Communities*, 313 – 14.

6. McKnight, *Light among the Gentiles*, 5.

7. Jeremias, *Jesus' Promise to the Nations*, 56 – 62.

far away, the inhabitants of the remotest parts of the earth to your holy name, bearing gifts in their hands for the King of heaven" (Tob 13.11). A more explicit reference to the conversion of these Gentiles is found in the following chapter of Tobit: "Then the nations in the whole world will all be converted and worship God in truth. They will all abandon their idols, which deceitfully have led them into their error; and in righteousness they will praise the eternal God" (Tob 14.6). Many other texts envisage the same thing: *1 Enoch* 10.21; 90.6 – 42; *2 Baruch* 72.2 – 4; *Sibylline Oracles* 3.716 – 20; *Testament of Levi* 18; *Testament of Judah* 24.6; *Testament of Naphtali* 8.3 – 4; *Testament of Benjamin* 10.9.

These references do not point to *actual* missionary activity on the part of Jews in the Second Temple era. They simply draw attention to the fact that Jews in the period did look forward to the conversion of Gentiles to the true God. The attitudinal framework for mission was therefore clearly in place. Jews were not disinterested in the religious practices of Gentiles; they hoped for their repentance. Goodman believes that "a logical prerequisite for a universal proselytizing mission to convert others to a new religion is a belief that their present religious behaviour is unsatisfactory."[8] This prerequisite seems to be present in, indeed central to, the eschatological pilgrimage motif found in many types of ancient Judaism.

This eschatological hope found tangible historical expression in the missionary activity of at least some Jews of the period.

2. Ethical Apologetic

Some Jews of the pre-Christian era believed that ethical conduct — specifically, obedience to the Torah — was one means of God's light shining to the Gentile world to give knowledge of the one true Lord. In a speech from the late Maccabean period the putative "Levi" says to his "sons": "you should be the lights of Israel [text *a* adds "for all the nations"] as the sun and the moon. For what will all the nations do if you become darkened with impiety? You will bring down a curse on our nation, because you want to destroy the light of the Law which was granted to you for the enlightenment of every man" (*T. Levi* 14.1 – 4).

According to the unknown author of this text, Jewish disobedience threatens one of the purposes of the Law: to bring light to "every man," which in context must include Gentiles. What is interesting here is that the normally *eschatological* theme of a universal light is brought into the present. Gentiles will see God's light not only at the end-time pilgrimage but also *now* through the daily lives of God's covenant people. A similar emphasis on ethical apologetic is found in *Testament of Benjamin* 5.5, 8.2 – 3, *Letter of Aristeas* 227 (possibly), and *Jewish Antiquities* 20.75 – 76.[9]

Philo, the great Alexandrian Jewish intellectual (10 – 15 BCE to 45 – 50 CE), echoes the same theme in his account of the biblical Joseph: "they [the prisoners] were rebuked by his wise words and doctrines of philosophy, while the conduct of their

---

8. Goodman, *Mission and Conversion*, 38.

9. On these passages (and the others below) see Dickson, *Mission-Commitment in Ancient Judaism and in the Pauline Communities*, 51 – 60.

teacher effected more than any words. For by setting before them his life of temperance and every virtue, like an original picture of skilled workmanship, he converted even those who seemed to be quite incurable, who as the long-standing distempers of their soul abated reproached themselves for their past and repented" (*On the Life of Joseph* 86 – 87).

It may be enough for our purposes simply to observe that Philo believed the good conduct of a Jew living in a Gentile land had the power to convert those around him. Given the rhetorical strategy of Philo's writings, it is difficult to imagine that he was not also recommending such a course of life for his Jewish readership and hoping for a similar outcome among their pagan neighbors. That Philo himself desired the conversion of pagan Alexandria is clear from *On Moses* 2.44, a passage discussed below.

Scot McKnight agrees that an ethical apologetic of the type described by Philo "is a consistent feature of the evidence and probably formed the very backbone for the majority of conversions to Judaism."[10] However, he believes that the connection between the good life and conversion was "probably unconscious" for Jews themselves. The evidence above suggests otherwise, at least for these Jewish writers.

Ethical apologetic forms a central part of the New Testament understanding of mission. In a passage reminiscent of Tobit 13 – 14 and *Testament of Levi* 14 Jesus himself is remembered as having declared: "You are the light of the world. A town built on a hill cannot be hidden. Neither do people light a lamp and put it under a bowl. Instead they put it on its stand, and it gives light to everyone in the house. In the same way, let your light shine before others, that they may see your good deeds and glorify your Father in heaven" (Matt 5:14 – 16).

The eschatological light of salvation is conveyed to the unbelieving world through the good conduct of disciples. That this includes Gentiles is suggested by (1) the use of *kosmos* ("world"), (2) the Isaianic background of this international light motif (Isa 42:6; 49:6; 51:4), and (3) the clear hints of Gentile mission elsewhere in Matthew's gospel (Matt 2:1 – 2; 28:19). In 1 Peter we find a specific example of Christians bringing glory to God through "good deeds" among the pagans. Wives are encouraged to live such good lives that, if any of their husbands do not believe the word, "they may be won over without words by the behavior of their wives, when they see the purity and reverence of your lives" (1 Pet 3:1 – 2). A similar thought is present in the call to Christian slaves to "beautify" (*kosmeo*) the teaching about God the Savior (Titus 2:9 – 10).[11]

3. Prayer for the Gentiles

As mentioned above, intercession for the salvation of others must be included as evidence in any nuanced account of mission-commitment. Already in the Hebrew Bible we observe a prayerful desire for Gentiles to worship the God of Israel. At the founding of the temple King Solomon beseeches the Lord: "that all the peoples of the earth may know your name and fear you, as do your own people Israel" (1 Kgs 8:43). The

---

10. McKnight, *Light among the Gentiles*, 67 – 68.

11. See the discussion of ethical apologetic in the New Testament in Dickson, *Mission-Commitment in Ancient Judaism and in the Pauline Communities*, 262 – 92.

words "as do your own people Israel" suggest that the "knowing" and "fearing" of these foreigners refers not to enforced submission but to covenant relationship.

Philo gives expression to the missionary impulse of intercession. He describes the Jewish people as a nation divinely appointed to pray for the deliverance of Gentiles: "[Israel is] a nation destined to be consecrated above all others to offer prayers for ever on behalf of the human race that it may be delivered from evil and participate in what is good" (*Mos.* 1.149).

"Escaping evil" and "sharing in good" are expressions obviously influenced by Philo's Hellenistic philosophical outlook, but for the Jew, Philo, such phrases can refer to nothing other than Gentiles leaving paganism and adopting the worship of the one true God. The sentiment is reiterated in *Special Laws* 1.84–97. Here Philo contrasts the attitude of Israel's high priest with the parochial intentions of pagan priests. The former "holds the world to be, as in very truth it is, his country, and in its behalf he is wont to propitiate the Ruler with supplication and intercession, beseeching Him to make His creature a partaker of His own kindly and merciful nature." Regardless of whether the high priest did in fact pray for Gentiles in this manner, we can assume that Philo here reflects his own, and perhaps his Alexandrian community's, intercession on behalf of non-Jews.

Readers of the New Testament will no doubt be reminded of the numerous requests for prayer found in specifically missionary contexts. Jesus urges disciples to plead with the Lord of the harvest to send out more heralds (Matt 9:38). Paul admits his fervent practice of praying for the salvation of his fellow Jews (Rom 10:1). In 2 Thessalonians 3:1 believers are urged to "pray for us that the message of the Lord may spread rapidly and be honored." Missionary-oriented requests are also found in Colossians 4:2–4 and Ephesians 6:19–20.[12]

4. Public Worship as Mission

Already in the biblical psalms we observe the occasional reference to the importance of public worship as a statement to the Gentiles of the majesty of YHWH (e.g., Ps 96:3–8). Jews of the Second Temple period were also aware of the attractive power of their liturgical life and believed that the maintenance of proper worship provided one means by which Gentiles would embrace the true worship of God.[13]

Philo (*Mos.* 2.41–44) waxes lyrical about an annual celebration on the island of Pharos in his day that commemorated the translation of the Torah into Greek, and to which "not only Jews but multitudes of others cross the water, both to do honour to the place in which the light of that Greek version first shone out, and also to thank God for the good gift so old yet ever young." For Philo, the festival is a picture of a much greater missionary possibility: "I believe that each nation would abandon its

---

12. For a discussion of the significance of prayer for mission in the New Testament see Dickson, *Mission-Commitment in Ancient Judaism and in the Pauline Communities*, 214–27.

13. Despite the contentions of Dieter Georgi, *The Opponents of Paul in Second Corinthians* (Edinburgh: T&T Clark, 1987), 83–89, the ancient synagogue does not appear to have been deliberately styled toward the conversion of outsiders.

peculiar ways, and, throwing overboard their ancestral customs, turn to honouring our laws alone."

Another example of the missionary effect of Jewish liturgical life is found in *Jewish War* 7.45. Here, Josephus explains that resentment toward Jews in first-century Antioch had to do with the fact that the Jewish community there was growing, partly because the Jews there "were constantly attracting (*prosagō*) to their religious ceremonies multitudes of Greeks, and these they had in some measure incorporated with themselves." The language is striking. As Goodman acknowledges, "The use of the verb *prosago* in the middle form implied action by the Antiochene Jews on their own behalf, so it may be surmised that they wanted such Gentiles to join their rites and to become 'in some way' attached to their community."[14] This was happening "constantly" and in great numbers, according to Josephus.

Bird thinks the significance of this passage for our question is minimized by the fact that these Gentiles are said to have become members of the Jewish community only "in some measure" (*tini moiran*). The "account documents attraction," he says, "not mission *per se*."[15] Rather than accept the passage as an odd but real piece of evidence for Jewish mission-commitment, Bird and others argue that the text does not fit exactly with their strict definition of "mission."[16] (I have often wondered how many New Testament passages usually thought to be relevant to Christian mission would, by a similar method, be excluded from the contemporary discussion of mission.) The expression "in some measure" does not diminish the missionary significance of this activity; it simply betrays an ambivalence on the part of Josephus toward the status of these would-be converts. Perhaps for political reasons he did not wish to suggest that joining in worship with Jews dehellenized Greeks entirely. Then again, perhaps Josephus, a sometime Pharisee, had scruples about describing (presumably uncircumcised) Gentiles as anything but *partial* members of the synagogue.

Syria may have been a place of particular success for Jewish mission activity. Hengel and Schwemer have drawn attention to the large numbers of "god-fearers" in another major city of Syria: Damascus.[17] In *Jewish War* 2.560 Josephus speaks of the wives of the local inhabitants of that city "who, with few exceptions, had all become converts to the Jewish religion." While nothing can be said from this description — which is probably somewhat exaggerated — about the means by which the women were "led" to the religion of the Jews, the example of the Antiochene Jews deliberately leading Greeks to their religious services provides a suggestive parallel.[18]

One passage in the New Testament provides clear evidence that some Christians, like some Jews, saw their worship services as potentially significant for outsiders'

---

14. Goodman, *Mission and Conversion*, 66–67.

15. Bird, *Crossing Over Sea and Land*, 100.

16. Scot McKnight plays down the significance of this reference by stressing that it says nothing clear about leading Gentiles to synagogue services so that the Gentiles can hear an "evangelistic or propagandistic sermon" on the Torah (McKnight, *Light among the Gentiles*, 65).

17. Martin Hengel and Anna Schwemer, *Paul between Damascus and Antioch: The Unknown Years* (trans. John Bowden; London: SCM, 1997), 50–54.

18. Hengel and Schwemer rightly point to *Jewish War* 2.462–63 as further evidence of the prevalence of Jewish "sympathizers" throughout Syria.

knowledge of God. In 1 Corinthians 14:23 – 26 Paul describes a would-be believer entering a Christian gathering while prophesying is already going on. The unbeliever "overhears" a typical utterance aimed at the gathered faithful and is brought to the worship of God. Paul's assumption is the same as that of Philo and Josephus: as the outsider observes true worship he or she is drawn to join in.[19]

5. Jewish "Missionaries"?

There are two examples of deliberate missionary persuasion on the part of some Jews in the period. Jews were expelled from Rome *en masse* in CE 19 (under Tiberius). The event is attested in four passages: Josephus, *Jewish Antiquities* 18.81 – 84; Tacitus, *Annals* 2.85; Suetonius, *Tiberius* 36; Cassius Dio 57.18.5a. The last of these explicitly connects the expulsion with proselytizing: "As the Jews had flocked to Rome in great numbers and were converting many of the natives to their ways, he banished most of them" (Cassius Dio 57.18.5a).

Because the text is the latest of the four,[20] Martin Goodman dismisses its information as irrelevant, insisting that none of the other three texts says anything about proselytizing. This is not quite accurate. The earliest of the texts, *Jewish Antiquities* 18.81 – 84, contains a thinly veiled reference to Jewish mission. Josephus blames the expulsion on just four rogue Jewish teachers who "played the part of an interpreter of the Mosaic law" and who swindled a certain aristocratic Roman woman named Fulvia, whose husband was a friend of Tiberius. Tellingly, Josephus describes Fulvia as "a woman of high rank who had become a Jewish proselyte." Here, then, is a specific example of Dio's more generalized reference to many "native" converts. Josephus's story reads like an historical smoke screen. Like Dio, he knew that proselytism was part of the controversy in Rome so, rather than denying it outright or attempting to defend it, he shifts the blame from Jewish mission *per se* to one isolated and corrupt example of that mission.

Another passage in *Jewish Antiquities* recounts the conversions of certain members of the royal house of Adiabene in northern Mesopotamia around CE 30.[21] Significantly, the Adiabene prince, Izates, is converted through the explicit instruction of a Jewish merchant and teacher named Ananias:[22] "Now during the time when Izates resided at Charax Spasini [SE Mesopotamia], a certain Jewish merchant named Ananias visited the king's wives and taught them to worship God after the manner of the Jewish tradition. It was through their agency that he was brought to the notice of Izates, whom he similarly won over with the co-operation of the women" (*Ant.* 20.34 – 35).

---

19. For a discussion of the significance of public worship in Judaism and early Christianity see Dickson, *Mission-Commitment in Ancient Judaism and in the Pauline Communities*, 74 – 84, 293 – 302.

20. The statement is preserved as a citation of Dio by the seventh-century writer John of Antioch.

21. The event is also referred to in rabbinic literature: *m. Nazir* 3.6; *t. Sukkah* 1.1; *Bereshith (Genesis) Rabbah* 46.11.

22. Goodman cites Ananias's attempt here to persuade the royal family at Charax Spasini "to worship God" as an example of "apologetic mission," merely an attempt to convince Gentiles of the power of the Jewish God (*Mission and Conversion*, 86 – 87). This is not a convincing reading of the story. For a fuller discussion see Dickson, *Mission-Commitment in Ancient Judaism and in the Pauline Communities*, 33 – 37.

Returning home to Adiabene the newly converted Izates discovers that his mother, Helena, has also become a Jew through another teacher (*Ant.* 20.35). Excited by his mother's newfound devotion to the Jewish law, Izates wants to confirm his faith by being circumcised. Ananias, the Jewish merchant and teacher, advises Izates against circumcision: "The king could, he said, worship God even without being circumcised if indeed he had fully decided to be a devoted adherent of Judaism, for it was this that counted more than circumcision" (*Ant.* 20.41). Nevertheless, some time later another Jew, named Eleazar, came from Galilee and urged the king to be circumcised.

It is sometimes pointed out that Josephus says nothing about Ananias and Eleazar being missionaries deliberately traveling in order to convert Gentiles.[23] That is true, but irrelevant. Josephus tells us nothing about why these two Jews ended up in Adiabene. It could have been commercial. It could have been missionary. An argument from silence will not do. What is clear is that, whatever the reason for visiting Izates, Ananias appears in the story only as the king's "teacher," being described as such in the same breath we are introduced to "the physician" of the king (*Ant.* 20.45 – 46). It is not difficult to accept Carleton Paget's suggestion that just as Paul the "tent maker" was also self-consciously Paul the "missionary" so too Ananias the "merchant" may have thought of himself as Ananias the "teacher" of Gentiles.[24]

It is striking that in this one story we find five examples of missionary persuasion: (1) Ananias's teaching of the royal wives; (2) Ananias's instruction of Izates with (3) the stated assistance of the royal wives; (4) Eleazar's persuasion of Izates to be circumcised; and (5) the unnamed teacher's earlier success in bringing the Queen Mother to Judaism.

The story of Ananias provides a fascinating analogy to another Jewish merchant and teacher named Paul, who likewise permitted Gentiles to worship God without circumcision and who urged his own converts to speak to outsiders about their faith (Col 4:5 – 6).

Conclusion

Not only did Second Temple Jews look forward to Gentile worship of God at the climax of history; some sought to encourage this worship in the normal course of history. They prayed for it, drew Gentile neighbours to the synagogue, engaged in ethical apologetic, and, on a few clear occasions, even took part in explicit teaching. This is not to say that Judaism was a "missionary religion," only that a missionary impulse found concrete expression among a variety of Jews, both East and West, in the period. The Christian mission that would develop within just a few years of the conversion of the royal house of Adiabene, was in no sense a "shocking novelty." Rather, it was an intense expression of an impulse already present in the Judaism from which Christianity came.

---

23. Goodman, *Mission and Conversion*, 84; McKnight, *Light among the Gentiles*, 56; Bird, *Crossing Over Sea and Land*, 98.

24. Carleton Paget, "Jewish Proselytism at the Time of Christian Origins," 65 – 103.

For Further Reading

Bird, Michael F. "The Case of the Proselytizing Pharisees? — Matthew 23.15." *Journal for the Study of the Historical Jesus* 2, no. 2 (2004): 117 – 37.

———. *Crossing Over Sea and Land: Jewish Missionary Activity in the Second Temple Period*. Peabody, Mass.: Hendrickson, 2010.

Borgen, Peder. "Proselytes, Conquest, and Mission." Pages 57 – 77 in *Recruitment, Conquest and Conflict: Strategies in Judaism, Early Christianity, and the Greco-Roman World*. Edited by P. Borgen, V. K. Robbins, and D. B. Gowler. Atlanta: Scholars, 1998.

Carleton Paget, James. "Jewish Proselytism at the Time of Christian Origins: Chimera or Reality?" *Journal for the Study of the New Testament* 62 (1996): 65 – 103.

Cohen, Shaye J. D. "Was Judaism in Antiquity a Missionary Religion?" Pages 14 – 23 in *Jewish Assimilation, Acculturation, and Accommodation: Past Traditions, Current Issues and Future Prospects*. Edited by Menachem Mor. New York: University Press of America, 1992.

Dickson, John P. *Mission-Commitment in Ancient Judaism and in the Pauline Communities*. Tübingen: Mohr Siebeck, 2003.

Donaldson, Terrence L. "Proselytes or 'Righteous Gentiles'? The Status of Gentiles in Eschatological Pilgrimage Patterns of Thought." *Journal for the Study of the Pseudepigrapha* 7 (1990): 3 – 27.

Feldman, Louis H. *Jew and Gentile in the Ancient World: Attitudes and Interactions from Alexander to Justinian*. Princeton: Princeton University Press, 1993.

———. "Jewish Proselytism." Pages 372 – 408 in *Eusebius, Christianity, and Judaism*. Edited by Harold W. Attridge and Gohei Hata. Detroit: Wayne State University Press, 1994.

———. "Was Judaism a Missionary Religion in Ancient Times?" Pages 24 – 37 in *Jewish Assimilation, Acculturation and Accommodation: Past Traditions, Current Issues and Future Prospects*. Edited by Menachem Mor. New York: University Press of America, 1992.

Goodman, Martin. "Jewish Proselytizing in the First Century." Pages 53 – 78 in *The Jews Among Pagans and Christians in the Roman Empire*. Edited by Judith Lieu, John North and Tessa Rajak. London: Routledge, 1994.

———. *Mission and Conversion: Proselytizing in the Religious History of the Roman Empire*. Oxford: Clarendon, 1994.

McKnight, Scot. *A Light among the Gentiles: Jewish Missionary Activity in the Second Temple Period*. Minneapolis: Fortress, 1991.

Nolland, J. "Uncircumcised Proselytes." *Journal for the Study of Judaism in the Persian, Hellenistic and Roman Period* 12 (1981): 173 – 94.

Riesner, Rainer. "A Pre-Christian Jewish Mission?" Pages 211 – 50 in *The Mission of the Early Church to Jews and Gentiles*. Edited by J. Ådna and H. Kvalbein. Tübingen: Mohr Siebeck, 2000.

CHAPTER 25

The Son of David and the Gospel

MARKUS BOCKMUEHL

Among the very earliest Christian affirmations about Jesus appears the assertion that he was "descended from David according to the flesh" (Rom 1:3 NRSV).[1] This simple and yet astonishing assertion was so important to the messianism of early Christian readers that they sought to support it in the gospel record without detriment to another, equally vital belief that would appear at first sight to be starkly incompatible with Davidic sonship: the virginal conception of Jesus. As we will see in this short chapter, that apparent contradiction was resolved by a fascinating exegesis of the Gospels' account of Joseph and especially of Mary. We will begin by comparing the affirmation of Jesus' Davidic descent with similar claims, both Jewish and Christian, for other known ancient individuals. Despite the uncertain genealogical record, such assertions were in fact more common than we might imagine.

In What Sense Is Jesus the Son of David?

Romans 1:3 is the earliest New Testament text to identify Jesus as David's descendant; the same theme recurs in one of the latest Pauline documents (2 Tim 2:8). It is particularly frequent in Matthew (about 12x), Mark (5x), and Luke (8x; cf. Acts 2:30; 13:22 – 23, etc.). And yet this seemingly clear attestation brings with it a number of challenges. There had been no Davidic king for over six hundred years. Can there really have been a biological "family of David" in the first century — or is this even what the New Testament authors have in mind?

Surprisingly, only Matthew and Luke associate the "Son of David" title with any genealogical implications at all. Yet it seems they trace Jesus' line of descent through Joseph (Matt 1:16; Luke 3:23), whom nevertheless they both rule out as his biological father. Commentators have long since concluded that these evangelists evidently affirm Jesus' Davidic descent as a matter of his legal adoption by Joseph. This has appeared to most interpreters to offer an elegant solution that renders the biblical text accessible to the modern reader. Recent scholarship, however, has pointed out that while it may seem compatible with modern and indeed ancient Roman assumptions, this view in fact falters on the nature of Jewish genealogy, which never recognized adoption as a way to legitimize descent.[2]

---

1. I gratefully acknowledge the editorial assistance of my student Benjamin A. Edsall. For fuller critical documentation of some of this chapter's underlying historical and exegetical arguments see also Markus Bockmuehl, "The Son of David and His Mother," *Journal of Theological Studies* 62 (2011): 476 – 93.

2. Cf. Yigal Levin, "Jesus, 'Son of God' and 'Son of David': The 'Adoption' of Jesus into the Davidic Line," *Journal*

264

Yet even if one were to accept the genealogies as tracing the legally adoptive rather than the biological line of descent, it soon transpires that the evangelists depict Joseph's family tree in two versions of strikingly contradictory form and substance, being traced through two *different* sons of David — Solomon in Matthew 1:6 (who generally follows Chronicles) and the nonroyal Nathan in Luke 3:31.

Sceptics since antiquity have pointed out the problems raised both within and between these two New Testament genealogies: Porphyry (ca. 234 – 305) famously mocked Matthew's genealogy for failing to spot that his scheme of 3x14 generations works only if one counts Jechoniah twice.[3] In modern times, the famous Tübingen critic David Friedrich Strauss (1808 – 74) was one of the first to expound the genealogies as comprehensively unhistorical "myth."[4] In reply, Christians since antiquity have attempted to cope with these differences by resorting to various ultimately speculative interpretative devices like the Jewish law of Levirate marriage[5] or by suggesting that Matthew's genealogy pertains to Joseph, but Luke's to Mary.

Moving on from these opening chapters of Matthew and Luke, we face four gospels in which the role and title of Jesus as Son of David are indeed repeatedly affirmed — but this is always associated with his messianic status as healer and eschatological ruler of Israel, rather than being connected in a concrete sense with his family background or biological descent. Mark, while acknowledging that Jesus claims for his Sabbath praxis the precedent of David (Mark 2:25) and that some contemporaries did indeed address Jesus as Son of David,[6] betrays no knowledge of the family tree, let alone of Bethlehem. Even Matthean statements like "Can this be the Son of David?" (Matt 12:23 NRSV) or "Hosanna to the Son of David" (Matt 21:9, 15; cf. Mark 11:9 – 10; John 12:13) are more patently preoccupied with Jesus' hoped-for messianic role and identity as political redeemer of Israel than with his gene pool.

In all this it is puzzling that Jesus never claims Davidic sonship for himself, and the gospel narratives show none of the Twelve ever referring to him in such terms. On the contrary, in the one episode that has Jesus specifically addressing the question of the expected Messiah's identity as Son of David, he seems clearly to employ Psalm 110 in order to *relativize or subvert* Davidic in favour of divine sonship (Matt 22:42 – 45; Mark 12:35 – 37; Luke 20:41 – 44). A Davidide theme does indeed feature unambiguously in the Marcan (11:10) and Matthean (21:9) accounts of the triumphal entry into Jerusalem, but despite the important allusions to Davidic lament psalms like Psalm 22 it never resurfaces in the remainder of the passion or resurrection accounts; and Luke has Jesus dismissing the disciples' postresurrection allusion to a "restoration of the kingship" as misguided (at least as to timing).

The fourth gospel seems virtually silent, not to say tone-deaf, on the question.

---

for the Study of the New Testament 28 (2006): 415 – 42 (esp. 421 – 23). Inner-familial insertions to secure the patrilinear line, whether by levirate marriage or the adoption of a domestic slave's son (e.g., 1 Chr 2:34 – 36), are clearly delimited exceptions that preserve the rule — and would not pertain in the case of Jesus.

3. See Jerome, *Commentary on Daniel* 1.1 (replying that Porphyry fails to distinguish Jehoiakim, whom Matthew omits, from Jehoiachin).

4. David Friedrich Strauss, *The Life of Jesus Critically Examined* (Philadelphia: Fortress, 1972), 108 – 18.

5. Thus Julius Africanus (early third century), in Eusebius, *Hist. eccl.* 1.7.1 – 17.

6. Mark 10:47 – 48; cf. 11:10; 12:35 – 37.

The sole exception is its (possibly ironic) report of the Jewish challenge that the true Messiah could not be a Galilean but must be a Davidic descendant born in Bethlehem (John 7:42). It also follows that the Messiah, unlike Jesus, cannot therefore be of doubtful paternity (cf. John 8:41).

To claim that Jesus is "Son of David," therefore, is historically problematic and yet evidently also somehow central to the New Testament message. The interpretative difficulties have long been familiar, being lampooned by Christianity's intellectual enemies — from Porphyry in antiquity all the way to the raspy pop neo-atheists of our own century. None of the difficulties are in principle unanswerable, even if they may be intractable.

Davidic Descent — Through Joseph or Mary?

Given this state of affairs, do the gospel genealogies reveal primarily what their authors believed in the first place, namely that Jesus was descended from David because he was Messiah? In an important sense we are indeed dealing with theological "mood music." And yet it is not merely circular to say that this is because the conviction of Davidic descent stands at the heart of Christian faith from the start. Readers of the Gospels found here the Christological particularity and authenticity of Jesus as Messiah, the fulfillment of prophecy and the continuity between the two Testaments of Scripture. Far from self-evident, these convictions were upheld in the face of powerful challenges and objections voiced by both Jewish and Gentile Christian critics.

Generally speaking, the earliest Christian readers of the Gospels assumed Davidic sonship to speak to Christ's humanity, a feature they thought of as an invariable part of Jewish messianic expectation.

A famous late first-century document of apostolic teaching known as the *Didache* connects the wine of the Eucharist with the "holy vine of David" identified in Jesus; and like later liturgies it appeals in this connection to the gospel exclamation "Hosanna to the Son of David" (*Did.* 9.2, 10.6). Early in the second century, the *Epistle of Barnabas* appeals to the citation of Psalm 110 in the Gospels (Matt 22:42 – 45) in order to call into question ideas of Jesus as *merely messianic* "Son of David," rather than also divine — notions that subsequent patristic literature connects with Jewish polemic and with the teaching of the Ebionite heresy (*Barn.* 12.10). Similarly, Ignatius of Antioch (ca. 37 – 110) repeatedly appeals to Jesus' Davidic descent in his articulation of a divine-human Christology in terms that echo Paul's phrasing in Romans 1:3 – 4.[7]

A little later Justin Martyr (ca. 103 – 65), a native of the Holy Land who moved to Rome, produced his famous dialogue with a (real or literary) Jewish interlocutor, Trypho, set in Ephesus. Here Justin understands Jesus' Davidic sonship to document Jesus' birth in fulfillment of Old Testament prophecy, a theme that recurs repeatedly in early Alexandrian fathers like Clement of Alexandria (ca. 150 – 215) and Origen (ca. 185 – 254), who wish to stress against Gnosticism that God is the same in the Old Testament as in the New.[8] Justin quite plausibly links Isaiah 7:14 ("Behold, the virgin

7. Cf. Ignatius, *Smyrn.* 1.1; *Eph.* 18.2; 20.2; *Trall.* 9.1; *Rom.* 7.3.
8. Clement of Alexandria, *Paed.* 1.5; 6.15; *Quis div.* 29. Origen, *Princ.* 2.4.2; 4.1.5; *Cels.* 1.35; *Comm. Jo.* 10.4, 17.

shall conceive and bear a son, and shall call his name Immanuel" [ESV]) with 7:13 ("Hear then, O house of David! Is it too little for you to weary men, that you weary my God also?" [ESV]).[9] Trypho, understandably, objects that contrary to Christian assertions of Jesus' divinity the Messiah's Davidic descent in fact clearly demonstrates his *humanity* (*Dial.* 48).

In a somewhat unexpected but important and influential departure from the apparent letter of the biblical text, Justin repeatedly insists that Mary the mother of Jesus is also a descendant of David (*Dial.* 43, 45, 100), a view that was already held by Ignatius and others before him.[10] Later in the same century, Irenaeus (ca. 130–200) explicitly stresses that Jesus' Davidic descent was *through Mary* rather than Joseph; he grounds this on the argument that Matthew's genealogy shows Joseph's descent to be from Jehoiakim and Jechoniah, who according to Jeremiah (22:24–30; 36:30–31) were disinherited from the kingdom — a fate that also awaits those who claim that Joseph was Jesus' biological father![11] Tertullian (ca. 160–225) similarly argues for Jesus' Davidic descent through Mary,[12] which to him is evident from the fact that she too went to Bethlehem for the census (Luke 2:5).[13]

Historically, the idea that Joseph might have married within the same extended clan is by no means implausible; Mary's Davidic descent is an assumption that helped get around the problem of how one could identify Jesus as "of the seed of David according to the flesh" (Rom 1:3 KJV) while avoiding reference to a human father.

One important additional insight is to note how the "Son of David" argument was consistently deployed as an argument against Marcionite and Gnostic views. This is particularly clear for Irenaeus and Tertullian (explicitly so in *Marc.* 4.36–37). The Nag Hammadi texts, by contrast, feature David very rarely — and then as a contemptible or even a demonic character.[14]

Other Supposed Descendants of David

David and his descendants feature prominently in the story of Israel as told in the books of the Latter Prophets and Chronicles. At the time of writing, they were remembered as the origin and high point of the divinely approved line of royal succession that had long since gone into terminal decline, and finally expired with Jerusalem's destruction in 586 BCE. Yet David retained an abiding symbolic significance in light of key dynastic prophecies like 2 Samuel 7, which proved to survive the utter political demise of the Davidide clan.

It is not difficult to demonstrate this continued interest in the royal line in postexilic appraisals of Zerubbabel and related genealogies. Nevertheless, a more specifically developed hope for a Davidic "Messiah" did not really surface until the second half of

---

9. Cf. *Dial.* 45, 46.

10. Cf. previously Ign. *Eph.* 18.2 (much less so in *Trall.* 9.1; *Smyrn.* 1.1), cited a few notes above. Two other clear second-century examples are *Prot. Jas.* 10.1 (ed. Strycker 1961, 21); *Asc. Isa.* 11.2.

11. So Irenaeus, *Haer.* 3.21.9. Cf. similarly *Haer.* 3.9.2 and 3.21.5, 9; *Epid.* 36–40, 59, 63; etc.

12. Tertullian, *Adv. Jud.* 9; *Marc.* 3.20; 4.1; 4.36; 5.1; *Carn. Chr.* 21–22. Cf. more generally *Prax.* 27.

13. *Apol.* 9.

14. *Second Treatise of the Great Seth* VII 63.4; *Testimony of Truth* IX 70.3, 25.

the second century BCE, four hundred or so years later. We can discern this recovery of messianic hope vested in the family of David most clearly in the Dead Sea Scrolls and Jewish pseudepigrapha like the *Psalms of Solomon*. A strongly Davidic strand of expectation now remained a standard part of the messianic "toolkit" for at least two centuries.

But what might this mean, more concretely? In what sense could this assertion of Davidic descent attach to real living contemporaries, whether messiahs or not?

Contrary to what is sometimes assumed, such Davidic claims did not in fact expire with Zerubbabel. Ancient Jewish literature repeatedly suggests that there were public genealogical records, in writings ranging from the early Second Temple period (Ezra 2:62; Neh 7:64) via Josephus (*C. Ap.* 1.31; *Life* 6) all the way to rabbinic literature (e.g., *m. Qidd.* 4.4; *Gen. Rab.* 98.8). Occasional Christian confirmation can also be identified: thus in the early third century Julius Africanus asserted that Herod the Great had in fact *destroyed* the genealogical evidence attesting the line of Davidic descent, a despotic move that he assumed would aid his own royal pretentions (Eusebius, *Hist. eccl.* 1.7).

Whether or not written genealogical sources may be deemed plausible as late as the first century BCE, it is not difficult to believe that oral genealogies were maintained among priestly and other distinctive families whose religious or social status depended on their pedigree.[15]

Perhaps most interestingly for our purposes, it is in fact very easy to document that Davidic descent was asserted for a considerable number of individuals ranging from the early postexilic period families of Zerubbabel and the house of Nathan (Zech 12:10, 12) all the way to medieval Judaism. Examples of this are understandably sporadic, but nevertheless sufficiently recurrent and politically significant in ancient Jewish and Christian sources to make it worth our while to take a closer look.

Some of the evidence has come to light only in modern times. So for example an excavation at Giv'at ha-Mivtar in Jerusalem in 1971 produced a first-century burial box (ossuary) with the inscription "of the hou[se of] David": this has been plausibly identified as designating a deceased member of that family.[16] Whether or not that reading of the bone box inscription is correct, we can easily demonstrate that it would be entirely in keeping with other Davidic traditions in contemporary sources from the late Second Temple period and beyond. The Mishnah, for example, assigns the family of David responsibility for the traditional wood offering in the Temple on the twentieth day of the month of Tammuz (*M. Taʿan.* 4.5; cf. Ezra 8:2).

In the mid-third century, the early rabbinic collection known as the Tosefta similarly assumes that the royal line of David and Solomon will identifiably continue forever: although by divine judgment it was divided and succumbed to its enemies, nevertheless in the end the kingdom will be returned to the sons of David.[17] So also

15. So e.g., Richard J. Bauckham, *Jude and the Relatives of Jesus in the Early Church* (Edinburgh: T&T Clark, 1990), 341. Julius Africanus's *Epistle to Aristides* asserts this explicitly.

16. David Flusser and R. Steven Notley, "The House of David on an Ossuary," in *Jesus* (Jerusalem: Magnes, 2001): 180–86; cf. Craig A. Evans, "Jesus and the Ossuaries," *Bulletin for Biblical Research* 13 (2003): 21–46, 36.

17. *T. Sanh.* 4.11; *t. Soṭah* 12.1 (with strikingly similar expectations at Mark 11:10; Acts 1:6). Cf. later *Num. Rab.* 3.2; 15.17.

the third petition of the so-called *Amidah* prayer, integral to Sabbath liturgies since antiquity, implores God to rebuild Jerusalem and reestablish "the throne of David."[18]

In relation to the family of Jesus, claims of Davidic lineage persisted for a considerable time. After the year 70, the Romans' ability to identify the Davidic line enabled its persecution during the reigns of Vespasian (69–79) as well as Domitian (81–96), and perhaps again at the time of Hadrian (117–38). According to one well-known tradition, Domitian interrogated the grandsons of Jude the brother of Jesus, who confirmed their own Davidic descent but were released as peasants posing no danger or consequence.[19] In the second century Hegesippus reports that Simon Clopas, a Jewish Christian bishop in Jerusalem, was said to have been betrayed by an opponent as belonging to the family of David.[20]

The persistent recurrence of these claims strongly suggests that identifiable individuals were asserted to have been Davidic descendants — not just among the descendants of the family of Jesus but also among other Jews. The question of genealogical historicity inevitably remains elusive and for our purposes may safely be left to one side. Here we must note only that from antiquity all the way to the Middle Ages there were repeated and apparently often unproblematic claims that specific Jewish leaders were descended from David. Among these figures were Hillel the Elder (fl. ca. 30–10 BCE) and his descendants in Palestine down to the fifth century,[21] Rabbi Judah the Prince[22] (the editor of the Mishnah), and several centuries of the Exilarchs in Babylonia. Davidic messiahship may have been affirmed for Bar Kokhba.[23] Medieval assertions — about Rashi (1040–1105), for instance — are even more tenuous and the associated genealogies in any case fragmentary at best. Nevertheless, we do witness even in these late attestations the continuation of a trope of Davidic descent that evidently dates back all the way to antiquity.

Jesus' Davidic Sonship: Why It Mattered

Here we have only been able to touch on a few aspects of what is clearly a topic of wide-ranging relevance for the messianic significance of Jesus the Jew. In antiquity, Jews and Christians shared a common concern for the royal and messianic line of David — a concern they were evidently willing to connect to a surprising number of identifiable Jewish figures of their own times.

Both Paul and the Synoptic Gospels assigned considerable theological importance to the "Son of David" title in their own Christology, thereby guaranteeing its ongoing prominence in Christian reflection despite the obvious historical and exegetical tensions besetting the gospel genealogies. Even the impact of these convictions among the earliest gospel readers already locates here an affirmation of enormous Christological and hermeneutical reach. It allowed Christians to hold together belief in Jesus

18. Cf. with similar concreteness of expectation *Pss. Sol.* 17.4, 21; also Acts 1:6 and Sir 45.24–25; 47.22.
19. Eusebius, *Hist. eccl.* 3.12–13 (Vespasian); 3.19–20; 3.32.2–6.
20. Hegesippus in Eusebius, *Eccl. Hist.* 3.32.3–4.
21. E.g., *Gen. Rab.* 98.8.
22. E.g., *b. Šab.* 113b.
23. Cf. *y. Taʿan.* 4.8, 68d; *Lam. Rab.* 1.20.

as prophecy's promised human Messiah with his divine kingship, thereby fending off "Gnostic" challengers to the former conviction and "Ebionite" ones to the latter.[24]

At the same time, Jesus' Davidic descent is decidedly underplayed in some parts of the New Testament, including Hebrews and the fourth gospel, and also (due in part perhaps to the second-century challenges) in the Apostolic and Nicene Creeds. It is perhaps true that these "portable summaries" of the faith were as good as one could expect in the circumstances. Nevertheless, their neglect of Jesus' lineage did little to alleviate the frequently inadequate theology of Israel that characterized the later church's interpretation of its two-Testament Scripture.

Nevertheless, the descent of *both* Joseph and Mary from David immediately turned out to be an inspired aid to interpretation: it allowed the Son of David to be the Son of God and vice versa, rejecting all false Christological dichotomies.[25]

But could this device claim exegetical justification? Luke 1:5 after all tells us that Mary's relative Elizabeth was "of the daughters of Aaron," which might instead point to priestly rather than royal lineage — a point potentially also reflected in the second-century *Infancy Gospel of James*. Nevertheless, Scriptural support for Mary's Davidic descent was located in Luke's infancy narrative, where Gabriel announces the conception, without Joseph's involvement, of a son from the line of David (1:32; cf. 1:69). Luke's account requires Mary also to be registered for the census of Davidides in Bethlehem (2:5). More specifically still, both Origen and Chrysostom went on to derive Mary's Davidic heritage explicitly from Luke 1:27, effectively reading "to a virgin (engaged to a man called Joseph) of the house of David. And the virgin's name was Mary."[26] Contemporary commentaries tend with very few exceptions to rule out such a reading, which appears to most of them to strain an already overloaded grammatical structure. Yet the early interpretive footprint of this passage supposes precisely such a reading. Exegetically, moreover, this may be rather less strained as a reading of Luke's admittedly complex text than the critics suppose: a Davidic Mary in 1:27 does make excellent exegetical and theological sense of the angel's announcement in the same context (1:32; cf. 1:69) that God will give to Mary's humanly unfathered child "the throne of his ancestor David" (1:32 NRSV).

In purely historical terms, these questions are not of course finally resolvable by recourse to DNA fingerprinting. What we do discover from the exegetical footprint of these texts, however, is a clear sense that belief in the Son of David came to safeguard the second-century struggle against Gnostic, Marcionite, and other attempts to devalue the biblical and Jewish roots of Jesus and the gospel.[27] And that concern is no less topical in the present age.

24. On the latter, see Oskar Skarsaune, "The Ebionites," in *Jewish Believers in Jesus: the Early Centuries* (ed. Oskar Skarsaune and Reidar Hvalvik; Peabody, Mass.: Hendrickson, 2007), 419–62.

25. Cf. explicitly Eusebius, *Dem. Ev.* 7.3.

26. Origen, *Hom. Luke*, frag. 20a; cf. Chrysostom, *Hom. Matt.* 2.7–8.

27. On this point see further Markus Bockmuehl, "God's Life as a Jew: Remembering the Son of God as Son of David," in *Seeking the Identity of Jesus: A Pilgrimage* (ed. Beverly Roberts Gaventa and Richard B. Hays; Grand Rapids: Eerdmans, 2008), 60–78.

The Son of David in Christian Faith Today

During some of the darkest days of Christian-Jewish relations Karl Barth, the twentieth century's leading theologian, famously drew attention to the fact that "the Word did not simply become any 'flesh,' any man humbled and suffering. It became Jewish flesh."[28] This observation bears directly on our theme in the present chapter: "[God] elects to make His fellowship with man radically true by becoming man Himself in the person of the Son of David, Jesus; when He elects the people of Israel for the purpose of assuming its flesh and blood. What is really meant by the humanity of the whole elected community of God, what it costs God to make Himself one with it, to be its God, emerges in its Israelite form."[29] For Barth this entailed that "in order to be elect ourselves, for good or evil we must either be Jews or belong to this Jew."[30]

The early Christians found Jesus' messianic identity definitively confirmed in his resurrection. And so they passionately confessed that the Jesus who died was the Jesus who rose again (Acts 2:36; 17:3; Rom 1:3 – 4; etc.): as Jesus of Nazareth was the Son of David, so also was the risen and ascended Lord — a point particularly explicit in the book of Revelation (5:5; 22:16). For Christian faith in the Jewish Messiah today that point matters no less, as Barth rightly notes. The Son of God "was incarnate of the Holy Spirit and the Virgin Mary" as the Son of David — and it is none other than this elect, crucified, and exalted Son of David "according to the flesh" who is "the Son of God with power by the resurrection of the dead."

For Further Reading

Ahearne-Kroll, Stephen P. *The Psalms of Lament in Mark's Passion: Jesus' Davidic Suffering.* Cambridge: Cambridge University Press, 2007.

Bockmuehl, Markus. "God's Life as a Jew: Remembering the Son of God as Son of David." Pages 60 – 78 in *Seeking the Identity of Jesus: A Pilgrimage.* Edited by Beverly R. Gaventa and Richard B. Hays. Grand Rapids: Eerdmans, 2008.

———. "Seeing the Son of David." Pages 189 – 228 in *Seeing the Word: Refocusing New Testament Study.* Grand Rapids: Baker Academic, 2006.

Chae, Young S. *Jesus as the Eschatological Davidic Shepherd: Studies in the Old Testament, Second Temple Judaism, and in the Gospel of Matthew.* Tübingen: Mohr Siebeck, 2006.

Daly-Denton, Margaret. *David in the Fourth Gospel: The Johannine Reception of the Psalms.* Leiden, Netherlands: Brill, 2000.

Henrix, Hans Hermann. "The Son of God Became Human as a Jew: Implications of the Jewishness of Jesus for Christology." Pages 114 – 43 in *Christ Jesus and the Jewish People Today: New Explorations of Theological Interrelationships.* Edited by Philip A. Cunningham, Joseph Sievers, Mary C. Boys, Hans Hermann Henrix, and Jesper Svartvik. Grand Rapids: Eerdmans, 2011.

Himmelfarb, Martha. "The Mother of the Messiah in the Talmud Yerushalmi and Sefer Zerubbabel." Pages 369 – 89 in *The Talmud Yerushalmi and Graeco-Roman Culture III.* Edited by Peter Schäfer and Catherine Hezser. Tübingen: Mohr Siebeck, 2002.

Kingsbury, Jack D. "The Title 'Son of David'

---

28. *Church Dogmatics* IV/1, 166.
29. *Church Dogmatics* II/2, 207.
30. *Church Dogmatics* III/3, 225.

in Matthew's Gospel." *Journal of Biblical Literature* 95 (1976): 591–602.

Malbon, Elizabeth Struthers. "The Jesus of Mark and the 'Son of David.'" Pages 162–85 in *Between Author and Audience in Mark*. Sheffield, UK: Phoenix, 2009.

Marshall, Bruce D. "Christ and the Cultures: The Jewish People and Christian Theology." Pages 81–100 in *Cambridge Companion to Christian Doctrine*. Edited by Colin E. Gunton. New York: Cambridge University Press, 1997.

Meyer, Barbara U. "The Dogmatic Significance of Christ Being Jewish." Pages 144–56 in *Christ Jesus and the Jewish People Today: New Explorations of Theological Interrelationships*. Edited by Philip A. Cunningham, Joseph Sievers, Mary C. Boys, Hans Hermann Henrix, and Jesper Svartvik. Grand Rapids: Eerdmans, 2011.

Miura, Yuzuru. *David in Luke-Acts: His Portrayal in the Light of Early Judaism*. Tübingen: Mohr Siebeck, 2007.

Novakovic, Lidija. *Messiah, the Healer of the Sick: A Study of Jesus as the Son of David in the Gospel of Matthew*. Tübingen: Mohr Siebeck, 2003.

Strauss, M. L. *The Davidic Messiah in Luke-Acts: The Promise and Its Fulfilment in Lukan Christology*. Sheffield, UK: Sheffield Academic Press, 1995.

Van Egmond, Richard. "The Messianic 'Son of David' in Matthew." *Journal of Greco-Roman Christianity and Judaism* 3 (2006): 41–71.

Willitts, Joel. *Matthew's Messianic Shepherd-King: In Search of the Lost Sheep of the House of Israel*. Vol. 147 BNZW. Berlin; New York: Walter de Gruyter, 2007.

CHAPTER 26

Jewish Priority, Election, and the Gospel

Douglas Harink

Taking our direction from the New Testament, we must say that, theologically speaking, there is nothing prior to the gospel. Whether we study the canonical Gospels, or the Epistles of Paul, Peter, and John, or Hebrews, or the book of Revelation, we learn that the one who *himself* comes *as the gospel* is both temporally and eternally prior to his arrival in history as Jesus of Nazareth. The titles *Christos* and *huios Theou* (Son of God) are in their first-century Jewish context *messianic* designations, but already in the earliest Christian documents they also (and perhaps just so) come to signify the preexistent one who is conceived in Mary through the Holy Spirit (Matthew and Luke) or "from above" (John; see 3:31), the one whom God sends "in the fullness of time" (Paul; see Gal 4:4 NRSV). This same one is declared emphatically (according to such classic Christological texts as 1 Cor 8:6; Col 1:15–20; Heb 1:1–4; John 1:1–18; Rev 5) to be the one through whom all things are created, by whom all things are sustained, and for whom all things are appointed as their final end. He is "the Alpha and the Omega, the First and the Last, the Beginning and the End" (Rev 22:13), the divine eternal life from which all creation is brought forth and into which all creation will finally be taken. These New Testament declarations about *Christos* and *huios Theou* come to theological fruition in the Nicene Creed.

The Priority of the Messiah

We must, therefore, speak of *messianic priority* before we speak of election and Jewish priority. The Messiah precedes creation, precedes the nations, precedes the election of Israel, precedes the historical reality of the Jewish people. Apart from the Messiah these other realities would not be. They are because the Messiah first is, and because the Father wills them to be through the Messiah. The Messiah, who himself is the gospel, is before all. When he is born in the flesh as Jesus of Nazareth, and is "apocalypsed" in Israel,[1] he comes to "his own" people (John 1:11). Before he belongs to this people, they belong to him. Because the messianic gospel is prior to all, the apostle Paul can declare that this gospel was announced beforehand (*proeuēngelisato*) to Abraham (Gal 3:8), and that its content — blessing to the nations and resurrection

---

1. I use the term "apocalypsed" rather than the usual "revealed" to indicate that, as the whole New Testament witnesses, the coming of the Messiah in history is far more than an unveiling or showing of previously hidden mysteries; it is God's dramatic, interruptive, critical, and rectifying *incursion* into the world of historical and cosmic injustice, oppression, and bondage, under which Israel, the nations, and all creation are suffering.

273

from the dead (Rom 4) — was the same in the time of Abraham as it is in the time
after the Messiah's historical arrival, for the Messiah himself is that content. As Paul
says remarkably in Galatians 3:16, collapsing all of the generations of Abraham into a
single moment, the Messiah is the singular "seed" of Abraham. The various historical
times of Abraham, Israel, the Prophets, Jesus, the apostles, and the Church are bound
together and in some measure even blended together, made contemporaneous, in the
differentiated but singular time of the Messiah. The transfiguration of Jesus on the
mountain is the clearest display of this in the Gospels: there, gathered in one place
and time, are Moses and Elijah representing Israel, the Law, and the Prophets; the
three apostles representing the Church; and the Messiah Jesus. All are enveloped by
the bright cloud of the Spirit. Jesus, whose glorious transfigured reality encompasses
all with his light, is declared by the Father to be the beloved Son: "Listen to him," the
Voice says (Matt 17:5). In this moment the divine messianic reality of the one with
whom Moses and Elijah (the past) are already in eternal conversation (the future) is
apocalypsed (in the present) to the church.

    The priority of the gospel — that is, the priority of the Messiah — is also declared
in the New Testament with respect to Israel's Torah. In the Gospels Jesus displays an
authority over the Torah that is noticed by all those who see his deeds and hear his
words. That authority is nowhere more evident than in the familiar section of the
Sermon on the Mount (Matt 5:21 – 48) where Jesus says, "You have heard that it was
said …; but I tell you …" The point here, as Jesus himself makes crystal clear, is not
that his authority cancels (*katalusai*) the Torah and the Prophets; rather, Jesus by his
own authority fulfills (*plērōsai*) the Torah and Prophets (Matt 5:17). By his authority
he authorizes their ongoing authority in Israel until "all is accomplished" (Matt 5:18
ESV), that is, until the messianic age arrives in fullness. But it is just as clear in the
Gospels that the authority of the Torah and the Prophets is subordinate to and dependent upon the authority of the Messiah as the Lord, and that their authority consists in
their being read in the light of, and as witnesses to, the singular, normative messianity
that is enacted by Jesus of Nazareth in his life, death, and resurrection.

    The relationship of the Messiah to the Torah in Paul's writings is a matter of
much debate — a debate that cannot be recounted here. Paul announces, famously,
in Romans 10:4 that "Christ is the [*telos*] of the Law." Debate rages over the meaning
of *telos* or "end." Does "end" mean "cancellation"; or "abrogation"; or "fulfillment"; or
"completion"; or "purpose"? Some help might be offered by considering the role of
Torah in the conceptual universe, indeed, in the "philosophy" of Judaism in the time
of Paul. From the great song of Wisdom in Proverbs 8, to the praise of Wisdom in
the Wisdom of Solomon (chaps. 6 – 8) and Sirach (chaps. 24, 43), powerful claims are
made about the priority and role of Wisdom in God's work of creating, ordering, and
sustaining all things. Wisdom then pitches her tent, takes up her dwelling, in Zion, in
the beloved city Jerusalem, in the chosen people of God: "I took root in an honored
people, in the portion of the Lord, his heritage" (Sir 24:10 – 12 NRSV). The *Torah* is
the concrete revelation in Israel of the Wisdom by which all things are created and
in which all things hold together. "All this [wisdom] is the book of the covenant of
the Most High God, the law that Moses commanded us as an inheritance for the

congregations of Jacob" (Sir 24:23 NRSV). To observe Torah, then, is not primarily or essentially to "obey the rules"; it is, rather, to participate through concrete bodily practices in the very goodness and order and beauty of creation brought about by God through preexistent Wisdom and revealed to Israel in Torah.

This philosophy of Torah that Paul no doubt shared as a Hellenistic Pharisee seems to stand behind Paul's understanding of Christ in such texts as 1 Corinthians 8:6, Colossians 1:15 – 2:4, and Ephesians 1:3 – 14. But where Paul the Pharisee would formerly have conceptually positioned the Torah, the earthly image of the preexistent invisible Wisdom of God, he now positions the Messiah, who is himself the Wisdom of God in person, and therefore also the concrete personal embodiment of the Torah of God.[2] So when Paul states in Romans 10:4, *telos gar nomou Christos* (Messiah is the *telos* of Torah), he is far from canceling or abrogating the Torah revealed to Israel. Rather, the Messiah assumes — indeed, has always assumed — Torah to himself, summing it up in his own person, fulfilling it in his faithfulness, obedience, and self-emptying humility (Rom 5:12 – 21; Phil 2:6 – 11), and rendering by his death and resurrection transparent witness to the creating, ordering, and sustaining Wisdom of God, which he himself also is. The Messiah "supercedes" the Torah, not by making it obsolete, but by enveloping it in his own personal divine reality. God's apocalypse in Jesus the Messiah is in this way the apocalypse of the *telos* of Torah.

The central issue, therefore, between Paul's messianic Judaism on the one hand and the Torah-Judaism of his contemporaries on the other should not be construed in terms of abstract principles such as "grace" and "law" or "faith" and "works." The central issue is this: Will the reality and significance of God's Wisdom and Torah be subsumed within and defined by the now-apocalypsed divine messianic reality of Jesus; or will the messianic reality of Jesus (if it is granted at all by Paul's Jewish compatriots) be subsumed within and defined by an already established conception of divine Wisdom and Torah? This central controversial issue between Paul's Judaism and the Judaism of those (whether messianic or not) who opposed his mission comes to its moment of greatest intensity (for Paul at least) in the Torah's assessment of the crucifixion of Jesus as "curse" (Gal 3:13), and in Wisdom's assessment of the crucifixion as "foolishness" and weakness (1 Cor 1:18 – 24). In view of this for Paul, to whom the crucified Jesus was apocalypsed as the risen and glorified Messiah, Wisdom and Torah themselves undergo a fundamental revaluation. They are thought and defined and qualified *within and by* the prior and greater reality of the Messiah crucified and resurrected, and only — but truly — thereby "saved"; for independent of this messianic *Aufhebung*[3] they do not provide the sufficient criteria for discerning the work of God in creation, in Israel, and among the nations. The messianic *Aufhebung* of Torah in Messiah Jesus remains perhaps the fundamental point of difference

---

2. Cf. Robert Jenson's rendering of John 1:14 ("The Torah became flesh and dwelt among us") in "Toward a Christian Theology of Judaism," in *Jews and Christians: People of God* (ed. Carl E. Braaten and Robert W. Jenson; Grand Rapids: Eerdmans, 2003), 3, 6, 11 – 13.

3. The German term *Aufhebung* (sublation) has a long and complex history within philosophical discussion and is particularly crucial in Hegelian philosophy. My use of the word here mildly harkens to that discussion, but more importantly it aims to capture the pattern of death and resurrection in the New Testament. Wisdom and Torah undergo a kind of death and resurrection when they are revalued through the crucifixion of the Messiah.

between Christianity and Judaism even to this day.[4] Messianic Judaism, on the other hand, aims to represent the place where this *Aufhebung* is again made manifest in the concrete historical practice of Torah by Jews in Jesus the Messiah.

The Election of Israel

As Jews and Christians throughout the centuries have often acknowledged, God's election of his people Israel constitutes the very heart of the biblical narrative. The dynamic of God's gracious election pervades the narratives of Genesis, the story of the Exodus and the giving of the Law, the history of the kings (particularly David and Solomon), and the proclamations of the Prophets. We cannot do justice here to the breadth, depth, and complexity of the theology of election in the Hebrew Scriptures.[5] Nevertheless, we must note some of its key features.

The reason *why* God chooses one person and one nation, and not others, remains largely a mystery. Why does God favor Jacob and not Esau? Paul, drawing on a text from Malachi (1:2 – 3) states the prophet's words bluntly, "I have loved Jacob, but Esau I have hated" — and this divine decision is made, Paul notes, "before the twins were born or had done anything good or bad" (Rom 9:10 – 13). To ask why God "loves" one and "hates" another (which for Paul is only to say that God "elects" Jacob and not Esau) is to attempt to get "behind" the concrete mystery of God's decision. Nevertheless, we are not left wholly without some clues to this mystery. If we ask, Why were Abraham and Sarah chosen, and not some other family among the apparently vast number of candidates in the ancient Near East? we are led to the single note about this family given in Genesis 11:30 (NIV 1984), "Now Sarai was barren; she had no children." This is the note that creates the narrative plot and tension that runs throughout the story of Abraham in Genesis 12 – 22. What is at stake in this note? It is the fact that, amidst all of the blessing, natural potency, and procreation going on in the post-flood generations recorded in Genesis 10 – 11, this family in its childlessness represents curse, impotence, uncreation. Mysteriously, "foolishly," God sets his eye and his heart upon a family that is at a *dead end*: as Paul aptly states it in Romans 4:17 – 19, if there is to be a history here, it can come about only through a new act of the creating and resurrecting God, "the God who gives life to the dead and calls into being things that were not." Israel comes into being and is set among the nations not as a product of natural generative powers, but as a new creative act of God, brought about by that power by which God creates a garden in the desert (Gen 2) and raises Jesus from the dead. God chooses this family devoid of natural human potential in order to demonstrate his everlasting covenant faithfulness in their now-dead flesh,

4. As, for example, the Jewish philosopher Jacob Taubes suggests: "Christian theology is based on Christology, which means that all things, human and divine, achieve relevance only as they refer to Jesus the Christ. Judaism, based on the law, grants relevance to all things, human and divine, only as they relate to halacha" (*From Cult to Culture: Fragments toward a Critique of Historical Reason* [Stanford: Stanford University Press, 2010], 56). As Taubes also recognizes, the doctrine of the Trinity is theologically dependent upon and therefore secondary to the prior valuation of the role of the Messiah vis-à-vis Wisdom and Torah in God's work of creation, revelation, and redemption.

5. A recent outstanding study that is also accessible to the general reader is Joel S. Kaminsky, *Yet I Loved Jacob: Reclaiming the Biblical Concept of Election* (Nashville: Abingdon, 2007).

by bringing about through them a history of blessing and fruitfulness against and beyond the powers of nature. By remaining faithful to Abraham and Sarah and their progeny God establishes for them (and for the "families of the earth"; Gen 12:3 NRSV) his own personal reality and character. *This* God is not a force of nature. Rather, *this is an electing, promising, covenanting God who evokes unqualified personal trust and risky venture.* Throughout the patriarchal narratives of Genesis this God continues to choose the "least of these" in order to display his creating, resurrecting power and steadfast faithfulness toward them. That is also the story of the Exodus. It is the constant message of the Former and Latter Prophets.

When God comes and calls Abram and Sarai, he makes the purpose *for which* he chooses them clear. He chooses them in order (1) to exalt them among the nations, contrary to all normal expectation; (2) to bless them in the midst of the nations; and (3) through them to bless the nations (Gen 12:1 – 3). But before we come to this election and call we must first take account (as the Genesis narrative does) of *the nations* — those that are there "naturally." The table of the nations in Genesis 10 represents the geographic spreading and cultural-linguistic pluralizing of the peoples of the earth according to God's blessing and command to the sons of Noah in Genesis 9:1. While this is indeed occurring in a "post-fall" world it is nevertheless clear that Genesis 10 is telling a story of God's continuing grace toward and blessing upon the "non-elect" peoples. Genesis 10 is not a history of "sin" and its historical (or eternal) effects, in the midst of which the story of Abraham's call enters simply as God's act of "redemption." In fact, if we look for a narrative of God's redemptive action, there is one more explicitly told in the story of Babel in Genesis 11:1 – 9. There, against the disobedient centralizing, self-exalting, and imperial intentions of the political community gathered on the plain of Shinar, God comes down and brings about the spreading and cultural-linguistic pluralizing of peoples that he intended according to Genesis 10. God's judgment upon Babel is God's redemptive grace at work for the nations.

For what purpose, then, are Abram and Sarai chosen, called, and resurrected? It is in order to set among the nations — already the recipients of God's blessing, judgment, and redemptive grace — an *other* nation beyond the power of *natura*, an *other* blessing beyond the natural blessing of spreading and pluralizing. This *other* will forever be the particular historical witness to *God's own Otherness as covenant-keeping faithfulness and mercy* in the midst of the nations. In his radical faithfulness and blessing toward *this* people, God will be made known as the God he is *to all the peoples of the earth.* From God's faithfulness to elect Israel, the non-elect nations may learn that God has mercy on the cursed that they might be blessed beyond expectation; on the despised that they might be vindicated; on the lowly that they might be exalted; on the nothings that they might be made something; on the enslaved that they might be liberated; on the dead that they might be raised to new life. In other words, from Israel the non-elect nations may learn the *messianic* shape and character of God's work, which is definitively apocalypsed in the Messiah of Israel, Jesus of Nazareth.

The revelation of God's being and character to the non-elect peoples through the chosen people is fundamentally predicated upon God's unconditional faithfulness toward the chosen people. If God does not remain faithful to *this* people to the end, not only in blessing but also in judgment upon their disobedience, then there is no clear witness among the nations that the God of Abraham and Sarah is the rightful object of unqualified trust. It is necessary to make this point against the all-too-frequent tendency among Christians to emphasize only the third "instrumental" aspect of God's promise to Abram, that is, that in or through Abram and his family all the nations of the earth shall be blessed. God's affection and favor comes to rest truly and uniquely upon Abram and Sarai and their people *for their own sake* — God loves *them* — and only as such for the sake of the non-elect peoples. The patriarchs and matriarchs and the people Israel are not merely the instruments or channels through which God will bless the nations, so that perhaps at some point later on they might be set aside when they have "served their purpose" — or perhaps have failed to do so. No. God's covenant with them is everlasting. He loves Israel; only in this way is his love for the nations made known.

The Messiah, Israel, and the Nations

When at the appointed time the Messiah comes in person in Jesus, he comes to *Israel* — to the *people* Israel. Only when he is raised from the dead does he send his emissaries to the *nations*. Jesus is in fact God's very own visitation and apocalypse to his chosen people for their corporate judgment and healing. The Messiah comes to Israel because, as we have already suggested, the people Israel itself belongs to the Messiah, is chosen in the Messiah, from the beginning, insofar as the Messiah is the one through whom the God of Israel creates, elects, redeems, renews. The Messiah is God to Israel. He is also Israel to God, the royal representative and corporate (indeed, incorporating) head of this theopolitical body. "Messiah" means nothing if it does not mean this. The whole logic of the gospel narrative depends upon this identity of the Messiah as God's own coming to Israel and as the whole corporate Israel standing before God.

Christian theology has largely forgotten the corporate, theopolitical character of the messianic mission of Jesus. It has forgotten that the advent of the Messiah is for the salvation of the people Israel, and not merely for the salvation of "individuals" — individuals construed in modern, liberal-democratic fashion as free choosers of their "religion." Those individuals who do become the apostles of Jesus the Messiah do not themselves choose this role: they are chosen, elected by the Messiah. According to each of the Gospels an inner circle of exactly twelve disciples is chosen in a representative way. These are the beginning, the firstfruits of Israel's corporate renewal as a people under their divinely appointed king. The disciples are not lifted out and separated from Israel as "Christians"; they, like the Messiah himself, are Israelites commissioned to enter ever more deeply into solidarity with and dependence upon the people as they announce the good news of the messianic era now breaking in upon Israel. "Go nowhere among the Gentiles, and enter no town of the Samaritans, but go rather to the lost sheep of the house of Israel. As you go, proclaim the good news, 'The kingdom of heaven has come near.' Cure the sick, raise the dead, cleanse the lepers, cast out demons" (Matt 10:5–8 NRSV). When Israel, through its other corporate representatives, the leaders in Jerusalem, refuses Jesus' messianic mission and message and calls for Jesus' crucifixion, this does not become the occasion when the apostles abandon Israel and go *instead* to the nations. The apostles remain in Jerusalem, and it is there that the Holy Spirit comes upon them and through them brings about further renewal in Israel. The apostles remain Israelites to the end and seek the salvation of Israel (Acts 1:6) even as they are commissioned as messianic witnesses to the ends of the earth (Matt 28:16–20; Acts 1:8).

It is no different for the apostle to the nations. For Paul there is no conflict between his appointment by Jesus the Messiah as apostle to the nations and his fundamental solidarity with and hope for the salvation of his people Israel. Quite the contrary: each is in direct proportion to the other in its level of intensity, and not just in "feeling," but also and primarily theologically. His messianic mission to the nations is for the sake of Israel; his solidarity with Israel is for the sake of the nations (Rom 11:11–12). The mystery of the gospel is *messianic peace between Israel and the nations*, a peace that is even now, in the single messianic "day" that reaches from the Messiah's arrival in suffering to his arrival in glory, being brought about between those from Israel and those from the nations who find themselves praising God and rejoicing together under the rule of the one Lord of all (Rom 15:7–13). The ancient distinction created by God between Israel and the nations is never dissolved in Paul — that is the whole burden of Romans, coming to a focus in chapters 9–11. The ancient hope, eagerly anticipated by the Prophets, that Israel and the nations might live at peace and in mutual blessing is never abrogated in Paul — that is the testimony of Ephesians 1–3.

There is no New Testament theological reason to think that the corporate, theopolitical vision of the Hebrew Scriptures for Israel and the nations comes to an end with the coming of Jesus. Rather, that vision is both intensified in and for Israel and announced as the true destiny of the Gentile nations in the Messiah. The sign, witness, sacrament, and down payment of that vision is the table fellowship and worship of Jews and Gentiles together in the messianic theopolitical reality called the *ekklēsia* — where Jews as Jews practice Torah, the *telos* of which is given in the Messiah, and Gentiles as Gentiles work out their own salvation in fear and trembling in the Messiah; where each group gives itself in cruciform service, indeed sacrifice, for the sake of the other; where each group seeks to build the other up in its unique form of witness; where each group displays toward its wider theopolitical body of origin, whether Israel or the nations, a testimony to the cruciform way of the Messiah in this time before the time of the restoration of all things and of the kingdom to Israel; where each group seeks blessing and to be a blessing in the midst of these wider theopolitical realities for their welfare and healing.

Precisely as sign, witness, sacrament, and down payment, the *ekklēsia* in its ongoing duality as messianic Jews and messianic Gentiles anticipates, hopes, and prays for the full theopolitical reality of Israel and the nations living at peace under the reign of Jesus the Messiah. Israel itself has continued in some form — not primarily through land and temple, but through the practice of halacha — for two millennia since the time of the destruction of Jerusalem. Its earlier attempts to restore itself as a nation among nations, often through its own "zeal" (cf. Rom 9:30–10:3) rather than through trust in God's own act of justice (10:4), came to an end in that event. Since then Israel, as "Judaism" and mostly in Diaspora, has learned to live peaceably among the nations, observing Torah faithfully and trusting God to preserve, deliver, and one day restore it.[6]

By contrast, the Gentile nations are as far from living peaceably as ever before, seeking to establish their own place in the world with violent zeal, often with the robust support and encouragement of the churches that claim Israel's Messiah as their Lord. More deeply troubling theologically, these same nations, often without protest from the churches and sometimes with their support, have from time to time sought the end of Israel and the end of the Jews. The churches themselves even from the earliest centuries have sought, often violently, to erase Judaism in its midst, such that Jewish "Christians" have consistently been required to cease being Jewish. The contradictions in these matters for the churches "of Jesus Christ" are so grave as to be damning (Rom 11:17 – 24), except for the grace of God through Jesus, Israel's Messiah.

We may in our time be seeing a new day in the history of Israel and the nations, one given by the Messiah himself. There are three encouraging signs. First, while in the past the Gentile churches have usually acknowledged that apart from Israel of old they would not now be "in the Messiah," they are now beginning to acknowledge that apart from the reality of Israel *today* — represented primarily in Judaism — they are equally cut adrift from the tree into which they were once grafted. Second, Jews within traditional Judaism are beginning to acknowledge the work of the God of Israel in the Gentile churches. Third, Jews who find themselves "in the Messiah Jesus" are attempting to recover their witness *as Jews within Judaism* despite the fact that wider Judaism is reluctant to recognize them as such. These are small, halting, and often vulnerable beginnings. They may appear weak, foolish, lacking any real potential or power to influence or "bless" the peoples and cultures of the modern world. But then we remember our father Abraham and our mother Sarah, and the crucified Messiah.

---

6. The most significant exception to this is the modern nation-state of Israel. In what sense this state, constituted and maintained as it is through political and military power, *is* Israel, is a matter of debate among Jews. It seems to me that contemporary *Messianic* Jews must carefully avoid giving any kind of assent to this state that is not fundamentally qualified by the normative cruciform political existence enacted in and for Israel by Jesus, Israel's Messiah. This may be one of the most significant cutting edges for Messianic Jews, for whom being "pro-Israel" often does not exclude militant Zionism. Some surprising resources for thinking through their *messianic* witness might be found in some recent Jewish philosophers such as Daniel and Jonathan Boyarin, Franz Rosenzweig, Walter Benjamin, and Jacob Taubes.

For Further Reading

Bader-Saye, Scott. *Church and Israel after Christendom: The Politics of Election.* Boulder: Westview, 1999.

Brueggemann, Walter. "Election." Pages 61 – 64 in *Reverberations of Faith: A Theological Handbook of Old Testament Themes.* Louisville: Westminster John Knox, 2002.

Givens, Tommy. "We the People: Israel and the Catholicity of Jesus." PhD diss., Duke University, 2012. Online: http://dukespace.lib.duke.edu/dspace/handle/10161/5733.

Harink, Douglas. "Israel: Who Will Bring Any Charge against God's Elect?" Pages 151 – 207 in *Paul among the Postliberals: Pauline Theology beyond Christendom and Modernity.* Grand Rapids: Brazos, 2003.

———. "Paul and Israel: An Apocalyptic Reading." *Pro Ecclesia* 16 (2007): 359 – 80.

Kaminsky, Joel S. *Yet I Loved Jacob: Reclaiming the Biblical Concept of Election.* Nashville: Abingdon, 2007.

Levenson, Jon D. *Death and Resurrection of the Beloved Son: The Transformation of Child Sacrifice in Judaism and Christianity.* New Haven: Yale University Press, 1993.

———. "Universal Horizon of Biblical Particularism." Pages 143 – 69 in *Ethnicity and the Bible.* Edited by M. G. Brett. Leiden, Netherlands: Brill, 1996.

Lohr, Joel N. *Chosen and Unchosen: Conceptions of Election in the Pentateuch and Jewish-Christian Interpretation.* Winona Lake, Ind.: Eisenbrauns, 2009.

Novak, David. *The Election of Israel: The Idea of the Chosen People.* Cambridge: Cambridge University Press, 1995.

Osten-Sacken, Peter von der. *Christian-Jewish Dialogue: Theological Foundations.* Philadelphia: Fortress, 1986.

Rudolph, David J. "Intertextual Issues: Understanding Paul's Jewishness in Relation to Being in Christ." Pages 23 – 89 in *A Jew to the Jews: Jewish Contours of Pauline Flexibility in 1 Corinthians 9:19 – 23.* Tübingen: Mohr Siebeck, 2011.

Runesson. Anders. "Particularistic Judaism and Universalistic Christianity? Some Critical Remarks on Terminology and Theology." *Journal of Greco-Roman Christianity and Judaism* 1 (2000): 120 – 44.

Sohn, Seock-Tae. *The Divine Election of Israel.* Grand Rapids: Eerdmans, 1991.

Wyschogrod, Michael. *The Body of Faith: Judaism as Corporeal Election.* Minneapolis: Seabury, 1983.

———. "Israel, the Church, and Election." Pages 79 – 87 in *Brothers in Hope.* Edited by John M. Oesterreicher. South Orange, N.Y.: Herder and Herder, 1970.

CHAPTER 27

The Standard Canonical Narrative and the Problem of Supersessionism

R. Kendall Soulen

The idea of a canonical narrative rests on the insight that interpreting a complex text such as the Bible requires one to move back and forth between smaller and larger units of meaning. To understand a sentence it is necessary to understand the words that make it up. But the opposite is also true. To understand a word in a sentence, one must make a judgment about the meaning of the sentence as a whole, for a sentence is not just a string of words but a semantic unit in its own right that determines the meaning of words according to rules of grammar and syntax. A similar relationship between part and whole repeats itself at larger levels of literary organization. To understand Romans 9 – 11, for example, one must make a host of judgments about individual sentences and the larger rhetorical units in which they appear. But one must also venture a judgment about the central aim or purpose of Romans as a whole (its *scopus*, in the terminology of older interpreters), for the letter's purpose governs how the various rhetorical units function in the total composition.

At the highest level of literary organization, making sense of the Bible requires one to venture a judgment that moves back and forth between the many elements that comprise the canon and the canon as a whole. It is true that not everyone thinks this last step is a valid one. The canon differs from Paul's letter to the Romans because it is not the product of a single human author, but a sprawling anthology of documents written and edited by different people in varied circumstances over a very long stretch of time. Many contemporary interpreters of the Bible are so impressed by the canon's variety that they resist any suggestion that it can be interpreted as a meaningful unity. The best that can be done, they insist, is to let each part of the canon speak in its own way, without any effort to hear the different voices as participating in or evoking a deeper unity.

Emphasis on the canon's internal variety, so characteristic of modern biblical studies, has yielded many benefits, much as ever-stronger microscopes yield sharper images of the fibers of a piece of cloth. Yet such an emphasis alone is incomplete, at least when measured by the approach to Scripture perennially practiced by Israel and the church, the communities that created the biblical canons in the first place. The *parts* of the Christian canon have indeed no single human author, but the canon as a *whole* does: the church. Moreover, the church assembled the canon in the conviction that this particular set of writings, beginning with Israel's holy books, is the privileged written instrument used by the Holy Spirit to instruct and edify the church in the things of God. Accordingly, Christians have routinely interpreted the canon as a unity, as a reflex of the unity and uniqueness of God, whose instrument and witness the canon is.

It is at this juncture that the concept of a canonical construal or narrative comes in handy.[1] A canonical narrative is a judgment about how the canon hangs together as a witness to and instrument of God. Such a judgment rests on innumerably many decisions about the meaning of individual words, sentences, rhetorical units, books, and so on. But a canonical narrative is more than just the sum of all such decisions. Just as bread is not simply certain quantities of flour, salt, oil, and yeast, but the product of their interaction, so the Bible interpreted by means of a canonical narrative is no mere anthology of writings; "it is the new instrument produced by the working together of these parts when they are taken in a certain way, that is, according to the canonical construal which has been adopted."[2]

St. Irenaeus, the Standard Canonical Narrative, and Supersessionism

At first glance, the concept of a canonical narrative may seem to introduce an intolerable element of relativism into biblical interpretation, by multiplying the possible grounds of disagreement *ad infinitum*. In fact, the concept points to a powerfully stabilizing and unifying factor in Christian tradition. A shared canonical narrative permits interpreters to disagree about the meaning of individual texts while still agreeing on the larger story of which they are a part, like artisans who differ about where best to place a stone in a mosaic, while still agreeing on the overall design.

The first theologian fully to articulate a Christian canonical narrative was Irenaeus of Lyon. Irenaeus's grand design accomplished two supremely important things. It showed how God the Father, in unity with the Word and Spirit, acts consistently and graciously in all his works, from creation to new creation, from Genesis to Revelation. And it focused on God's Word made flesh, Jesus Christ, so as to render intelligible the central place accorded to him by Christian worship. Indeed, Irenaeus did these things with such extraordinary power, breadth, and detail that his vision of the unity of the Christian canon has been determinative for the Christian tradition ever since. Irenaeus, we might say, made it possible for Christians to argue productively about the interpretation of this or that part of Scripture, by articulating a vision of the whole to which all could subscribe.

It is in light of Irenaeus's accomplishment that we can properly estimate the enormity of the challenge posed by the rejection of supersessionism by significant parts of contemporary Christianity.[3] This development is perhaps the single most dramatic

---

1. Charles Wood proposed the term "canonical construal" in *The Formation of Christian Understanding: Theological Hermeneutics* (Philadelphia: Westminster, 1981), 78. I prefer the term "canonical narrative," in view of the prominent role played by narrative in the church's traditional canonical construal. See R. Kendall Soulen, *The God of Israel and Christian Theology* (Minneapolis: Fortress, 1996), 14.

2. Wood, *Formation of Christian Understanding*, 109.

3. For documentation, see the important new anthology by Franklin Sherman, *Bridges: Documents of the Christian-Jewish Dialogue* (New York: Paulist, 2011).

change in ecclesial self-understanding to have occurred since the close of the conciliar era. The difficulty is that the churches' new convictions regarding Israel do not jibe easily with the Irenaean conception of the unity of the Bible. The problem is not just tensions between the new convictions and the traditional interpretation of a few isolated passages, such as, for example, the parable of the wicked tenants (Mark 12:1 – 12) or the crowd's answer to Pilate (Mark 15:6 – 15). Rather, the problem is with the inner configurations of the canon at a larger scale, as represented, for example, by the Irenaean account of the relationship of Old and New Testaments (cf. *Against Heresies*, 4.9.2). At the outer limit, the church's new posture toward the Jewish people raises questions about the adequacy of its traditional canonical narrative as a whole.

Now, if this analysis is roughly correct, there would seem to be three basic ways one could try to resolve the tension between the church's new posture toward the Jewish people and its traditional canonical narrative.

At one extreme, one could aim to preserve the traditional canonical narrative unchanged, by denying that supersessionism was really a problem, or by defining it so narrowly that it was easily avoided.[4] At the other extreme, one might seek to replace the traditional canonical narrative with a new one that was more obviously compatible with the church's new posture toward the Jewish people. Although opposed to each other, these two strategies have something important in common. Both envisage the relationship between the church's traditional canonical narrative and its new doctrinal posture toward the Jewish people as a zero-sum game, where fidelity to one requires a corresponding rejection of the other. A third strategy does not share this zero-sum analysis. According to it, the church's new posture toward the Jewish people provides an occasion to renew and reinvigorate the traditional canonical narrative from within, according to its own criteria and insights, in a way that is simultaneously true to the traditional construal's trinitarian and christological logic, and to the church's contemporary witness to God's faithfulness toward the Jewish people.

The God of Israel and Christian Theology

In *The God of Israel and Christian Theology*, I adopted a version of the second strategy noted above. I first diagnosed the weaknesses I perceived in the traditional canonical construal and then proposed an alternative to take its place. Looking back on that work today, I still agree with several claims I made at the time. I still find it is useful to distinguish between three different forms of supersessionism that are rooted in the standard model at different "depths" and in different ways — namely, punitive, economic, and structural supersessionism (more on these in a moment). And I remain convinced that Christians can fully overcome supersessionism in all its forms only if they rethink the theological significance of the biblical distinction between Israel and the nations, between Gentiles and Jews. If God's election of Israel is "irrevocable," as

---

4. While I will not discuss this strategy at length in this essay, I think it is represented today by, e.g., Matthew Levering, who recognizes supersessionism as a problem but defines it so narrowly that it is easily avoided. See Matthew Levering, *Jewish-Christian Dialogue and the Life of Wisdom: Engagements with the Theology of David Novak* (London: Continuum, 2010), 12.

many churches now officially maintain in continuity with Romans 11:29, then God desires a world irrevocably characterized by the distinction between Israel and the nations. But why? The answer, it seems to me, is at least in part because it is characteristic of the biblical God to grace creation through economies of mutual blessing between creatures who are themselves different. This theme is introduced in the opening chapters of Genesis, reiterated in a new key in God's election of Abraham and his descendants, and sustained into John's vision of the new heavens and the new earth. The church of Jesus Christ is a sphere of mutual blessing between Jew and Gentile where the distinction between them (like that between male and female) is not erased, but recreated in a promissory way, as the eschatological sign and foretaste of messianic peace and mutual blessing among all the peoples of the world.

At the same time, I am no longer satisfied with some things I wrote in *The God of Israel and Christian Theology*. Basically, I failed to give christology and the doctrine of the Trinity a central and constitutive place in my canonical narrative. However unintentionally, I treated these affirmations as necessary but secondary truths to be fitted into the preexisting framework of God's consummating work as "the God of Israel." Even at the time, I had misgivings about this approach. Still, I could not imagine how else to formulate a canonical narrative without supersessionism.

The Standard Canonical Narrative Revisited

In retrospect, I regard the cost of my earlier strategy as too high. Moreover, I now think the strategy itself was unnecessary. I am as convinced as ever that Christians can articulate a canonical narrative that is thoroughly non-supersessionistic. Now, however, I do not think this must be *an alternative* to the traditional canonical narrative. What has changed is that I no longer think that supersessionism is an essential or necessary feature of the standard canonical narrative. I think of it rather as a deformation of that narrative, which can be overcome from within, by making it truer to the canon's witness to Jesus Christ and to the Holy Trinity revealed in him.

The key to delivering on this conviction, as I now see it, is at heart quite simple (which is not to say that it is easy). What is required is that Christians pay more — and more careful — attention to the canon's cumulative witness to the Tetragrammaton, the sacred and unspoken name of God. The Old and New Testaments testify to the Tetragrammaton on virtually every page. They do so, however, in ways that are deeply shaped by distinctively Jewish forms of piety for the Divine Name. Ancient translations of the Old Testament, for example, typically render the Tetragrammaton with distinctive characters or by means of a surrogate in place of the name, while the New Testament, for its part, is pervasively shaped by the practice of alluding to the Divine Name indirectly, in keeping with the Second Temple custom of avoiding its direct use. Since the second century, Gentile Christians have commonly lacked the skills needed to fully understand these practices. Sadly this was already true of Irenaeus, who seems to have had little knowledge of the Tetragrammaton and its place in the Scriptures he sought to interpret. I think this lack contributed greatly to the supersessionistic form his canonical narrative took, a bit like scurvy is caused by a deficiency of vitamin C. Conversely, I think the Irenaean canonical narrative can be made vastly more resistant to the deformation of supersessionism by recovering a lively sense of the canon's witness to the unspoken Divine Name. Such a reinvigoration, moreover, would profoundly strengthen the standard model's trinitarian and christocentric character. Let me briefly suggest how this might be so, addressing the three forms of supersessionism in turn.

Reclaiming the Standard Canonical Narrative from Structural Supersessionism

Structural supersessionism unifies the canon in an "Israel-forgetful" way. In the standard canonical narrative, it operates by foregrounding the story of creation, fall, redemption, and consummation, leaving the bulk of the Old Testament in the background. The result is a "bleached" portrait of God and God's purposes, one that lacks the vivid marks of divine uniqueness that are so prominently revealed in the context of God's covenant with Israel.

As soon as one begins to attend carefully to the Tetragrammaton, however, a funny thing happens to structural supersessionism. The uniqueness of the biblical God comes roaring back into the picture, driving away the bleached portraits of God like dry leaves before a summer storm. The Tetragrammaton is an incommunicable name, one that belongs exclusively to the God attested by the Bible. It is also by a wide margin the name most commonly used to identify God. In the Scriptures of Israel, it appears some six thousand times (more than twice as often as all other theonyms combined), beginning with the opening chapters of Genesis. While Genesis 1 speaks simply of "God," the following chapter deepens and expands this identification by employing the double-barreled name "Lord God," thereby assigning priority to the Tetragrammaton in a way that remains determinative for the rest of the canon. Nor is the prominence of the Divine Name restricted to the Old Testament. In the Apostolic Witness, we find (by one estimate) some *two thousand* forms of speech shaped by the practice of showing reverence for the Tetragrammaton by avoiding its direct use.[5] Allowing for differences of length, this means the density of allusion to the Divine Name is about the same in the New Testament as in the Old, if not greater still.

In recent decades, scholars such as Richard Bauckham, Markus Bockmuehl, and Larry Hurtado have shown that the Divine Name is not merely frequently attested in the New Testament. More significantly, it is something like the matrix out of which the church's christology and trinitarian faith emerges.[6] Consider, for example, a passage from Paul's Letter to the Philippians, one of the earliest writings in the Apostolic Witness:

---

5. Julius Boehmer, *Die Neutestamentliche Gottescheu und die ersten drei Bitten des Vaterunsers* (Halle, Germany: Richard Mühlmann Verlagsbuchhandlung, 1917). The work includes an eighty-page inventory of every instance of speech shaped by name avoidance in the New Testament.

6. See esp. Larry W. Hurtado, *Lord Jesus Christ: Devotion to Jesus in Earliest Christianity* (Grand Rapids: Eerdmans, 2003), and Richard Bauckham, *Jesus and the God of Israel: God Crucified and Other Studies on the New Testament's Christology of Divine Identity* (Grand Rapids: Eerdmans, 2008).

Let the same mind be in you that was in Christ Jesus,

[who] humbled himself and became obedient to the point of death —
even death on a cross.
Therefore God also highly exalted him
and gave him the name that is above every name,
so that at the name of Jesus every knee should bend,
in heaven and on earth and under the earth,
and every tongue should confess that Jesus Christ is Lord,
to the glory of God the Father.

— PHILIPPIANS 2:5, 8 – 11 NRSV

Over the centuries, Christians have interpreted Paul's reference to "the name that is above every name" in different ways. Some have held that it refers to God's name-lessness; others, the word "Lord"; and still others, the name "Jesus." When one takes into account the passage's Jewish context, however, a more likely possibility suggests itself. "The name that is above every name" refers to the Tetragrammaton, the name that first-century Jews — whether Christian or not — referred to *obliquely*, by means of phrases such as this one. If this interpretation is correct, then Paul in Philippians 2 uses oblique reference to the Tetragrammaton to articulate a christology of the highest conceivable kind. What is more, he expresses a sophisticated form of *trinitarian* faith that remains strictly continuous with the Old Testament's exclusive worship of YHWH as God. Paul identifies the first person of the Trinity as the one who gives the Divine Name, the second person as the one who receives it, and the third person as the one who awakens its acknowledgement and glorification. (While the Holy Spirit is not explicitly mentioned by the text, its activity is implied by the cosmic acclamation of Jesus as "Lord," which Paul elsewhere says is possible only as a work of the Spirit [1 Cor. 12:3]). This way of identifying the persons of the Trinity, as the Giver, Receiver, and Glorifer of the Divine Name, does not replace or demote the ones already identified in the Irenaean tradition, such as "Father, Son, and Holy Spirit," "God, Word, Breath," "Lover, Beloved, Love," etc. It does, however, supplement their meaning in a quite decisive way, by anchoring them to the incommunicable name God revealed to Moses at the burning bush (Exod 3:15). This name, so central to *Jewish* liturgical practice, and so long overlooked by the Christian tradition, turns out to be the wellspring of the church's trinitarian and Christ-centered life.[7]

What these considerations suggest is that *even if* one interprets the Bible in light of a canonical narrative that privileges the story of creation, fall, redemption, and consummation (as the standard canonical narrative does), *one is continuously faced with scriptural testimony to the Divine Name and the primordial mystery of divine uniqueness to which it points.* This fact militates powerfully against the logic of structural supersessionism. It introduces the incomparable uniqueness of the biblical God into the "foreground" story itself, including its portrait of Jesus Christ and the Trinity,

---

7. I develop the argument of this paragraph in greater detail in my book *The Divine Name(s) and the Holy Trinity: Distinguishing the Voices* (Louisville: Westminster John Knox, 2011).

thus cutting off the marginalization of the God who spoke to Moses before it can even arise.

Reclaiming the Standard Canonical Narrative from Economic Supersessionism

Economic supersessionism holds that God designed carnal Israel from the very beginning to become obsolete with the coming of Christ. In the standard model, it operates by insisting that *everything* characteristic of Israel's life under the "Old Covenant" is fulfilled and rendered obsolete by its ecclesial equivalent: the written Mosaic law by Christ's spiritual law, circumcision by baptism, natural descent by faith, and so on. The implication is that carnal Israel itself becomes obsolete. Many Christian theologians have interpreted the Divine Name itself along these lines, as the German theologian Otto Weber does in this passage: "Why then, we must ask, do [Christians] not say 'Yahweh'? The only possible answer is that the name Yahweh belongs to the old covenant.... It does not occur in the New Testament." Weber continues: "Just as Christ is the goal and thus the 'end' of the law, the name Yahweh attains its goal and its 'end' in him.... The name Yahweh belongs as a name to the unfulfilled law, to the promise, to the old covenant.... If the Church still wanted to say 'Yahweh' or (perhaps) 'Jehovah,' then it would be denying what God has done."[8]

Here Weber applies the logic of economic supersessionism to the Tetragrammaton. Just as Christ's coming rendered the ceremonial Law superfluous and abhorrent to God, so also the Divine Name itself. The upshot is that Christ's coming marks the divinely intended end both of carnal Israel and of its distinctive way of identifying God.

Once again, however, a funny thing happens to this whole line of reasoning as soon as one attends more carefully to the canon's witness to the Tetragrammaton. As we have already noted, this witness is not restricted to the Scriptures of Israel but continues powerfully into the Apostolic Witness as well. What is more, it assumes a form in the New Testament that is thoroughly determined by distinctively Jewish religious practice. Jesus Christ, the apostles, and the writers of the New Testament show reverence for the Divine Name by *avoiding its direct use, in keeping with the norms of Jewish tradition.* As soon as one becomes cognizant of this, Weber's answer to the question he poses in the quotation above vanishes like a puff of smoke. Why do Christians not pronounce the Divine Name in their worship of God, Christ, and the Spirit? The reason is not that the name has become obsolete, but *because they conform to the model of Jesus and the apostles, who themselves follow the precedent of Jewish practice.* Far from testifying to the wholesale obsolescence of the Old Covenant, the nonpronunciation of the Tetragrammaton in Christian worship testifies to the continuing presence and influence of Jewish practice at the heart of the church's liturgical life! Every time a Christian prays the Lord's Prayer, he or she renders up silent witness to the sanctity of the unspoken name and demonstrates in the most concrete way imaginable that

---

8. Otto Weber, *Foundations of Dogmatics* (trans. Darrell L. Guder; Grand Rapids: Eerdmans, 1981 – 83), 1:418.

Jewish religious practice remains alive and well at the heart of the church's own worship of God.

Slight though it may seem, the discovery of living Jewish tradition at the heart of Christian worship sends a shiver through the logic of economic supersessionism, a bit like blades of grass peeking up through the snow after a hundred-year winter. The discovery does not imply that the distinction between Old and New Covenants is wholly mistaken. Christ's coming, it seems, does fulfill *some* aspects of the Old Covenant in a way that render some aspects of its continued observance obsolete, most obviously, perhaps, sacrificial worship in the Temple. But the nonpronunciation of the Divine Name in the New Testament does imply that it is a mistake to *universalize* this precedent to every feature of Jewish tradition. This fact creates a space in which it is possible to imagine a distinctively Jewish form of Christian discipleship, one that is both rooted in traditional Jewish practice and normed by the precedent of Jesus Christ, the living Torah for Jew and for Gentile.

Reclaiming the Standard Canonical Narrative from Punitive Supersessionism

But even if all of the previous considerations are valid, might not YHWH still reject carnal Israel on account of its sins, as punitive supersessionism maintains? Here I think we must answer carefully. As Michael Wyschogrod has observed, "I do not think the Bible is very sympathetic to human preconceptions about what God will or will not, can or cannot do."[9] Moreover, it is important to remember that YHWH and "the God of Israel" are not synonyms. YHWH would still be YHWH, even if he had not chosen Israel, or had chosen otherwise, or were to reject it as his people (cf. Exod 32:10). That is why Paul can truthfully declare that God "has mercy on whomever he chooses, and he hardens the heart of whomever he chooses" (Rom 9:18 NRSV). And yet this truth alone does not exhaust the mystery of YHWH's identity as YHWH, as Paul goes on to argue in the remainder of Romans 9–11. Though the Divine Name is a "pure" proper name, devoid of conventional semantic meaning, its connotations fill the pages of the canon, much as the glory of the LORD filled the tabernacle of old (Exod 40:34). Within its cloud of connotation, the Divine Name encompasses the truth of God's eternal being and the ontological distinction between Creator and creation (cf. Gen 21:23; Isa 40:28; Pss 90; 103; 145; etc.). Yet it also encompasses in a quite particular way the truth of God's gracious condescension toward and faithfulness to Abraham and his chosen descendants: "Thus says the LORD, who gives the sun for light by day and the fixed order of the moon and the stars for light by night, who stirs up the sea so that its waves roar—the LORD of hosts is his name: If this fixed order were ever to cease from my presence, says the LORD, then also the offspring of Israel would cease to be a nation before me forever" (Jer 31:35–36 NRSV).

---

9. Michael Wyschogrod, "Why Was and Is the Theology of Karl Barth of Interest to a Jewish Theologian?" in *Footnotes to a Theology: The Karl Barth Colloquium of 1972* (ed. Martin Rumscheidt; Waterloo, Ontario: Corporation for the Publication of Academic Studies in Religion in Canada, 1974), 99.

The LORD's covenant with Israel, we might say, is the outworking of his desire to be praised by name, by Israel, the nations, and all creation. If Paul ultimately declares that "the gifts and the calling of God are irrevocable" (Rom 11:29 NRSV), it is not because YHWH owes it to his creatures, but because he owes it to himself, to who he is as YHWH and to the oaths and promises he has made in this name. But because the LORD owes it to himself and to his name, therefore Christ "has become a servant of the circumcised *on behalf of the truth of God* in order that he might confirm the promises given to the patriarchs, and in order that the Gentiles might glorify God for his mercy. As it is written, 'Therefore I will confess you among the Gentiles, and sing praises to your name'" (Rom 15:8–9 NRSV).

I suggested a moment ago that overcoming supersessionism in the standard canonical narrative, though simple in principle, was not necessarily easy in practice. Certainly, I do not think this essay suffices on the latter score. But I do hope it helps explain why I believe more careful attention to the Divine Name can remedy the deformation of supersessionism from within the contours of the standard canonical narrative, in a manner that strengthens, deepens, and renews what is best about the standard narrative, which is its profoundly trinitarian and Christ-centered orientation.

For Further Reading

Blaising, Craig A. "The Future of Israel as a Theological Question." Pages 102–21 in *To the Jew First: The Case for Jewish Evangelism in Scripture and History*. Edited by Darrell L. Bock and Mitch Glaser. Grand Rapids: Kregel, 2008.

Bock, Darrell L. "Replacement Theology with Implications for Messianic Jewish Relations." Pages 235–47 in *Jesus, Salvation and the Jewish People: The Uniqueness of Jesus and Jewish Evangelism*. Edited by David Parker. Milton Keynes, UK: Paternoster, 2011.

Diprose, Ronald E. *Israel and the Church: The Origin and Effects of Replacement Theology*. Rome: Instituto Biblico Evangelico Italiano, 2004.

Eby, Aaron, and Toby Janicki. *Hallowed Be Your Name: Sanctifying God's Sacred Name*. (Mayim Chayim Series; Marshfield: First Fruits of Zion, 2008), 1–75.

House, H. Wayne. "The Church's Appropriation of Israel's Blessings." Pages 77–110 in *Israel the Land and the People: An Evangelical Affirmation of God's Promises*. Edited by H. Wayne House. Grand Rapids: Kregel, 1998.

Kaiser, Walter C. "An Assessment of 'Replacement Theology.'" *Mishkan: A Forum on the Gospel and the Jewish People* 21 (1994): 9–20.

Lindbeck, George. "The Church as Israel: Ecclesiology and Ecumenism." Pages 78–94 in *Jews and Christians: People of God*. Edited by Carl E. Braaten and Robert W. Jenson. Grand Rapids: Eerdmans, 2003.

Novak, David. "From Supersessionism to Parallelism in Jewish-Christian Dialogue." Pages 95–113 in *Jews and Christians: People of God*. Edited by Carl E. Braaten and Robert W. Jenson. Grand Rapids: Eerdmans, 2003.

Ochs, Peter. *Another Reformation: Postliberal Christianity and the Jews*. Grand Rapids: Baker Academic, 2011.

Remaud, Michel. *Israel, Servant of God*. London: T&T Clark, 2003.

Rosner, Jennifer. "Election and Law: An Exploration of Am Israel and the Halachic

Life." Paper presented at the Consultation on Jewish Continuity in the Body of Messiah, Paris, November 2011. Online: http://www.mjstudies.com.

Rudolph, David, Joel Willitts, Justin K. Hardin, and J. Brian Tucker. *New Testament Interpretation after Supersessionism: Changing Paradigms*. Eugene, Oreg.: Cascade, forthcoming.

Soulen, R. Kendall. *The God of Israel and Christian Theology*. Minneapolis: Fortress, 1996.

———. "Post-supersessionism." Pages 350–51 in *A Dictionary of Jewish-Christian Relations*. Edited by Edward Kessler and Neil Wenborn. Cambridge: Cambridge University Press, 2005.

Vlach, Michael J. *The Church as a Replacement of Israel: An Analysis of Supersessionism*. Frankfurt am Main: Peter Lang, 2009.

Wyschogrod, Michael. *Abraham's Promise: Judaism and Jewish-Christian Relations*. Edited by R. Kendall Soulen. Grand Rapids: Eerdmans, 2004.

Willitts, Joel, David Rudolph, and Justin K. Hardin. *The Jewish New Testament: An Introduction to Its Jewish Social and Conceptual Context*. Grand Rapids: Eerdmans, forthcoming.

Zoccali, Christopher. *Whom God Has Called: The Relationship of Church and Israel in Pauline Interpretation, 1920 to the Present*. Eugene, Oreg.: Pickwick, 2010.

PART 3

Summary
and Conclusion

CHAPTER 28

Summary of the Chapters

Joel Willitts

This chapter presents a summary of each essay in the book. These summaries are not intended to replace the careful reading of each chapter but simply to provide an overview of each chapter's contents for quick consultation. We hope this chapter will serve as a point of reference to facilitate the book's use.

Part 1: The Messianic Jewish Community

Chapter 1: Messianic Judaism in Antiquity and in the Modern Era
David Rudolph

"Messianic Judaism in Antiquity and in the Modern Era" briefly sketches the history of Messianic Judaism in its two historical manifestations, the first four centuries of the Common Era and the modern movement beginning in the eighteenth century. David Rudolph defines Messianic Judaism as a religious tradition in which Jews who claim to follow Yeshua as the Messiah of Israel continue to live as Jews within the orbit of Judaism. He makes several important observations about the history of the movement.

To begin with, Rudolph shows that the New Testament, and Acts in particular, presents a dual-track ecclesiology in which, on the one side, Jewish believers in Yeshua maintain their covenant responsibilities as followers of Yeshua and, on the other, Yeshua-believing Gentiles worship the God of Israel as Gentiles. Furthermore, Rudolph notes that there is a growing scholarly objection to the long-standing assumption that Judaism and Christianity parted ways during the New Testament period. Recent scholarship has persuasively shown that Messianic Jews existed into the fourth century. The only apparent reason Messianic Jews disappear from history after that period was because it became illegal and heretical to be a Messianic Jew in the post-Constantinian era.

Rudolph also observes that the first Jewish believers in Yeshua to refer to themselves as "Messianic Jews," and to their religious tradition as "Messianic Judaism," were those who in the early twentieth century practiced Judaism and wished to distinguish themselves from Hebrew Christians, believers in Yeshua who were Jews by birth but who assimilated into Gentile Protestant churches.

The contemporary expression of Messianic Judaism, especially in North America, grew out of a grassroots movement of twentysomething Jewish believers in Yeshua who in the 1970s in significant numbers established Messianic Jewish congregations. Rudolph observes that today, among those using the terms "Messianic Jew" and "Messianic Jewish," there is a great diversity of belief and practice. Still, the essence of what "Messianic Judaism" has meant for more than a century, and continues to mean, centers on a belief in Yeshua that includes a commitment to live as a Jew as a matter of covenant responsibility or calling before God.

Chapter 2: Messianic Jewish Synagogues
David Rudolph and Elliot Klayman

"Messianic Jewish Synagogues" defines the synagogue as a sacred community of Jewish people who gather for worship, prayer, fellowship, study, celebrations, and other Jewish community activities. What distinguishes Messianic synagogues is the centrality of Yeshua, the prominent place of the New Covenant, and the presence of Gentiles who come alongside Messianic Jews to build a congregation for Yeshua within the house of Israel.

Yeshua and the New Covenant are woven throughout the fabric of the Messianic Jewish synagogue. So while the community life, symbols, ritual objects, and cultural forms would be largely the same as in mainstream synagogues, the content of these forms is transformed by the living reality of Yeshua.

A primary purpose of Messianic synagogues is to be a place where Jews who follow the Jewish Messiah can remain Jews and become better Jews in keeping with the eternal purposes of the God of Israel. This includes conveying Jewish identity to their children and being a visible testimony of Yeshua from within the Jewish community.

The significant Gentile presence in Messianic Jewish congregations is due to a number of factors ranging from intermarriage to *ahavat Yisrael* (love for Israel) to attraction to Judaism. The demographic reality of Messianic Gentiles, including a second and third generation, raises a number of questions that the Messianic Jewish community is currently engaging. Many of these questions relate to time-honored traditions in the Jewish world concerning the participation of non-Jews in Jewish life. Because of the large number of Gentile Christian visitors, synagogue leaders have to walk a fine line between being inclusive and upholding the Messianic Jewish vision and traditions of their congregation.

Chapter 3: Messianic Jewish Worship and Prayer
Seth N. Klayman

"Messianic Jewish Worship and Prayer" presents a description of worship and prayer in the Messianic Jewish community. Seth Klayman begins by noting a conundrum faced by Messianic Jewish leaders as the modern movement emerged in the late twentieth century: there were no models that combined Jewish modes of worship with a focus on Yeshua. In Klayman's words, the last two millennia did not prepare the modern Messianic Jewish community to worship and pray in a way that was at once Messianic and Jewish. Into this vacuum, leaders of the Messianic Jewish movement in the 1960s and '70s began creating expressions of worship that were theologically consistent with the faith of the Jewish apostles while at the same time being something a Jew would recognize today as Jewish.

Messianic Jewish music and dance in the congregational context are among the distinctive forms of worship associated with Messianic Judaism. Moreover, Messianic Jews celebrate the Jewish festivals in light of the life, death, resurrection, and return of the Messiah Yeshua. They celebrate *Shabbat, Pesach/Hag HaMatzot, Bikkurim, Hag HaShavu'ot, Yom Teruah, Rosh HaShanah, Yom Kippur, Hag HaSukkot, Hanukkah* and *Purim* among other observances.

The infusing of Jewish worship forms with Christological significance is also reflected in Messianic Jewish liturgy. Published Messianic Jewish prayer books for Shabbat and festivals (*Siddurim* and *Machzorim*) make Yeshua-faith explicit in the context of traditional Jewish prayer. At the same time, Klayman underscores that worship and prayer in the Messianic Jewish community is not monolithic. He attributes the diverse expressions of Messianic Jewish worship and prayer to the priority placed on the leading of the *Ruach HaKodesh* (the Holy Spirit).

Finally, Klayman argues, provocatively, that Messianic Jewish worship and prayer challenge both Jews and Gentile Christians to reassess their long-held assumptions about the relationship between belief in the Messiah Yeshua and Jewish identity.

Chapter 4: Messianic Jews and Scripture
Carl Kinbar

"Messianic Jews and Scripture" details the Messianic Jewish perspective on Scripture and its use in congregational life. Carl Kinbar notes that the consensus among Messianic Jews is that the Bible is divinely inspired, infallible, and authoritative. Concerning the question of the relationship between Scripture and tradition, there is a divide presently within Messianic Judaism. Kinbar refers to the writings of two Messianic Jewish leaders, both of whom are contributors to this book, to illustrate the differences of opinion.

Dan Juster affirms the perspicuity of Scripture and the importance of using critical scholarship judiciously to bridge the gap between the ancient and contemporary world. He is cautious about the role of tradition in interpretation and maintains that tradition should always be accountable to Scripture.

On the other side is Mark Kinzer, who makes a distinction between Scripture and tradition but believes that a tradition must be employed in a Messianic Jewish approach to Scripture. To hold any other view would be to ignore the fact that a person's understanding of Scripture is informed by the community within which Scripture is read. Recognizing the influence of one's own tradition on interpretation is an essential element of interpretation according to Kinzer.

A second area that Kinbar surveys in the chapter is the canonical narrative employed to bring unity to the diverse parts of the canon. Messianic Jews reject the classic Gentile Christian canonical reading that fails to account for God's ongoing relationship with Israel and the existence of the movement of Jewish followers of Yeshua. Messianic Jews have sought alternatives that place the person and work of

Yeshua in the context of the ongoing life and vocation of Israel rather than its replacement. As yet, however, no one particular alternative has emerged as normative for Messianic Judaism.

In Messianic Jewish congregations, as in all Jewish synagogues, the Torah is given special honor. Messianic Jews recognize with the wider Jewish world the holiness of the thirty-nine writings that make up the Tanakh. The New Testament, referred to by many Messianic Jews as the B'rit Chadashah, is also accorded authoritative status alongside the Tanakh. So in unity with all Christians, Messianic Jews have a canon comprised of both the Hebrew Scriptures and the Apostolic Writings.

Chapter 5: Messianic Jews and Jewish Tradition
Carl Kinbar

"Messianic Jews and Jewish Tradition" sketches the diverse perspectives on the authority and use of Jewish tradition in Messianic Judaism. Jewish tradition, says Kinbar, is a network of interrelated practices, texts, and concepts that has been developed and passed down in Jewish communities from generation to generation.

Within contemporary Messianic Judaism there is intense debate over the normativity of Jewish tradition. These disagreements reflect significant theological differences evident in Messianic Judaism today. As illustrations of the debate over tradition, Kinbar discusses Passover, the Talmud, and Jewish prayers.

Most Messianic Jews take an eclectic approach to Jewish tradition and choose elements from Jewish tradition that seem relevant to them and that are consistent with Scripture. At the same time, there are more traditional segments of modern Messianic Judaism, such as those represented by Hashivenu, the Union of Messianic Jewish Congregations (UMJC), and the Messianic Jewish Rabbinical Council (MJRC), that advocate the normativity, to a greater or lesser degree, of those traditions recognized by the whole Jewish community through the centuries. In Kinbar's words, the latter minority seeks to express Yeshua-faith shaped by a form of tradition that originated with the rabbis (i.e., Rabbinic Judaism) and Jewish communities of the past, while also engaging with the Jewish consensus of the present. This debate represents one of the significant tensions in the movement today.

Chapter 6: Messianic Jewish Ethics
Russ Resnik

"Messianic Jewish Ethics" offers a distinctively Messianic Jewish approach to ethics. Messianic Jewish ethics, according to Russ Resnik, arise from the ethical teachings of Yeshua. Yeshua's ethics, from this point of view, are Jewish ethics brought to their highest point and embodied in Yeshua's way of life. Jewish ethics are built on the concept of divine emulation. As Resnik puts it, God does ethics before humanity does. In Judaism, ethics derive from identity, from being God's image-bearers, and not primarily from God's commandments. Thus, as the revelation of God, Yeshua, through his life and teachings, revealed the God of Israel in a way that was climactic and definitive.

What's more, for Resnik, Yeshua's ethics mean something unique for Messianic

Jews. First, Messianic Jews must live the ethics of Yeshua among the Jewish people, as the Messiah did. Yeshua's example of love for Israel and loyalty to the Torah of Moses and related Jewish traditions suggest that Messianic Jews should also place these commitments at the center of their ethics.

Second, Messianic Jews should embrace their marginalized position within the wider Jewish community in sacrificial service, as Yeshua did. Resnik points out that the wider Jewish community accuses the Messianic Jewish community of being unethical because it insists on identifying itself as a form of Judaism while affirming Yeshua as the Messiah. The false accusation and the accompanying exclusion should not dissuade Messianic Jews from firmly maintaining their loyalty to the Jewish community. Resnik argues that it is from this marginalized place, the same position as Yeshua, that Messianic Jews witness for Yeshua, displaying God's love and favor. In doing so, Messianic Jews share in the sufferings of Messiah and his ethics.

Chapter 7: Messianic Jewish Outreach
Stuart Dauermann

"Messianic Jewish Outreach" examines paradigms of outreach among Jewish mission agencies and Hebrew Christians in the nineteenth and twentieth centuries, on the one hand, and the emerging Messianic Jewish movement in the late twentieth and early twenty-first centuries, on the other. Stuart Dauermann first summarizes the message, milieu, and methods of the Jewish missions agencies and Hebrew Christians. He characterizes their message as a gospel of personal salvation through faith in Yeshua the Messiah understood as the true faith over against Judaism. In this regard, the evidence of faith in such a context is (1) a personal statement of belief with (2) an accompanying testimony of an inward spiritual experience and (3) socialization in the context of a Gentile Christian church.

The methods employed by nineteenth- and twentieth-century Jewish mission agencies and Hebrew Christians were largely focused on a center. A center was usually a facility in close proximity to a Jewish population where basic needs for poor Jews and especially immigrants were provided. While meeting the social needs of Jews, the center sought to share the gospel of personal salvation through Bible studies, evangelistic meetings, literature distribution, and Jewish religious services.

In contrast to early Hebrew Christian evangelistic efforts and Jewish mission agencies today, the Messianic Jewish congregational movement, which emerged in the 1970s, has a different message and milieu, while sharing some of the methods of Hebrew Christianity. Dauermann refers to this new perspective as an eschatologically driven Messianic Jewish outreach. What distinguishes this approach from earlier ones is that it moves the primary focus away from individual salvation and toward the communal and covenantal aspect of the good news. In Dauermann's words, the New Testament presents a gospel as good news not simply for individuals, but for the Jewish people. Eschatologically driven outreach, according to Dauermann, returns the gospel to a Jewish covenantal/communal context.

What's more, Dauermann argues that "outreach" in the Messianic Jewish paradigm

is not simply another word for evangelism. While outreach includes evangelism traditionally defined in personal terms, it encompasses more. It involves calling Jews to
repent and follow Yeshua in the context of a renewed vision of Jewish community,
covenant, and consummation. This repentance and discipleship, in the framework of
Messianic Jewish outreach, is measured in part in terms of a return to "the paths of
Torah" in the context of Messianic Jewish congregations.

Chapter 8: Messianic Judaism and Women
Rachel Wolf

"Messianic Judaism and Women" presents Rachel Wolf's first-person perspective on
women in the Messianic Jewish community. Messianic Jewish women, according to
Wolf, are pioneers of a new way of life in faithfulness to the God of Israel and the Messiah Yeshua. Their pioneering work is done as they negotiate the conflicting voices
that seek to shape their identity and social roles.

Messianic Jewish women have been co-laborers with men from the earliest stages
of the development of the modern movement, although often without recognition.
Many Messianic Jewish women experience significant difficulty establishing their
identity as Jews and females, and navigating their social roles as Messianic Jewish
women. This situation is in part due to the diverse backgrounds that influence the
developing Messianic Jewish culture—from traditional Judaism on the one hand to
evangelical Gentile Christianity on the other.

Women fill a wide range of roles in the public sphere of the Messianic Jewish community. Many synagogues today, according to Wolf, have an egalitarian policy about
leading worship. Women can be seen serving as cantors, Torah readers, and teachers. Also, women serve as co-founders and leaders of their congregations with their
husbands. Many women work as congregational administrators and board members
or serve as president of their synagogue. Women have also founded Messianic Jewish
organizations that serve women within the movement and beyond.

In addition to the important public roles that women increasingly fill in the Messianic Jewish community, Wolf underscores the fundamental role that women fill as
mothers. She eloquently expresses the irreplaceable role of mothers in the history of
the Jewish people, both past and present. From Wolf's perspective, motherhood is far
from a holdover from a patriarchal society. For most Messianic Jewish women, the
private life of motherhood, away from the public eye, is where the future generations
of the people of Israel, faithful to Messiah Yeshua, are secured.

Chapter 9: Messianic Jews in the Land of Israel
Akiva Cohen

"Messianic Jews in the Land of Israel" addresses the presence of Messianic Jews in
Israel. Beginning with the historical precursors to the contemporary Messianic Jewish
community in Israel, Akiva Cohen observes that the rise of indigenous Israeli followers of Yeshua started with the "Hebrew Christian Prayer Union" and the "Jerusalem
Hebrew Christian Association."

Several formative developments took place in the twentieth and twenty-first centuries. First, Cohen notes that from the 1950s through the 1990s, Israel experienced a significant influx of immigrants from Eastern Europe, Russia, and Ethiopia, some of whom were Messianic Jews. These immigrants represent a significant percentage of the Messianic Jewish community today.

Second, while there is a strong national identity among the Israeli Messianic Jewish community that stems in part from required military service and the celebration of Jewish High Holy Days (which are national holidays), the majority of Israeli Messianic Jews do not embrace a traditional Jewish identity. This, however, may be changing. Cohen observes that recently there is a growing number of young Messianic Jews who are seeking connection to their Jewish spiritual heritage while maintaining their faith in Yeshua as Messiah.

The current expression of Messianic Judaism in Israel, then, is the result of (1) early, predominantly Western, foreign missionary efforts, (2) immigration, particularly of Eastern Europeans and Russians, and (3) a burgeoning indigenous Yeshua-believing community.

Cohen lists the following as challenges and opportunities that the contemporary Messianic Jewish community needs to embrace: (1) discipleship training for the next generation of Israeli Messianic Jews, (2) education and professional development for financial independence from foreign missionary agencies, (3) formal theological training of Messianic Jewish leaders, (4) the development of resources and paradigms for the proper integration of Israeli national identity with one's identity as a Jewish follower of Yeshua, and (5) intentional dialogue between the Messianic Jewish community and Palestinian Christians.

Chapter 10: Messianic Jewish National Organizations
Mitch Glaser

"Messianic Jewish National Organizations" surveys the major Messianic Jewish national organizations and Jewish mission agencies and examines the Jewish fidelity of these organizations. By way of definition, Mitch Glaser describes a Messianic Jewish national organization as an institution that brings Messianic Jews and Messianic synagogues together for conferences, fellowship, teaching, and benevolent activities. They function much like denominations by providing ordination, accountability in doctrine and practice, and educational and leadership development opportunities. Examples of Messianic Jewish national organizations are the Messianic Jewish Alliance of America (MJAA), the International Messianic Jewish Alliance (IMJA), and the Union of Messianic Jewish Congregations (UMJC).

A Jewish mission agency, by contrast, is an organization established for the purpose of evangelizing Jewish people. Examples of Jewish mission agencies are Chosen People Ministries (CPM), Friends of Israel (FOI), and Jews for Jesus (JFJ). Traditionally, tension has existed between Messianic Jewish national organizations and Jewish mission agencies, as David Rudolph in chapter 1 also noted. The significant point of tension relates to the question of commitment to ongoing Jewish identity. Some

within the Messianic Jewish national organizations believe that mission agencies are
not concerned about Jewish calling and continuity, while some within the mission
agencies think that the Messianic Jewish national organizations promote separatism.

Glaser provides criteria that more objectively evaluates the Jewish fidelity of these
organizations and agencies. He identifies five critical issues that can serve as a measure of Jewish fidelity: (1) commitment to Israel, (2) concern about assimilation, (3)
involvement in the Jewish community, (4) Torah observance and Jewish tradition,
and (5) a vision for the next generation. When these criteria are applied to Messianic
Jewish national organizations and mission agencies, according to Glaser, they demonstrate that both groups are closer in their commitment to Jewish fidelity than is
usually assumed.

Chapter 11: Messianic Jews and the Jewish World
Mark S. Kinzer

"Messianic Jews and the Jewish World" provides a historically oriented summary of
the Messianic Jewish outlook toward the wider Jewish world. Mark Kinzer shows that
the early history of the Messianic Jewish movement in the late twentieth century, with
its roots in evangelical Protestant Christianity, found itself in an ambivalent position
in relation to the wider Jewish community.

On the one side, early Messianic Judaism claimed to be fully part of the Jewish
community. Messianic Judaism, although birthed from Hebrew Christianity, pushed
beyond it by reclaiming Torah observance and saw itself no longer as a Jewish version of Christianity but as a Yeshua-version of Judaism. On the other side, this early
Messianic Judaism was still very much influenced, according to Kinzer, by the theological tenets of traditional evangelicalism. The combination of elements such as a
distrust of tradition as well as evangelicalism's unique ecclesiology, eschatology, and
soteriology alienated the wider Jewish community from the burgeoning Messianic
Judaism.

To the Jewish world, Messianic Judaism is not disconnected from its Hebrew
Christian mother. The wider Jewish community in the late twentieth and early twenty-
first centuries has considered Messianic Judaism a disingenuous — even an insidious
— attempt to missionize Jews. All the major branches of Judaism in America have
condemned Messianic Judaism and ruled that a Messianic Jew should be denied the
privileges of membership in the Jewish community. Kinzer notes, with evident disappointment, that Messianic Jews are the only Jews who are treated this way.

Kinzer, however, also highlights that at the beginning of the twenty-first century
Messianic Judaism's relationship to the wider Jewish world is changing. A vocal minority in Messianic Judaism — Hashivenu and the UMJC most notably — has labored to
distinguish the movement from evangelical Protestantism and to identify Messianic
Judaism as a branch of Judaism. While this direction is still very much debated within
the movement, and it has had little to no impact on the wider Jewish world's view
of Messianic Jews, there are signs that the Messianic Jewish community's view of its
relationship to the wider Jewish community is evolving.

Chapter 12: Messianic Jews and the Gentile Christian World
Daniel C. Juster

"Messianic Jews and the Gentile Christian World" describes the Messianic Jewish community's relationship with their Gentile Christian family. Dan Juster writes that the Messianic Jewish movement's perspective on the Gentile wing of the church is best delineated by the terms "interdependence" and "mutual blessing," although there remain highly problematic issues such as Christian supersessionism (i.e., the view that the church replaces Israel as God's people) that create tensions for Messianic Jews as they relate to the Gentile Christian world.

Simply put, Messianic Judaism holds to a "bilateral ecclesiology" — a term coined by Mark Kinzer. This view asserts that the one Body of Messiah, the *ekklesia*, exists in two distinguishable expressions, a Jewish and a Gentile one. Messianic Jews contend that this perspective is biblical and consistent with God's irrevocable covenant relationship with the Jewish people.

Furthermore, with regard to terminology and self-designation, many Messianic Jews today are uncomfortable using the term "Christian" and avoid it completely. The reason for this sensitivity is that the term "Christian" in the wider Jewish world means "Gentile" — to be a Christian means to no longer be Jewish. Thus, "Christian church," for many Messianic Jews, is equivalent to "Gentile church." When speaking of the worldwide community of Jewish and Gentile believers in Yeshua, they prefer the term "Body of Messiah" or the untranslated Greek term *ekklesia* since these terms do not have the connotation "Gentile church."

Juster also describes the major dialogues taking place between Messianic Jewish leaders and officials from major Christian church traditions and denominations. These official meetings, statements, and affirmations are evidence that the Messianic Jewish community is reestablishing itself after a sixteen-hundred-year absence as the essential, inseparable partner of the predominantly Gentile Christian church.

Chapter 13: Messianic Jews and Jewish-Christian Dialogue
Jennifer M. Rosner

"Messianic Jews and Jewish-Christian Dialogue" examines the challenge Messianic Judaism presents for contemporary Jewish-Christian dialogue. Jennifer Rosner posits that Messianic Judaism is a challenge for both sides because of the difficulty of mapping Messianic Jews on the religious landscape. Messianic Jews blur the lines upon which the dialogue has depended. In fact, some of the strongest advocates of Jewish-Christian dialogue have spoken out against Messianic Judaism definitively, maintaining there is an impassable chasm between Judaism and Christianity, and consequently label Messianic Judaism as "a syncretistic aberration."

However, describing Judaism and Christianity as mutually exclusive is not the only, or even the most logical, way of understanding their relationship. Rosner presents a perspective on Judaism and Christianity that centers on their historical relationship and stresses their interdependence. When the two entities are construed in this way, there is room for Messianic Judaism in the dialogue. But not just room. Because

Messianic Judaism views the divide between Judaism and Christianity as a destructive and tragic rupture of the one people of God, Messianic Judaism has the potential to be a bridge over the chasm — to be a means of healing the historic rupture.

Rosner surveys three areas in which Messianic Judaism makes a contribution to Jewish-Christian dialogue: (1) intra – Messianic Jewish dialogue, (2) Messianic Jewish – Christian dialogue, and (3) Messianic Jewish – mainstream Jewish dialogue.

Part 2: The Church and Messianic Judaism

Chapter 14: Matthew's Christian-Jewish Community
Daniel J. Harrington

"Matthew's Christian-Jewish Community" presents a reading of Matthew's Gospel that highlights its late first-century Jewish context. Daniel Harrington contends that the gospel was most likely written in the wake of the destruction of the Temple in 70 CE as a Christian-Jewish response to the tragedy. In contrast to other similar Jewish responses (e.g., the Apocalypses of *4 Ezra* and *2 Baruch* or nascent Rabbinic Judaism promoted at this time by Rabban Yohanan ben Zakkai), Matthew sought to give vision in two areas. First, in the wake of the destruction of the Temple, Jewish heritage would be best carried on in the community gathered around Jesus of Nazareth. Second, Matthew's goal was to recapture the Jewish roots of Jesus and the movement he began, which by the late first century may have been lost on some uninformed Christians.

Harrington presents the Christian-Jewish nature of the first gospel by demonstrating its unique Jewish themes and features. Harrington highlights several aspects of Matthew's Jewish message: (1) Jesus as the fulfillment of Jewish Scripture, (2) Jesus as the herald of the kingdom of heaven, (3) the very Jewish Messiah, (4) Jesus as an interpreter of the Torah, (5) Jesus' debate with other Jewish teachers, (6) Jesus' ethical teaching, (7) Christian-Jewish communal life, and (8) intra-Jewish polemical dialogue.

In Harrington's view, a Christian Jewish author wrote Matthew's gospel for a Christian Jewish community at a pivotal time in Jewish history. The gospel reminds all Christians of their Jewish roots and enables them to see the central role that Christian Jews played in the early history of the church. What's more, Matthew's Christian Judaism definitively reveals that Messianic Judaism has been and should be part of the Christian movement in every age.

Chapter 15: The Restoration of Israel in Luke-Acts
Darrell Bock

"The Restoration of Israel in Luke-Acts" redresses the widespread belief within the Gentile wing of the church that the church has replaced the Jewish people as the people of God in some form — a belief commonly referred to as "supersessionism."

Darrell Bock shows that in the narrative Luke lays out in his two-volume work, Israel's story is at no point eclipsed or set aside by some other story, be that the story of Jesus or the story of the expansion of the church in the Greco-Roman world. In both cases, Luke-Acts teaches that these realities are developments of the same Israel story of the Hebrew Scriptures.

Bock asserts that, for Luke, Israel's story remains at the center of the plot. In the story of Jesus and the early church, Israel's story remains, but is developed. This fact should caution readers of the New Testament about arriving at interpretations that present a landless and nationless theology. While the New Testament generally, and Luke-Acts in particular, teaches a theology of equality between Jew and Gentile and stresses the inclusion of the Gentiles into eschatological salvation, Bock contends that New Testament theology never forgets that it is Israel's story and Israel's hope that brings blessing to the world.

Chapter 16: James and the Jerusalem Council Decision
Richard Bauckham

"James and the Jerusalem Council Decision" presents the early church's twin affirmations that (1) Gentiles become members of the eschatological people of God by faith without the requirement of a fully Torah-observant lifestyle, and (2) Jewish believers in Jesus continue to maintain a fully Torah-observant lifestyle. Richard Bauckham shows that these affirmations in the story retold by Luke in Acts 15 were based on two facts: first, the miraculous experiences of the Holy Spirit among Gentiles witnessed to by Peter, Paul, and Barnabas and, second, James's interpretation of Scripture.

With regard to Gentile inclusion, Bauckham notes that Cornelius's story in Acts 10 is paradigmatic. Cornelius and his household received the gift of the Spirit apart from proselyte conversion. Through a dream, God made clear to Peter that he should make no distinction between impure and profane people (Acts 10:28). Peter was thus encouraged by God to go with the servants of Cornelius and associate intimately with Gentiles. It seems that such intimate contact with Gentiles was taboo among some Judeans (less so among Diaspora Jews), although there is no direct Torah command that mandates this level of separation. At the council, Peter bore witness to this experience, which was corroborated by the work of Paul and Barnabas.

James brought the council to conclusion with an appeal to Scripture (particularly Amos 9:11–12) in support of that experience. James concluded that in view of the restoration of the messianic kingdom of David, Gentiles become members of God's eschatological people, as Gentiles, through faith and loyalty to Messiah Jesus. As part of the resolution, James added four "essential" instructions for the Gentiles that dealt with immorality and idolatry. Bauckham believes that these "laws" derive from four laws for resident aliens given in the Torah (Lev 17–18). He believes that James saw that these four prohibitions applied to the situation at hand. Moreover, Bauckham asserts that these prohibitions related not to matters of eating certain foods, but addressed the issue of moral impurity. As such, the "essentials" were more than simply standards to assist in table fellowship among a mixed Jew/Gentile community. Rather, these commandments were the necessary and appropriate expression of Gentile Christ-faith, as, likewise, were the wider Torah commandments essential for the appropriate Jewish expression of Christ-faith.

Chapter 17: Interdependence and Mutual Blessing in the Church
Craig Keener

"Interdependence and Mutual Blessing in the Church" addresses Paul's admonition to Gentiles and Jews in Romans 14–15. Craig Keener understands Paul's letter to address primarily a disagreement between Jewish and Gentile Jesus-believers. As such, Romans provides both a vision and a model for Jewish-Gentile reconciliation.

According to Keener, the argument of the whole letter supports Paul's call to unity, climactically stated in Romans 15:5–6. Paul accomplished this, first, by showing the universal lostness of all humanity and the insufficiency of Jewish ethnic identity alone for eschatological blessing (Rom 1–10). Then, Paul similarly warned Gentile Jesus-believers against spiritual and ethnic arrogance in view of their status as "spiritual proselytes" to Judaism (Rom 9–11).

In Romans Paul has proven that Jews and Gentiles are interdependent; both are dependent on the other soteriologically. For Gentiles this is a backward-looking fact in view of the Jewish foundation of their salvation. But it is also a present reality through the ministry of those Jewish believers like Paul who are Messiah's ambassadors to the Gentiles. For Jews, it is both present and forward-looking, as Paul believed that his Gentile mission would spur Jews to faith in Jesus. Paul looked forward to the day when a great number within Israel would repent and turn to the Messiah.

Consequently, Paul calls both groups, although primarily focusing on his predominately Gentile audience in Romans, to unity and mutual acceptance (Rom 15:5–6). This mutual blessing is grounded on the example of Jesus himself, who, Paul claimed, served both Jew and Gentile (Rom 15:8–9). And it is a tangible blessing—the example of the Messiah should be expressed in concrete acts of service between Jesus-believing Gentiles and Messianic Jews, including the wider Jewish world.

Keener concludes with a challenge to Gentile Christians today to repent of disobeying Paul's command. In his words, Gentile Christianity did the opposite of what Paul commanded in Romans, and through anti-Judaism and anti-Semitism it marred the Gentile Christian witness to the Jewish people. But with the emergence of Messianic Judaism, says Keener, there is a new opportunity to live out Paul's teaching and be a positive witness to Jews today.

Chapter 18: The Relationship between Israel and the Church
William S. Campbell

"The Relationship between Israel and the Church" focuses on Romans 9–11, the most comprehensive statement in Paul's letters on the relationship between Israel and the church. William Campbell notes at the outset that the addressees of Paul's letter were primarily Gentile and not Jewish, which means that Paul's focus largely, if not singularly, concerns Gentiles and not Jews. Second, Paul's rhetorical strategy is didactic or instructive in nature. Rather than browbeat his audience, Paul attempted to lead his envisaged Gentile students to their own conclusions about Israel through a dialogical style. Ultimately Paul's desired outcome, according to Campbell, was that his Gentile hearers' perception about Israel would be transformed and they would abandon their ill-formed biases against Jews.

Paul tackled head-on assumptions that may have been current among the Gentile Christ-believers in Rome about Jewish rejection of the gospel. Paul made plain that although the majority of Israel had rejected the Messiah, God in his freedom had not rejected her. Second, God's impartial justice did not require the conclusion that Israel had no future. It is incorrect to infer from Israel's disobedience that God could not restore her.

Paul made several arguments in response to these incorrect assumptions by the Roman Gentile Christ-believers. First, he reminded his readers of God's actions on Israel's behalf even to the present day. Particularly important is the existence of a present remnant through which God is saving both Jew and Gentile. Second, Paul's metaphors in Romans 9 of "stumbling" and "hardening" are presented as temporary problems and do not denote a final destiny. Third, the nation's inability to embrace the new message is temporary. Furthermore, their present rejection resulting from ignorance is a means of blessing for the Gentiles.

Campbell brings the chapter to a close by making four points. First, the church and Israel must coexist. The church of Gentile Christ-followers does not replace the Jewish people in God's economy of salvation. Second, Israel and the church share in God's blessings. Gentiles therefore should acknowledge that they share in the riches of God's grace with Israel. Third, the posture required toward Israel on the part of Gentiles is humility. Finally, Gentile Christ-believers should recognize the mystery of God's purposes for Israel.

Campbell emphasizes that for Paul there can be no totally separate existence for the two ethnic groups who claim allegiance to the God of Israel. In Campbell's words Israel is not merely a historical antecedent to the church. Israel belongs in the foreground of the church and not only to its background.

Chapter 19: The Redemption of Israel for the Sake of the Gentiles
Scott J. Hafemann

"The Redemption of Israel for the Sake of the Gentiles" presents an exegetical discussion of Romans 15:9–12. Scott Hafemann shows that Paul's use of scriptural quotations serves his thoroughly Jewish eschatology. Paul's scriptural exegesis and its consequential eschatological framework provided the basis (15:4) for his exhortation to the Gentiles to (1) glorify God for his work on their behalf in and through the Jewish people (15:9a) and (2) accept the Jew since Christ was a servant to both Jew and Gentile (15:7–8).

Paul's argument, according to Hafemann, makes clear that the present Church comprised of a small group of Jews and Gentiles is not the final fulfillment of Israel's hope for restoration. Paul leaves no room to conclude either that Israel's history has climaxed with the coming of the Messiah or that God has reconfigured Israel's identity and eschatological hopes into the exclusively present reality of the Church.

According to Hafemann's reading of Romans 15:7–13, Israel's history continues on after Christ's coming and the establishment of the Church just as concretely and historically as it did before. Israel's complete restoration at the return of Christ is the basis of the hope for salvation of the Gentiles. God's commitment to Israel for the sake of the nations, says Hafemann, is the bedrock of the Gentile Church's hope.

The Church in the present is made up of a remnant of Jews and Gentiles who already glorify God and live under the Lordship of Messiah. The future hope for Israel's full restoration expresses itself in the present through the Gentiles joining Israel in living lives of praise to the one true God.

Chapter 20: Paul's Rule in All the *Ekklēsiai*
Anders Runesson

"Paul's Rule in All the *Ekklēsiai*" attempts to find a center for Paul's theology in his first letter to the Corinthians. Anders Runesson presents Paul's "hermeneutical hub," which is drawn from Paul's universal rule in 1 Corinthians 7:7 – 24 that he applied in ethnic and economic advice to the church.

With respect to ethnicity, and particularly the question of circumcision, Paul stated that Jews ("the circumcised") must remain Jewish, while Gentiles ("the uncir-cumcised") should maintain their non-Jewish status since both those who are circum-cised and those who are not can keep God's commandments (7:19). For the Jew, these commandments are nothing less than the Jewish law because of the inextricable link between following the Torah and ethnicity.

Paul's view of equality is based, according to Runesson, on the "higher principle" by which such obedience is possible, namely, the gift of the Spirit. Since the Spirit is given through faith to both Jew and non-Jew, being Jew or Gentile means nothing in relation to keeping God's commands and salvation. But that demoting of ethnic identity on a theological hierarchy does not at the same time erase ethnic distinction. Paul's rule relativizes while simultaneously upholding the distinction between Jew and Gentile.

The same principle of relativization with distinction is applied to the economic sphere in regard to slavery. The result was that in the social context of ancient Greco-Roman associations Paul theologized that the *ekklēsiai* comprised Spirit-filled non-Jews and Jews, slave and free, male and female, all expressing faith in Messiah and displaying behavior appropriate to their specific stations in life. Runesson additionally concludes that Paul more than likely applied this rule of remaining a Jew to his own experience of being in Messiah. Thus, Paul was a Torah-observant Jew.

The center of Paul's theology for Runesson, then, is faith as an entrance point for the Spirit. The gift of the Holy Spirit empowered all people, without distinction, to keep the commandments of God. In Runesson's words, maintaining the status quo made plain God's borderless grace as the world was about to be transformed. The faith-leading-to-Spirit conviction constituted one of Paul's core theological convictions.

Chapter 21: Equality in the Church
Justin K. Hardin

"Equality in the Church" unpacks two statements in separate Pauline letters that have been taken to mean that faith in Jesus erases ethnic distinction. In contrast to the conventional interpretations of both of these texts, Justin Hardin argues that Paul's message is one of equality without collapse of ethnicity. In these passages Paul demonstrated the full equality of both Jews and Gentiles in Messiah without obliterating ethnic distinction.

The first of these statements is Galatians 3:28. Hardin concludes that in this text Paul announced the glorious universal reality that, through faith in Messiah, there is equality as children of Abraham across ethnic, social, and gender lines. Paul's universalizing statement both relativized and maintained social distinctions. Paul's rhetoric was directed at Gentiles who were at risk of shipwrecking their faith by submitting to circumcision. If Gentiles followed the advice of the agitators, they would deny the truth of the gospel that in the messianic age, which had dawned in the coming of Jesus the Messiah, Gentiles are children of Abraham through faith and not by becoming Jewish converts.

Paul's insistence against circumcision should not be taken as a rejection of a Jewish Torah-observant lifestyle. Rather, more contextually read, Paul is explaining that circumcision is not the means by which Gentiles in Galatia are included as Abraham's children.

Ephesians 2:14–18 is the other related statement. As with Galatians 3:28, Hardin shows that when read closely it too does not support a raceless race in Messiah. Hardin argues that the Jewish Messiah transformed everything when he appeared. With respect to ethnicity, the Messiah secured peace between Jew and Gentile, and between each group and God. But this unity in the Messiah does not simultaneously result in an ethnic collapse. Instead, Paul's argument actually presupposes an Israel-centric view of the world.

Chapter 22: The Supersession and Superfluity of the Law? Another Look at Galatians
Todd A. Wilson

"The Supersession and Superfluity of the Law? Another Look at Galatians" presents the claim that the common understanding of Paul's view of the law is a misreading of Galatians. Todd Wilson argues that instead of attempting to convince his primarily Gentile audience that the law was both superseded in redemptive history and superfluous for shaping behavior, Paul's chief burden was to convince them that the law's curse had been removed. For Paul, the validity and authority of the Mosaic Torah continued after the messianic age, and those that have faith in Messiah and walk by the Spirit actually fulfill it. Thus the law for Paul is neither superseded nor superfluous.

Wilson briefly considers the message of Galatians 3:23–25, 5:18, and 6:2. With respect to the first of these, Paul's chronological argument served to point to the suspension of the law's curse, but not the law's supersession as is so often assumed. What Paul sought to show was not that the law itself was of a limited duration, but that the law's function as a curse was temporally limited. As Wilson puts it, the law's perpetuity after the advent of Messiah was not at issue.

Wilson elucidates Galatians 5:18, where Paul states that when the Galatians are led by the Spirit they are not "under law," as a shorthand reference to the law's curse. He interprets this in context to mean, "If you are led by the Spirit, you are not under the curse of the law." Consequently, for Wilson, Paul is persuading his hearers that the leading of the Spirit and its chief marker, love, are sufficient to avoid falling under the law's curse.

Galatians 6:2 is Paul's assertion that the Galatian believers will fulfill "the law of Messiah" when they bear one another's burdens. Wilson sees this as a clear reference to the abiding nature of Mosaic Torah in the lives of believers in Jesus, both Jew and Gentile. Thus, he agrees with the growing minority of voices that see Paul's statements about the Mosaic law along a Jew/Gentile axis. From this perspective the Mosaic law relates to both Jew and Gentile, but in different ways.

Moreover, Paul's positive views about the law in Galatians and elsewhere can be taken as statements of the abiding nature of the Torah in the lives of God's people after the coming of Messiah. Thus, Paul's negative and positive statements about the Mosaic law have an adequate explanation without resorting to supersessionist eschatology.

Chapter 23: The Bride of Messiah and the Israel-ness of the New Heavens and New Earth
Joel Willitts

"The Bride of Messiah and the Israel-ness of the New Heavens and New Earth" presents a reading of the last four chapters of Revelation that is informed by its Jewish context. Joel Willitts contends that Revelation 19–22 reflects the story of the God of Israel's redemption of creation with an abiding Israel-centric vision of an earthly city of David.

At the end of the story, Israel's distinctive role continues into eternity. In the eternal state, Israel's history and Israel's kingdom encompass the history and kingdoms of the new world. At the end, the picture is not simply a return to Eden as many assume, but the coming of an Edenic and Davidic city—a political capital city where the throne of God and Messiah resides.

From this perspective, Israel's uniqueness in God's administration of his creation appears never to be superseded. Instead, in fulfillment of Old Testament prophecy and in line with Second Temple Jewish tradition, the kingdom of Israel, with the New Jerusalem at its center, remains the locus of God's glory and the infrastructure of God's eternal kingdom on earth.

Chapter 24: Mission-Commitment in Second Temple Judaism and the New Testament
John Dickson

"Mission-Commitment in Second Temple Judaism and the New Testament" presents the Jewish roots of mission activity in the early Jesus movement. John Dickson demonstrates that the scholarly consensus regarding the absence of a mission impulse in Second Temple Judaism is mistaken. The Jewish eschatological hope for Gentile conversion found tangible expression in the deliberate missionary activities of some Second Temple Jews.

Dickson notes that the definition of mission that previous scholars worked with was flawed. Instead of defining mission as universal proselytism, Dickson broadens the definition to include any activity that aimed to move outsiders toward embracing one's own religion. With this broader definition, Dickson surveys several examples within Second Temple Judaism that represent attempts by Jews to move Gentiles toward worshiping the God of Israel. These included the hope of eschatological conversion of Gentiles, ethical apologetics, prayers for Gentiles, public worship, and the possibility of Jewish missionaries.

In light of these activities on the part of some Second Temple Jews, Dickson concludes that a missionary impulse found concrete expression in Second Temple Judaism. This evidence, however, falls short of the claim that the Judaism of the period was a missionary religion. Still, Christian mission appears to have solid Jewish roots.

Chapter 25: The Son of David and the Gospel
Markus Bockmuehl

"The Son of David and the Gospel" discusses the early Christian claim that Jesus was a descendant of David. Markus Bockmuehl shows that while the claim is central to the New Testament message, it is a historically problematic idea. The historical difficulties emerge out of the seemingly contradictory assertion that Jesus is both a descendant of David and born supernaturally through a virginal conception.

Yet in spite of the historical difficulty, the claim that Jesus was in fact a Son of David is not as historically suspect as critics, both ancient and modern, claim, for four reasons. First, there is evidence of genealogical records from the time of Jesus as well as testimonies of other Jews who claimed Davidic descent. Second, evidence points to a continued belief in the Davidic descent of Jesus. Third, early church fathers found the Davidic identity of Jesus powerful ammunition against Gnostic and sub-orthodox Christologies that devalued or erased the Jewish roots of Jesus and the gospel. Finally, many early church interpreters argued, and not without exegetical merit, that Jesus' Davidic ancestry came through Mary, not Joseph, based on Luke 1:27, 32, and 69.

Despite this background, the Davidic descent of Jesus was underplayed in the earliest Christian creeds and in the subsequent imagination of the church. The consequence was a lack of appreciation for the Jewish substructure of the Christian faith and a resultant inadequate theology of Israel that came to characterize the church's interpretation of the Bible. This was indeed unfortunate, for, as Bockmuehl eloquently summarizes, the Son of God was incarnate of the Holy Spirit and the Virgin Mary as the Son of David. God became Jewish flesh.

Chapter 26: Jewish Priority, Election, and the Gospel
Douglas Harink

"Jewish Priority, Election, and the Gospel" presents the theological consequences of what Douglas Harink labels the "messianic priority." Harink defines messianic priority as the idea that nothing precedes the priority of the gospel. In his words, the New Testament teaches that the Messiah, Son of God, who comes as the gospel, is both temporally and eternally prior to his arrival in history as Jesus of Nazareth. Thus, Christ comes before creation; he precedes nations, the election of Israel, and the historical reality of the Jewish people. From the perspective of the New Testament, according to Harink, various historical times are blended together in the singular time of the Messiah.

This messianic priority, therefore, means that the Messiah assumes even Israel's Torah. But the implication of this is far from an abrogation of the Torah. Instead, Harink affirms the validity of the Torah by showing that the Messiah envelops it in his own personal divine reality. In comparison with non-Christ-believing Jews, both past and present, Jewish believers in Jesus take the view that Torah is now defined and qualified within and by the prior and greater reality of the crucified and resurrected Messiah. Messiah, not the Torah, is the only sufficient criteria for discerning the work of God in creation, in Israel, and among the nations.

Turning to the election of Israel, Harink argues provocatively that the choice of Abram and Sarai, and God's faithfulness to Israel, was to show the messianic shape and character of God's work. In stressing only the third aspect of God's promise to Abram in Genesis 12:1 – 3, the promise of blessing the peoples of the earth through Abram, some have unwittingly (or perhaps wittingly) rendered Israel nothing more than an instrument. Harink protests that Israel is no mere instrument. God loves Israel for its own sake. And, according to Harink, it is only through God's faithful, eternal love for Israel that his love for the non-elect nations is made known.

Therefore, concludes Harink, when Messiah "apocalypsed" in Jesus of Nazareth it was for Israel and the nations as a theopolitical entity in continuity with the Hebrew Scriptures. As such, the ancient distinction made by God between Israel and the nations is maintained in the Messianic Jew and Messianic Gentile *ekklesia*.

Chapter 27: The Standard Canonical Narrative and the Problem of Supersessionism
R. Kendall Soulen

"The Standard Canonical Narrative and the Problem of Supersessionism" discusses the church's dominant canonical narrative. R. Kendall Soulen says that although the church's canonical narrative — a certain perspective on the unity of the message of the Testaments — has resulted in supersessionism, it is not a necessary consequence of that narrative. Soulen believes that a non-supersessionistic canonical narrative is not only possible, but also the most natural implication of the traditional canonical narrative. His contention in the chapter is that, when more careful attention is given to usage of the Divine Name in both Testaments, the deformation of supersessionism in the standard canonical narrative is overcome. The result of this move is that the trinitarian and christocentric character of the model is strengthened.

Soulen shows that reflection on the Divine Name helps to overcome the three kinds of supersessionism: structural, economic, and punitive. "Structural supersessionism" is a term that refers to a model that unifies the canon at the expense of Israel by backgrounding Israel's story. This kind of supersessionism can be overcome when one realizes the consistent testimony of Scripture to the Divine Name in both Testaments. Attention to the Divine Name in the New Testament moves the God of Israel and the history of Israel to the foreground of the Bible's canonical narrative. In Soulen's terms, the unique God who spoke to Moses is the same God revealed in and through Jesus the Messiah. This undermines the logic of structural supersessionism.

"Economic supersessionism" holds that God designed carnal Israel from the very beginning to become obsolete with the coming of Christ. This form of supersessionism is countered by the realization that Christian tradition concerning the Divine Name is rooted in Jewish tradition, which came into the church through the teachings of the Jewish Messiah, the Jewish apostles, and the first-century community of Jesus-believing Jews. Soulen's point is that this has theological significance. The non-pronunciation of the Divine Name in Christian worship should remind Christians that there remains significant continuity between the covenants in contrast to the view of economic supersessionism. Moreover, the continuation of Jewish tradition concerning the Divine Name in the church makes it possible to imagine a distinctively Jewish form of Christian discipleship, one that is both rooted in traditional Jewish practice and normed by the precedent of Jesus the Messiah, the living Torah for Jew and Gentile.

Finally, "punitive supersessionism," the view that God rejected carnal Israel because of her sins, is itself rejected in view of the Divine Name as a testimony of the irrevocable gift and calling of Israel by God. The Divine Name is a reminder of the God of Israel's covenant commitment to Abraham and his descendants. It points back to the oaths and promises the LORD made to his people Israel. Moreover, because the LORD owes it to himself and to his name to keep his promises to the Jewish people, Christ "has become a servant of the circumcised *on behalf of the truth of God* in order that he might confirm the promises given to the patriarchs" (Rom 15:8 NRSV).

Conclusion

JOEL WILLITTS

My interest in Messianic Judaism, as for most things in life, is the result of relationship. In this case, there are two relationships in particular: my relationship to the text and context of the New Testament and my relationship with David Rudolph, my co-editor.

While I am sure I heard of Messianic Judaism before 1999, the first time I distinctly remember encountering it was on a three-week archaeological dig in Israel during the final year of my ThM program at Dallas Theological Seminary. This was my first experience in the Holy Land, and it had a profound impact on me. The accommodations for our three-week stay in Israel were at the Messianic Jewish Kibbutz, *Yad Hashmona*, mentioned in Akiva Cohen's essay. Although I have forgotten much about my time at *Yad Hashmona*, I distinctly remember the Shabbat celebration on Friday nights.

At the time I was completely ignorant about the Messianic Jewish movement. I naively assumed that Jewish Christians in Israel worshiped like traditional (Gentile) Christians. Also, I equated Messianic Judaism with Jewish mission agencies like Jews for Jesus, which I had knowledge of through my local church. There I was in Israel, a seminary student, getting a ThM no less, and I had no idea what Messianic Judaism was. I can't remember any professors in seminary either mentioning Messianic Judaism or teaching that Messianic Judaism represented one of the streams of the contemporary church.

It was in the first year of my PhD program at Cambridge University that I began to learn about Messianic Judaism through my friendship with David Rudolph. David and I began our doctoral work in New Testament at the same time under Professor Markus Bockmuehl. David is one of a growing number of second-generation Messianic Jews who have earned advanced degrees in biblical and theological studies. During our four years together at Cambridge, between 2002 and 2006, David and I had many conversations. Just the other day I remembered a significant chat we had sitting next to each other on a flight from Edinburgh to Cambridge as we were returning from the British New Testament Conference. There were so many of these conversations during our time at Cambridge. As a result of our friendship I became very interested in the Messianic Jewish movement. Of course, I will never forget the Shabbat evening my wife, Karla, and I spent with David, his wife, Harumi, and their children.

In addition to my relationship with David, my own personal and academic interests in the Jewish context of the New Testament contributed to my growing curiosity about Messianic Judaism. As a young theological student in seminary, I became

315

increasingly disenchanted with the *ahistorical* gospel on which I had been reared in my church and home. I was raised in a fundamentalist-evangelical tradition that had reduced the gospel to ethereal spiritual laws about an individual's personal relationship with God. Studying the New Testament and its Jewish milieu in my New Testament courses in seminary, this de-storied, de-Judaized gospel seemed like a distortion of the New Testament gospel, or, at the very least, a severely abbreviated individualization of the message. As a result, I became driven to know the Jewish context of the New Testament and its message as thoroughly as I could. This is why I pursued a PhD in the first place, and it is how I found myself a colleague of David's at Cambridge. My doctoral research focused on Matthew's gospel.

The many conversations I had with David about Messianic Judaism were fascinating in part because he and his community were similar to what I imagined Matthew's audience — and more broadly the first-century community of Jewish believers in Jesus — to be like. David's Messianic Judaism was like a contemporary expression of early Christian Judaism.

When I would talk with David about my research and the implications I was drawing about the more concrete elements of Jewish faith such as the Land, he thought it was natural that first-century Jews who followed Jesus would remain committed to the pillars of Judaism, including its territorial dimension. Thus while I found the academic guild did not have much imagination for such Israel-centric readings of Matthew, David and his Messianic Judaism intuitively affirmed these readings. Over time, as my research confirmed the direction of my thesis, I began to value and weigh more heavily David's perspective over against that of the commentaries and monographs with which I was interacting. So my relationship with David grew as did my conviction that the New Testament was a Jewish book from front to back.

It is because of our friendship and my continued interest in the Jewish context of the New Testament that the present book has emerged. Its two parts neatly parallel my relationship with David and his community on the one hand, and my passion for reading the New Testament and its message in more thoroughly Jewish ways on the other.

In the thirteen chapters of part 1 we provided a sketch of the ecclesial context of Messianic Judaism as it is practiced today. Contributors from the Messianic Jewish movement, representing a variety of institutional affiliations, wrote the chapters. While not exhaustive, part 1 provides an introduction to the Messianic Jewish movement historically, theologically, and socially.

What do these chapters teach us about the contemporary Messianic Jewish movement? Below are seven observations about Messianic Judaism from part 1. Since I am an outsider to the movement, these observations are my way of summarizing what I took away from listening carefully to those who are on the inside.

1. Messianic Judaism is historically both ancient and modern.
2. Messianic Judaism is a multilingual, worldwide movement of Messianic Jews and Messianic Gentiles who have come alongside them.
3. Messianic Judaism is a diverse movement theologically, culturally, halachically, and ecclesially.

4. Messianic Judaism is a growing movement that remains very much in process.
5. Messianic Judaism is in the midst of an intense period of identity formation.
6. Messianic Judaism is developing young leaders who are theologically and biblically trained at the highest levels, ensuring a strong future.
7. Messianic Judaism is experiencing positive development in its relationship with the wider Jewish and Christian worlds.

Part 2 consisted of fourteen chapters written largely by Gentile Christian scholars in the fields of New Testament and systematic theology. It is an unprecedented collection of accessibly written essays by some of the most recognized New Testament scholars and theologians of our day. This section, while addressing a number of different topics, focused on biblical, theological, and historical issues central to the question of the validity of Messianic Judaism. While not all of the contributors would agree at every point, their contributions in this volume represent an emerging post-supersessionist approach to the New Testament. This approach can be characterized by at least four assumptions:

1. God's covenant relationship with the Jewish people (Israel) is present and future.
2. Israel has a distinctive role and priority in God's redemptive activity through Messiah Jesus.
3. By God's design and calling, there is a continuing distinction between Jew and Gentile in the church today.
4. For Jews, distinction takes shape fundamentally through Torah observance as an expression of covenant faithfulness to the God of Israel and the Messiah Jesus.

At every stage of this project, David and I have kept in mind a religiously diverse audience. We hope, for example, that this book will help Messianic Jews to have a better grasp of their own history and theology, and the changing contours of their community. For Jews who are not Messianic, we hope that this volume will inform, break down stereotypes, and result in a new appreciation for Messianic Judaism. For Gentile Christians of all traditions, we hope these essays will lead to a deepening of relationship with Messianic Jews.

For my part, as a Christian in a Protestant evangelical context, I would like to conclude with a conversation I recently had with a friend and colleague from my church. I believe this story is illustrative of the potential significance of *Introduction to Messianic Judaism* for the Gentile Christian church.

Mark is an intelligent guy without formal theological training. He is a mature Christian and intellectually curious. Mark asked me what I was writing and I mentioned this book. He had heard of Messianic Judaism before, but like most Gentile Christians he knew nothing about it. So I began to describe what the book was about. After giving Mark the big picture, he asked the million-dollar question, "So what is its significance for *our* church?" Mark's "our church" is *my* church; it is a large seeker-sensitive suburban Chicago upper-middle-class church full of Gentile Christians. What does *Introduction to Messianic Judaism* have to say to us? What a great question.

This is what I told Mark: First, this book informs the church of a modern move of

God's Spirit of which it is largely ignorant. Learning about the Messianic Jewish community should result in resounding praise and glory to the God of Israel for "making good his promises" to his people (Rom 15:8 CJB).

Second, *Introduction to Messianic Judaism* introduces a post-supersessionist reading of the New Testament. Most Christians naturally read the Bible in a supersessionist way. Such an approach is largely unintentional for most. It is the by-product of uncritical assumptions concerning what the Scriptures teach about the Jewish people. *Introduction to Messianic Judaism* offers a new paradigm for reading the Bible, one that is more consistent with its message of the fulfillment of Israel's story in the story of Jesus, Israel's Messiah.

Third, *Introduction to Messianic Judaism* presents a robust ecclesiology that strengthens evangelical Christian ministry by reimagining church planting and mission. An Israel-centered reading of the Bible makes room for a New Testament ecclesiology that celebrates diversity, fights cultural hegemony, and supports diverse ethnic expressions of faith in Jesus, whether they be Jewish or Gentile (one of the over sixteen thousand ethnic people groups among the nations).[1]

This is of particular concern for Jewish believers in Jesus because Jewish ethnicity is wrapped up with God-given markers of identity like circumcision, food laws, and Sabbath observance, practices that the Gentile Christian church, from the patristic period, stigmatized because of the belief that these practices had been set aside with the coming of Christ and replaced with a new Christian identity. By making normative this perspective in church teaching and practice, Gentile Christian leaders ensured that there would no longer be an ethnic representation of Jews in the body of Messiah—a most egregious irony since the Messiah lived as a Torah-observant Jew. The church cannot champion a message of ethnic diversity while at the same time maintaining a theological perspective that strips God-given ethnic boundary markers of identity from Jewish people who follow Jesus.

Fourth, the book reminds Gentile Christians of the Jewish roots of their Christian faith. It reminds us that, in the language of Paul's olive tree analogy (Rom 11:17–21), we are not the root of the tree, but "wild shoots" that in God's kindness have been "grafted" in. The more we appreciate the Jewishness of our confession that Jesus is Lord and Messiah, the truer we will represent Israel's God to the world and the more authentic we will be as the people of Messiah in our unique historical and cultural contexts.

Finally, *Introduction to Messianic Judaism* helps to inform Christians about how they can help meet the communal and individual needs of Jewish people who believe in Jesus. This book makes the argument that Jews who find themselves in Gentile Christian churches should be encouraged to maintain their Jewish identity and lifestyle in keeping with their calling from God. While Jewish identity and lifestyle can take shape in a variety of ways, Christian leaders should view it as their pastoral responsibility to help Jewish believers in Jesus remain Jews and become better Jews.

---

1. Cited 21 January 2012. Online: http://www.joshuaproject.net/how-many-people-groups.php.

So, to answer Mark's question, *Introduction to Messianic Judaism* offers our church an opportunity to grow and be stretched in the areas of worship, hermeneutics, mission, Christian identity, and spiritual formation. It is our hope that the relationship David and I share, which resulted in the fruit of this book, will inspire other "Jew and Gentile" partnerships for the sake of Messiah and the gospel of the kingdom.

εἰρήνη ἐπ᾽ αὐτοὺς καὶ ἔλεος καὶ ἐπὶ τὸν Ἰσραὴλ τοῦ θεοῦ.
Peace on them, and mercy also on the Israel of God.
— GALATIANS 6:16 (MY ENG. TRANS.)

Subject Index

Note: page numbers in italics refer to photos or figures.

(churches, *cont.*)
interdependence and, 187–95
Israel and, 14, 196–205, 306–7
Messianic Judaism and, 157, 304
models of, 15
mutual blessing in, 187–95, 306
starting, 30
circumcision
covenant of, 39
obligation of, 23–29, 207, 225–28, 308–9, 318
opposing, 242, 262
requirement of, 138, 153, 175, 180, 183, 213, 288
rules for, 215–18
Claudius, Emperor, 187
Clement of Alexandria, 184, 266
Clopas, Simon, 269
Coh, Rabbi Leopold, 118
Cohen, Akiva, 9, 107, 300–301, 315
Cohen, Philip, 27, 45
community. *See also* Jewish community
Christian-Jewish community, 159–67
Scripture and, 65–69
synagogues and, 37–40, 49–50
women and, 102–3
Community, Law and Mission in Matthew's Gospel, 21
community life, 37–40, 49–50, 165–66
"Competing Trends in Messianic Judaism: The Debate over Evangelicalism," 131
conflict, mediating, 111
congregational leadership, 44–45, 111
congregational movement, 29–31
conversion, 121, 152–53, 178–83, 219, 255–62
core values, 74–75
covenantal duty, 23
covenant faithfulness, 15, 69, 93, 276, 317
covenant relationship, 46, 95, 138, 259, 303, 317
covenant responsibility, 11, 33, 45, 48, 62, 76, 122, 136, 295–96
Crossing Over Sea and Land, 255
current trends, 69–70

Dabru Emet, 145–46
dance, 53–54, 297
Dauermann, Stuart, 9, 52–53, 64, 90, 299–300
David, Son of, 16–17, 93–95, 264–72, 311–12
David, star of, 40
Davidic Dance, 53
Davidic descent, 266–69
Davidic Sonship, 269–71
Dead Sea Scrolls, 268
"Defining Messianic Judaism Statement," 34n36, 75–79, 136–37, 142

Deines, Roland, 21
dialogue, 15, 145–47. *See also* Jewish-Christian dialogue
Diaspora, 23, 139, 193, 220, 245–46, 280, 305
Dickson, John, 9, 255, 311
Dillon, Richard J., 173
Divine Name, 65, 285–90, 313
Divine Word, 16, 16n13, 38
Domitian, 269
Duff-Forbes, Lawrence, 30
Dunn, J. D. G., 240

ekklesia, 33, 92n6, 136–37, 214–23, 279, 303, 308, 312
Ephesians, 229–33
Epiphanius, 24
Episcopal Jews' Chapel Abrahamic Society, 26
equality, 224–34, 309
eschatological conversion, 256–57
eternal light, 41
eternal rule, 170
ethical apologetic, 257–58
ethics
ethical teachings, 165
Jewish ethics, 82–90, 298–99
loyalty and, 85–86
of margins, 86–87
revelatory ethics, 84–85
evangelism, 94–96

faithfulness, "remnant" of, 191–94
Felix, Minucius, 184
festivals, 53–54, 297
First Things, 137
Foster, Paul, 21
Fredriksen, Paula, 24
Friends of Israel (FOI), 118, 122, 301
Fruchtenbaum, Arnold, 118
Fuller, Michael, 22
Funkenstein, Amos, 148

Gager, John, 24
Galatians, 224–29, 233, 235, 309–10
Gentile believers, 23, 121, 140, 181–90
Gentile Christians, 13–18, 49, 49n48, 136–40, 180–94
Gentile Christian visitors, 49, 49n48, 296
Gentile Christian world, 136–44, 303
Gentiles, 47–50, 258–59. *See also* Messianic Gentiles
Gervitz, Rabbi, 37
Geyser, Albert, 246
Glaser, Mitch, 9, 91, 116, 133, 301–2
God, Son of, 16, 85, 148, 163, 270–73, 312

rabbis, 39–40, 44–45
Rabinowitz, Joseph, 27, 29–30
Rashkover, Randi, 146
Rausch, David, 90
Ravens, David, 171
Reason, Gabriela Karabelnik, 131–32
Reed, Annette Yoshiko, 24
"Re-Judaizing Jesus," 83
"remnant," 191–94
Resnik, Russ, 10, 82, 298–99
Revelation, 249–51
revelatory ethics, 84–85
ritual objects, 40–44
rituals, 54–55
Roman Catholic dialogue, 137–38
Romans
    argument from Scripture, 208–12
    eschatology and, 206–7
    ethics and, 206–7
    main point of, 206–7
    promises of, 207–8
Rosen, Moishe, 118
Rosenthal, Marv, 118
Rosenzweig, Frank, 148–49
Rosner, Jennifer M., 10, 145, 303–4
Rottenberg, Isaac, 14
Rudolph, David, 10, 11, 21, 37, 295–96, 301,
    315–17
Rudolph, Harumi, 315
Runesson, Anders, 10, 21, 214, 308–9

Saal, Paul, 64, 70
Sabbath, 25–29, 37–41, 52, 57, 69, 91, 120–21,
    161, 164, 175, 187, 265, 269, 318
sabras, 109–10
Saldarini, Anthony, 21
Sanders, E. P., 17
Scattered Nation, The, 28
Schnabel, Eckhard, 255
Schönborn, Cardinal Christoff, 137, 138
Schwemer, Anna, 260
Scripture
    argument from, 208–12
    canonical narrative and, 63–65
    Christian-Jewish community, 161–62
    community and, 65–69
    current trends and, 69–70
    Jesus as fulfillment of, 161–62
    Messianic Jews and, 61–71, 297–98
    Statement of Faith, 66–67, 75–77
    traditions and, 61–63
Second Temple Judaism
    Acts and, 175
    bounds of, 22, 147

Luke and, 170
    mission-commitment in, 255–63, 311
Sermon on the Mount, 82, 84, 162, 165, 274
Seven Affirmations, 141–42
Shabbat, 37–41, 52–57, 65, 91, 104–5, 120, 127
shared blessing, 203
Sheldon, 37
shlichim, 44, 47
Siddur, 30, 37, 52, 57, 59, 73–74
Siddur for Messianic Jews, 57
Siddurim, 41, 56–57, 297
Sigal, Phillip, 21
simchas, 49
slavery, 219
socioritual behavior, 216–17
Son of David, 16–17, 93–95, 264–72, 311–12
Son of God, 16, 85, 148, 163, 270–73, 312
Soulen, R. Kendall, 10, 15, 63–65, 95, 282,
    312–13
Spencer, F. Scott, 23
spiritual calling, 98–99
Standards of Observance, 77–79
star of David, 40
Statement of Faith, 66–67, 75–77
State of Israel, 35, 46, 91, 99, 112–13, 119, 121,
    191, 280n6
Stern, David, 69, 154
stoicheia, 228
Strauss, David Friedrich, 265
"stumbling," 200
Sukkot, 55
summer camps, 46, 123
superfluity of law, 235–44, 309–10
supersessionism
    canonical narrative and, 286–88, 312–13
    economic supersessionism, 288–89, 313
    problem of, 282–92, 312–13
    punitive supersessionism, 289–90, 313
    structural supersessionism, 286–88, 313
supersession of law, 235–44, 309–10
symbols, 40–44
synagogues
    Jewish community and, 37–40, 49–50, 296–97
    leadership of, 44–48
    Messianic Jews and, 12–13
    number of, 11
    photos of, *42–43*
    purpose of, 45–47
    services at, 37–50
    symbols and, 40–44

Tallitot, 41
Talmud, 73
Tanakh, 41, 52, 53

Scripture Index

1 Corinthians

2 Corinthians

Galatians

Share Your Thoughts

With the Author: Your comments will be forwarded to
the author when you send them to *zauthor@zondervan.com*.

With Zondervan: Submit your review of this book
by writing to *zreview@zondervan.com*.

Free Online Resources at
www.zondervan.com

Zondervan AuthorTracker: Be notified whenever your favorite
authors publish new books, go on tour, or post an update
about what's happening in their lives at www.zondervan.com/
authortracker.

Daily Bible Verses and Devotions: Enrich your life with daily
Bible verses or devotions that help you start every morning
focused on God. Visit www.zondervan.com/newsletters.

Free Email Publications: Sign up for newsletters on Christian
living, academic resources, church ministry, fiction, children's
resources, and more. Visit www.zondervan.com/newsletters.

Zondervan Bible Search: Find and compare Bible passages in
a variety of translations at www.zondervanbiblesearch.com.

Other Benefits: Register to receive online benefits like
coupons and special offers, or to participate in research.

ZONDERVAN®

ZONDERVAN.com/
AUTHORTRACKER
follow your favorite authors